Praise for This Book

It is truly a ground breaking volume that is long overdue and the first of its kind. It provides all the information hunters need to start using tracking dogs. It also includes details about what breeds to consider, how to select a dog and how to train hounds to locate dead deer. This book should be required reading by all state and provincial commissions and administrators who are responsible for setting regulations regarding the recovery of whitetails with dogs.
—*Richard P. Smith, Deer and Deer Hunting, October 2004*

This book speaks for itself in indicating that the author knows where he's coming from; has "been there, done that" when it comes to hunting, tracking, dog training and breeding.

Jeanneney's favorite breed for blood tracking will surprise most sportsmen: the Dachshund, specifically the wirehaired variety out of hunting stock, which he breeds and trains himself. But what makes this book so valuable and interesting is his inclusion and excellent evaluation of the potential use of virtually all the gun dog breeds in recovering wounded and dead deer; from the well-known pointing, flushing, retrieving, versatile and hound breeds to virtually unknown Wachtelhunds, Jagdterriers and curs. Anyone who hunts deer with gun or bow, even if not a dog owner, will find the book worthwhile as an aid in "sign reading" so a hunter stands a better chance of finding what he's hit, rather then moan about "the one that got away".
—*Dave Duffey, April/May 2004 issue of Gun Dog Magazine*

After nearly 30 years of personal experience and investigating how others adapt tracking to their areas, John Jeanneney has written a book on the subject, *Tracking Dogs for Finding Wounded Deer*. Chapters 11 and 12 alone are worth the price, even for hunters with no interest in tracking dogs. They detail how not to be fooled about where the deer was hit.
—*Larry Mueller, Outdoor Life, June 2005*

Whether you would like to add a tracking dog to your list of hunting equipment, or you would like to improve your own ability to choose effective shots and read the signs left by wounded deer, John Jeanneney's book will be a valuable addition to your hunting library. Throughout the chapters on wound types and their signs, John goes into detail on the indicators of every type of wound imaginable. His aim is to help prospective dog owners read these signs and determine the nature of the wound they are dealing with, information that will help them better understand their dog's behavior and response. This information, however, is extremely useful to hunters who are tracking wounded deer without the aid of a dog.
—*Lindsay Thomas Jr., Quality Whitetails, vol. 11, issue 1, 2004*

About the best book on the subject I have ever read in 40 years of shooting.
—*GCW Baron van Tuyll, V-President of the Game Conservancy Trust, UK*

The abundant wealth of this book lies in what it can do for a hunter before he goes out hunting and wounds a deer. Once a deer has been wounded, Jeanneney's suggestions become priceless for identifying wound sites and tracking approaches before making that call to a Deer Search volunteer handler.
—*Will Elliott, New York Outdoor News 2005*

There are some books which are a necessity for the bookshelf. This is one of those books. As someone who is in the process of training a dog for the following up of deer this book has proved extremely useful. It has an easy to read style about it and the useful summary at the end of each chapter serves as a reinforcement of the items covered. The book covers all aspects of using a dog; from breeds suitable for the task to equipment, techniques and wound identification from ground sign. There is even a chapter on following up wounded bear. I would advise anyone involved in deer management to obtain a copy of this book. The chapters on wound identification are some of the best I have read. The book covers shot reaction other than the classical "text book" reactions and prompts the stalker/manager to investigate the ground closely to confirm their original assumptions.
—*Guy Hagg, Deer-UK.com*

The book covers all aspects of using dogs to blood trail mortally wounded whitetail deer, and I do mean ALL! Chapters 11 and 12, which cover special tracking situations, offer expertise and advice that may be applied to tracking wounded game with both bow and firearms. Even for the hunter who has no dog, these two chapters present useful and detailed information concerning reading the sign left by a wounded whitetail that I've never seen before in any publication.It is invaluable in aiding hunters in the tracking of a wounded whitetail.
—*Milton Whitmore, Woods-N-Water News, September 2005*

John's book *Tracking Dogs for Finding Wounded Deer* is a must-read for deer hunters whether you train a tracking dog or not. It will, without a doubt, improve your understanding of wounded deer and how to recover them.
—*Les Davenport, Deer and Deer Hunting December 2008*

John Jeanneney has done a truly admirable job of assembling the facts so hunters can develop their own informed opinions. (...) While the author's passion for tracking dogs is obvious, he still manages a nicely balanced overview of the subject's controversial aspects. While he may or may not change the minds of diehard skeptics, anyone who reads this authoritative book will come away better informed. If only all bowhunters would take the time to gather the facts before expressing their opinions...
—*Don Thomas, Traditional Bowhunter June/July 2008*

Tracking Dogs for Finding Wounded Deer deserves a place along side the very best dog training books ever published. I had some small inkling of its quality when I ordered it. Now that it has arrived, I'm blown away by its comprehensiveness, clarity, and practical orientation. My wife and I have dozens of dog training books at home, and yours is easily among the top three or four in quality. You've done a tremendous service over the years. Publication of this book ensures that the value of your work will continue for a very long time. Thanks.

—Charles Elk, Executive Director, Kittery Trading Post Outdoor Academy, Kittery, ME; October 2006

John, I can't tell you how much I have enjoyed your book. It is a classic. It should be the bible for trackers of wounded game.

—Louis Taxiarchis, M.D., Maine, March 2008

John's logical and scientific approach to the issues of both dog training and practical blood tracking is very thorough and still easy to understand and to put into practice. Very, very recommended reading, very entertaining. too.

—Dirk Uwe Kern, Stuttgart, Germany, February 2008 www.accuratereloading.com

I would like to say thank you for the wonderful information you have shared in your book. I have found it very informative and I look forward to using the knowledge to train my lab and other dogs down the road in my hunting adventures in Louisiana and Texas. Although I started training my lab to trail blood before I knew about your book, it certainly helps to learn from someone with so much knowledge. I have thoroughly enjoyed reading it so far and will more than likely re-read it over time to stay fresh.

—Jared Politz, LA, February 2008

John's book is excellent! I don't know what more a person could have hoped for. I have just started reading it again, for the third time. I want to absorb as much of the information and experience as possible. I believe reading this book has made my dog and myself more efficient at tracking than would have been possible after many years of learning by trial and error.

—Dave Mundy, February 2008

I am in my first year of tracking, and am pretty severely hooked on it. I bought your book almost a year ago, and I can't count the number of ways it has helped me with my dog and with tracking in general. I really don't know how I would have even got my dog started without it.

—Lance Falzone, TX, January 2008

Dear John, Lately I bought your book, fantastic, it has been very useful for me and my young dachshund. Here in Quebec city, we are few conductors of blood tracking dogs. As I see that you signed my book in French, nice, thanks.

—Jacques Dion, September 2007

I can truly recommend this book to anyone who is interested in learning more about tracking wounded deer. I paid more than twice what this book actually costs (shipping to Norway is expensive!) and it was worth every penny I paid for it. I am looking forward to the third edition of the book, which I will order as soon as it is published, just to read the updates.

—*Terje Wangsholm - hunting instructor, deer tracking instructor and proud owner of a wire haired dachshund - Bergen, Norway*

The best—and possibly only—book on the subject is *Tracking Dogs for Finding Wounded Deer* by John Jeanneney

—*David DiBenedetto, Field and Stream, 2009*

If one is interested in training a dog to trail wounded deer, a must-have book will help you on your endeavor is *"Tracking Dogs For Finding Wounded Deer"* by John Jeanneney. It is by far the most extensive book published on the subject and a great read for any hunter planning to train a dog or not.

—*Drew Hall, OutdoorWriter.net, 2010*

John Jeanneney's first book on the topic of recovering wounded big game with leashed tracking dogs opened the door to the American blood tracking culture to me. Before I was half way through I was on the phone to Jeanneney and had placed my name on a waiting list for a pup from his lines. Six years later I'm a seasoned tracker with a couple hundred trails and scores of game recoveries under my belt. John Jeanneney's three books on tracking wounded game have been a constant source of both inspiration and practical advice on all phases of game tracking. I suggest that anyone who wants to learn the art of tracking wounded game with a leashed tracking dog purchase and study this book before they ever pull on a pair of pack boots and clip a lead to a dog.

—*Kevin Armstrong, 2011*

"Tracking Dogs For Finding Wounded Deer" is the bible of blood tracking. It provides all the information needed for choosing, training and maintaing a blood tracking dog. The best part about this book is the commitment the author and his wife have to the sport. Their blog is always full of news about blood tracking events, reports, and personal tracking stories. John is also an active blood tracker and an educator that loves to track and does everything possible to promote the use of blood tracking dogs to recover wounded deer and bear. No doubt then that, his book is all from personal experience and not from having read other sources on the market and rewriting what's been written before. Don't hesitate to even call him, and you will speak directly to the author of the book who will give you advice and tutoring at any time.

I keep this book in my truck during the tracking season and whenever I come upon an obstacle or have a question, my answer is in the book. I highly recommend it!

—*Gentian Shero, Tracking Dog Supply, 2011*

Tracking Dogs
for
Finding Wounded Deer

John Jeanneney

Tracking Dogs
for
Finding Wounded Deer

New, Expanded & Revised 2nd Edition

John Jeanneney

Teckel Time, Inc.
Berne, NY
www.born-to-track.com

Tracking Dogs for Finding Wounded Deer
by John Jeanneney

Published by

Teckel Time Inc.
Jolanta Jeanneney
1584 Helderberg Trail
Berne, NY 12023-2920
teckeltime@born-to-track.com
www.born-to-track.com

Photographs by Jolanta and John Jeanneney unless otherwise credited
Illustrations by Marilyn Wood and Paul Jeanneney

Cover design by Cathi Stevenson

2nd Edition, Revised and Expanded
Printed in the United States

Paperback ISBN: 978-0972508926
Library of Congress Control Number: 2006901301

This book is dedicated with love to my wife Jolanta,

my toughest critic and my best friend.

Acknowledgements

Many years have passed since we published the first edition of *Tracking Dogs for Finding Wounded Deer* in 2004. Many people have contributed insights and advice to help this revised second edition expand in breadth and depth.

Andy Bensing, a professional dog trainer and passionate tracker contributed training ideas and GPS expertise. Larry Gohlke explained the Midwest perspective on tracking and presented original approaches to almost everything! Susanne Hamilton demonstrated that even in Maine hunters could be persuaded to try something new. Roy Hindes invited me to his ranch in Texas and showed the very effective Texas way of finding wounded deer. Several times this book draws upon Roy's description of how Texas tracking started. Ken Parker shared the complex, international world of Bavarian Mountain Hounds.

Philippe Rainaud introduced me to the refinements of French *recherche au sang* with teckels. Wolfgang Ransleben, as President of the Deutscher Teckelklub, opened to me the tracking test events of the DTK in Germany, and he extended his organization to include the North American Teckel Club. With Alain Ridel in Quebec, I learned about the art and science of moose tracking. Alain also compiled an excellent collection of tracking statistics in Quebec that he has allowed me to draw upon for this book.

Linda Sanborn of Ontario, a retired English professor and dog scholar, is an accomplished editor. She gave wonderful advice on the training chapters, which were of special interest to her. JJ Scarborough, an extraordinary handler with an extraordinary dog, contributed much to the chapter on tracking off lead in the South. Mike Lopez demonstrated just how efficient off-lead tracking in the South can be. Lore Schlechtingen, who died in 2012, provided us with some gifted tracking Dachshunds and long e-mails of valuable advice on how to develop them. Hubert Stoquert in eastern France, provided the initial instructions and inspiration to launch European style tracking in the United States. Years later Hubert's son, Patrice Stoquert, also known as the "Dog Whisperer", showed me what his responsive Labradors can do as they track wounded wild boar in the Vosges Mountains. Randy Vick invited me to his home in south Georgia, and provided useful lessons about terrain and techniques of the South.

So many people have contributed to this book that it has become impossible to devote a well-deserved paragraph to all of them. I am reduced to listing these individuals in alphabetical order, but this does not reflect my deep appreciation for what they have shared with us all: Mark Bowen, Andre

Brun, Ron Dupont, Chris Eberhart, John Engelken, Hank Hearn, Henry Holt, David Johnson, Dan Kendall, Tim Nichols, Bill Wadsworth, Martin Zander.

Of course I owe my wife Jolanta extraordinary thanks for providing a judicious balance of criticism and support. Without her this book would never have come into being.

Jolanta knows both dogs and blood tracking, and she has no inhibitions about blasting my unsupported statements. What is most amazing is Jolanta's sense of organization and her ear for good clear English (English is her second language). She designed and formatted the whole book so that it could be sent directly to the printer, photos and all. I am fortunate indeed to have had her as editor/publisher.

I would like to conclude my praises with this quotation from a letter Jolanta wrote to the many mentors who advise new trackers. It illustrates both her command of language and her wisdom.

When you give advice to novices, give them your opinion and relate your experiences without trying to be dogmatic (opinionated, peremptory, assertive, insistent, emphatic, adamant, doctrinaire, authoritarian, imperious, dictatorial, uncompromising, unyielding, inflexible, rigid). There is no ONE right way to train a tracking dog that works for all dogs. What might be working for you and your dog, might not be working for another dog and another handler. I see that there are a lot of people on the mentor list with relatively little experience. That's OK as long as you support another member, encourage him/her, point to good resources and share your own experience. But please do not say "the only way to train a dog is my way". A much better approach is to say "this worked for me", or "I did not have a good luck with that method of training".

I couldn't have said it better myself.

TABLE OF CONTENTS

About This Book

If you have hunted very long, you have come to realize that you, or one of your friends, will shoot a deer and not be able to find it. Despite all precautions your shot will not go where you wished.

This happened to me in 1970 when I shot a big doe in Dutchess County, New York. The shotgun slug was deflected a little too far back by a branch that I did not see. The blood trail ended after 50 yards, and although I spent the whole day combing the area, I never found the deer. A week later I met two hunters who had found the spoiled carcass in a small swale a quarter mile away. This set me thinking; this experience was the seed out of which this book grew. I know today that this deer would have been found easily had I been able to call upon someone with a leashed tracking dog. But in 1970 even leashed tracking dogs were illegal in New York State. I had read about the use of dogs to find big game in Europe, but I had no practical experience. I did not even know that trained dogs were already being used off lead for this specific purpose in Texas, and in a different way, in the Deep South. I had much to learn.

In this book I will share with you, as a fellow hunter, what I did learn over the next 40 years through field experience and other research. At the time I wounded and lost the deer, I was already raising and hunting with wirehaired Dachshunds from German hunting stock. I knew that such Dachshunds were one of the breeds used to track wounded deer in Europe. I applied to New York State's Department of Environmental Conservation for a research permit to investigate the feasibility of leashed tracking dogs to find wounded deer in my state. I received this permit in 1976 after much persistence and because of the intervention of Bill Wadsworth, a visionary pioneer of legalized bowhunting in the Northeast.

Learning whether tracking dogs could have a place in modern deer hunting was not a one-man project; needed was a broader base of information and a wider contact with the hunting and non-hunting public to learn how they would react to the "heresy" of using dogs, even on a leash, to find wounded deer. Others were added to the research permit list as "designated agents". The success of this group, which had organized itself as Deer Search Inc., was responsible for legalizing the use of leashed tracking dogs in New York State. This came in 1986, and by May 2016 the total number of "legal" states has expanded to 35. Information about this can be found in Chapter 27, which deals with regional traditions and different types of regulations. Even here the historical treatment will be held to a minimum. Although I was a history professor by trade, I know that a straightforward, how-to book on tracking with dogs was needed right away. In this book I will spare you the history. My own passion for looking forward and backward is restricted to the appendices.

This book may be read by some non-hunters, so I must say a few things that true hunters know in their bones. Hunting involves much more than killing, but killing is a part of it. Hunting does include the art and the science of killing so quickly that the animal dies before it has any awareness of what has happened. The clean kill is the ideal, but in practice clean kills do not always happen. Every hunter should be concerned about the minority of cases in which death comes slowly. Central to ethical hunting is a determination to account for any game animal that has been shot and wounded.

Second in importance to killing quickly and humanely comes the concern to avoid wasting the animal. Humans are at the top of the food chain, but we have a moral responsibility to use our game resources wisely. Ethical hunting means making every possible effort to recover the venison, hide and antlers of deer that we shoot.

Knowing how to avoid losing deer involves a grasp of physical details and what they mean. The description of deer wounds in this book is graphic and often ugly because this is necessary information for those who must deal with such situations. If you are squeamish by nature and mostly interested in dogs, I advise you to skip Chapters 14 and 15. Enjoy this book and read it on a need to know basis. If you are going to be a handler of a tracking dog, then you do need to know as much as possible about all the problems that arise when a wounded deer eludes the hunter.

There are several good books in English on the art of tracking wounded deer by eye. Richard P. Smith's *Tracking Wounded Deer* is my favorite, but John Trout Jr.'s *Finding Wounded Deer* also has much useful information. Then there are a number of books on tracking by eye by Tom Brown Jr., who is not a hunter. His books do not deal with hunting, but his *The Science and Art of Tracking* will make you aware of how much can be involved in tracking by eye. This book will help you interpret the evidence that your dog shows you.

The book you now have in your hands will take you a step farther, beyond eyetracking, beyond Smith and Trout, and even beyond Brown. It deals with those situations where eyetracking does not work. Tracking the visible may not work because of weather conditions (rain, snow) or because the lack of visible blood sign leaves the hunter unable to proceed. I have had the privilege of seeing the work of some fine game trackers. Even they will admit that there are times when a good tracking dog will take the line farther than they can, especially when there are many similar sized deer leaving footprints. I know several eyetrackers who have gone on to be excellent handlers of tracking dogs as well. They understand the need for both approaches. In partnership with a tracking dog, a human can track much faster, covering a hundred yards of line in minutes, while an eyetracker alone might spend a half hour to accomplish the same thing. Sometimes, as we shall see in this book, speed does make a big difference. The coyotes do not wait.

Since this book is about finding wounded deer that cannot be tracked by eye, the perspective is different from most how-to hunting books. It deals with the problems of finding wounded deer from the dog handler's point of view. It goes into considerable detail about situations where a mortally hit deer does not leave a good blood trail, but it omits discussion of all of the clean kill situations where a dog is not needed.

This book is also written as if you would be accepting numerous invitations to track wounded deer with your dog each season. This will not be the actual case, of course, for many readers. The majority of people with a trained tracking dog will want to track only for themselves and for those in their hunting group. Readers should not be turned off by references to many "deer calls" or generalizations about "most calls". You don't *have* to go overboard and take 30 plus calls each season from people you do not know. But you will discover that the more you track, the more skilled you and your dog will become.

The use of tracking dogs to find wounded game is almost as old as hunting itself. Throughout the Middle Ages Europeans wrote about such dogs and their use, but the language used was seldom English. Today excellent books are available in German, French and other European languages, but at present there is only one European book that has been translated in English. This is Niels Sondergaard's *Working With Dogs for Deer*, and it is well worth reading. One of the problems with all the European books is that they do not completely meet the special needs of American hunters. Our hunting traditions are different, our game and field conditions are different, and bowhunting is much more important in North America than in Europe.

Tracking Dogs for Finding Wounded Deer deals with both firearms hunting and bowhunting. The bowhunting parts of this book are the most original. The use of tracking dogs for bowhunters is a virgin subject that the Europeans have not yet seriously examined. Until very recently there was no bowhunting in Europe. Bowhunting ended there with the development of suitable firearms. Now modern bowhunting has been legalized in some countries, and interest in the sport is growing.

From the standpoint of the tracking dog handler, a bowshot deer is usually much more difficult to track than a deer shot with a rifle or a slug gun. True, modern arrows kill by hemorrhage, but the hemorrhage is sometimes internal. When the wound is sealed by moving layers of muscle or plugs of fat, there is little scent that comes down from the wound. The edges of the wound close. In contrast, the wound made by a bullet or a shotgun slug usually leaves an open, ragged hole, which allows more scent particles to drift down to the ground from the wound. Handlers and their dogs, who track for and with bowhunters in the United States and Canada, face unique challenges. As you will learn from this book, the tactics and techniques of finding a deer in bow season are quite different from those required during the firearms seasons.

This book is written from the perspective of a Northeasterner, who was first introduced to European methods and then adapted them to his home state of New York. I have been using leashed tracking dogs for 40 years and in that time I have found 304 deer that hunters were unable to find for themselves. I am still learning and sometimes changing my mind.

I think it is important to realize that the leashed tracking dog methods, which I focus upon through most of this book, are not the only ways to do it. There are other American methods and traditions of finding wounded deer with dogs. These are adapted to the regions of America in which they originated. I have tried to give them the attention and serious treatment they deserve, particularly in the chapters on breeds of dogs, and in Chapter 13, "Working Dogs Off Lead", and in Chapter 27, "Regional Tracking Traditions". I hope that there is information in the other chapters that any handler anywhere in North America can use. When I was in Texas with rancher/tracker Roy Hindes, we found that we held much of our lore in common. I hope that this book will inspire or provoke other experienced handlers from different parts of the United States and Canada to write books of their own on the basis of their regional experience. Videos can also play an important role.

Experienced dog trainers, who read the training chapters of this book, will note that there is no discussion of modern, "behaviorist" training methods. There is no mention of "operant conditioning" or "negative reinforcement". It is this author's position that these methods can be very useful for training a tracking/companion dog for living in a household. But they have little application in training a tracking dog to actually track wounded game.

The methods of training for tracking are compatible with behaviorist theories even if they differ in the details. We always advocate positive reinforcement, which is natural since the dog wants to track in order to get the to the deer skin and the treats at the end of the line. We do not punish the dog when he gets off the line or is distracted by fresh game scent.

A desire to pursue game by its scent is inherent in the genetic inheritance of most dogs. A dog may need to be "conditioned" to track a human being, which he does not perceive as prey, but the natural desire to track a blood line appears in very young puppies. The trainer's role is to encourage and shape this desire. In a good tracking prospect this does not require structured behaviorist methods.

An exception to this generalization is discussed in Appendix D that treats the training of dogs to track when they have little natural desire to get their noses down to follow a scent line. No doubt there will be some other applications of modern behaviorist techniques in tracking dog training, but I do not see it ever playing a fundamental role. Introducing the complex vocabulary and analysis of modern behaviorist training into this book would confuse more than it would enlighten.

This expanded update of *Tracking Dogs for Finding Wounded Deer* is not a definitive book. It attempts to deal with state of the art methods at the beginning of the 21st century. At this point, I am confident that a good tracking dog will find many wounded deer that will not be found by such technological means as hand-held infra-red sensors, electronic transmitters on arrows, or even string trackers. In the past ten years it is GPS equipment that has had the greatest impact upon searching for wounded big game with tracking dogs.

My strategy in this book is to plunge right into Chapter 1 with a how-to overview explaining what a dog and handler must do in the field when tracking wounded deer. Once the reader has covered this, he will be in a better position to appreciate what is expected of a tracking dog and how he must be trained to develop his initiative and concentration.

Chapter 2 is an introduction to scent, how dogs perceive it and how it is affected by weather and surface conditions.

Chapters 3 through 7 deal with the selection of tracking dog prospects. A general chapter on what to look for in a young dog is followed by chapters on breeds used for blood tracking. It is useful to know what tracking styles one is likely to find in each breed, but keep in mind that dogs are individuals. There are canine geniuses and dimwits in every breed, and there are always some dogs that defy any breed generalizations that we apply to them.

After the discussion of breeds, Chapters 8 through 13 deal with the training of tracking dogs. The discussion of training has been greatly expanded beyond the original two chapters written in 2004. By the time you reach these chapters it will be clear that there are mental differences between breeds and between individual dogs within a breed. Your methods must be adapted to the dog that you are working with. This situation does not lend itself to simple, cookbook recipes for training dogs. We see too much of that in the canine literature. I have tried to explain various training options as clearly as possible, but I rely on the trainer's good judgment to decide which training procedures will work best on his own dog. Training dogs is not like manufacturing wing nuts. To avoid confusion while reading the training chapters you might consider reading the "Summary" at the end of each chapter first. In the summaries the main points of each chapter are listed.

Chapters 14 and 15 on "Special Tracking Situations" are a must for readers who are actually going to track wounded deer, although the discussion of the range of bad hit possibilities does not make for pleasant reading. These chapters are quite technical, and it will not be easy to absorb all the detail right away unless you are an experienced hunter. Observing wounded deer cases, as I took over 1000 calls, has made me a much more conservative hunter. I pass up many shots, and I hope that these chapters will have a similar effect upon hunters who read it.

The short Chapter 16 on "Tracking Wounded Bears" takes the position that most dogs experienced in wounded deer tracking will readily make the transition to tracking a wounded bear without specialized training. However, the handler should be prepared for the different characteristics of bear scent and bear behavior.

The new Chapter 17, "Tracking Wounded Moose and Elk", based on my tracking experiences in Quebec, deals with the importance of tracking dogs to find wounded moose quickly before the meat spoils. This chapter ends with a report of how and why tracking dogs are catching on in the western elk states.

Chapter 18, "Putting Down Wounded Deer", deals with a subject that is still politically sensitive in many states. You will appreciate it more after you have had to deal with aggressive big game. We must also realize that it is our mission to abbreviate animal suffering.

Chapters 19, "Basic Equipment", discusses all the things that you can buy to make your tracking more efficient. The bare minimum of equipment that you need to begin is simple and not expensive. Personally, I started out with only a collar, long leash, flashlight and a handgun. If you enjoy browsing in the Cabela's catalog, you will find entertainment value in this chapter. You will also become aware of the full list of equipment that you might like to have at some point.

Chapter 20, "Hi-Tech Equipment", explains what you can do with the new, constantly improving GPS equipment. This technology can be very useful in the woods. We leave the detailed "how to" to the GPS instruction manuals.

Chapter 21, "The Makings of a Good Handler", is tucked away near the end of the book, but it is important. If you hope to have maximum impact on the problem of unfound wounded deer, you must know how to establish contacts with the deer hunters in your area. In this chapter we also explore that curious human type, the tracking "addict". I confess that I am one of them! How did this minority of extremists, both male and female, get that way? Why does everything, except family and job, get pushed aside when the next deer call comes in?

Chapter 22, "Working with the Hunter", points out that what the average hunter sees and tells you about his wounded deer is often very different from what you, as an experienced handler, are going to want to know. For you, the art of asking the right questions may be almost as important as the art of handling your dog. Those who track only for themselves and a small circle of friends will find useful information on interpreting evidence.

Chapters 23, "The Tracking Dog in the Family", and 24, "Tracking Dogs for Guides and Outfitters", are two chapters which grew out of a clear need for more information. As the tracking movement has grown, both families and professional outfitters have found that working dogs are now part of their lives.

Chapter 25, "Tests" deals with tracking tests. This is a specialized subject that you may want to skip until you have an occasion to enter your dog in one. We know from our own school days that good test takers do not always do so well in the practical world. The same is true for canine blood trackers. I hope that you will concentrate on training your dog for the real thing rather than just for tests.

Chapter 26, "Questions and Some Answers", grew out of the long phone conversations that I have had with readers over the last ten years. It's up to you to come up with even better answers to these eternal questions!

Chapter 27 on "Regional Tracking Traditions" shows how diverse hunting and tracking are in different parts of the United States and Canada. While we are all different as hunters and trackers from the North, South and West, there is much that we have in common concerning our methods, goals and our feelings about our tracking dogs. The diversity of state and provincial tracking regulations is discussed, but we have found that there is no longer any way to present a summary which remains up to date.

The final Chapter 28, "Conclusion", is at once a summary and a look forward to the possible futures of blood tracking in America.

When I finished the first edition of this book, back in 2004, Jolanta and I hoped that we would sell a thousand copies in the next ten years. It would have a small, niche market, we were sure. Most people we talked to thought that it was a pretty weird subject. We are still amazed that so far we have sold over 11,000 copies. Orders came in not just from the United States but also from the United Kingdom and the rest of the English speaking world.

Of course it helped that there wasn't any competition in the English language, but it also seemed that the time for the new idea had come. In North America the fascination with deer hunting, and especially the quest for trophy bucks, had much to do with the growing interest in tracking dogs. Hunters especially hated to lose what might be the buck of a lifetime. But there was also a growing ethical concern about hunting cleanly and without waste.

We sold most of the copies of our self-published book ourselves. Some good magazine reviews and the Internet helped sales in ways that we had not expected. We discovered that more and more people are searching the Web for information about their special interests; they found our website (www. born-to-track.com) and were able to purchase the book without middlemen or intermediaries. One of the many good things about this arrangement was that we learned who was purchasing our book. When buyers ordered by phone, we were able to chat with them and discover their special concerns and expectations. We encouraged readers to call back, and often they did so with enthusiasm. You will appreciate their inputs in the four new training chapters and in expansions of many of the older ones.

Throughout this book I consistently refer to "tracking dogs" although these dogs actually find wounded big game by a combination of tracking and trailing. This can be confusing to some because the parallel literature on tracking humans with dogs deals with "tracking" and "trailing" as two distinctly different actions.

A man-tracking dog works footprint scent, the scent of shoe contact and crushed earth and vegetation. Such a tracking dog works very close to the footprint line in a methodical way with a "deep nose".

A man-trailing dog, by contrast, works body scent particles that may have drifted over ten yards or more, particularly down wind.

In most cases an experienced dog, when following a wounded deer, does trail more than he tracks. With nose fairly high he follows the body scent that has settled in a broad zone of the deer's travel. This includes tarsal gland scent, scent from the interdigital glands, which are located between the cloves of the hoof, and drifting scent particles from the wound. But he also tracks dried blood droplets that stay in a precise place on the track line much like a footprint scent.

When I first began my career of using a dog to find wounded deer I tried to use the term "trailing dog". My original application for a research permit from the Fish and Wildlife authorities was entitled *"Proposal for Research on the Public Acceptance of the Practice of Recovering Wounded Deer by Means of a Leashed Trailing Dog"*. I soon found that the most commonly used terms for what I wanted to do were "tracking" and "blood tracking." To ease a communications problem, which at the time was quite real, I began to speak of leashed tracking dogs.

Early in the 21st century the useful distinction between tracking and trailing seems to be breaking down among those who hunt game with hounds. I suppose that I have played my own small part in this process. My apologies.

Separate from the trailing vs. tracking confusions there is confusion about the use of the word "blood" as in blood tracking. Everywhere in North America, and in Europe too, the activity of tracking wounded big game with a dog is described as blood tracking. These words can be misleading. Most of the time the dogs are not tracking blood; they are tracking other scents left by the deer, particularly scent from the body and the interdigital glands. In this book we have sometimes followed convention. To be better understood we have used the term blood tracking even when we are referring to tracking when there is little or no blood.

What's New in This Expanded and Revised Version of the 2nd Edition?

This new version of the 2nd edition constitutes a major update and expansion. It was produced ten years after the second edition was originally published, and it reflects the development of big game tracking to include moose in Quebec and elk in the Rocky Mountains.

The chapters on training have been increased from two to six. There is an entirely new chapter on "canine adolescence" and the training problems associated with it.

Thanks to the inputs of my southern and Texas friends, there is much more information on training and working with tracking dogs off lead.

We have done our best to keep up with the rapidly changing technologies in equipment used in tracking. This extends from GPS equipment to better lights for night work.

The state legislations pertaining to tracking dogs have been expanding and changing so rapidly that it has been impossible to keep up with it all. We refer you to state Fish and Wildlife websites for current information.

Chapter 1

General Tracking Techniques

In later chapters of this book we will go into detail on such matters as selecting tracking dogs, training them and actually using them to find real wounded deer. These topics will make more sense if you have an overview, right from the start, of what is involved when you go out to find a wounded deer. I hope that this will give you an early feel for the subject, and an understanding of how the details fit into the big picture.

Collars, Harnesses and Leashes

Later on in this book you will find more information about equipment, but to get started we will introduce only those most basic items for tracking: a tracking collar or harness, and a tracking leash. In certain states dogs are allowed to work off lead, but even there it is best to train and start natural tracking with the dog on a leash. You have a lot more control over the young dog when he makes mistakes or gets off on the wrong line.

It is very important that the tracking collar or harness be different from what the dog wears on a day-to-day basis. When it is buckled on the dog,

Tracking collar on Vars, a Bavarian Mountain Hound.
Photo courtesy of Dan Kendall

the collar sends a message to focus on tracking, which requires a special sort of attention. Because of this, the collar or harness should be used only for wounded big game tracking or training. It should not be placed on the dog until he is brought to the blood or scent line to be tracked.

The dog's regular collar, with name and phone number of the owner, should always remain on the dog in front of the tracking collar.

The choice of collar or harness is a matter of personal preference. If your dog pulls very hard or has a sensitive windpipe, the harness will prevent choking, coughing and wheezing.

The Germans manufacture specialized leather tracking collars for all sizes of dogs. These are high quality, expensive leather collars 1¼ inch to 1¾ inch wide. A brass ring bolt is mounted in the thick leather and projects upward for attaching the leash. These collars are very nice to have, but certainly not essential. The important thing is to have a dedicated piece of equipment that the dog knows is just for blood tracking. It should be wide enough to distribute strain over a broad area of the dog's neck. Narrow rolled collars, chain collars or choke collars are out.

If you use a harness, it should be durable and have wide bearing surfaces. Make sure that it has no sharp edges that will chafe your dog.

The tracking leash is the most important part of your tracking equipment, and we would recommend one of "good" length. Personally, I think a good length is 30 feet for all sizes of dogs. Until you have tried working in dense cover, it is natural to assume that a short leash will tangle less and be more convenient. The reverse is true. Some handlers actually prefer 50 feet when working in very dense cover.

A tracking harness is suitable for a large dog like this Bloodhound.

A long leash snakes flat along the ground, and the handler lets it drag ahead of him and behind him as he moves backward and forward along the leash. He can double it forward when the dog goes on one side of a tree and the handler passes on the other side. At a deadfall, or in a patch of briars, he can let the hunter hold the very end of the leash while he runs up to take it again near the dog's collar. Don't attempt to carry this leash in coils as you track. Letting the length of leash drag and slide back and forth in your hands is an essential part of avoiding tangles. With a leash of proper length and material, handling becomes automatic, and it is amazing how fast you can go through dense undergrowth.

Well what is the proper material for a tracking leash? This is not a simple question because the material must be appropriate for the vegetation you will be tracking in. After trying many different materials my personal choice, for the country I track in, is stiff mountain climbing rope. This rope has a stranded nylon core covered by a braided nylon sheath. Eight or nine millimeter diameter seems to be the best for dogs under 30 pounds while eleven millimeter is best for the big, powerful dogs because the thicker rope is easier to hold onto when a dog is pulling hard. This cord is much stronger than it has to be, but its desirable quality is just the right degree of permanent semi-stiffness. Try a broken-in length of cotton clothesline and you will find that it whips back and forth, wrapping around snags and brush.

To get started most trackers will do fine with the flexible plastic leashes that are about 30 feet long. Many handlers find them well-suited to the conditions in which they track, although they are not as stiff as the best climbing rope. In certain types of vegetation light, polypropylene marine cord works amazingly

German tracking collar and American 30-foot leash of mountain climbing rope

well. The tracking leash is a very important piece of equipment; detailed information about various leashes is available in Chapter 19 on equipment.

Your First Deer Call

In later chapters we will discuss the various ways to train a dog, but for now we will assume that you have a dog with a basic understanding of what he is expected to do. You start out with a situation in which a fellow hunter in your club or hunting lease believes that he has hit a deer hard and mortally wounded it. He cannot come up with enough blood sign or identifiable footprints to track the deer to where it must be down. The finer points of all this are discussed in the next chapter; in this chapter we are reviewing the basic techniques of finding that deer with your dog.

You hope that your dog's first deer call involves a fairly fresh line only a few hours old. It takes most dogs a number of outings to learn just how hard they have to "dig" with their noses in the grass roots and under the leaves to find the last traces of scent on an old, cold line left by a deer wounded the previous day.

The hunter should be able to take you to the exact place where he shot the deer as well as to the point where he lost the line. In almost every case it is well worthwhile to begin tracking at the hit site where the hunter shot the deer. You may see something (blood smears, bone chips) that gives you a better idea of where in the body and how hard the deer is hit. Deer don't always bleed immediately, so you may have to go a little way with the hunter's guidance to see and start working the actual bloodline. Working over the easy part of the blood trail, which has already been tracked by eye, will familiarize your dog with the scent characteristics of the particular wounded deer that you have been asked to track.

The hunter's point of loss is the real beginning of your own tracking work, and this beginning is the most difficult part of the whole search. In the first place, the point of loss will be thoroughly tracked up by the hunter, who searched to pick up the blood trail again before he called you. Almost always the hunter has stepped in blood and deer scent as he tracked, and this will confuse things at the point of loss. He may have avoided the big drops and puddles of blood, but some muddling of the scent line cannot be avoided. Ask the hunter to show you where he finally left the area because there is a chance that the dog will follow his blood-contaminated tracks away from the point of loss.

If the dog has memorized the whole combination of blood scent, deer body scent and hoof scent on the easy part of the line before the loss, he has a better chance to solve the puzzle of the point of loss afterwards.

As you begin to track, the hunter may say, "The deer didn't go that way." If you are not seeing any blood, it is good practice to restart the dog where the hunter saw the deer. At the restart, if the dog still insists on going in another direction, then go with the dog's opinion. Sometimes hunters see another deer running and incorrectly assume that it is the deer they shot at. In such situations a good dog is more reliable than a person. When dog and hunter disagree, or when you as handler doubt your dog, remember that it is the dog who has the nose and is most likely to be correct. Trust your dog!

If you are dealing with one of the more difficult situations, you may find your dog making several tentative starts in wrong directions before settling on the correct line. I do not like to go out more than a hundred yards or so without some confirming blood sign, unless I know the dog well, and the dog seems very positive. This is a matter of reading the dog's body language. Once you begin seeing new, previously undiscovered drops of blood, you can be assured that the tracking will become much easier because you are now past the tracked up, contaminated area.

Often the hunter has lost the line because the deer suddenly changed the direction in which it was traveling. If the start is difficult, which is often the case, the dog will want to check back over the trail leading to the point of loss. Let the dog try this for a hundred yards. The deer may have reversed its direction, traveling back over the original line. "Fingers" on the blood splatters will point in the direction that the deer was moving. You may see blood splatters pointing in both directions, and this suggests a back track. Your dog must find the point where the deer broke off the back track and headed in a new direction.

Sometimes it takes a lot of patience to overcome the problems of following the line on past the hunter's point of loss. You may even resort to walking some big circles around this loss point before your dog shows you a new drop of blood and you know that you are on your way.

"Fingers" on the blood spatters indicate the direction the deer traveled.

Dead Spots

The technique of walking circles around a spot where the dog has a great deal of trouble works for getting you out of a "dead spot" at any point along the trail. Dead spots are small pockets of terrain, where there seems to be no scent for reasons that we cannot always explain. In some cases, there will be a masking of scent by such things as fallen apples in an orchard. The area beneath an active high-tension electrical transmission line becomes "dead" for scent. The strong magnetic field from the electrical current extends down to ground level, and this ionizes scent particles. It is sometimes necessary to give a less experienced dog some help by leading him into a circling maneuver around the problem area.

Marking Line

To keep track of what the dog is doing, it is a great help to use biodegradable, orange surveyor's tape or flagging. It is especially valuable at the beginning, when the dog may start off on the scent of another deer. Fastening the tape on branches above the places where you see blood makes it much easier to come back to the spot if you get stuck and lose the line later. Tie the tape at eye level with a loose end about a foot long to make it more visible.

At the take-off from the point of loss, you may be tentatively marking lines about which you and your dog are not absolutely certain. To distinguish these "I'm not positive." lines from a confirmed line with visible blood, I like to tie a simple knot into the tail of the hanging tape to indicate that this is an unconfirmed line.

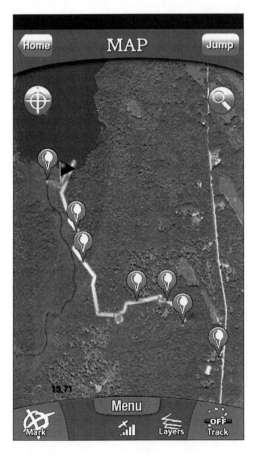

GPS handhelds and smartphone apps are of great help in marking the line and recording a real track of a wounded deer. We will have more information about them in Chapter 20 on High-Tech Equipment. This picture shows a real track that Susanne Hamilton and Lindsay Ware did on November 9, 2014. They were using the Trimble Hunt Pro app. The markers indicate where blood was found.

Orange surveyor's tape marks where blood was found in a patch of spruce.

Crossing a Field

Frequently a wounded deer is tracked by eye into an open field, where the expanse of semi-vertical grass blades makes the small drops of blood very difficult to see. The line is lost out in the field, and the tracking dog is expected to continue from this point. Unless the air is still and the humidity is high, this can be very difficult. If there was or is currently any breeze at all, the scent will have been wafted out over a broad zone paralleling the deer's direction of travel. This scent will tend to drift downwind. In a breezy field a tracking dog will find it difficult to work in a well-defined line. If the dog does get started in the field, you will notice that he works in broad "S" curves through a zone of scent.

If little progress can be made across the field, then the best solution is to go around the perimeter of the field working the edges. When deer cross a field, whether wounded or not, they will stick to their old habits and reenter cover on a well-defined deer run. Lead your dog to each deer trail exiting from the field and follow it for ten to fifty yards. You may actually see blood there; in any case, by reading your dog's body language you will realize when he has the right line.

If the field is fenced, you can quickly identify the places where a deer would exit. This could be an open gateway, a broken or downed strand of barbed wire, or a spot where deer habitually duck under the wire. Wherever deer are forced by fence wire to jump over or duck under is an excellent place to look for that telltale droplet, which confirms that you have the line. A deer

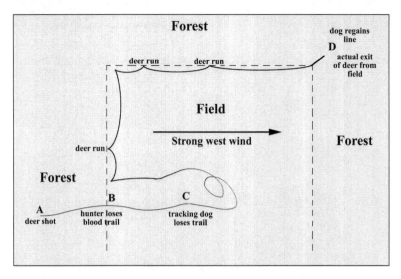

*If strong winds make it difficult to track across an open field,
lead your dog around the perimeter to check each deer run.*

that has almost stopped bleeding is most likely to leave a few drops when it exerts itself or stretches from its normal body posture. Crossings on stone walls are always a good place to look for blood.

Cold Tracking

Deer calls begin with a cold tracking phase, which may be followed by a hot line phase if the deer is not dead and leaves its bed at the tracker's approach. In the cold tracking phase the tracker and dog should work slowly and deliberately while trying to observe all evidence that offers information about the wounded deer. Most new handlers work much too fast because their dog wants to work fast. They slow the dog down as they gain experience. Marking the line as more blood is found may seem time-consuming, but almost always this will save time in the long run.

Watch for blood smears on brush and weeds, since the highest level of blood will help you determine how high the deer is hit. There is no point in spending hours tracking a deer that has been creased across the back.

Beds are easy to miss if you are working too fast. How much blood is in the bed? Where is the blood located in the bed and what does it look like and smell like? Is the bed warm, indicating that the deer took off at your approach, or did the deer voluntarily leave the bed at some time earlier? Details for interpreting this sort of evidence are given in the following chapters.

Sometimes when you are tracking through thick cover, you will hear the deer go out, or your dog will become excited and begin to bark or whine. Before you fly off in hot pursuit take the time to look for a wound bed or the place where the wounded deer was standing. This will save you time and embarrassment because it is all too easy to bump a healthy deer standing or bedded right on the line. The best dogs will sometimes get confused in this situation.

Hills

Something must be said about hills. The conventional hunting wisdom holds that wounded deer do not go uphill and prefer to go downhill if possible. Anyone who has tracked very much learns that deer go where they want to go, as if ups and downs did not exist. Deer climb hills when they are pushed, but they also willingly climb without pressure. If your dog indicates that the line goes up a steep hill, trust your dog! Often a deer will seek a knoll or a ridge crest as a bedding place because it offers good visibility of any danger approaching. A deer that has been wounded will not alter its behavior in this respect.

Fresh, Bright Blood on the Trail

When you begin to see fresh, bright blood on the trail that your dog is tracking, you naturally assume that the deer is moving out ahead of you and bleeding once more. You may be correct, but check your dog for briar cuts that can also produce surprising amounts of blood.

In 1976, early in my tracking career, I failed to find a deer for a hunter, who was an official in the New York State Department of Environmental Conservation. The dead buck was almost under my dog's nose, but we missed it. This is how it happened.

Bill had bowshot the buck late one afternoon, and he called me the next morning. We began working the line across an overgrown field where the blood sign had run out the previous evening. We had tracked about 200 yards when Clary veered suddenly off to the left on a fresh, hot line. We saw fresh blood low on the weeds, and I assumed too quickly that we had the buck up and bleeding. We had a line and we pushed it hard, right up into the high ridges from where Bill had tracked the buck the previous afternoon. After about a mile and some very steep slopes, we began to have our doubts about ever catching up. The deer was just too strong and we quit. The problem, as we learned later, was that we were tracking the hot line of another unwounded deer. The fresh blood from Clary's briar-torn ears had fooled me into thinking that we had jumped the deer from its wound bed.

Two days later Bill called me. He had found the buck, spoiled and inedible, 50 yards from where we had been when we took off on the fresh line. It was my fault. I had not checked for a wound bed. I had not inspected my dog's ears for briar cuts. I had taken off on impulse and enthusiasm, but I had learned my lesson.

Distractions of Wildlife and Staying on the Right Line

As the story of Bill's deer suggests, a major problem in finding wounded deer is distinguishing them from the healthy ones that abound in the area. An accomplished tracking dog learns that different deer have different scents, just as humans do. Scent from the interdigital glands in particular seems to be unique for each deer. Dogs learn to follow a particular deer, even if there is no visible blood, but this discrimination does not develop over night. Different dogs learn at different rates, and some never learn.

Part of the art of handling is being able to recognize when your tracking dog has taken a hot line and is likely to be following the wrong deer. Even old experienced dogs occasionally make mistakes and will confuse a healthy deer with a deer with a sealed arrow wound or some other wound that leaves little scent.

Bucks in rut have an overwhelmingly strong tarsal gland scent. A number of handlers have reported that even an experienced dog may have difficulty distinguishing one rutting buck from another.

When you are fairly sure that your dog is off on the wrong line, take him back to a point where you feel confident that the dog was correct. You can scold him mildly, but the main thing is to settle the dog down and make him realize that you are interested in the original line. If you punish the dog severely, you will turn him off to the whole idea of tracking. Learning to stay on the line comes primarily from positive reinforcement. And never forget the possibility that the dog may be correct, and you are the one who has made a mistake.

Never do anything that will weaken the bond between you and your dog. On a long, tough search, mutual trust is what keeps the team working. With some dogs in some activities there is a need for force training and hard measures. This is not the case in tracking work, which is driven by desire not fear.

Wild turkeys are also a problem for inexperienced dogs. A flock of turkeys scratching and feeding through the woods leaves an exciting cloud of scent that blows the mind of a young dog. Personally, I find fresh, strong turkey scent on a wounded deer track creates more problems than healthy deer scent. At least fresh turkey scratchings are a visual trace of their recent passage, so the handler knows what he is getting into. The best tactic is to calm your dog and restart him away from the scuffed-up area.

Staying on the right line, no matter what, is usually the most difficult skill that a tracking dog must learn. My old Sabina demonstrated how reliable an experienced dog can become:

> Jolanta and I tracked a buck together. On the phone it sounded like an easy one so we took one of our young wire males, Alec, who had training but no natural experience. Jolanta handled Alec and I handled Sabina behind as a backup in case the young dog had trouble. Alec did a pretty good job, trailed out past the hunter's point of loss and went on for another quarter mile without help.

Then came misfortune. Young Alec tracked right into a fresh gut pile, still warm. Alec thought the guts were better than nothing, and he munched a bit. The hunters and the handlers were down-hearted for sure. They had called us, and we had driven a long way; now it was all for nothing. Someone else had finished off their deer and dragged him out.

Then I thought of something. There had been some grains of corn in the track on the way to the gut pile. They had leaked out of the deer. It was funny that there was no corn in the gut pile that we were standing over. I took Sabina back on the trail about 50 yards and let her work the line; she tracked right past the gut pile, never looking at it. All concentration, she worked another 50 yards into some thick bush, and there he was, the original buck, corn, guts and all.

For Clary, an experienced tracker, this fawn was domestic livestock.

Night Work

Fortunately for those of us who deer hunt and who also track wounded deer for others, deer calls usually come in at times when they do not conflict very much with our own hunting. We receive calls for the services of a tracking dog either around midday or after dark, which is, in either case, several hours after the prime moving times when most deer are shot. Hunters in the Northeast and Midwest will try to track any wounded deer themselves and then call for tracking dog assistance if they are unsuccessful. A majority of these calls are night calls. As explained later in Chapter 27, tracking tactics and timing do vary in different parts of the country.

In my own area of northeastern New York State, night calls have become more popular with both hunters and trackers in recent years because of the rapid expansion of coyote populations. In many areas postponing the search until morning is not really an option because the odds are strong that coyotes will find the deer first. A family pack does not leave anything worthwhile for the hunter who arrives at 8 AM the following day. Even in early evening we have driven coyotes off "their" venison just as they were beginning their banquet. Coyotes are not pleased by such interruptions, and from a safe distance back in the brush they will yap at you in frustration. This is a good time to keep small tracking dogs on lead!

For those who work standard hours, as well as for those who hunt, it is actually more convenient to track after dark. You will need a suitable flashlight. Even if you track in the afternoon, darkness comes soon during the short days of deer season. Again, you should be prepared to complete your search for the deer in darkness, and you need to carry a suitable light with you. If I go out to track after lunch, I always carry a light with me.

We will pursue the subject of lights at greater length in the Chapter 19 on equipment. Here, we will touch upon the basics only. An expensive light is not necessary, but it does have to be powerful enough and reliable enough to do the job of lighting your way for four or five hours. After this, you must be able to muster enough candlepower to see and possibly shoot the deer you have been tracking. For this service we are not talking about a penlight or a two-cell flashlight from the supermarket. A LED flashlight or headlamp will work well, but be sure that it has a brightness of at least 150 lumens. Eventually you will probably want to buy one of the more expensive LED coon hunters' lights mounted on a plastic bump cap.

Those who go with you can be of little help if they do not have individual lights. More important, it is mandatory that everyone indicates their position with a shining flashlight if there is to be any shooting. If you really become involved in tracking wounded deer, you will find that it is best to have some extra lights for the accompanying hunters who are not well equipped.

After dark the handler should work more slowly, especially in rough, ledgy country. Even familiar woods look different at night. You may find that your hunter, "who knows these woods like his own backyard", is less reliable as a guide at night than he expected. Keep track of things for yourself; carry a compass or GPS and be aware of your directions. This is particularly true in flat, featureless country.

Even though the hunter has assured you that he has carefully marked the way to where he lost the deer, he may have a problem finding his markers in the dark. A scuff mark in the leaves is not all that obvious when you don't know exactly where you are. What we wrote about the use of surveyor's marking tape is doubly true at night. When you begin tracking at night, use plenty of tape and place it high so that it will catch the beam of your light.

The distractions and the hazards of wildlife are different at night. Agricultural fields, which were barren during the day, may be teaming with deer at night. This can unsettle an inexperienced dog. Mature woods may be empty of deer at night if there is no acorn mast. The deer will be out in the fields feeding. When working with an inexperienced dog, it is often best to postpone

Coyotes are excellent blood trackers!

tracking the wounded deer until an hour when the area is relatively deer-free. Dawn and dusk can be difficult times to track because deer are on the move.

During warm weather, poisonous snakes in the South are much more active after dark. If rattlesnakes, cottonmouths, copperheads or coral snakes are common in your area, a dog may have no business at all in the woods at night unless the temperature is below 50 degrees Fahrenheit. Certainly I would not want to work with a small, low set dog like a Dachshund if snakes were a hazard. A dog is not likely to survive a bite on the neck or chest.

As you track at night, keep looking ahead at the same time that you look for blood sign behind your dog. It is a big advantage to spot a wounded deer before it bolts, and they will often hold tight in their bed hoping that they will be overlooked.

Rarely but inevitably, if you track long enough, a charging wounded deer will suddenly materialize from beneath a deadfall or out of a thicket. It is startling to see those pale antler tines bearing down on your dog; even your dog will be impressed. Stay alert.

Perseverance

One of the most important traits of an outstanding handler/dog team is perseverance. When all seems hopeless, when there has not been a drop of blood seen in the last half mile the team pushes on for another quarter mile. Yes, this takes more time, and usually it is the dejected hunter who wants to quit, but surprisingly often it is that extra final push that produces the deer.

Part of this phenomenon is due to a situation in which internal bleeding has reduced the deer's blood pressure to a point that all external bleeding stops. Finally the deer collapses.

Extreme perseverance pays off. You will be spared the regrets that I felt in the 2012 season. I had tracked the deer nearly a mile without blood and I picked up my dog. Days later I learned that the dead buck had been found 100 yards farther on. Usually I do a better job of following my own advice.

Dealing With a Live Wounded Deer

About ⅔ of the deer that you find will be dead, but you must be prepared to deal with those that are still alive, including those that are aggressive. This is not only a matter of humane concern; it is also a matter of safety for your dog and even safety for your own person. Deciding upon the correct way to put down a wounded deer can be complicated. It is not a simple matter of good judgment. Assuming that tracking wounded deer with a leashed dog is legal in your state or province, the way that the deer is "humanely destroyed" may also be a matter of individual state regulation. The details of the various state regulations go beyond the scope of this book, but a general review and analysis is presented in Chapters 18 and 27.

In New York State the hunter accompanying the dog handler is permitted to put down the wounded deer during legal shooting hours, that is from sunrise to sunset. For this he must use a weapon that is legal during that particular hunting season. During bow season he must use a legal bow and so forth. If there are considerations of safety or of abbreviating animal suffering, the handler may use a firearm, at his discretion, at any time.

After legal shooting hours only the dog handler may shoot a wounded deer. The regulations in Vermont, Maine and New Hampshire, which were modeled after those in New York, are substantially the same. In certain states of the Midwest the use of a firearm or a bow to put down wounded deer is currently prohibited at all times. Other techniques must be used.

I prefer to let the hunter put down his own deer in the daytime if he chooses to do so. In that way the hunter has a sense that he has personally fulfilled the responsibility he undertook when he shot the deer. Generally, gun hunters do wish to put down their own deer, but the attitudes of bowhunters tend to be different.

Many bowhunters are not keen about the idea of carrying a compound bow long distances through heavy cover. They also recognize that an arrow is not very well suited for the sort of finishing shot that arises when a leashed tracking dog is used. In these circumstances the deer is likely to end up in thick cover through which it is difficult to thread an arrow without it being deflected. Since the deer is almost always lying down, the heart and lungs are not easily accessible because of the angle. The heavy handgun bullet that can smash through brush seems to be a better solution.

In bowhunting the final killing shot is more an anticlimax, and bowhunters are not as concerned about making it themselves. It seems more important that the killing be quick and clean. This attitude is compatible with the traditional bowhunting ethic, which bases "credit" and rightful ownership of the deer on the first, ultimately lethal, shot. It is right and proper for another to finish off a deer for his fellow hunter.

In the equipment chapter we will have more to say about handguns, long guns, sights, holsters and so on. Here we can only stress that a deer has much more vitality than a human of equal weight. Since there is always the possibility of having to stop an aggressive deer under circumstances of surprise, the handgun must have some real authority. Anyone who has seen law enforcement officers try to put down a deer with a .38 or a 9mm will realize that these cartridges are completely inadequate. The .357 magnum is a safe minimum, and I prefer a .44 magnum.

No matter how weak a wounded deer appears, approach with caution and respect. I can remember one incident where we pushed a bowshot buck hard for two miles and finally caught up to him lying out in the open on a little knoll. The deer was inert, but the eyes were closed and he was still breathing, He was not dead but seemed completely spent. When the bowhunter's finishing arrow caught the buck in the chest he leaped straight up. I clearly remember looking above my head at the deer. The first jump came directly at me and then he veered away. The buck was down again within 50 yards, but what power that last surge of adrenaline had given him!

Shooting can seldom be done under ideal circumstances. As in hunting, the largest reliable target is the heart-lung area, and it is best to try for this. If the bullet is placed behind the shoulder in the rib cage, little venison will be damaged. Avoid head shots especially on bucks. You have a good chance of shooting off a trophy antler, and the hunter will not be pleased. When the deer has already been put through so much, it seems a sacrilege to wait additional five minutes for the last breaths to come. A close, finishing shot in the neck behind the head is a better ending. Have respect for the game.

When a handler is making a decision to finish off a large antlered buck with a firearm during bow season, he should be aware that his bullet may make the deer ineligible for the record book. For example, the Pope and Young Club maintains a record book for bowhunters who take trophy deer with antlers scoring above a certain minimum. Pope and Young's fair chase rules for bowhunters do not allow for the use of a firearm.

There is much more involved with putting down wounded deer than we can deal with in this first chapter, which is designed to give the reader an overview of wounded deer tracking. Chapter 18 is totally focused on this subject.

Reward

When a deer has been found and is being dressed out, the question of "reward" arises. Should we give the dog a piece of liver or a strip of belly meat so that he will want to track next time? For some dogs a warm treat from the deer fulfills their prey drive and is obviously important for them.

Other highly motivated dogs are so transported by the emotions of finding the deer that they aren't interested in eating at all. Sabina, one of my best tracking Dachshunds, relished a chew on the tail. After she had sheared off a few tails, I was able to transfer her fetish to a hind hoof. Munching on a hind hoof was much more important to her than a mouthful of raw venison. For Sabina, and for most of the highly motivated tracking dogs that I have known, it is the joy and praise of the handler, the hunter and everyone else in the party which means the most.

Tracking is a participatory experience and your dog soon realizes that this is a joint effort. For the handler, who is a true believer, this close involvement takes the experience a notch higher than watching and hearing what a hound does hundreds of yards away. The psychic bonding that takes place on a tough but successful deer call is akin to what members of a sports team experience in the exaltation of victory. You and your dog will be closer than ever before, and this is the greatest reward of all.

Summary

• Use a tracking leash that is at least 30 feet long. Mountain climbing rope and flexible plastic leashes work well.

• Try to start tracking at the hit site where the hunter shot the deer instead of at the hunter's point of loss.

• Mark your tracking progress with biodegradable, blaze orange marking tape.

• If your dog has trouble tracking across an open field, check the deer runs around the edges of the field.

• If you suddenly see fresh blood on the ground, check your dog to make sure that you are not seeing blood from briar cuts.

• Be alert. A wounded deer may attack your dog. Wounded deer have attacked handlers.

• Respect the game. If you must put the deer down, do it quickly and humanely with a handgun or other legal firearm of adequate power.

Chapter 2

The Tracking Dog and Scent

What Is Scent?

Even scientists admit that there is much that we don't know about scent and the means that animals use to interpret it. Scent seems to be composed of particles scaling down to molecular size. These may be rubbed off an animal or shed like a cloud of microscopic dandruff. Scent from a deer has many components. It includes tiny flakes of bacteria-laden dead skin; scent may also contain traces of secretions from the deer's various scent glands such as the interdigital glands between the cloves of the hoofs and the tarsal glands above the hocks. Scent of a wounded deer can also be emitted from droplets of blood or other body fluids that have leaked from the wound onto the ground. Scent particles drift with the wind or on minor air currents, much like smoke. The effectiveness with which a dog recognizes these different forms of scent is very much influenced by atmospheric conditions. We have already touched upon the role that wind plays in the tracking process, but there are many other factors involved, and not all of them are clearly understood.

In the morning, as the air warms to a temperature greater than that of the ground, air from the ground level tends to rise carrying with it scent particles. Body scent particles, which have been resting on the ground all night, tend to be borne aloft beyond reach of the dog. If you are tracking body scent from the night before, it can make for tough conditions as the dew or frost burns off. On the other hand, if there are actual drops of blood on the ground giving off scent, the task will not be so difficult because there will be a flow of blood scent particles upward to the dog's nose. The dog may work with a high head.

In the evening the reverse is the case. The air settles and body scent hangs at the ground surface. Cooling air flows down from the ridges into the valleys carrying scent particles with it. Tracking is at its best in the evening as the air becomes heavier and moisture begins to condense out of the atmosphere as dew. Generally, superior scenting conditions are one of the reasons why many experienced handlers prefer to track with their dogs at night. A background of coon hunting may also contribute to this preference. On the whole, the windiest part of the day tends to be early in the afternoon and the calmest times come with darkness. The best times for tracking begin with the hours when work and deer hunting are over for the day.

Barometric pressure must be involved in some way in the whole complex explanation of scenting conditions. On a falling barometer, before a storm front, I have seen a seasoned tracking dog become as helpless as a newborn puppy when it came to following a blood line. Once, with big drops of raunchy, gut blood right under her nose, my best tracking dog ever could not follow what I could track easily by eye.

Everyone wants to know "How old can a blood line be before you can't track it?" Everything depends on scenting conditions. On a cold, damp day in January, during the Long Island bow season, my tracking dog Clary successfully worked a wounded deer line without visible blood that was 48 hours old. I am sure that some cold nosed big game hounds and Bloodhounds could do better than this. Bear scent "holds" better than deer scent. In the Northeast of the United States you seldom need a dog capable of tracking lines more than 24 hours old. Hunters will almost always contact you before a day and a night have elapsed. A dog that can regularly track natural lines that have aged eight hours in daylight is very useful. Scent lines age much more during the daytime than at night.

Reading Your Dog

It is essential for the handler to recognize what his dog is doing with the scent line. Has he been distracted by fresh deer scent? Has he overshot a turn and lost scent contact? Understanding the dog's work is done by "reading" the dog's "body language". Dogs don't speak in human fashion when tracking, but they express themselves through their body language of special movements. Body language can be expressed by head carriage, ear positioning, tail set and tail movement, or arching of the back.

Reading your dog is complicated by the fact that not all dogs do use the same body language. The handler must learn to interpret each individual dog he works with.

Scent and the Direction of Track

A good dog has considerable capacity to determine the direction of passage on the line by scent. The fresher the scent line, the more reliable the dog will be in going the right direction. I have had some very good dogs, who had problems figuring out which direction the deer went if the line was older than 12 hours. Generally, on older lines the handler will end up combining his skills and perceptions with those of his canine partner. If the dog can show you right where the line is, you can usually find a footprint clear enough to show the direction of travel. Fingers on occasional drops of splattered blood are another indicator. They point in the direction the deer was headed.

There has been endless speculation on the question of how dogs pick the proper direction of a track. A common explanation is that the dog can tell the direction because the scent is slightly fresher, and therefore stronger, going in the proper direction of travel. I find this hard to swallow. Even on a four-hour-old track, the difference in intensity of scent is infinitesimal.

Another explanation is that the front of a hoof or paw smells different than the heel part, and that a dog can detect this and determine direction.

Ripples made by a swimming beaver
Photo courtesy of James Pitcher

My own contribution to these speculations concerning direction involves some different assumptions and depends upon some different models to explain what we observe. We know that scent drifts with the flow of air movements. Imagine a beaver swimming across a tranquil pond. A "V" shaped wave or ripple extends back from the point of the beaver's advancing nose.

Now imagine this "V" of ripples flash frozen into solid ice just after the beaver has passed. In the distribution pattern of the frozen ripples, or the distribution pattern of all the plankton and other particles floating in the ripples, there would be visible evidence of the direction of passage.

As a deer passes there is a cloud of body scent particles that drifts out from either side. The configuration of this cloud and the distribution of scent particles onto the ground and surrounding cover is certainly going to be influenced by the minor turbulence created by the deer as it moves forward.

As our eyes can detect the direction-oriented pattern of the ripples and ripple-borne particles, it just may be possible that a dog's nose can "scan" the distribution pattern of scent particles from a moving animal in a similar way.

Research by Noam Sobel and Jess Porter at the University of California at Berkeley demonstrates that humans have a "directional" scenting capacity. The human brain can localize the source of a certain scent by processing how it comes into the left and right nostril. This is the same principle that gives us directional hearing. It is not much of a stretch to assume that dogs have a similar capacity, and that this enhances their ability to "scan" a scent path to determine its direction.

This matter deserves serious research. It is easy to see that dogs have a better sense of direction when tracking in cover than when tracking on a hard, uncluttered surface. Also when a dog determines direction, he does not minutely examine each track with his nose. Rather he seems to scan a broader area before taking off in the right direction. Perhaps the scent leavings of the deer have ripple marks and "tails" instead of "fingers".

The older the line the more difficult it is for the dog to determine direction. This could be explained by the fading and blurring of the scent distribution pattern over time.

Tracking Conditions

After you have tracked a number of deer under different conditions you will begin to realize that the age of a wounded deer trail is not as significant as the conditions existing as you track. Generally, moisture, including rain, is your friend, while dryness and wind are your enemies.

As the temperature falls toward the dew point in late afternoon, tracking conditions improve. A line that was very difficult for a dog at 3 PM generally becomes easier at dusk two hours later. This is one reason why it is attractive to track at night.

Rain is usually helpful; it has to be very heavy or prolonged to completely wash away the scent. A steady rain dilutes and spreads the blood out so that nothing is visible, but at the same time the scent is actually freshened.

I can remember tracking a buck across a 50-acre hillside covered with red cedars. Rainwater was flowing in sheets across the ground with only the high patches not immersed. It seemed like an impossible undertaking, but old Max picked his way from one high spot to another along the shoulder of the hill, down across a major highway and to the edge of a swamp. There lay the buck very much alive.

Tracking blood in the rain seems to be a miraculous feat to inexperienced observers. Enjoy the praise, but prepare to have your pride humbled when you try to track on one of those dry, windy days of early bow season. Crisp, new fallen leaves are swept along the ridge tops, and your dog finds only occasional traces of ground scent. It can be almost impossible to work a line by ground scent, and the best strategy may be to work the wind according to techniques described later in the chapter.

Don't be intimidated by snow that lies two to four inches deep on the blood line. Wet, heavy snow seems to preserve the scent so that the dog can "snowplow" along with his nose, following the scent line slowly but with great accuracy. Very dry, dusty snow is another matter; it tends to be drawn up the dog's nose, closing down effective scenting.

Snow is often a plus when tracking but there is one circumstance in which it becomes a problem. If snow melts out from **under** a trail of blood and scent, it becomes very difficult for the dog to follow.

Scents and Surfaces

The surface on which the scent line is to be followed has a lot to do with the difficulty of the track. Fortunately, what is difficult for the dog can be easy for the handler. Dog and handler work as a team, which is more effective than either team partner would be if working alone.

Freshly plowed fields are a problem for the tracking dog. The abundance of earth scent seems to mask the scent of the wounded animal. Sandy beaches and gravel pits also seem to retain little scent but for different reasons. Smooth dry surfaces do not hold scent well. On such surfaces your eyes can assist the dog.

As you would expect, it is much easier for a dog to pick up scent in brush or high grass than it is in a closely grazed pasture.

Conifer forests make for more difficult tracking. Generally, there is little undergrowth under the dense canopy of branches. The needles on the ground have slick surfaces, and they have an aromatic scent that may mask other fainter scents to some degree.

Generally, the thicker the cover the easier it is for a dog to track scent. There are more uneven surfaces to retain the scent particles. Scent from animal passers-by rubs off on to the surrounding cover. I have seen a Dachshund stand on her hind legs to examine with her nose a blackberry briar hanging out into a deer trail.

Scent Discrimination

Every deer has an individual scent, just like humans. The interdigital glands between the cloves of the hoofs are very important for leaving the individual "signature" of each deer. Staying on that individual scent line is one of the most important things that a young tracking dog must learn. He was born with the nose and brain that permit him to discriminate between scents. Training and natural scent lines will help him to develop this inborn ability.

You may already have encountered the familiar example illustrating the difference between human and dog when it comes to smelling things. "When a human comes into the kitchen, he smells the whole smell of the stew cooking on the burner." Good stew! When the family dog comes into the kitchen he smells all the different ingredients of the stew. "Meat, that's beef not venison. Cabbage, I don't like that, potatoes, they're OK....." To better understand scent work we must try to think like a dog!

Here's a practical example of what a tracking dog has to do. The hunter calls you at 6 PM, and an hour later you start tracking in the hardwoods at the hit site. No problem! No problem that is until you track to the edge of a hay field where eight deer are grazing. The deer take off, but their fresh scent lingers. This is a tough situation for a year-old dog, but an experienced dog will recognize and tune out the fresh deer scent. He will track across the field following the much fainter scent of the wounded deer.

The scent discriminating powers of an experienced dog never cease to amaze me. Here's a case for you.

I was tracking a difficult deer line at night with my old dog Clary. This bitch had few faults, but one of them was a passion for skunks. That night we bumped into Mr. Skunk crossing the scent line of the deer. Clary veered off and grabbed the skunk before I could stop her. Clary killed him, but not before he saturated her with spray. The whole area reeked of skunk. I told the hunter, "Sorry, I guess that's it!" But no! Clary rolled in the leaves a bit, then got back on the line, showing us some blood drops for the next quarter mile. We never caught up to that deer, but we couldn't blame it on the skunk. All I could smell for the next few days was skunk, but Clary had no such problem.

Water Hazards

Deer recognize the relationship between scent retention and surfaces very well. They track one another, and they are chased by dogs, coyotes and wolves. Water is the deer's favorite avenue of escape from its pursuers. When the opportunity presents itself, the wounded deer will use all its tricks and experience to stump the tracking dog and handler.

When your tracking dog brings you to a running stream do not assume that the deer went directly across. The deer may have gone up or down stream a hundred yards or more. It may have exited from the stream on the same side that it entered. The deer understood that running water does not hold scent.

If you are a few hundred yards behind the deer, you may be able to see muddied water or splashes of water on stones that can guide you and the dog. An experienced dog always checks the other side of the stream and then checks up and down the banks, first on the far shore and then on the near one. As a handler you can help the dog. You are better equipped than the dog to judge the likely exit points from a stream.

Roads

From a deer's viewpoint roads are almost as useful as streams, and they use them in very much the same way to elude their pursuers. The smooth surface of the road holds scent poorly as it is swept away by the rush of passing traffic. Exhaust fumes also mask the scent. Don't count on a deer to go straight across the road; they may use it as they would a stream, and your dog should check it out in the same way also. An experienced dog does not have to be told to do this. They check across, up and down the far side, and then up and down the near side. Your job is to watch the traffic and not let your dog be run over!

I tracked a large wounded doe that had been shot within 100 yards of the Taconic Parkway in Dutchess County, New York. The bowhunters had been able to track her into dense brush along the Parkway, but there all traces of the blood trail seemed to disappear. Four hours later, after dark, my tracking dog Max was able to carry the line another 100 yards parallel to the Parkway. Then Max turned, went to the edge of the pavement and made ready to cross.

We waited until there was a safe break in the traffic flow before crossing to the median, which was 25 yards wide and lightly wooded. It was not easy to pick up the line there, but after some casting Max showed us drops of blood farther north on the median. The doe had traveled north along the median about 150 yards, and had then cut back across the south bound lanes to the side from which she had originally come. She must have done all this when traffic was heavy in late afternoon. She finally bedded in a patch of purple loosestrife in the middle of a hay field close to the parkway.

Although wounded, the doe had kept her wits. She had known that she was being tracked by the bowhunters, and she had done all she could to make their pursuit impossible. Without Max to get us across some of the long and critical gaps in the blood trail, the doe certainly would have been lost.

Water Tactics

Ponds, lakes and big rivers will also be used by deer in their effort to put a scent-free barrier between them and their pursuer. Leg-hit deer seem particularly likely to do this. If you are pressing a deer hard and it heads for big water, this can create problems for you; it is best to ease off and try to work the deer gently away from this place where you have a good chance of losing it.

It is generally true that young, wounded deer quit quickly, if they move out of their bed at all as the tracking dog approaches. However, in deer tracking there are exceptions to every rule.

On Long Island in January of 1980, Clary and I tracked a leg-hit fawn that dressed out at less than fifty pounds. Most fawns are easy, but this little one would not quit. After some difficulty reconstructing a back track, we got the deer moving. There was enough fresh blood to suggest that the deer would soon weaken and stop.

Skirting a large tidal pond, we were about 100 yards behind the deer when it decided that there was no safety on land. The fawn veered out into the salt water and headed for the far shore a quarter of a mile away. The Park Ranger, who was accompanying me and the hunter, took several shots with his handgun, but the deer kept on swimming. We might well have lost her if the deer had not swum into a floating barrier of ice crystals on the other side of the pond. It struggled in the ice and died. Finally we were able to borrow a boat, row out and take the deer from its last icy bed.

Such stories do not always end with finding the deer. In another case I pushed the deer too hard and lost it in a long, narrow pond, which had been created by damming a steep gorge. If the deer ever came back out of the water, we never found the place. At this point I had not learned that a deer will float to the surface after gas builds up in its belly. I should have told the hunter to return and check in 12 hours.

In December 2015 we got an interesting message from a tracker down south. Her gifted young dog had tracked a gut shot deer to a pond. But there was no deer to be seen! "Mossy", the tracking dog, insisted that the deer had gone no farther than the pond and had to be there. Well, where was it? After Mossy and her handler Judy Catrett had gone home, the hunter checked the pond again. Behold! The deer had now risen to the surface; the bulge of its body was visible. How can this be explained?

When a dead deer is in light summer coat (no air in the thick winter hairs), it will usually sink. The same is true throughout the year for southern deer that don't develop dense winter coats, even late in the season. Mossy's southern deer had gone into the pond, drank some water, died and sank out of sight. When gas began to form in it's stomach and intestines, the deer had become more buoyant and had floated to the surface.

Swamps

Swamps are a combination of land and water. The water may be a few inches deep or waist deep. For the deer they offer a means of putting gaps in their scent line, and often the deer bed down on dry mounds and hummocks that are surrounded by water and swamp vegetation.

Dogs track in watery swamps much better than you would think. I have waded behind Dachshunds as they swam from bog to bog, picking up traces of body scent on the vegetation and following the line to the deer's hiding place or across to solid ground (color Fig. 15). If you are right behind the deer, body scent will hang over the sheltered waters for some time. For swamp work you need a dog with some body mass to withstand the cold if it is late in the season. A strong standard Dachshund will do the job, but big dogs like retrievers, pointing dogs and cur dogs are even better. I considered Cleo, my Southern Black Mouth Cur, to be my swamp dog of choice.

Checks

"Checks" occur when dog and handler encounter a place where the line of scent is temporarily lost. Surfaces, water, roads and many other problems create such checks. At a check forward progress ceases while the tracking team searches to regain the line and to determine its direction. If the deer makes a sharp turn or backtracks, that will create a check. In these cases the dog tends to overrun the turn or end of the line, and then has to come back to regain it. Some checks result from distractions created by other deer or game such as wild turkeys. Sometimes checks do not have any apparent cause, or the cause lies within the dog rather than in external circumstances. Dogs make some dumb mistakes, just as people do, but smart, experienced dogs make very few tracking mistakes on their own. If they have a problem following the line, there is usually a good reason.

Most checks last for less than a minute, but some are prolonged. I have worked for 45 minutes on a single check with the dog going back to the point of loss repeatedly with an accuracy and sense of spatial relations that would be completely beyond the capacity of most human beings. Finally the puzzle was solved, and we continued.

The handler assists on the check by giving the dog support and focusing his concentration. A dog will stay much longer on a check if the handler encourages and supports him. "Where is it? Where is it? Work it out. Work it out." The message is in the tone and inflection of the voice. The calm repetition of encouragement transmits the superior patience and attention span of the handler to the tracking dog. This communication flows both ways and is mutually reinforcing. Most dogs answer with their body language and nose talk. "I'm trying. I'm taking it all in. I'm checking everything."

When the good scent comes to the dog and the puzzle of the check falls away, the response of the dog is clear. The tempo and swing of the tail increase. "I've got it."

Don Hickman's great tracking dog Addie was extraordinary in her check-work communications. Like most tracking dogs Addie worked silently on lines unless she was very close to the deer. With her outstanding nose and her will to find, she would work a check diligently like a good mother checking over her child for ticks. When Addie did regain that golden thread of the line, she would always announce it with two quick barks. "Got it." And off she would go.

A new handler once told me, "I was just a dope on a rope." It is especially through check work that a handler grows past this phase of feeling like an awkward bystander. Through check work dog and handler come together and become a tracking team. The handler gains a window on the world beyond his own senses; he enters animal consciousness without losing his own.

Working the Wind

Working the wind should be in your arsenal of skills. Work the wind when the wind is your enemy and ground scent will not hold. If branches sway in the wind, if individual dry leaves skip and tumble across the forest floor, then the whole scent line will become fragmented and scattered after a few hours. In a roaring wind the usual ground scenting strategies must be altered so that the wind will work for you rather than against you. Rather than trying to track down the scent line as it disintegrates, you are often better off letting the wounded deer's body scent come to you as you deliberately work downwind of its suspected hiding places.

If a good wind-scenting dog is downwind of a wounded or dead deer, he can pick up the scent of that deer (or a pile of guts) 200 yards away. Some cur dog breeders from Texas claim that their dogs can wind scent a squirrel in a tree a quarter mile away! Half that distance is a long way.

Watch your dog and follow your dog as he passes downwind of potential bedding places. Scent discrimination between one deer and another does not seem to be very good on the wind at a distance. Possibly he will take you in to where some healthy deer were bedded, but he will also find the wounded deer if it is there.

If you have ever steered a sailboat, you will be aware that the wind is often shifting. In fitful winds before a storm it may swing around 180 degrees. Your dog can be ten feet upwind of the dead deer and not scent a thing. Be aware that wind direction can change as you work.

The ability to wind scent and the ability to track ground scent are not the same. Most dogs are better at one than the other, and only a few excel at both. Pointing dogs were developed by selecting individuals that could "wind" a bird in the bush at long distances. The southern cattle and hog dogs like the Southern Black Mouth Curs were selected in part for their ability to wind semi-wild cattle and hogs at a distance in thick brush. These types of dogs wind scent best, but good ground scent trackers certainly have some wind scenting capability as well.

Even on a still day there are subtle air currents that an experienced deer tracking dog will use. For example in the warming morning hours air currents flow uphill; in the cooling evening hours they flow downward.

Whatever the specialty of your personal tracking dog, working the wind will not spoil him provided that he already has established line sense that comes out of tracking experience. It would be a mistake to take a young tracking dog and lead him around for wind scenting before he knew what it means to dig in and work a line step-by-step or drop-by-drop. To work the wind too soon with an inexperienced dog may well produce a sloppy worker, which inappropriately switches back and forth from one mode of scenting to the other.

Blood Tracking Without Blood

Throughout this book we refer to "blood tracking" because this is the standard and established term applied to tracking wounded big game. They call it "blood tracking", but at its highest level it's really about tracking when there is no blood.

Deer, and probably other mammals, have distinctive individual scents just as people do. Everyone knows that a man-tracking Bloodhound sticks to the right line, but hunters are usually amazed to learn that a good game dog can make the same distinctions on a wounded deer if encouraged to do so.

In bow season we get called in to track a certain number of wounded deer shot from a tree stand at a steep downward angle with a high entry wound and no exit. A little blood will trickle down at the beginning, and then all the bleeding is internal. The tracking dog must follow the individual scent of the deer. This consists of body scent, scent from the tarsal glands at the hocks and particularly scent from the interdigital glands located in between the cloven hoofs at the top of each foot. High wounds with no exit can make for tough tracking, and scenting conditions will be a major factor in determining how long the trail will last for the dog. A pup can't do this in his first tracking season. Usually it takes 20 or 30 calls worth of experience.

When we are called upon to track deer on snow, it provides a good opportunity to learn how much dogs are dependent upon blood in tracking. In 2002, snow cover came with the first day of the deer gun season. This cut down on the need for tracking dogs considerably, but we had an instructive call on Thanksgiving Day.

This Thanksgiving Day deer was a "buck of a lifetime", a nice ten pointer, and there aren't too many of these in our part of New York State. There was some blood on the snow for about 300 yards, but then it stopped and the dry snow was so loose that it was impossible to pick out a particular deer track from all the others. The hunter called just before noon after searching all morning, but I didn't want to take the call until after dark when all the hunters were out of the woods. If a wounded, big-racked buck is still alive and you get him up and parade him around the woods in front of other hunters, it is almost inevitable that someone else will drop him. Darren, the hunter, really wanted this deer.

Late afternoon Thanksgiving dinner was postponed a bit, and we got to the hit site just as it was getting dark. We wanted to miss other hunters, but

Sabina with a buck she tracked on dry, dusty snow with no blood visible.

we also wanted to beat out the coyotes, which begin to move at dusk. We worked out over the part of the line with blood, and then we came to the point where Darren and his father had lost it in a maze of deer tracks. The temperature was dropping to ten degrees, which didn't make things any easier. On the six inches of dry white snow, we would have been able to see a pinhead-sized spot of blood, but there wasn't any. Still there was some scent for my Dachshund Sabina to work. Probably there were microscopic scent particles from the wound, and of course the individual scent of the deer.

It was slow going. Once Sabina went off 50 yards on the wrong track and then corrected herself and came back. It was easy to read her level of confidence by her tail and body language. We worked about 200 yards through heavy evergreen cover, and then there was a bloody bed and another and another. In the fourth bed, the buck lay dead.

They call it "blood tracking" but very often it includes tracking where there is no blood.

Summary

- To better understand your dog's work it is important to know as much as possible about the nature of scent.

- Atmospheric conditions are more important than the age of the track.

- Dogs have the ability to distinguish between many different scents at the same time.

- Each deer has an individual scent.

- Under the right conditions dogs can locate deer by body scent carried by wind or air currents.

- Dogs do not need blood to track a wounded deer!

Chapter 3

Selecting a Tracking Dog Prospect

Guidelines for All Breeds

Perhaps you already have a dog that you believe will become a good blood tracker. By all means experiment with the dog you have, following the instructions in the training chapters. If you are satisfied with your dog's work, you may choose to skip this chapter or put it on the back burner. However, there are many prospective handlers, starting from scratch, with a need to acquire a dog that is a strong tracking prospect. Others may not be sure about the potential of a dog they currently own. If a dog lacks the basic requirements of a tracking dog, it does not make sense to invest a great deal of time in attempting to train him to blood track.

This chapter deals primarily with the psychological factors and the scenting abilities required in a tracking dog prospect. But it goes without saying that the physical soundness of a tracking dog is also tremendously important. You cannot have a tracking dog unable to work many miles of a track through rough terrain. Since different breeds of dogs tend to have different weaknesses, it makes sense to discuss these in the following breed Chapters, 4-7.

Individual Dogs Within a Breed

You will have to think about dog breeds in your selection process, but finding the individual puppy or dog within the breed is just as important. From the standpoint of selecting a dog to work, breeds are simply useful categories in which to start evaluating individual dogs.

"Where can I get a Wirehaired Dachshund? I hear that they are great for tracking wounded deer." This question comes in frequently to our website. Unfortunately, there is no magic in the Wirehaired Dachshund label, or any other breed label. Within the category of Wirehaired Dachshunds you can expect to find certain individuals who will have the useful behavior traits for blood tracking. However, these traits will not necessarily be present in every individual of the breed and coat variety. In selecting a puppy for tracking you should ask a lot of questions about the working abilities of the ancestors and particularly of the sire and dam. If the litter comes out of a repeat breeding, it is very useful to find out what the pups of earlier litters accomplished. If you can visit the breeder and observe the behavior patterns of the puppies, this is very valuable. Otherwise, you must rely on the knowledge, skill and the honesty of the breeder. Puppies are always a gamble to some degree, but you can greatly reduce the risks if you do your research.

It would seem that the safest solution is to buy a mature, trained dog whose accomplishments can be evaluated. Unfortunately, mature, experienced blood trackers are seldom available, and when they are sold, they do not come cheap. After many tracking adventures, handlers bond closely with their very best dogs, and normally these are not for sale at any price.

Also keep in mind that a trained blood tracking dog is not like a piece of equipment, ready to be used when you need it. It may take you months of time spent with your dog, and also a number of live deer calls, to establish the kind of working relationship that your dog had with his original trainer. There is much to be said for training your own dog.

There are only a few breeds of dogs such as the Bavarian Mountain Hound that are bred exclusively for blood tracking. Not all of these will be good trackers because of their breed label, but the odds are very good that they will excel. The Bloodhound strains bred for man tracking in Law Enforcement are also specialists, and these can be adapted to big game tracking. In practice, only a small percentage of handlers work with the specialized breeds. In most breeds used for tracking, the dogs are not bred for one specific purpose. Versatility has a strong appeal for most of us, but selecting the right multi-purpose dog requires research. This research can be both educational and a lot of fun.

Show, Pet and Hunting Stock

In most "working" or "hunting" breeds, three different physical and psychological types exist: **show, pet or companion, and hunting or working**. To be sure, these categories overlap, but they still are useful to help you sort things out. More categories might be added, but for our purposes here it isn't necessary to warn about pet shops and puppy mills. In some breeds, such as the setters, there has been a split into show and hunting types. You should be aware of this.

Most show breeders are interested in producing show champions. Because of the complexities and competitiveness of the dog show game, they can seldom give hunting or tracking abilities a high priority. These show people are not necessarily against hunting or tracking, but they ignore working ability in selecting breeding animals.

There are also some show-oriented breeders who couldn't care less about hunting ability or tracking ability. Many of these "show only" breeders sincerely believe there is little or no genetic basis for working ability. They believe that all any dog needs is good training. Wistfully, these show people say "My champion could certainly do it if only I had the time to give him an opportunity." It is up to you to decide whether you can accept this on faith without supporting evidence. Amazingly, in certain breeds hunting and tracking abilities do survive many generations of selection for show purposes. One good example is the miniature Dachshund.

Pet or companion dogs come from several sources. Many pets come from show breeders who recognize that certain pups will not make the grade in the show ring. Hunter/breeders sometimes do the same thing when they realize that certain puppies "don't have it" for work in the field.

Of course, there are "pet breeders", who produce puppies with no intention of either showing them or developing them as workers or hunters. Some of them breed out of an honest desire to provide sound, stable and attractive companions for people. Even though these breeders are not interested in working their dogs at the traditional tasks of the breed, they find that many of the original breed traits, such as responsiveness and intelligence, enhance the quality of a dog as a companion.

In some breeds, such as Golden Retrievers, the great majority of dogs are bred to be companion dogs rather than hunters. By and large, these Goldens serve very well as a family dog. The problem is that many pet owners, who know very little, breed a litter or two to immortalize their canine family member, and perhaps to make a few extra dollars. These people are not necessarily knowledgeable about such things as hip dysplasia and other genetically influenced defects. They assume that the closest male of the breed will be as suitable a sire as any other.

It does happen that there are some products of pet breeding that have all the necessary qualities of desire, capability and common sense. This is particularly true in blood tracking. Here intelligence, coupled with a reasonable amount of nose, is the single most important trait that we need in a dog.

In the summer of 2000, I helped Gary Salisbury train his Golden Retriever of pet breeding for blood tracking. The dog showed the right moves and had excellent focus when working old lines. But don't count on this good fortune. My daughter purchased another golden, of unrelated pet breeding, as a long distance hiking companion. The dog had no interest in game, probably a good thing for a hiker's dog, but hip dysplasia limited the dog's capabilities to plod more than three miles. You have the best chance of getting a useful dog if you purchase from a knowledgeable breeder, who breeds physically sound dogs that are intelligent and nose-oriented.

We have been critical of the show and pet breeders, but don't jump to the conclusion that the dogs bred by hunters are always good. All too often the hunter/breeder is a guy who likes his dog, and thinks about having a "chip off the old block" to replace him when he passes on. His buddy, who lives in the next town, has a hunting bitch of the same breed, so they put them together at the amorous moment. The two prospective parents may be very ordinary dogs, or they may have similar physical or psychological weaknesses; no thought is given to this. It is a one-litter affair, bred for sentimental reasons, and no particular effort is made to follow up on the pups to see how they work out. A hunter/breeder like this, who has seen few dogs work except his own, does not learn much more by selling a few pups who disappear into the great unknown at seven weeks. The casual hunter/breeder may have the best intentions of producing fine hunting dogs, but his hit-or-miss methods are not very likely to produce them.

There are also hunter/breeders with much more experience. They understand their bloodlines, and they have produced enough litters to know which matings produce a high percentage of intelligent, trainable puppies. They work with their young puppies, and they keep informed about them after they are sold. Their own hunting and tracking work in the field gives them a thorough understanding of what a young puppy needs to succeed.

Sometimes these experienced breeders become overconfident and lose all humility. "Breeding is simply a matter of understanding genetics. All of my puppies are good". The breeder who says these things is either a liar or a fool. Dog breeding is still a long way from being a science. There are too many variables, and there is still much to be learned. But a conscientious hunter/breeder can learn from trial and error. He develops an "eye" for how pups of his breeding will develop into working adults. If you can tell him what you need, he can see the foreshadowing of this in the puppy he helps you select.

Mixed Breeds

Purebred dogs don't have a monopoly on tracking aptitudes. There are excellent mixed breed tracking dogs working, particularly in the South. A Lab-Beagle cross is often an effective combination. We are not advocating that breeds should be intentionally crossed, but we all know that accidents happen in the real world. A buyer on a tight budget may find a good pup at a quarter of the purebred price. However, all mixed breeds are not equal.

In the parents, if they are known, look for a combination of working dog smarts and responsiveness on one parent's side and superior nose on the other. The intended blending of qualities from two distinct breeds, may present itself in the first generation, but in successive generations there is little control over how the ancestral breed aptitudes will appear.

The breeds used for tracking are bred for a purpose, and in the long run, it is in everyone's interest to preserve these traits in the dogs of the future.

The Role of Genetics

A tracking dog's genetics, that is his ancestry, is certainly an important factor determining his future potential as a blood tracker. However, genetics can't be relied on to overcome the neglect of breeders who ignore their puppies and leave them in a pen until they are sold. Some breeders of hunting dogs overemphasize the importance of genetics while ignoring the very important role played by environment and early conditioning. Recent psychological research on infant humans and other young mammals clearly shows that the development of the brain circuitry is influenced in part by the stimulation that the developing brain receives and not simply by the programmed genetic codes that come down from the parents. In practice, this means that a very "well-bred" puppy, left in a dull kennel environment for its formative months, may mature with inferior tracking abilities.

Over 40 years of breeding experience, we have become much more successful in producing a high percentage of Wirehaired Dachshunds with a strong drive to track blood scent from point "A" to point "B". We have always used good working dogs in our pedigrees but the improvement that we have seen in our puppies seems too great to be explained by "better genetics".

We have to attribute part of the improvement to early conditioning starting when, or even before, the puppies are weaned. We have gone from about 25% "good ones" to about 80% that we can sell with guarantees of a strong desire to track. This tracking desire will already be clearly evident when the pups are 10 or 12 weeks old.

We cannot scientifically prove that our gains are to be explained by a much greater emphasis on early psychological conditioning or by other factors. However, the improvements that we are seeing in our own attempts to produce good tracking puppies are consistent with current research on brain development. If a puppy is stimulated to use his nose at a very young age, the "wiring" to the olfactory (scenting) center of the brain will be more extensive.

Research on how much scenting ability is inherited in dogs is still in its early stages, but the early results suggest that the genetic control of this nose power is lower than hunting dog breeders have generally assumed. The whole topic of what is inherited, and what is not, is still very much up in the air as of 2016. As practical dog people, we can leave the issue to the scientists equipped to deal with it. The important thing to know is that both, genetics and environment, are important. We should provide the best we can in both departments.

To sum up, the *ideal* solution would be to breed your own tracking dog, using parents of strong tracking abilities and then offering to the pup, from very

A seven-week-old puppy checks out her enriched environment.

early on, the best of stimulation to develop the blood tracking processes of its brain. Obviously, this is not practical for most people who want to get started in blood tracking! The next best thing is to find a knowledgeable breeder, who understands that all dogs are not equally suitable for the purposes that you have in mind. He will not blandly tell you "All of my pups are good." This person selects his breeding stock carefully and will have discovered which matings work and which do not. Beyond this, he will spend time with the puppies, letting them relate to humans and receive at least some introduction to the fascinating world of scent. Selecting the breeder can be as important as selecting the puppy.

A "guarantee to track" is a risky document from the breeder's point of view. Even if he has seen the puppy's work enough to be confident of his raw ability, the breeder can never be absolutely sure of what kind of treatment and training the pup will receive after he goes to his new home. There is also the problem that some puppies regress for a while during adolescence. Personally we do not give a formal guarantee to track, but we stand behind our puppies and return the sale price when we are convinced that pup has been given a fair opportunity to develop.

The most important thing is trust and communication between the breeder and the new owner. Don't buy a dog from someone who has little time to talk with you. Don't buy from a breeder unless he is interested in keeping in touch with you and learning about the progress of your puppy.

Intelligence and the Use of Nose

What are the most important things to look for in a tracking dog prospect?

Obviously your tracking prospect needs a good nose, but you must also think about what kind of nose will be needed for your own special situation. If you are tracking for yourself and for fellow partners in a deer hunting lease, you will not need a dog with the capability to follow scent lines, without visible blood, that are 24 hours old. An intelligent dog with ability to track four-hour-old lines and work the wind to find downed game, will serve very well. But if you find that many of your deer calls come from afar, after the hunter has searched for a day on his own, you may need a cold nosed type of dog. This tends to be the situation in the Northeast.

The sense of smell may be comparatively simple in the case of humans, but in dogs this olfactory sense has many rich and complex variations. What follows may seem overly detailed and technical, but it is worth considering some of the basics.

You may have read that a dog has from 125 to 200 million olfactory receptors and that each of these scenting cells has 100 to 150 cilia (microscopic hair-like extensions that receive the scent particles). This is vastly more sensory capacity than that of humans, who have only about 5 million olfactory cells with 6 to 8 cilia each. Dogs have the equipment to gather much more scent information than humans, and they have a much larger olfactory center within their brain to process this information. The neurological wiring within this canine olfactory center is complex and varies from dog to dog. In other mammals it has been shown that both genetics and environment are involved in creating these wiring patterns. Much is still unknown in the rapidly advancing field of scientific brain research. For practical dog people, such as those who wrote and are reading this book, there is enough evidence to conclude the following: *Different dogs process scent information in different ways; they also use their noses and their brains in different ways when working in the field. These differences are breed-related to a considerable degree.*

If this seems farfetched, just consider what you know about human intelligence and how we deal with problem solving. We all learn that there are different kinds of human "smarts". Some of us are good with numbers, and some are good with words. Some are fortunate to be gifted in both categories. Some of us, who were never very good at scoring well on tests, have an uncanny focus and intuition for craftsmanship or running a small people-oriented business. The brains of different people operate in different ways. So it is with dogs when the subject is narrowed down to a category of performance like smelling things.

For example, some dogs excel at scent discrimination; they can detect a bag of cocaine in a truckload of onions. This same dog may not be particularly good at working an old, cold scent line from point A to point B. From a game finder's perspective, the most important distinction is the one between air scenters and ground scenters. A good example of an air scenter is the English Pointer, who runs high headed, and is able to locate and point a covey of quail at 50 yards if the wind is right. At the other side of the spectrum is the patient, deliberate brace trial-type Beagle that "digs" rabbit scent out of the grass roots and slowly follows every twist and turn of the cottontail's passage. In performance most hunting dogs are somewhere between these two extremes, but tend to be better at one sort of scenting than the other. My Southern Black Mouth Cur, Stone Apple Cleo, was a good example. As a deer finder she was at her best on a very windy day when she could locate a wounded deer, or a pile of guts, at 200 yards. I did not take her out on a dry, still night to find a deer wounded and lost at dawn the previous morning.

Just as there are a very few multi-talented human geniuses, who can do just about anything, there are rare dogs that excel in all types of scenting and can maybe herd cattle as well. But don't count on this. You will find breeders and breed publications claiming that their dogs can do it all. It is easier to make such claims if you have never seen the best specialists of other breeds do their work.

Intelligence in the tracking dog is so tied to the actual process of using the nose that it is difficult to treat it independently. As I use the term "intelligence" here, I am referring more to the ability to learn from experience than to any abstract reasoning ability. There are very important things that a good dog learns from experience, and there are unintelligent dogs that learn these things slowly or not at all. For example, a dog must use intelligence to realize that a back track is a possibility when a scent line comes to a dead end. In the same way, tracking dogs learn that when a scent line terminates at a stream, they must "reach" across even if they have to swim. If they don't pick up the line right away on the other side, they must work up and down stream along that far bank and finally check up and down on the side where they started. They apply such intelligently processed experience in developing similar techniques for tracking across well-traveled highways.

One cold windy night I was working a line on hard, crusted snow. There was no blood to be seen and no way to follow an individual deer track by eye. Wise, old Clary, my first tracking dog, repeatedly left the line by twenty feet or more to put her nose down in the depressions that had formed at the base of trees downwind. She knew that the last vestiges of windblown deer scent would collect in these little snow hollows. This could be called intelligent application of experience.

The effectiveness of a dog's nose is also influenced by his temperament. A patient, focused dog will get more done than a dog who is checking out everything within reach like a hyperactive child. The way the nose is used is even more important than the sensitivity of the nose.

Nose Power

As you consider what type of tracking dog you need, it's inevitable that you will consider "nose power." We have pointed out that there are wind scenters and ground scenters and a few dogs that combine both abilities.

Beyond this there is something else which I'll call "nose power" and the experts would call olfactory capability. For example a Bloodhound usually has more olfactory receptors than a Dachshund or a Labrador Retriever. He will usually have a greater power to recognize scent particles even if they are extremely diluted in other particles.

It might seem obvious that the more nose power a dog has the more useful he will be as a tracking dog. This is true for certain kinds of wounded game tracking, but this is not always the case. For example, a good Bloodhound has so much nose power that he can often work 10 yards or more off the wounded animal's line of travel. His working style will be quite different from that of a dog with less "nose". The Bloodhound does not have to straddle the scent line to follow it. This is not the best thing for the handler who needs to see and read the blood sign.

When a handler and dog are out in the woods tracking for a hunter they can seldom be sure that the animal is dead or destined to die in a short time. The hunter may be sure that he hit him "good", but this is often not the case, particularly during bow season. A majority of the deer I track are not mortally wounded.

It is important to be able to read the sign, occurring at long intervals along the scent trail, in order to figure out if it is going to be possible to find or catch up to the deer. The height of blood smears on brush and saplings can be critical. Many deer are hit too high with an arrow or a bullet above the spine; these deer can keep going forever.

Gut-shot deer almost always die, but the blood from a gut-shot deer may be bright red and very misleading. Most of the blood on the ground comes from the outside, not the stomach or guts of the deer. One brownish muddy-looking drop of blood out of 50 drops of bright red muscle blood tells the real story. You need a dog that will keep you on the line so that you see all 50 drops!

Years ago I had an experience which demonstrates that there are draw-backs in tracking with a dog that doesn't have to stay on the line to follow it. The pointing dogs often have this capability. It was gun season and I was working with a man with a very good German Shorthaired Pointer. I was following his dog, Buckshot, with my own Clary, a Wirehaired Dachshund that was the best I ever owned. The line was old and difficult with no visible blood, but each dog could follow in his or her own individual style. The GSP had a very good nose and did not have to stay right on the line to follow it. Working 15 feet off the line, Buckshot drifted past the one wound bed we found and his handler never saw it. Clary coming along behind but right on the scent line took me right over the bed that the GSP had missed.

That wound bed told us everything. There was no blood in the imprint of the buck's body. The few drops of stringy, diluted blood were more than a foot outside of the body imprint. Jaw shot! A deer destined to die.... but not for many days. Basically the deer was ungettable in that vast area of brushy woods with no open areas where we could get a clear shot. We concluded that the case was hopeless and headed back to the truck.

In other situations the more nose the better. The primary objective is to follow the wounded deer, no matter what. This is often the case with a big trophy buck that handler and dog have traveled a 100 miles to track. After three hours on the road the handler is not going to say after the first quarter mile, "There's no point in tracking this one!" For many reasons the professional handler, who is called in to track trophy bucks, will have more need for a Bloodhound class nose than the ordinary handler/dog team tracking to save venison from spoilage or coyotes.

The importance of nose power is a complicated and controversial subject that we will examine more closely in our chapters on various tracking breeds. For many of us the dog that will work 24-hour tracks under decent conditions and stay close to the line, is most useful. The nose power factor has to be considered in combination with many other things. Working style is important. A dog with a "24-hour nose", may not be very useful if his good, but not exceptional nose, is combined with too much nervous energy and a working style that has him swinging all over the place.

On the other hand the dog with an exceptional, Bloodhound class nose may have great intelligence and close relationship with his handler. The

Germans train their dogs to show sign to the handler. They call this action Verweisen, and for some dogs it comes naturally.

Sometimes it makes good sense to see all the evidence to determine what kind of wound you are dealing with. It may seem strange to argue that the "biggest nose" is not always the most useful, but I have found this to be the case up North.

Prey Drive and Desire to Track

Prey drive is the most basic instinct of a meat-eating animal who needs to eat in order to survive. It is the instinct to search, chase, kill, and rip apart his meal. When a bouncing rubber ball triggers a puppy's desire to chase and grab it, the pup is exhibiting prey drive instinct.

The instinctive desire to track and find a game animal is an indispensable attribute of the tracking dog. Not all dogs have prey drive to a sufficient degree, and they don't always relate prey drive to tracking with their nose. They use their eyes instead. They may lack any desire to follow a blood trail until they are taught that there is "prey" at the end. This prey may be a piece of raw deer liver to munch on or a deer tail to play with. Once introduced to the "prey" we expect to see a strong desire to track by 14 weeks at the latest. This is an indication that your pup will have a strong motivation to be shaped by your training. It is safest not to gamble on a puppy unless he shows prey drive guided by his nose.

Training by harnessing prey drive is much easier than training for man tracking with food treats, or as an extension of retrieving. Some dogs manifest their prey drive through possessiveness and they become possessive of their finds. This behavior must be addressed early so that hunters and bystanders are not at risk. This is discussed in Chapter 9.

Persistence to the point of die-hard stubbornness also flows out of prey drive. This is the trait of character that keeps a dog working overtime under grueling conditions. Blood tracking dogs need this, even though stubbornness is not the most endearing trait of a house dog.

"Biddability" and Responsiveness

"Biddability", the responsiveness of a dog to his handler and his desires, is an essential trait for tracking dogs. Part of this does have a genetic basis. The herding dogs, from Border Collies to Black Mouth Curs are noted for their abilities to round up livestock in accordance with their handlers' wishes and needs. But there is also an environmental factor that influences development of cooperation between handler and dog.

Scientists of canine behavior, "ethologists", have established that there is a critical period in early puppyhood when "socialization" with humans is most effectively established. The emotional response developed during the socialization stays with the puppy through life, if he is not abused. If the puppy does not have experiences that stimulate development of the brain circuitry for social interaction when he is a very young, he will have difficulty in relating to people and cooperating with his handler later on.

The socialization period, when puppies become conscious of their dam and litter mates, begins at two or three weeks. This is when "empty headed" little puppies begin to learn how to be dogs and how to act in canine social situations. Learning to socialize with people begins a little later, at around six weeks and extends to around 14 weeks. Make sure that the breeder who sells you a pup has played with all the pups and has given them lots of attention. When you pick up your puppy it should be friendly and relaxed with you.

There is a big difference between a seven week and a ten week old puppy. With the older puppy you have a much clearer idea of what you are buying in terms of temperament and ability. Be prepared to pay a little more for a ten week old puppy that is less of a gamble.

Tracking is a cooperative effort, and a natural retrieving instinct has proved to be a reliable indicator of a dog's cooperative attitude. In selecting guide dogs for the blind, a natural tendency to retrieve is the single most important sign of potential guide dog character. It's a good sign if a puppy bounds off after a ball or chew toy in prey drive mode and then brings it back to you for more fun. Retrieving is a positive sign, but it is not essential. I have had excellent, cooperative trackers like Sabina that were not interested in retrieving.

High Energy and Excitability

Some traits desirable in a tracking dog are quite malleable and can be shaped by training. But you should also be aware that certain traits are hardwired, and it is very difficult or almost impossible to modify them. Two examples of hardwired traits that have significance here are high energy and excitability. Some dogs, like some people, have high energy levels and seem to be in a constant motion. Be wary of this psychological type, but don't automatically reject such a puppy as a tracking dog prospect. Check to see if she becomes steady and focused on a short, liver dragged training line.

Our Tommy is a good example of the complexity of high energy dogs. To see him frisking around the house and yard, you would never expect him to be the outstanding, steady tracker that he is. His emotional steadiness and his willingness to focus explain the difference.

Another of our German imports, Asko, was equally energetic. He was intelligent and learned to work an artificial line very well, provided that there were no distractions. But in the woods on a real wounded deer track, he was all over the place. Asko displayed a much higher level of excitability than Tommy, and this explains the difference between the work of the two dogs.

High energy dogs can be great tracking dogs provided that they do not become so emotionally excited that they lose their capacity to concentrate on something important.

Stability and Courage

Temperament, which includes stability and courage, is certainly influenced by both genetics and the puppy's experiences. By the time that you purchase a puppy, certain traits will have become established and will continue through life. In some ways the temperament you prefer in your tracking dogs is a matter of individual preference. If you desire a versatile dog that does other things in addition to tracking, you will find that the other aptitudes have an influence upon temperament of the dog you select. Pound for pound most hunting Dachshunds are going to be more aggressive on all game than a soft-mouthed Golden Retriever. But even within breeds there are wide variations.

It is highly desirable to have a dog with an outgoing, friendly disposition toward humans. Some otherwise capable dogs shut down and work poorly, or not at all, if a stranger accompanies the handler. An active tracking dog is going to encounter many different hunters, who want to go along and be part of the search process. It is a disadvantage if you have to keep them a long way back from your dog because he is man shy or aggressive toward strangers. It is a big disadvantage if your dog tries to take the arm off the hunter as he approaches the deer that has been found.

Sometimes a man-shy dog will be bold and aggressive on game, and sometimes the reverse is true. In dogs there is little relationship between aggressiveness on game and aggressiveness to humans. A dog should be friendly to an introduced guest coming into the house; that same dog should be deadly serious and aggressive when confronting game. It is possible to track with a dog that is fearful about confronting big game, but it is not recommended.

Years ago my young son had a tracking Dachshund dog named Eda, whom I trained and worked with for a time. She was intelligent, friendly toward everyone, and she had an excellent nose. When she was a young dog we used her to track a big eight pointer one dark night; he rose suddenly out of a thicket and shook his antlers at Eda from a range of ten feet. The wounded buck was put down without any problem, and it was some time before we realized just how much Eda had been shaken up by the encounter. Gradually, it became clear that she lacked the natural courage and aggressiveness on game to overcome the surprise and shock of the incident.

Later, as I tracked with Eda, I found she would work very competently on an old, cold line. However, if we jumped the deer, and it moved out well ahead, Eda would begin to discover "problems" with the track, even though it was now a fresh, easy line to follow. She would invent checks, points of temporary loss, and she would potter and waste time in resolving them. When I got to the point where I could see the collapsed deer, I would have to tie her up and go in with the hunter to dispatch it.

The situation finally degenerated to the point where Eda would make up a fantasy line to avoid tracking the real line that might bring her to danger.

I remember one time when she took me over a mile in the wrong direction, going through the whole charade of showing me that she was working out a difficult line. Needless-to-say, Eda became purely a pet and was never asked to track again. Since she was not afraid of rabbits, she remained one of the very best competitors in AKC field trials. She was never used for breeding.

Somewhat timid dogs, who track wounded deer well, have been known to refuse to track wounded bear. For a dog, the strong ground scent left by bear can be just as scary as his sounds and appearance. Even if they have never seen a bear, some dogs seem to know from the scent that this is something big that can hurt them. In a courageous dog, it is his strong prey drive that overcomes any fears that he may have.

Temperament problems can also reveal themselves in the form of gun-shyness. This condition may grow out of a sudden and unpleasant introduction to gunfire, but the tendency to gun-shyness is likely to be genetic. Gun-shyness usually goes with a nervous and fearful temperament. When you are observing a litter, or an individual pup, ask the breeder to make a loud noise such as beating a food pan with a large spoon. In New York State, where I track, it is legal for the handler to put down a wounded deer with a firearm. If a handler has a gun-shy dog and does happen to miss with his first shot, it may be difficult to get the dog tracking again.

One of the best ways to avoid gun-shyness to expose very young puppies to gunfire at a distance. Before five weeks puppies react to loud noises simply as a part of the environment they are discovering. They don't associate loud noise with danger at this early age. If your breeder has taken the time to condition the pups to gunfire at a distance of 50 yards, it is a real plus. Gun-shyness, however, can be avoided by other means later in the puppy's life.

Working Style

The future working style of a dog can usually be predicted in the young puppy, and this is important. Working style is almost as important as intelligence and courage. It is influenced by both nature (genetics) and nurture (training). You do not want to select a wild, flighty puppy that does not stay on a scent line. As an adult he is likely to bounce around all over the place when asked to track a wounded deer. This style is not good for an old, cold line. Training will seldom overcome strong, undesirable tendencies that are genetically based so it pays to observe the puppy and how he responds to a blood line.

Of course, not everyone prefers the same working style, but everyone does agree that the important thing is getting a job done. A dog may work the line rapidly or slowly and deliberately. In tracking for bowhunters there is much to be said for the slower dog who works rather close to the line, allowing the handler to see whatever visible sign is present. The blood appearance and its placement allow the handler to determine whether the deer is mortally wounded or likely to recover.

Dachshund puppy works a liver drag marked with surveyor flags.

A chew on the deer liver at the end is the reward for the tracking work.

From what I have seen of European judging and European trained dogs, a faster tracking pace is preferred on the Continent. The game animal is likely to have been hit by a rifle bullet; usually there is more wound scent. When hit in the body the animal is not likely to go very far. In North America, if you track for gun and rifle hunters, you may prefer to get the job done as quickly as possible. On the other hand, if you are going to track very much for bowhunters, you do not want a lightning fast dog. The handler must check all blood sign that the dog points out to him. An informed decision must be made as to whether the deer can survive or not.

The age of the handler may also influence his ideas about appropriate tracking speed. It is a curious thing, but in my own case, a preference for slow dogs increased as I tracked on into my seventies. There may be other gray beards, who prefer to slow down rather than retire.

Generally, the natural working speed of the individual dog can be modified to some degree by training, by holding back on the leash and by telling the dog in a drawling tone to slow down. Out of eagerness, most young dogs of all breeds tend to go too fast at the beginning.

Dogs also vary in their tendency to stay close to the deer's line of passage. When a deer goes a long way, as in the case of a leg hit, it can be efficient for the dog to "drift" the line, following the trend of it, while working back and forth over it in gentle "S" curves. However, as we have previously stated, with this style of work the handler will see much less sign and may miss wound beds and other valuable evidence. Bird dogs, selected over many generations for a tendency to quarter back and forth, are especially likely to work this way. A searching German Shepherd often has similar moves, although the quartering tendency will be less pronounced than in a bird dog.

Puppy Tests

When you visit a breeder and look over puppies offered for sale, there are many questions you can answer for yourself. One cannot overemphasize the physical things because the health and character of a dog will be strongly influenced by his early nurture. Are the pups clean, well fed and well housed? If the pups are thin and scrawny, there is a strong probability that they have intestinal parasites. Are the pups getting plenty of human attention during the very critical weeks after they have been weaned from their mother? Beyond these basics there are specific ways that puppies can be evaluated for psychological stability and for interest in tracking.

First, there are a number of puppy tests, administered at seven weeks, which are designed to predict adult temperaments. The most widely used is the Puppy Aptitude Test (P.A.T.) developed by Jack and Wendy Volhard. P.A.T. is not a specific test of hunting aptitudes, but it can reveal exreme temperament traits that have a real bearing on how useful a dog will be in blood tracking. As explained above, you do not want a people-shy dog or a dog that is aggressive to humans. You also want to avoid sound sensitivity. The test will pick up tendencies toward these exaggerated extremes. The P.A.T. is most reliable and useful for identifying future behavioral traits that will be a problem such as fearfulness or aggressiveness toward humans. Recent research has proved that puppy tests at seven weeks do not reliably predict what will develop within the normal spectrum of dog behavior.

Concerning the P.A.T., it is not practical for a prospective buyer to conduct the seven component parts of the test on a litter for himself. It is the breeder, who should arrange for this test when the puppies are about seven weeks old. The test should be conducted in a place that is unfamiliar to the puppies. The individual doing the testing should be a stranger to the puppies, and he or she should carry out the tests in a consistent and objective way.

If the breeder sets up the aptitude test for his puppies, he should be willing to share the results with you. Puppies are scored on a scale of 1 to 6. In one test, for example, the pup is turned over on his back and gently held down by the person doing the testing. You should probably avoid the puppy that gets a "5" in this test because it goes completely limp and passive. You would also want to avoid the puppy at the other extreme that gets a "1" because it struggles violently and tries to bite. You would want to select a strong but stable puppy, with a "2", "3" or "4". This particular test is one that you, as a prospective buyer, might try yourself on a puppy that impresses you in other ways.

The puppy aptitude test is most useful in identifying puppies with extreme personality traits. In most of the tests the middle numbers can vary depending on whether the puppy is sleepy, hungry or just having an off day. The results of one test session should not be taken too seriously. Puppy temperaments evolve through later life in response to their environment. A somewhat retiring puppy may blossom when separated from his more dominant littermates. Suddenly he is Mr. Important in the eyes of his new family. With self-confidence there develops a striving, can-do attitude to new challenges including blood tracking.

Some animal psychologists have questioned the validity of canine puppy aptitude tests altogether. I think they are most useful in identifying a pronounced tendency to be shy and fearful around humans, or to be aggressive. These are traits that are least likely to be modified by a good social environment later on. All too often a shy puppy becomes a shy adult dog. You cannot afford to take the chance.

Puppy tests can tell us more about responsiveness than about intelligence. In domestic dogs the traits of responsiveness and intelligence do tend to be related; this would not be true in a coyote. For the tracking dog who works for and with humans, responsiveness is tremendously important. This is especially true for the dog who is going to be worked off lead, as is possible in the South and in Texas. On lead or off lead, the dog must be able to learn that he is part of a team, and that the teammates need one another to be successful. Off lead, a GPS electronic tracking collar can be very useful to locate the dog, but it is still best to have a dog that will return on his own if he cannot come up with the deer.

It is not a natural thing for a canine to work a very old, difficult line when fresh prey is bouncing out of the cover through which he tracks. Most young dogs need the verbal support of the handler to keep them on the proper line despite distractions. A dog, who has no concern for the handler's voice and just wants to run game, will not be very useful.

The Volhards' P.A.T. was designed to evaluate the potential of puppies as companion dogs, but there are other aptitude tests, which focus more specifically on the traits needed in working and hunting dogs. One of these is the PAWS Working Dog Evaluation developed and copyrighted by Jona Decker. If your breeder is "into" tests, he may have administered PAWS or some other test.

PAWS evaluates such things as willingness to take responsibility. Readiness to take responsibility is an important quality in dogs who work in close partnership with humans. For example, guide dogs for the blind must have the strength of character to override the commands of their handler at a dangerous highway crossing. In tracking wounded deer, a dog must solve difficult problems on his own. Dogs with the "right stuff" will also correct their masters, as a good Seeing Eye dog will do at a busy intersection. I can remember a time, before I knew better, when a wise tracking dog insisted three times that she knew where the deer went, and that I was wrong. The third time I gave in, and she went her own way to find the deer.

The letters of the acronym PAWS stand for Possessiveness, Attention, Willingness and Strength (of character). Within PAWS there are tests for seven behavior patterns: prey drive, retrieving, persistence, tugging on an object, possessiveness, recall and attention span. Certain of these are very important for the tracking dog.

As you can see the PAWS Evaluation can help you assess the potential of a tracking dog candidate. It can be given considerably later than the P.A.T. As a matter of fact, it will tell you more about an older puppy. The test is designed especially for dogs that use both their eyes and noses, such as German Shepherds. When we gave PAWS to our Dachshund puppies, which are primarily nose-oriented, we found that we had to make allowances for this.

The details of PAWS Working Dog Evaluation are available on the Internet at malinut.com/ref/write/paws/.

Blood tracking is a specialized canine task, and "aptitude" tests for adult dogs are administered by a number of hunting dog organizations in North America and Europe. Some of these are discussed in Appendix F. However, these tests are not suitable for young puppies.

We have developed several informal tests or exercises that we have found useful for evaluating puppies from 10 to 12 weeks. They reveal something about a puppy's desire to track deer blood, and they also help predict his working style as he does the job.

The Process of Selecting Your Puppy

The breed and the parentage of your tracking candidate will give you some idea of what to expect at maturity. Their working style in searching for downed pheasants or tracking a rabbit can tell you much, even if they have done little or no blood tracking. The same talents come into play in these different activities.

There are also some specific tests or exercises that the breeder can use to help evaluate individual puppies for blood tracking. We find that little can be decided about a pup's working style at seven weeks, but by the tenth week certain natural traits begin to reveal themselves. Let's assume that you are looking over some ten-week-old puppies that have had a lot of attention and affection from the breeder or his family. What can you do to help make a decision to buy a particular pup?

An informal test that we have found very informative is to drag a thawed-out deer liver or heart on a piece of cord. Make the trail 25 to 100 yards long (it depends on the ages and size of the pups), and around the middle put a right angle turn in it. Let it age a half hour. Leave the deer part at the end so that the puppy can find it, lick and chew on it. The scent line can also be laid with deer blood dribbled or dabbed at one foot intervals and allowed to dry. At the end, a deer leg, scrap of deer hide or even a deer tail can be placed.

How a young puppy works a line will give valuable clues of what to expect in his mature working style. Does he stay close to the line, which should be marked in some way, or does he ramble back and forth? Does he stay focused and remember what he is doing? Does he correct himself when he gets out of scent contact with the line?

Puppies should be worked individually and preferably on individual lines. If they are released together, they will race one another, play and distract each other. At this early age a tracking leash is not necessary, and it is likely to be a distraction.

We have come to prefer a small drag like a deer liver to a whole deer skin. The skin leaves a much broader scent line, and you do not learn as much from seeing pups track it.

Good things that you see early in a pup's development will almost always be there at maturity. Of course, they may disappear for a while during adolescence! You can have some confidence in buying a puppy that stays on the line and shows an intense interest in it. This test will not tell you how good a nose the puppy will have, but it will show you how the puppy uses the nose that he has. This is actually more important.

Short of exercises with a liver drag on a big lawn or a mowed field, there are some other things that you can do. You can throw out pieces of hot dog into the grass and see how the pups use their noses to find it. A dog whose first resource is his eyes rather than his nose is not as strong a prospect as the pup that is definitely nose-oriented.

A breeder who has older puppies should be able to show you even more on a line that has been laid out in the woods with deer blood. As explained in the chapters on training, the blood laid on an artificial trail stays and continues to give off scent for days. A puppy of five months or more should be able to work a 300-yard blood line, twelve hours old, without difficulty. You should be understanding, however, if his concentration is interrupted by the hot scent of deer or wild turkeys. At less than a year, a puppy cannot be expected to ignore such distractions; it is up to the handler to read his young dog and keep him focused on the blood line. What you should avoid is the puppy who does not settle down when placed back on the blood line. Don't be put off by a few mistakes and brief departures from the line. The most important thing is to identify the puppy who will correct his mistakes on his own. When you are tracking the real thing, the dog will not be able to rely on you for correction.

When a breeder is demonstrating a young dog, make sure that he is not running the dog on a line that is already familiar. Dogs, including puppies, have excellent memories of scent, space and terrain; they will race expertly over a familiar line without using their noses at all. You should not be fooled by this.

It will not always be possible to buy a puppy from a breeder who is knowledgeable about blood tracking, and seldom will any breeder be in a position to provide you with all the details you would like to have concerning your puppy.

A breeder must win your confidence in his honesty. Beware the braggart, who assures you that everything he breeds will be excellent. Even in the best of litters from the best of parents, there is usually at least one dog that doesn't measure up to expectations. Avoid getting stuck with that puppy. You and the breeder should work together to select a puppy who will fulfill your needs.

Evaluating an Older Dog

Some new handlers will have an opportunity to acquire an adult dog to train for tracking. It does not make sense to begin work with an elderly dog, who will have to retire before he becomes experienced. However, a talented dog, four or five years old, can save you time because the mental maturity is already there. His attention span will be longer, and he will be more able to tune out distractions. It helps if the dog has already learned to use his nose in hunting or other kinds of scent oriented work. Of course, it is very important that the dog has not developed bad habits like chasing healthy deer.

A good way to check out an adult dog as a blood tracking prospect is to lay out a 300-yard blood line with a thawed-out deer skin at the end. Details on this will be found in the Chapter 8 on puppy training. Make sure that you have some 90-degree turns in the line. And use no more than a half pint of blood. Age the line for four to eight hours.

Does the dog show interest in the blood scent? Does he have a desire to follow the line? When he gets off the line, does he search to regain it? Does he seem to lose interest and wander off? A dog who shows indifference on this simple test will be hard to motivate later. If he works through the line with enthusiasm, he is a good prospect. Don't be concerned if he is not too interested in the hide itself. Good dogs differ greatly in how they react to the hide. Your concern is his desire to work the blood line; the hide is there as a symbol of accomplishment and an occasion for praise. Keep in mind that some dogs stay in the adolescent phase for up to two years of age. It is impossible to evaluate a dog's tracking potential during adolescence. For more information on adolescence check Chapter 10.

Conclusion

The conclusion of this chapter comes back to the point made at the beginning. Mature, experienced tracking dogs are very difficult to find. That is why most of this chapter has focused on the process of buying a puppy, even though many busy people would prefer to buy a trained and experienced dog. In most cases it makes more sense to begin with a well-chosen puppy who has had some training on artificial blood lines.

Don't let yourself be talked into buying a seven week old puppy. At this age they are cute and ready to start relating to their new owners. However, if the breeder is doing a good job, he will see that the pups get plenty of people time at this critical age. The drawback of selecting a pup at seven weeks is that you can't learn much about the individual puppy's tracking desire and line sense. At ten to twelve weeks much more of his future abilities will be evident.

Points to Remember When You Pick Your Puppy

- Pick a puppy from parents with a proven ability to use their noses well. In most cases the ability to work ground scent is more important than a specialized wind-scenting aptitude.

- Select a dog that relies first on his nose to find things. If possible, ask to see the puppy track a dragged deer liver or heart.

- Make sure that your pup has the physical conformation to work in tough conditions. Such factors as coat and ground clearance must be considered.

- Avoid selecting your puppy when he is very young. Evaluation of ability and working style can be done more reliably at 10 or 12 weeks.

- Pick a pup who is bold, friendly and not sound sensitive.

- Make sure that your breeder is honest and experienced in dog breeding. A backyard breeder, who does not understand what is involved in blood tracking, may mislead you about his dogs.

Chapter 4

Dog Breeds I: The Scent Hounds

Scent hounds are a category of hunting dogs that were specifically developed to find game by following ground scent. Of course they will use their eyes and ears as well in their search, but their nose dominates their other sensory organs; they are nose oriented. Their brain tends to process scent in terms of a line leading to the quarry. Dogs in the scent hound category do not have a monopoly of these abilities, but one can say that following game by scent comes very naturally to them. There are at least 68 breeds of hounds from around the world, and most of these breeds probably have individuals suitable for blood tracking. We can discuss only a few of the most important breeds. These are in order of presentation: Dachshunds, Beagles, Bassets, coonhounds, Bloodhounds, Hanover Hounds, and Bavarian Mountain Hounds.

Dachshunds

I am going to begin by writing about the breed that I know best, the standard-sized European Dachshund or Teckel. I don't pretend to be totally objective about this breed, which I have bred, hunted and tracked with for half a century. For the Northeast, where I live, and for the Midwest, I truly believe that they are best suited as blood trackers for most people. Of course, if I were primarily a bird hunter, I would choose one of the versatile hunting dog breeds that can point and retrieve game birds as well as blood track. If I tracked in snake infested country of the South or the Southwest during warm weather, I would want a bigger, higher stationed dog than a Dachshund. If a Dachshund gets bitten on the head, neck or shoulders, the results are almost always fatal.

To North American hunters, American or Anglo-Canadian, it probably seems a bit strange that a Dachshund would be considered at all as a serious choice for a hunting activity. The image of the plump, cylindrical couch potato, as depicted by the cartoonists, is firmly imprinted in everyone's mind. If you search through the American books on hunting hounds, from the coffee table sort to the serious texts, the Dachshund is absent. But this situation has begun to change. Dachshunds of European ancestry, especially the wirehaired coat variety, are being used extensively for finding whitetails in the Northeast and Midwest. They are used for tracking wounded moose in Quebec, and they are catching on in the Rockies for tracking elk.

Why did it take so long for the Dachshund to be recognized as a hunting dog outside of continental Europe? This is partly due to the fact that much of our North American hunting tradition comes originally from England. English hunters have never taken the Dachshund very seriously either, although now this is beginning to change. The British developed excellent terriers to do underground work, and for above ground they developed Beagles and other hare hounds; there was never very much interest in specialized blood trackers. At the end of the 20th century Dachshunds for blood tracking were just being discovered in the UK.

On the European continent the Dachshund situation is different. The Dachshund, also called Teckel or Dackel, holds firmly to the top position as a versatile, small hunting dog for above and underground work. In Germany, the Deutscher Teckelklub is a very large club with thousands of members who own Dachshunds. Certainly most of them don't hunt, but the official club policy is that the Dachshund should be bred so that it is a "useful" hunting dog.

The German vision of the Dachshund is very different from what developed in the United States. The German Dachshund image, rooted in the traditions of an orderly rural landscape, is that of a "forester's dog". To be sure foresters were not the actual breeder/developers of the early standard Dachshund. And by the early 1900s most Dachshunds in Germany were actually household companions of town and city dwellers.

Yet the identity of the Dachshund, its mystique, was still tied to a vision of the loyal, responsive small hunting dog, who accompanied the local forester on his daily rounds of inspection of the forests and game under his jurisdiction. There were a few supremely fortunate Dachshunds who actually lived this life.

It was the role of the forester's working Dachshund to extend his master's awareness of what was going on in the forest. The nose and inquisitiveness of the Dachshund, the vision and the intelligence of the man came together in a superior symbiosis, a mixed pack of two working together.

The Dachshund ranged out, but not too far, 200 meters at most, and he checked back frequently with the forester. Voice and body language expressed what the Dachshund had discovered: Perhaps the wild boars were back again, rooting out the young transplants in the pine plantation, or the old fox den was reoccupied, its entrance graced with the bones of a roe deer fawn.

Underground work on fox and badger was very important. After all, "Dachshund" means "badger dog" in German. Badgers and foxes were seen as vermin, and hunting them with a Dachshund was the best means of keeping them under control. This was the idealized role of the Dachshund: a devoted and responsive working partner.

In Germany, Dachshunds may not be as specialized as certain hound breeds like the Hanover Hound, but because there are so many Dachshunds trained for blood tracking, they find a great deal of big game, primarily roe deer and boar.

The North American Teckel Club, based in the United States and Canada, is an extension of the Deutscher Teckelklub (DTK). Periodic conformation shows, combined with hunting tests, are given. The tracking tests are conducted by a visiting Chief Judge, usually from Germany. For Americans, who use Dachshunds for blood tracking, much can be learned from these events. The DTK blood tracking tests are very instructive.

The Dachshund or Teckel network extends through the rest of Europe. There are international standards, tests and competitions. Considerable breeding of the best working dogs takes place between the various European countries, and a large international gene pool of hunting Dachshunds does exist.

There are three coat varieties of Dachshunds: smooth, longhaired and wirehaired. In Germany, where the coat varieties are considered different breeds, their relative popularity is very different from what it is in North America. According to the statistics of the German Dachshund Club for 2015, Standard Dachshunds registered for that year were: wirehaired 74%, smooth 14% and longhaired 12%. The "wires" are the most widely used for hunting.

It is important to realize that today there are significant differences between the European and the Anglo-American Dachshund physical types. The FCI (International Cynological Federation) defines the ideal size of the standard Dachshund as 9 kilos (20 pounds) or less. This is considerably smaller than the standard American counterpart. The European dogs are also supposed to be higher on the leg; the FCI standard, which was written by the Germans, states that the ground clearance of the dog should be one third of the shoulder height. They are also shorter in the back than the North American and English Dachshunds and generally they are less extreme in their typically "Dachshund" appearance.

Tommy, owned by John and Jolanta Jeanneney, is a good example of the Deutscher Teckelklub type of Wirehaired Dachshund.

Good trackers and indifferent ones are to be found in both types, but European breeders have selected for working ability much more seriously than American show breeders.

Even though there is a real difference between the hunting Dachshund of European ancestry and the American show Dachshund, in America both types are registered as the same breed by the AKC. It is possible for an American to register his European-type Dachshund with the Deutscher Teckelklub through its branch, the North American Teckel Club. Very few American owners of tracking Dachshunds actually do this. Since the North American club is a subsidiary of the DTK, all the rules of the parent German Club apply. These DTK rules are so intricate and so poorly adapted to American conditions that AKC registration has been accepted as the best solution.

We have talked about the way Dachshunds are put together physically, but it is actually the behavioral tendencies of the dog that are most important for getting the tracking job done.

The Germans see the Dachshund's instincts and behavior as something so unique that Dachshunds are given an FCI classification separate and distinct from hounds. On the other hand, the Americans and the English classify them as scent hounds. To add to the confusion some Dachshunds are houndier than others. Some can be quite terrier-like and visually oriented, but the most useful for tracking are those that rely on their noses first to solve problems. It is easy to spot this in puppies when they are two months old. An important point is that the blood tracker, while he needs a good nose, does not gain very much for practical work by having the exceptional scenting ability of a good Bloodhound.

Dachshunds have very good noses, but I have seen some Beagles, for example, that could follow a rabbit track that the best Dachshunds could not recognize. In practical deer recovery work, intelligence and attitude are even more important than nose. What the Dachshund has over most other hound breeds is "biddability". They are easy to train, and they are handler oriented. The Dachshunds have less tendency to run the freshest track because it is the most exciting. They are willing to please their handler by working the faint, cold line of the wounded deer, even when it is crossed by the steaming hot line of a healthy deer that passed 30 seconds before. Many, but not all Dachshunds learn to discriminate between the designated deer and others. This is essential for a useful blood tracker, and for a "hound" they learn it very quickly. Since they are worked on a long leash, they soon realize that the only deer they will catch up to is the one that is wounded. The desire to please is reinforced by practical experience behind wounded game. They soon understand that to find wounded game they must work with the handler as a team.

Dachshunds often relate better to people than to other dogs. They were not bred to be pack hounds, and as pack hounds they are not impressive; most of them do not hark into one another very well. They were used extensively for solo underground work on fox and badger, and their partner was the hunter/digger who accompanied them.

Because of this people orientation, the Dachshund is not the dog for the person who wants to use the dog like a tool; you cannot take a Dachshund out of the kennel, like a gun out of a gun cabinet, only when you need to use it. A Beagle will endure a kennel existence with minimum human contact much better than a Dachshund.

Dachshunds are small and adaptable. They are easy to transport, and enjoy riding on an all-terrain vehicle to get to and back from the tracking site. Once on the scent line they should work rather closely and slowly. It is true that most Dachshunds want to work too fast in their first working season, but in any case they are easy to slow down. The value of a deliberate speed and staying close to the line is that it gives the handler time to see and evaluate the blood smears and other indications of how the deer is hit. In many searches for bowshot deer, it turns out that the deer is not mortally wounded. The sign the handler sees in the first 1000 yards is essential for making a decision about how far to follow. You can't follow every deer for miles when the chances of catching up are close to zero.

The small size of the Dachshund can be a disadvantage in southern states and Texas where dogs can be legally used to track off lead, catch up to a deer and bay it until the handler arrives to put it down. A Dachshund is not as well suited for this as a dog weighing more than 50 pounds.

Dachshunds come in very small sizes. The desire to track can certainly be found in what Americans call the Miniature Dachshund and what the Germans call the Zwergteckel (literally dwarf teckel). As a matter of fact, in the American Dachshund breeding, hunting desire has been better retained, overall, in the miniature size than in the standard. Fifty years of Dachshund field trials have convinced me, against my expectations, that this is true. However, there are some trade-offs that come as size is reduced below 15 pounds. The Miniature Dachshund has less body mass and power to overcome the friction and weight of the tracking lead if the track is a long one. To counteract this the owner should use a lighter tracking leash and one with a friction-free finish. In cold, wet conditions the small dog is going to lose body heat faster than a standard-sized Dachshund of greater mass. Minis are not at their best when the temperature drops below freezing, but for a small group of bowhunters who want to have a small, handy dog available, they can be a solution.

In New York State's Deer Search Chapters there are a number of mini longhairs tracking and finding wounded deer. One of them, Chester Swierk's mini longhair Moby actually won the Deer Search Blood Tracking Competition in 2011.

The size of the dog that you can relate to is really a matter of personal taste. Some people just feel ridiculous to work with a 10-pound or even a 20-pound dog. If they feel more comfortable and confident with a 60-pound dog, then they should go with their feelings. Their hunter's intuition will work better as a result.

As previously explained, Dachshunds come in three types of coats, and this generates much confusion in this country. Everyone is familiar with

Rob Miller's Sypris, a Smooth Dachshund bred out of European bloodlines, explodes the myth that only Dachshunds of the wirehaired variety can be good trackers. Sypris is an outstanding tracker in central Michigan.

Photo courtesy of Rob Miller

the Smooth Dachshunds; the Longhairs are less numerous here, but most people with some interest in dogs know what they are. The wires are almost unknown outside of dog shows and areas where dogs are used for tracking wounded deer. I have become accustomed to having people ask, "What kind of a mixture is that? Is it part Dachshund?"

In Germany Wirehaired Dachshunds are by far the most numerous, and a majority of hunters who use Dachshunds in Europe use wires. Part of the dominance of Wirehaired Dachshunds as blood trackers in Europe can be explained by the nature of their coat. If it is a correct double coat, it is warmer, more water-resistant and better protection against briars than any of the other coats. A good wire coat is made up of very dense undercoat covered by an overcoat of coarse, straight guard hairs. A dog with a correct wire coat is almost as well protected in water as the double coated beaver. A good wire can swim a stream, give a shake and still be dry at the base of the undercoat. Air trapped in the fine undercoat keeps the water out almost as well as it does for the swimming beaver.

You noticed that the term "good coat" was used repeatedly in the last paragraph. There lies the problem; not all wire coats are good. A bad coat,

Tasha, a Longhaired Dachshund, was imported from Denmark by Cliff Shrader from Louisiana. She is a very talented and successful tracker. The picture shows Tasha wearing Ruffwear Front Range Harness.

Photo courtesy of Cliff Shrader

a soft woolly coat without guard hairs, gets soaked quickly, picks up burrs, and if there is wet snow, loads up with little snowballs. A bad wire coat is the worst imaginable coat. Moreover, good coats are not easy to breed on a consistent basis. In Europe, under FCI rules, the Dachshunds of each coat type are regarded as a separate breed and cross-coat matings are not allowed for registered dogs. Yet even under FCI rules the wire coats do not always breed true. A sire and dam may both have excellent coats and still produce a litter that has 25% of the coats unacceptable for hunters. Coats may be too soft and long. At the other extreme, coats may actually be almost as short as a smooth. In Dachshunds, and in other wirehaired breeds like the German Drahthaars, no breeder has succeeded in breeding all ideal coats generation after generation.

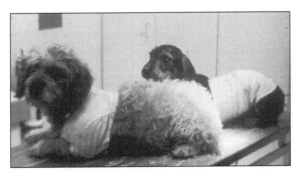

Oyat du Bellerstein at the vets after disagreement with a French wild boar. Oyat was a great tracker with a poor wire coat.

Photo courtesy of Hubert Stoquert

You cannot assume that puppies from two parents with good working coats are destined to have good coats themselves. You must look at the puppies themselves; the cutest, fuzziest puppies will invariably grow up to have poor coats. At first glance, the best puppy prospects from the coat standpoint will look more like smooths than wires at eight weeks. Look for a hard stiff coat with some undercoat already present on the sides; there should be the barest beginnings of a beard. A wire will have hair between the paw pads. The full characteristics of a correct wire coat often appear only after a year.

It is easier to find good coats in the wild boar colored Dachshunds than in black and tans. Generally it is easier to find good wire coats in standard sized Dachshunds than in miniatures or zwergs. There are exceptions to every generalization. Closely examine the puppy that you are considering as a blood tracking candidate.

Excellent blood trackers are to be found in all three coat varieties. Make your choice on the basis of the field conditions in which you will be working. In country with fields full of burrs and stick-tights, only slick smooth or good wire coats will get you through. These burr situations are not very numerous. In most circumstances, a long coat, bred without excessive show dog feathering, is a good working coat. Certainly it is much easier to produce these long coats with consistency than good wire coats. The leading American breeder of small Miniature Dachshunds for bolting rabbits from underground dens originally used wires. The best of the wire coats were excellent, but the average mini-wire coat was not very good, and little Dachshunds that were not blessed with the best of coats chilled rapidly on cold wet days. She shifted to breeding longs and got a very high percentage of long coats that were quite adequate for most conditions. The problem of producing good wire coats is greater in miniatures than in standards, but it is a problem for all wire breeders.

Smooth coats are fine in most weather conditions and vegetation, but avoid those with very short fine hair. In general a smooth coat is not as warm as a wire or long coat, and it offers less protection in thorny cover. A strong, standard smooth, when active, will generate enough internal heat to keep warm in all but the coldest temperatures. Desire will carry him through the briars with only a few extra scratches.

Breeders can argue for days about coats; coats are important, but this importance can be exaggerated. I found 51 deer with Max, a French wirehaired male, who had a rather soft coat that gave him poor protection. Sometimes I worked him with a blaze orange Cordura nylon vest of which he became quite proud. Only once, in a huge field infested with cockle burrs, did we have to close down. Max had a football helmet of burrs, which came down over his eyes. The burrs were too tangled in the hair to be removed in the field. I picked him up on the line and told the hunter to check out ahead. He found the buck within a hundred yards the next morning.

More important than the coat is the dog under the coat. Recognize and avoid the poor coats unsuitable for your climate and vegetation. To get the perfect coat don't sacrifice on intelligence, nose and desire. The choice of tracking bloodlines will be largest in wires. A Dachshund that has a German pedigree emphasizing underground fox work may be too high strung to excel in the calm, focused work of the tracking dog.

In Dachshunds, as with other breeds, don't get so caught up in generalities that you miss the qualities of the individual dog. My advice would be that if you are starting from scratch in Dachshunds for blood tracking, your best bet is to first investigate the blood trackers that trace back directly to European hunting Dachshunds. This is no 100% guarantee of success. Good blood tracking potential is where you find it.

Generally Dachshunds suffer few health issues, and on average they live to be 12-13. But almost every breed has some serious physical problems that grow out of genetically inherited tendencies, and the Dachshund is not an exception. Most insidious are those that appear in middle age after a dog has had extensive training and experience. Bonding grows out of tracking, and when disabling illness befalls your working partner of many cold nights, it is truly a disaster.

Intervertebral disk disease (IVDD), which involves premature aging of the spine, is number one problem in Dachshunds. It usually occurs at the age of 3-7 years. The disk disease involves one or more of the disks of cartilage, which lie between the spinal vertebrae. These structures allow for normal movement between the vertebrae, and they also act as shock absorbers. If the disk ruptures and presses on the spinal cord, the severity of symptoms may range from mild neck or back pain to severe pain, paralysis and loss of bladder and bowel control. If there is no swift intervention, the damage may be irreversible. Even if expensive surgery is undertaken, there is no assurance that the dog will ever work again. The genetics of disk disease is complex and not yet fully understood. IVDD does tend to run in families, but it can occur in any breeding. The condition is less common among Dachshunds bred to the less exaggerated FCI standard and in Dachshunds maintained in athletic physical condition. If you purchase a Dachshund for tracking, you should inquire about the disk problems that may have appeared in his genetic background. The excellent source of information and support can be found on the web at Dodgerslist (www.dodgerslist.com).

In standard wires the number two health problem is heart disease due to the degeneration of the heart valves. This is the most common heart disease in dogs, and the most common cause of Congestive Heart Failure.

When selecting a tracking dog it pays to ask questions. What is the present physical state of the sire, dam and grandparents? If they are no longer alive, what problems did they have and what did they die of? You can't choose your own parents, but you can choose the parents of your dog.

Beagles

Beagles should be a simple topic but unfortunately this is not the case. Even if we consider only Beagles that are worked in the field, there is no single working type, no generic Beagle type that we can generalize about in a few paragraphs. If you want to keep your life simple, skip this section.

Physically Beagles are divided into two size categories: 15-inch Beagles that are 13" to 15" at the shoulder, and a smaller type that is under 13 inches. This is the simple part. Through selective breeding three, or possibly four, genetically programmed working styles have emerged. Each type of Beagle is evaluated in field trials, which have different structures and judging criteria.

Fastest are the hare hounds, or large pack hounds, which are run on northern hares and run competitively in large packs of 20 hounds or more. These hounds have enormous hunting desire and drive. Their desire to overtake game may overwhelm any tendencies to listen to and be responsive to the handler. Many will not be very willing to work out an old, cold line of a wounded deer when the distractions of fresher game abound. If you choose a tracking prospect from hare hound breeding, make your selection carefully.

At the other end of the working spectrum are the brace Beagles. These are strains of Beagles that were developed to work a cottontail rabbit line very slowly and with great accuracy. In AKC field trials they compete in braces, and the best hounds move up to subsequent "series" in the trial. Beagles that win in brace trials "straddle the line" at a slow walking pace, tonguing continuously on every track. There is a minimum of overshooting at turns, and at a check these hounds are expected to work out very slowly and carefully from the point of loss. A dog that uses experience or intelligence to "reach" ahead to a promising bit of cover risks being dropped as too "rabbit wise" or "running too much rabbit".

The field trial ideal of brace Beagle behavior is not suitable for a tracking dog, which must be willing to reach to regain the line across a creek or on the other side of a highway.

Intermediate, between the extremes of hare hounds and brace hounds, are the Beagles that perform to the standards of "gun dog" field trials, sometimes referred to as small pack option (SPO) or small pack. These dogs are run on cottontails in small packs of six or seven. Their resourcefulness in solving problems and keeping the chase going are considered more important than precision of style. These hounds seldom run flat-out; they slow their speed to the scenting conditions and other circumstances in which they are trailing. The approved working characteristics for "gun dog" field trials are adaptable to the requirements for tracking wounded big game.

Formal foot packs are another device for packaging Beagle talents. The Beagles are selected for their ability to run together as a pack. Appearance and voice are also important considerations. These hounds are handled by a huntsman and his assistants or whips, who are on foot and wear green jackets rather than the red coats of mounted fox hunters. These hounds must handle well, and those that are too bullheaded or independent are culled from the pack. You don't want a Beagle who was culled from the pack because he was stupid or stubborn, but sometimes good hounds are let go because they are the wrong size, the wrong speed or have a poor voice. These can be good prospects.

Avoid Beagles from any background that are for sale cheap because they are determined deer chasers. These hotheaded, stubborn hounds are likely to give you the same problems that they gave their original owners. They will want to take off on a smoking fresh deer track just as you are trying to persuade them to follow the old, cold line of a wounded deer.

Avoid Beagles bred exclusively as show dogs or as pets; you will have no idea of what working pattern to expect when these puppies mature. Also keep in mind that even the owner of working Beagles will have some pups of questionable ability, which he is hoping to place in a good home. There is always a surplus of hounds that don't make the grade, but there are always a few young dogs of great potential if you take the trouble to look.

Not all Beagle backgrounds fall into a neat category. Maybe you know an old country boy, who rides around with a Beagle on the front seat of his pickup truck. If that Beagle is completely in tune with his owner, hunts rabbits, pheasants, and trees a coon at night, consider buying one of her pups. Good old boys and good old Beagles are getting scarcer every year.

Mickey, the Beagle pictured here, was owned by Tim Nichols, who provides tracking services in New York and Vermont. Mickey passed in 2007 at the age of 12 ½ years. He found 160 deer and three bears in his tracking career.

Considering the talents of the right sort of Beagle, it is surprising that only a small number of them are being used for wounded game tracking as of 2016. In the beagling world there has been considerable exposure to the tracking dog idea, but little interest. Beaglers, who have always been concerned about rabbit hounds running deer, become vaccinated against the whole idea of the Beagle as a tracking dog.

Beagle noses tend to be more than sufficient for blood tracking, it is the intelligence, responsiveness and adaptability that you have to worry about. These last three traits are going to be much more developed in the hound that grows up in an interesting, "enriched" environment. This is something that Beagles do not always get. The year-old Beagle, which has spent most of his young life in an isolated kennel is not a strong prospect. This unsocialized tracking dog may have a difficult time forming a productive working relationship with a handler.

Tim Nichols, who established the use of leashed tracking dogs in Vermont, used a Beagle and consistently found more than ten deer a year. Tim used Mickey, his 15-inch male exclusively for tracking wounded deer and bear. Mickey was not the quickest dog to learn to stay on the right line, but he developed into a tough, reliable dog. Unlike most tracking dogs, Mickey would voice on a wounded deer trail, if it was less than a half hour old. I once observed a Beagle/Walker Coonhound cross that tongued on a six hour line. Tonguing while tracking wounded deer is not a trait desired by every handler, or by nearby hunters waiting quietly in their tree stands

From a thousand miles to the south, Ronny Smith of Washington, Georgia talked to me about his seven-year-old male Beagle who knows well how to find a wounded deer. When hunters in the area can't find a deer, they just go over to Ronny's. If Ronny isn't home, the tracking leash is always hanging on the kennel. The local custom, which seems pretty laid back for uptight Northern types, is to take the old Beagle out yourself if Ronny isn't around. The old Beagle rides out in the hunter's pickup truck, does the job and then is driven back to his kennel. He loves his work so much that he will do it for anyone.

Bassets

There are two kinds of Bassets readily available in North America. The American AKC Basset is a big, heavy, low dog. Many weigh 70 pounds or more and with their long ears and heavy flews they resemble small, short-legged Bloodhounds. The English Basset, sometimes used in formal foot packs like Beagles, is higher on the leg and about half the weight of the American counterpart.

The English Basset, which is not recognized by the AKC, is much more agile. From this standpoint he is better suited for blood tracking work than the American type. The English Bassets were perfected in the UK for hunting and as formal foot pack hounds to work on hares. These hounds have considerable speed and drive. The English Bassets made available in the United States are likely to be drafts or surplus from formal foot packs. As in the case of Beagles, ask plenty of questions as to why they did not fit into the home pack.

Both types of Bassets have powerful noses and strong line sense. The AKC show types are sometimes so massive and passive that they lack enterprise for a demanding search. However, there are some fine working dogs to be found in the AKC field trialing system, which is run similarly to Beagle brace trials. Despite their appearance, AKC field trial Bassets are faster and more aggressive than their brace Beagle counterparts.

Remember that American Bassets are big, strong dogs and not the easiest to handle. The American show fancier's passion for exaggeration is expressed in the form of extra long ears, little ground clearance and very heavy bone. These features are not appropriate for tracking in briars and rough terrain. Massive bone does not mean sound, strong bone, and Bassets have more than their share of joint problems.

The first legal tracking dog in Vermont was an AKC Basset owned by Tim Nichols. Barney found nine deer and a bear in his first working season, but his brilliant beginning could not be sustained. Joint problems crippled Barney while he was still a young hound.

Coonhounds

"Coonhound" is a very broad generic term covering many different breeds and strains within breeds, which have different working characteristics. What all these dogs have in common is a bred-in trait to trail raccoons with a trail bark, and to announce "treed" with another bark that is distinctly different. There are many breeds: Black and Tans, Blue Ticks, English, Redbones, Treeing Walkers and Plotts. All but the Plotts have a strong Foxhound component in their ancestry. For decades most of the coonhound registries were opened to good hounds of undetermined ancestries. Breed distinctions were frequently made on the basis of color alone; a registered Blue Tick and a registered English (red ticked) might come out of the same litter. Today there are many registration organizations, but the largest by far for coonhounds is the United Kennel Club (UKC). The breed history of coonhounds is both complex and contested; this is not a book about that history.

The coonhound breeds were developed in rural, agricultural America. Farmers hunted their hounds after work for extra income and sometimes for food as well. They wanted a sensible hound that would handle well at night and stay out of trouble around the place during the daytime. After World War II the growth of the UKC's coonhound competitions, called Nite Hunts, had a major impact upon the coonhound breeds. Many of the most serious and competitive breeders began to breed hounds that could excel in this kind of competition hunting. In order to win, that is to get the first "strikes" and first "trees" that piled up points, an aggressive, far ranging dog was needed. For Nite Hunts a handler did not want hounds that checked back with him every 15 or 20 minutes. In a timed Nite Hunt checking in meant wasted minutes; the job of the dog was to hunt coons, the job of the handler was to listen for his hound, call "strike", call "tree" and then go in, find his dog, and prove that it had a coon up. One competition expert advocated giving a hound a good licking if it checked in to the handler and did not stay out in the timber until treed.

The rules of this new kind of competition had a major impact on the coonhound breeds. Within each coonhound breed, some breeders started to produce hounds primarily for competition. These hounds searched very widely, ran a line at top speed and barked with fanatical rage on tree. These competition dogs had so much "hunt" that they were difficult to control. It helped a great deal when tracking collars were developed in the 80s, and hounds could be more easily located when they had gone out of hearing.

Then there were the breeders of pleasure hounds, who wanted a more moderate searching hound, a responsive hound that could be called in if it got on posted property or near a dangerous highway. The pleasure people would argue that they actually put more coon hides on the board than the people with competition hounds. We spend our time hunting for coons, they say, rather than hunting for their dogs.

For the purposes of finding wounded deer and bear, responsive hounds that lean toward the pleasure hunt side are in order. A hound pup, with a pedigree loaded with Nite Hunt Champions and Grand Champions, is not likely to be a better dog for blood tracking; he is more likely to lack the steady patience required.

These temperament distinctions within each coonhound breed are more important than generalizations about breeds as a whole. It makes more sense to buy a puppy bred from dogs that you know firsthand than to buy a hound a 1000 miles away from a breeder that you know only through his magazine ads or his "Nite Hunt" record.

No one keeps statistics on the psychological types of coonhounds being bred. It can be said that Treeing Walkers command widespread respect both as practical hunters and at competitions. There is a wide variation of psychological types within the Treeing Walker breed, and some of these hounds handle extremely well. These big, tri-colored hounds are often seen as farm dogs that ride calmly in the front seat of pick-up trucks and have the country smarts of an old farm shepherd. They are out in the fields during haying, and they nail any number of woodchucks by cleverly cutting them off from their dens. They quickly learn that some animals are game or varmints, and others, like healthy deer, should be ignored.

This is the sort of tree hound to look for as a tracking dog. If he is the color of a Redbone or the color of a Bluetick, it should not make much difference. What counts is what is under the hide and especially between the ears. As is the case with Beagles and Bassets, the nose of a coonhound will probably be more than sufficient for blood tracking. What the brain does with the scent encountered will be the critical question.

Sometimes coonhounds and foxhounds are given away because they run deer rather than the intended game. The huntsman of a formal Foxhound pack

Bob, owned by Randy Vick of Georgia, was a cross of Beagle and Tree-ing Walker Coonhound. Bob had a big voice and an outstanding nose.

once said, "John, I have just the tracking dogs for you. These hounds really like to chase deer". I said "no", but I thanked him for his well-intentioned offer. If a hound is so hardheaded that it can't be broken off deer by a coon hunter or fox hunter, you can be sure that he is going to run deer for you too, healthy deer that is, and not the faint, cold traces of a wounded deer.

Bloodhounds

For pure scenting power there is nothing that can beat a Bloodhound. It is a fascinating breed, but in this book we can only deal with those aspects of the breed that have a bearing on blood tracking. Anyone who has read the well-documented reports of what the finest man tracking Bloodhounds have accomplished will share my own feelings of awe for the nose and for the brain that processes the data that the nose brings.

The truth is that olfactory power of this magnitude is very seldom needed in practical tracking of wounded big game. In most circumstances there is little to be gained in being able to track a wounded deer a week after it has been shot. Nothing will be salvageable but the skull and antlers. In that length of time the meat will certainly be spoiled or devoured by coyotes.

Of course there are some circumstances in which hunters are primarily concerned with the skull and antlers. A record book buck's skull and antlers can be remounted with a new cape. Cases certainly arise when a hunter wants to track and find a deer that was shot four or five days before. When such a call comes in, it may require the ultimate nose of a Bloodhound.

One problem with Bloodhound-class noses is that they are so good that they permit the dog to track drifted scent particles well off the line from where the deer actually passed and probably left some visible blood sign. Particularly in bow season, it is all-important for the handler to observe the very occasional spots and smears that a close-working dog can show him. He would be very unlikely to find this sign on his own, but it is essential for evaluating how the deer is hit and whether it is likely to survive. There can be more to tracking than just following the deer.

To have at hand the awesome scenting powers of the Bloodhound, one must, at the same time, be prepared to tolerate the disadvantages that come with this breed, especially when it is used for blood tracking. First, the Bloodhound is a powerful dog that can weigh a hundred pounds or more, and he pulls hard when locked in on the trail. Bloodhound people are recognizable by the greater length of their leash arm. Handlers in law enforcement will tell you that they can have a real problem holding back the dog when man tracking. Tracking wounded game is much worse because a deer or bear will travel through thick cover that a human would avoid. Imagine yourself being dragged through a deadfall or a patch of multiflora rose thorns while attached to dog with a powerful engine and four-legged drive. Obviously Bloodhounds need to be trained on the meaning of "whoa."

Most of the people who start out tracking wounded deer with Bloodhounds either drop out or shift to a smaller breed of dog. Physically, it is just too tough to work a Bloodhound while tracking in heavy cover or on rough terrain. If you have good reasons to want a Bloodhound despite the disadvantages of size, consider a bitch. In the Bloodhound breed, females are considerably smaller than males, and this can make them easier to handle.

There are some Bloodhounds that handle very well. The great Bloodhound handler and innovator Bill Tollhurst showed me a video of a young law enforcement officer in the South, who worked with a Bloodhound bitch off lead in man tracking. She would work ahead 50 yards, come back to her handler and then work out another 50. Man and Bloodhound were perfectly attuned. If the right Bloodhound could be trained to work like this with a handler on wounded game, it would be a truly great team. However, any Bloodhound handler will tell you that this level of cooperation is not easy to attain with most Bloodhounds.

John Engelken, of Apulia Station, New York, is a professional guide and dog handler, who finds Bloodhounds to his liking. He has worked with bitches weighing well under 100 pounds, and finds that they have responded well to intensive training (see color Fig. 2). According to John, Bloodhounds are tracking dogs suitable for the dedicated professional. "Bloodhounds are not for everyone".

In the semi-desert conditions of the Southwest, scenting conditions can be extremely poor. Bloodhounds are not much used in Texas, but there are circumstances where the awesome nose might have an application on the more difficult calls.

Bloodhounds, like so many great breeds, have been "improved" by the show fancy. The Bloodhound features of long ears, heavy dewlaps and flews have been exaggerated, which makes them more subject to injury in heavy, thorny cover. The show Bloodhounds have been bred very large in the past although somewhat smaller dogs have recently become fashionable. Most important, Bloodhounds have been judged and used for breeding on the basis of the external dog. Intelligence and tracking aptitudes were not factors in serious consideration.

Bloodhounds of man tracking breeding are a much better prospect for the blood trackers. These come from a very different gene pool managed by breeders who provide Bloodhounds for law enforcement and search and rescue work. These Bloodhounds are somewhat smaller and "drier" than the show hounds. Their willingness to cooperate with a handler is likely to be much greater. The distance from man tracking to deer tracking is much shorter than the distance from the show ring.

Bloat is a serious health problem, which occurs much more frequently in Bloodhounds than in most breeds. Anyone acquiring a Bloodhound should be aware of this and take proper precautions. A Bloodhound's stomach, when full, has a tendency to rotate enough so that the entry and exit from the stomach are twisted closed. Gas building up in the stomach can't escape and the dog may die very quickly. The risk can be minimized by feeding moistened food in at least two meals a day, and by not exercising the dog on a full stomach.

Here is one final problem associated with this truly great breed. Like most large breeds, Bloodhounds tend to be short lived. As a general rule, large dogs do not live as long as small ones. This means that you get fewer good working years from a Bloodhound. A nine-year-old Bloodhound is elderly and very near the end of his career. A blood tracking Dachshund or a Beagle of the same age is at the peak of his usefulness.

Hanover Hounds

The Hanover Hound (Hannoverscher Schweißhund) is a German dog that was developed specifically for blood tracking. Physically, it is somewhat smaller than an American Bloodhound, and the Bloodhound features are less pronounced. Still it is a big, heavy-boned hound weighing around 80 pounds. The Hanover Hounds come down from the same ancient stock of heavy, long eared scent hounds as the modern English/American Bloodhounds, but these German dogs were modified by breeding in a faster hunting hound, the Heidebracke from northern Germany (color Fig. 5).

Attractive as the Hanover Hound might appear as a solution to many American blood tracking situations, it is not an easy dog for an American to acquire. You can't just go out and buy a pup as you might buy a Beagle. The breed is monitored and controlled very closely by the German National Hanover Hound Club, which regards the breed as a cherished treasure to be preserved for hunters of the highest commitment and ethical standards. There is a virtual cult of the Hanover Hound, with roots going back to the 18th century when the famous hunting school, the Jaegerhof, was established by the Hanoverian Court. Hanover Hounds are also bred in other European countries where the breed clubs hold to German standards. Breeders of these specialized dogs are very determined to prevent them from falling into the hands of untrained people and those who might breed indiscriminately without rigorous quality control.

The Hanover Hound was developed and is trained as a dog that will work both on and off lead. The usual procedure is to work on lead over the cold line and then to release the dog if the wounded animal leaves the point where it has bedded. In traditional training, these patient, deliberate dogs are first asked to track healthy deer that their trainer has observed several hours earlier. The dog must follow the exact scent line of the individual deer and distinguish it from all others. This painstaking and time-consuming method of training, which does not depend on artificial blood lines, produces a dog capable of following any wounded deer regardless of whether there is a blood trail. Because of their exceptional noses and the type of training that they can absorb, the Hanover Hounds are considered in Europe to be the finest of all blood tracking dogs. These are the dogs that are called in for the extremely difficult tasks or for the cases that dogs of lesser breeds have failed to solve.

The capabilities of the properly trained Hanover Hound would be of great value in tracking for bow hunters. It is unfortunate that these dogs have been so difficult for an American to buy. Probably there are very few Americans that would have the time to train one in the traditional way but of course Hanover Hounds can also be trained by the blood and tracking shoe methods. Trained Hanover Hounds are very expensive.

An important new development is the importation into Quebec of Hanoverians from French sources. As of 2014 there were 14 dogs of this breed working within the Quebec tracking organization, the ACCSQ.

The quality of nose in a good "Hannoverscher" is hard to match, but keep in mind that dogs of other breeds also develop the capability of following an individual deer, even when there is no blood. Of course this only comes in the more intelligent dogs, which have worked at least 30 natural deer calls. Hanover Hounds come from the same part of Germany as the ancestors of American Plott hounds. Their brindle coloration is similar, but no one has established a connection between the two breeds.

Bavarian Mountain Hounds

In the mountainous terrain of the Bavarian Alps the massive Hanover Hound was found to lack agility, and a smaller, lighter blood tracking specialist, the Bavarian Mountain Hound (Bayerischer Gebirgsschweißhund), was developed. In America the breed is often referred to as the Bavarian Mountain Scent Hound, Bavarian, BGS or BMH.

The starting point in developing this breed was the Hanover Hound, but the blood of more agile trail hounds was carefully introduced. What emerged was a short-coated dog, the color of a Redbone Coonhound or Vizsla. Like the

Hanover Hounds, these dogs are very houndy in appearance, but they are lighter boned and better suited to working in very rough country. According to the German breed standard, Bavarians stand from 17.3 to 21 inches at the shoulder, with the males slightly taller than the females (color Figs. 3 and 4).

In December of 2008, after the snow in upstate New York had closed down most tracking, I went to Alsace in eastern France to see tracking dogs work. While there in the Vosges Mountains I went out on 11 calls with Meyer Didier, who had an experienced, truly excellent Bavarian bitch named Tikka. She was a light Redbone color and weighed about 45 pounds. Most of the time we were tracking wounded wild boars, but she also found a little roe deer that a less experienced dog had been unable to locate.

Wild boars have a lot of scent, but they are not easy to track. They don't bleed much, they are very tough, and they go a long way. The younger ones are most comfortable in a herd, so often it's hard to keep track of the wounded animal, which is not bleeding and running with a half dozen healthy animals.

In France and Germany there is sufficient manpower and dog power to check out "possible" hits in what is called a "Control Search". Control Searches are surprisingly productive. Typical was a case where a good-sized sow had been shot at while crossing a wood road during a drive the day before. There was no sign on the road, just scuff marks. The sow went up a steep slope of the type you climb by hanging onto tree trunks. There was no visible blood on the way up, but Tikka found the sow dead on top. No problem!

What impressed me about Tikka was the quality of her nose combined with intelligence and responsiveness. She worked with her handler on the long leash, but she did not drag him around.

Tikka was a hound that adjusted to the needs of her handler and also to the scenting conditions. We tracked a boar that had been hit down in the plains the day before. Wind was blasting across the open fields and Tikka had to search hard for scent in the short mowed grass that the boar had traversed. She took the leg-hit sow a long way before she finally ran out of line. Often you learn most about a dog in seeing her work in nearly impossible conditions.

The Bavarian Mountain Hound is bred and used today in a number of European countries. The Bavarian Club of Germany has very tight breeding restrictions. Hounds used for breeding have to be judged sound in conformation. Then they must prove their tracking ability on both artificially laid blood lines and on actual tracks of wounded game. The standard for Bavarians suitable for breeding is set very high, and the Club does everything it can to prevent indiscriminate breeding.

Bavarian puppies are bred and sold in other countries, and registered with the FCI, the same international registry that the German club uses. However, all of the rigorous controls of the German Bavarian Club are not applied in other countries. It's important to realize that even in Germany the parents may be registered by the FCI, but this does not mean that they have been validated by the working tests and real hunting. Some of these dogs may be good; some are purely ornamental.

Years ago I went to a big dog show in Dortmund, Germany, to check out the Dachshunds. In the great hall of the dog show I ran into a German gentleman all decked out in a traditional loden green hunting suit. He had a Bavarian on a leash, and I stopped to chat with him. "No, he didn't really track with his Bavarians, but he liked the way they looked." He was into the whole bit of German hunting folklore; he liked the atmosphere and the tradition of it all, and he was obviously not too concerned about working ability. There are people like this in Europe, and they breed and sell puppies too. Do not rush into buying a BMH from any source!

For Americans, Bavarians are certainly more accessible than the Hanover Hounds. Puppies have been imported to the United States from Germany, Sweden, Norway, England, Slovakia and Poland by at least a dozen different handlers, who wanted a medium-sized tracking dog with a truly superior nose.

By 2015 some tension had developed between the Americans, who adhere to the very strict rules of the German Bavarian Club, and those who don't want to be constrained by these rules, which make it difficult to acquire a puppy and often involves years of waiting.

The best source of current information on registered Bavarian imports from the official German Club is Ken Parker of Williamson, GA, (www. hillockkennels.com). Ken uses Bavarians himself for tracking, and he is a discriminating breeder. The waiting list for his registered pups is a long one, but Ken is generous with his experienced advice. He is a founder of BGS-GNA, a North American Group of Bayerischer Gebirgsschweißhund Club (www.kbgs.de).

An independent Bavarian Mountain Hound Club of America (BMHCA) was founded in 2015. The Club encourages owners to register their Bavarians with the United Kennel Club of America. More information can be found at www.bavarianmountainhoundclubofamerica.com.

When the demand for a breed exceeds the supply a bell rings for the money hungry puppy producers. If they can find some dogs to breed together, they are ready to start cranking out puppies for buyers inexperienced enough to buy on the basis of a breed labels. Today you can buy Bavarian pups on the Internet that have nothing going for them but the names of their untested parents.

Most of the "Bavarians" in America are doing very good work. They have proved that they handle the heat of Georgia and Texas well, and they are long-legged enough to have a low lethal risk from poisonous snakes.

Tim Nichols, who tracked with Mickey the Beagle for many years, now has a Bavarian from Poland. Bruno at age 9 has a total of 209 finds, which include 6 bear, 1 moose and a bobcat. As is the case with many BMH trackers, Bruno had an adolescent period when he could not bring his abilities together. Once his "teenage" years were behind him he became a legend in northeastern New York and Vermont.

Every breed of dog has characteristics that will not appeal to all handlers. Americans are drawn to the big nose, convenient size and responsiveness of the BMH, but on the downside they are not prepared for the delayed psychological maturity. Everyone I talked to in France and Germany agreed that you don't see most Bavarians settling down to do consistent, focused work until they are three years old.

Game aggressiveness in Bavarians is often slow to come, and this can be a problem when the dog works off lead. The European method is to release the tracking dog from the leash when a game animal is bumped from its wound bed and takes off. A good bay dog is required, and bay power is not something that comes early to Bavarians and Hanoverians. They need time to mature in this respect. We Americans, who like to see results fast, are often unprepared for a long wait.

This is a breed for the tracking specialist who takes 30 or more calls a year and has the patience to develop the dog's potential. The Bavarian doesn't make much sense for the ordinary guy who wants a household companion with which he will track two or three deer a season for his buddies.

Rommel, a Bavarian, with the hunter and a fine buck. Rommel is owned by Fred Zoeller from Cooperstown, NY.

Slovensky Kopov (Slovakian Hound)

The Slovensky Kopov from Eastern Europe is a newcomer to North America. They were first used very successfully as tracking dogs by Michael Schneider, a guide and outfitter in British Columbia.

The Kopov has an excellent nose and the willingness to keep it down on an old, cold line. They are smaller than the Bavarians, ranging from 30 pounds for bitches to 45 pounds for males. This is a handy size for transport, and they make good house dogs. As of 2016 the use of Kopovs for tracking is expanding in both the USA and Canada.

An example of young Slovensky Kopov that was bred in the USA.

Summary

- Dachshunds of appropriate agility are well suited for those who will track in states where the dog must be worked on a leash.

- Beagles have excellent noses, but the breed embraces hounds of many types and working styles. Don't just buy "a Beagle".

- Big hounds such as Bassets and coonhounds must be selected with particular concern for a calm temperament and responsiveness.

- A good Bloodhound is without equal for sensitivity of nose, but they are heavy, powerful dogs that can be difficult to handle in dense cover.

- In Europe, for good reasons, the Hanover Hound and the Bavarian Mountain Hound are considered the true blood tracking specialists.

Chapter 5

Dog Breeds II:
Spaniels, Pointing Dogs, and Retrievers

A common characteristic shared by dogs in these categories is a tendency to quarter back and forth as they search for live birds. In the best blood trackers of these breeds, the instinct to work back and forth is suppressed when they are working the scent line of wounded big game. This can be achieved in spaniels and pointers by starting training on blood before training to find birds in the field. A dog that works on and off the scent line will still find wounded big game, but it may take longer, and the handler will miss much of the blood sign that is so valuable in evaluating how an animal is wounded. This is particularly important when working with bowhunters.

The majority of the spaniels and pointers I have seen worked a line rather fast and in a pattern of broad "S" curves. However, the best and the most experienced stayed on the line like a good hound. Working behind these dogs, it would be possible to learn something about where or how seriously an animal is wounded. Particularly, with strong dogs over 70 pounds, it is not much fun to track unless the dog works at a reasonable speed and is trained to stop on command. On a steep mountainside, with wet, slippery rocks, it should be the handler, not the dog, who sets the pace.

The great advantage of most bird dogs is that they are bred to please and to be responsive to the handler. The value of this should not be underestimated. The training and practice you will give them in bird work will strengthen this partnership so that it becomes second nature to both of you. There may be some moments when a game bird will distract your dog while he is tracking a deer. This may create a minor delay until things are straightened out, but you will still accomplish what needs to be done in searching for the deer. The advantages of having a dog with which you hunt for other kinds of game will usually outweigh the disadvantages by far.

Running a few training bloodlines in the off season will never accomplish much in the way of exercise and conditioning. Field work, retriever training and water work in hot weather will be much more important.

Spaniels

There are so many different spaniel breeds that it is impossible to comment upon every one. Search for the individual and avoid the show bloodlines. The exaggerations of coat and conformation, and the single focus on winning in the show ring are at their worst in the spaniel breeds. A problem with the real hunting spaniels is that some have such an abundance of energy and hunting zest that it is out of character for them to slow down and work a faint scent line foot by foot.

It is hard to fit the German Wachtelhund into a chapter category, but we have grouped it with the "spaniels" because it does, among other things hunt birds in flushing style. The Wachtelhund, at 44-66 pounds, looks like a large spaniel when adorned with its full coat, but its appearance is much more hound-like when the coat is closely cropped. This duality of appearance is also carried over into the Wachtelhund's working style. It is both an air scenter and a ground tracker. As a versatile dog, it is used to hunt all manner of game, both furred and feathered, and excels at retrieving. While hunting birds, the Wachtelhund may "track" with its nose in the air, but during blood tracking, the breed is most likely to keep its nose down on the ground as it "digs" for scent.

Like many larger breeds, the Wachtelhund has a tendency to cover ground quickly and give the handler a workout while on lead. This faster pace will need to be reduced for those wishing to have a tracking dog that works more slowly and deliberately. This is especially important when tracking bow-shot game where blood sign may be difficult to detect.

Caliber, a Wachtelhund used for tracking wounded deer, is owned by Brady Hensington, MD, from Missouri.

The Wachtelhund is also adept at baying large furred game including wild hogs and wounded deer. There is even a documented case of a Wachtelhund having bayed up a nuisance grizzly bear in Alaska! As the wild hog extends its range across the United States, and as growing populations of larger predators such as wolves and coyotes become an increasing threat to smaller dogs, the Wachtelhund's popularity is likely to grow.

For the handler who wants a strong, tough, and determined dog for all kinds of hunting, and one that is also bright and responsive, the Wachtelhund is a good choice.

Versatile Hunting Dog Breeds From Europe

To avoid misunderstandings we must define our terms at the outset. The "versatile hunting dogs" are pointers, but not all pointing dogs are suitable for blood tracking. English Pointers and English Setters, for example, were developed exclusively for scenting upland game birds at a distance and pointing them. They are bird-finding and pointing specialists, but no one has expected these dogs to put their noses down and follow ground scent of a wounded deer.

On the continent of Europe more versatile breeds of dogs were developed that would point, retrieve over land and water, find and drive furred game and

Nova, this VDD Drahthaar, excelled in blood tracking tests and did equally well when asked to find a real wounded deer. She was one of the best blood trackers we have observed. Nova was owned by Andrei Nicolau.
Photo courtesy of Andrei Nicolau

finally track wounded big game. These European pointers are now correctly referred to as "versatile hunting dogs", a more descriptive title that the older term "continental pointing dogs". The most important of these breeds from the blood tracker's point of view are the Drahthaar, Americanized as the German Wirehaired Pointer, and the Kurzhaar, known here as the German Shorthaired Pointer. There are many other European pointing breeds: the Pointing Griffon, the Weimeraner, the Pudelpointer. The list can be extended for several lines.

Before the "versatiles" appeared in significant numbers, Americans thought of pointers and setters as bird dogs exclusively. The English Pointer has set the standard in the most prestigious American, multi-breed field trials. For this reason the English Pointer prototype has had a strong influence in shaping all pointing breeds of other origins once they were brought to this country. English Pointers tend to be big running, high headed dogs that detect bird scent and point at remarkable distances. Retrieving is much less important than bird finding, and in some trials pointers are not expected to retrieve at all.

In multi-breed field trials owners and handlers of the "other" pointing breeds sensed a competitive need to have dogs that ran like English Pointers. To many American field trial judges the Drahthaars and Kurzhaars, just off the boat, appeared to be plodding, too close working and too unexciting.

Who is to say how it happened that "American" German Shorthaired Pointers, especially, began to look and work more and more like English Pointers? Many of them had white markings. Perhaps, it was the simple result of selective breeding; perhaps a few GSP bitches were bred, under the table, to English Pointer studs. In any case, the result did not please admirers of the versatile hunting breeds in their original European form. These practical hunters wanted a pointing dog that could be followed on foot and that excelled in finding and retrieving dead birds and runners. They also wanted a dog that was competent at retrieving both waterfowl and furred game. In short they wanted a versatile dog.

The comparison of continental or European dogs to their American counterparts has become a very sensitive subject. The German breed clubs have been unhappy with the fate of their breeds on American shores. For example, the Verein Deutsch Drahthaar considers that the AKC German Wirehaired Pointer has become another breed, which they do not recognize or allow to be used for breeding purposes.

Similar tensions exist between some Americans and the Europeans in the cases of other breeds of continental origin. Another example is the Brittany, a pointing dog formerly known as the Brittany Spaniel. The American Brittany has become an entirely different dog from the cobby, close-working French original. Several of the European breed clubs have established outposts or "Groups" in North America for the minority of hunters here who are not happy with the mainstream American product.

This book was not written to analyze the controversies or assign blame. The arguments are complex and involve much more than alleged hunting ability. However, it is true that European pointers in America have tended to

---

become different after several generations. These differences can be significant for the blood tracker.

The versatile hunting dog, in his work on birds and small furred game, has to be a good tracker. As a matter of fact, tracking wounded deer and boar is one of his assigned tasks in Europe. Today, it is not surprising that pointing breeds that have been maintained to work as versatile hunting dogs offer much better prospects for blood tracking in North America. If you want to have a pointing dog that can also track wounded game, avoid the racy, high headed field trial prospect that does not care to find dead birds and retrieve them.

German Drahthaars and Kurzhaars are tough dogs psychologically. Training them does require a firm hand, but these versatile pointers have a reputation as aggressive bay dogs for stopping a big buck in the southern "off-lead" sections of the country.

As mentioned above, the German breed clubs have established a presence in North America. They conduct performance tests here, including blood tracking, which reward the working qualities that they favor. Dogs in America and their performances are recorded in the German registries.

The North American Versatile Hunting Dog Association does not have direct organizational links to Europe. The NAVHDA working tests, however, are similar and clearly inspired by the European concept of what a versatile hunting dog should be. A pedigree strong in NAVHDA performance tests is a big plus when you select a puppy. Unfortunately the NAVHDA organization has never demonstrated a specific interest in blood tracking, and unlike the German based clubs they do not offer blood tracking tests.

There are performance distinctions between the various pointers in the versatile hunting dog category, but supporters of the various breeds can't agree on just where the lines of distinction should be drawn. Clearly the overlap in styles, from one breed to another, is more significant than the differences between them. If you already have a breed preference, look for the right individual dog within that breed. Otherwise, there is no reason to limit your search to a single breed. Select on the basis of the breeder's reputation for producing the qualities you are looking for. Observe the parents of the puppy, their working style and their performance record. If you can thoroughly inspect the green grass close to home, you may find that it is the greenest of all.

Labrador Retrievers

The Labrador Retriever dominates the working retrievers by his numbers in the field. In America the Golden Retriever is second in popularity. The rugged Chesapeake Bay Retriever is a distant third, and then there are a few Flat Coated Retrievers from England. It will be a surprise to many that the Lab is widely used for tracking wounded deer in the South, where it can legally be worked off lead. In England and Scotland the "British" Lab is the most important tracking dog, and this type of Lab plays a significant role in France. The Lab has to be taken very seriously as a blood tracking prospect, but there are many caveats.

First, the Lab suffers from being too popular. There are more AKC registered Labs than any other breed. Labs are usually intelligent, stable and friendly; because of this a real cult of the Lab has grown up with prints, rugs and even dish towels extolling its appealing beauty. Almost every suburban family thinks about getting a Lab to be part of the family. Even if the family does not hunt, Labs are great companions and great with kids; the next step is to breed a litter of pups to teach the kids about birth, carry on the family tradition and immortalize the family member through another dog generation. In emotional terms this is fine, but it does not have much to do with preserving the working qualities of the breed. Many, possibly most of the Lab puppies out there in America were bred with absolutely no thought to what is needed in a gun dog, let alone a blood tracker. Choose your puppy and its parents carefully.

Show Labs are different in appearance from the working kind, being larger and not as athletic looking. However, the show people have paid more attention to function and soundness in the breed than the backyard pet breeders. Among Lab people there are a few who try to find a balance between working and showing. As you would expect, those involved in breed activities are most likely to be aware of hip dysplasia and seriously committed to weeding it out of their breeding stock.

Field trialing has been a very mixed blessing to the breed. The influence of the competitive AKC retriever trial actually led to a revolt and split in the ranks of field trial competitors. The nature of the controversy and its consequences has a direct relationship to the problems of selecting a Lab that has the best chances to become a fine blood tracker.

As AKC retriever trials evolved, it became more and more difficult for judges to decide which performance was best when so many performances were all but flawless. More and more difficult challenges were introduced, double blind retrieves, triple blinds. Today the dog is required to follow the handler's whistle and hand signals to perfection, even if it involves overriding practical dog sense. For example, a dog has to swim directly, in a straight line to a bird. If he uses his natural smarts and runs along the shore so that he can make the shortest swim, and therefore the fastest retrieve, he is dropped. Obedience to the handler's signals has to override use of nose. A superior nose does not have much to do with winning field trials, although nose has a great deal to do with being a practical gun dog in the marsh or on the uplands. Also, in contrast to the AKC field trial type retriever, the tracking Lab must rise above the level of "command and obey".

In reaction to the AKC retriever trials, a European type system of non-competitive tests was developed by a new organization, the North American Hunting Retriever Association, NAHRA. The AKC, acknowledging that there was something to the dissident position, came forth with their own system of "non-competitive" hunting tests, which soon became very competitive. David Michael Duffey, a columnist for Gun Dog Magazine, has pointed out how difficult it is in practice to relate retriever field trials, and even tests, to the practical needs of the hunter.

The competitive atmosphere of AKC field trials and even AKC tests has created another problem. To score really well in either type of event, dogs have to retrieve with great dash and splash. Labs have to demonstrate high style on retrieves with magnificent leaps into the water and high energy zest throughout the performance. Such a Lab is usually "wrapped too tight" to wait calmly and patiently for hours in a duck blind. He is not the dog for a practical duck hunter, and he is probably not the best prospect for blood tracking either.

What does all this mean for the ordinary dog person who wants a dog for bird hunting and also to find wounded deer? Look for a sire and dam with strong local reputations as practical flushing dogs and resourceful retrievers. A pup from this breeding will probably serve you better than one with papers showing that he is from national class field trial breeding. Certainly he will be cheaper to buy. Also keep in mind that in the dog world few rules are absolute. A dog from a certain background may not fit into it well. He may be too independent or not hard driving enough, but he may be just what you want.

Tracking Labs in America

In America the strong role of Labs as tracking dogs first developed in the Deep South along the Mississippi Flyway. Hank Hearn of Vicksburg, MS demonstrated Lab possibilities while he was working as a hunting guide on the 27,000 acre Tara Plantation nearby. Tara, in the 1980s was becoming famous for its quality bowhunting for whitetail deer. In 1988 Hank took his Lab puppy J-J and began to develop him as tracker for Tara's hunters. J-J was a highly intelligent dog out of Mississippi duck hunting stock. He was constantly with Hank, and after a few uncertain attempts as a puppy he found his calling doing what he and Hank realized they had been born to do, find wounded deer.

J-J was a hunting dog that could do almost anything. Duck retrieving and coon hunting were minor parts of his repertoire. However, by the time of his death in 1998 it was J-J's fame as a wounded deer tracker that had spread through the South. Today, there are many blood tracking Labs at work in the South that come out of J-J's duck retriever bloodlines. Today Mississippi and Louisiana are probably the best places to look for American Lab litters from strong blood tracking backgrounds.

Most of the Labs in the South track off lead, which means that they must handle easily with an intuitive sense of what their handler expects of them. More information on this type of tracking is to be found in the Tara Section of the chapter, "Tracking Dogs for Guides and Outfitters." Labs are also discussed in Chapter 13, "Tracking Off Lead". What struck me about the Labs I saw at Tara in 2005 was their calmness combined with their athleticism. For example Bo, a great grandson of J-J, was a big 80 pounder, with the speed and power to stop a buck twice his weight. But to see him lounging around on the porches of the Tara lodge, you would not imagine what he is like in his action mode. Most Labs that do a great deal of deer tracking work end up being

Al Wade with Scout, an outstanding chocolate Lab of American hunting breeding.

jabbed, rolled or thrown by an aggressive buck with formidable antlers. J-J and his descendants have been psychologically tough enough to survive such an experience and come back for more.

In Louisiana Al Wade and his chocolate Lab, Scout, are now on the leading edge of the tracking wave that originated at Tara. Al tracks professionally for outfitters, and Scout is a big strong dog that weighs just shy of 100 pounds. At age eight Scout has found 133 deer in Louisiana, Alabama and Illinois, where Al has been working under contract for Golden Triangle Outfitters. Conditions, traditions and regulations in the Gulf States are not at all like those in Illinois. In response Al has developed two different tracking methods.

In Louisiana and Alabama working the tracking dog off lead is officially tolerated; Scout works on or off lead as conditions require. Off lead he handles like a Lab, that is extremely well, and he wears a Garmin Astro GPS collar. Even if the wounded deer takes him a long way, Al can locate Scout easily with his hand-held receiver. Scout has frequently found deer 12 to 24 hours after they were shot, even when there was little or no visible blood. He is an excellent bay dog.

Up north Al works for an outfitter with Scout in the big buck country of Illinois. There Al must, by law, keep Scout on a tracking lead at all times. In open hardwoods he uses a 45 foot lead of stiff mountain climbing rope. In the northern tradition the tracking dog is brought in only when the hunter, or the guide, has exhausted the possibilities of eye-tracking.

Tracking Labs in Europe

I gained another perspective on the Lab as a tracking dog in eastern France, where I went on ten wounded wild boar calls with Patrice Stoquert, a forester in the Vosges Mountains. Raoul, his seven-year-old yellow Lab of Scottish bloodlines was a revelation. He reenforced what I had already learned from several decades of practical tracking in New York State. While nose is essential, the quality of intelligence is even more fundamental. A dog that uses his nose intelligently on an old, cold line of ground scent can be more effective than a dog of superior scenting power that lacks intuition and persistence to search for scent beyond the point of loss. The brain processing the olfactory stimuli must recognize the right game scent from all the other distracting scent in the area.

Getting a good start on the right line is an important part of tracking. When the wounded animal is a wild boar this can be especially difficult. Boars, when shot during drives, are usually running in a group so there is individual scent from many different pigs lingering in the same place. Also wild boars, even when shot with big, center-fire rifles, don't bleed very much. Patrice would release Raoul at the general hit site and then let him cast slowly in a 100 meter circle as he stood and watched. When Raoul found the right scent line he would sit down and bark. If Patrice did not approach him quickly enough, he would go to Patrice and nuzzle the tracking collar and leash in Patrice's hand. Clearly this dog understood that the cold tracking itself was to be done on the leash. It was Raoul's job to follow the line, Patrice's function was to observe and interpret what little blood was there to be seen.

I am not suggesting that this is typical Lab tracking work. Stoquert is a gifted handler, referred to in these borderlands of France and Germany as the "dog whisperer". He is unconventional in some of his handling techniques, and it must be remembered that Raoul is a mature, very experienced dog, thoroughly in tune with his human partner. Close cooperation, built on intelligence and an emotional bond, is necessary to some degree in all effective tracking dogs, but the psychological make-up of the Lab facilitates this.

In Europe it is customary and legal to release the tracking dog at the wound bed if the animal is still alive. When the boar or deer takes off the rapid chase begins; it is usually a short one before the game is pulled down or bayed by the tracking dog. Releasing the dog when the animal is jumped increases the percentage of wounded game that does not get away, but it can be hard on a tracking dog that confronts a large wild boar or a wounded red deer of up to 400 pounds live weight. A Lab-sized dog must have courage and physical toughness to prevail.

Patrice Stoquert has worked with three Labs. The first lab and his son Raoul were psychologically hard enough to be effective bay or catch dogs, depending on the size of the game. Raoul's dam, however, was not willing to press hard enough or close enough to be effective.

Raoul, is owned by Patrice Stoquert, a French forester. Raoul has just tracked and bayed this wild boar.

In France doubts were raised by certain Lab breeders, who worried that selecting for tracking and baying ability might produce aggressive, hard mouthed dogs unsuitable for the retrieving that is the breed's primary purpose. Patrice qualified all of his Labs in retriever field tests, and bird crunching was not a problem with any of them. Retriever training and bird flushing were completely compatible with their experience in tracking wounded big game. And Raoul, like his dam, was completely relaxed and friendly in the company of strangers.

Labs in Europe are what we Americans would call British Labs, usually smaller and stockier than the hunting Labs that have evolved here. Richard Wolters, in his book, *The Labrador Retriever...The History...The People*, wrote that he found greater initiative and nose in the British hunting Labs; he believed that this was the result of a more practical process of selection. To this day, American promoters of British Labs claim that their dogs are bred to be more laid-back, and they are expected to use their own intelligence and initiative to find wounded and dead birds.

British-bred Labs are available in the United States, and of course they are not cheap. I would not say that the Brits have a monopoly on good Labs for tracking wounded big game, but their Labs are worth investigating if you cannot find an "Americanized" individual that pleases you. I prefer to avoid the debate about differences of temperament and simply affirm that some American Labs have more than proved their usefulness as tracking dogs on this side of the Atlantic.

The Importance of the Lab in the United States

At present in 2016 the Lab is one of the most popular breeds for tracking wounded deer in the United States. The tracking Lab is useful anywhere, especially in water, but I personally think that his greatest value is in parts of the US where it is legal for dogs to track wounded deer off lead and where they can safely do so. His intelligence helps make him an ideal working partner, and with this same intelligence he can learn to stay away from many dangers when off lead in the field. For example, a Lab will readily learn to avoid a poisonous cottonmouth in a swamp. They will be more traffic-wise on a highway than most hounds. They handle well, and they are not likely to be aggressive toward the hunter who comes up to "his" dead deer. Their size permits them to either bay a wounded deer or pull it down. In situations like this they are prudent enough to do the right thing and not get themselves killed. The value of the Lab in the American South has been greatly enhanced by the development of the Garmin Alpha GPS collar. The Labs value off lead is further discussed in Chapter 13 which relates the experiences of Rosie, a Lab owned by JJ Scarborough.

Worked on a tracking leash, some of the Lab's advantages disappear. They are bigger dogs than you really need, and they tend to "drift" a line rather than stay right on it. A Dachshund is more likely to show the handler all of the blood signs that will permit him to judge how seriously the deer has been wounded.

Compared to some other breeds Labs are healthy, long-lived dogs. The most serious physical ailment common in Labs and the other retriever breeds is hip dysplasia. This is a crippling disease, and it seldom can be detected in the young puppy. The characteristically shallow hip sockets are partly a consequence of the pup's genetics, but there are environmental factors as well. Puppies, which are fed too much and grow too rapidly, are more prone to the disease than others. Avoid the problem as much as possible; ask to see the OFA hip soundness rating for the sire and dam of a pup that you are considering. If the breeder doesn't seem to know what you are talking about, be extremely cautious. A Lab may look fine trotting around in the yard, but he could come up too lame to track after an hour in the field. It is sad to be forced to leave your experienced, but hopelessly lame dog at home and begin all over again with a sounder, young dog.

Golden Retrievers

Goldens, like Labs, are hugely popular as family dogs, so most of the litters of this hunting dog were planned with no thoughts about hunting abilities. Many of the dogs bred as pets trace back to show breeding, and these dogs tend to be much larger than the Goldens used for hunting and field trialing. In temperament the generic Golden Retriever tends to be intelligent, but more easygoing than the Lab. Most suburban families do not want a hyper dog. The Goldens that I have observed did not show much intensity, but they had a way of getting the job done.

Goldens, with their heavy coats, are definitely not hot weather dogs. This can be a disadvantage in the South and during early bow season in the North.

If I wanted a retriever for bird work and for tracking wounded deer, I would choose a Lab over a Golden Retriever. The Labs have an established record; they are tougher dogs psychologically, with more suitable coats. But if I were a dedicated "swamp collie" man, I would stick with what I had. Steve Price of Madison, Wisconsin has clearly shown that a dedicated Golden and a dedicated handler can find wounded deer.

Josh Prouty of Steuben County in south central New York has clearly demonstrated that a Golden Retriever of the right breeding can be very capable tracker and a tough dog when need be. Josh's Rosston is a 65 pound Golden, who lives in the house as a member of the family. In two years of tracking he has found 31 deer with a high percentage of recoveries. Josh's account of a Rosston find tells us much about this dog's character.

> "I noticed that Rosston was pulling me toward what I thought was a large boulder. We approached and then right in front of me Rosston had this very large back by the throat with the deer's horns underneath his back legs so that he was being lifted off the ground. My first shot missed, and the buck stood up. This time the deer was standing broadside with this head and neck being dragged down by my dog; I had never seen this side of Rosston before! At my second shot the buck dropped and lay motionless with a tame and docile Golden Retriever sitting next to him, wagging his tail a thousand times a minute.

Chesapeakes and Flat Coats

The Chesapeake Bay Retriever is a big, hard dog. This is what it takes to swim out into an icy winter ocean and retrieve ducks. No one ever claimed they were easy to train, but they can take cold, and they don't know how to quit. For a strong, experienced handler ready to work in extreme conditions, a Chessie might serve well. The tawny coat is very much like the color of a deer. In light of this and their size such a dog should not be used to find wounded deer unless it is wearing a flame orange vest.

Rosston, a Golden Retriever, with his owner Josh Prouty, the hunter Lisa Luther, and the buck he fought.

Photo courtesy of Josh Prouty

Flat-Coated Retrievers are rare but obtainable in this country. These black dogs are highly regarded in the UK as intelligent natural hunters, unspoiled by those who wished to have them solely as pets or as show dogs. Much easier to handle than a Chesapeake, the Flat-Coat has been formed by natural hunting influences rather than those of competition. For a retriever person seeking to get back to the basic roots of hunting, this might be the dog.

One gateway into the world of versatile bird hunting dogs is through *Gun Dog* magazine. The articles contain a wealth of information useful to the owners of any breed. The advertisements will put you in touch with breeders and breed organizations.

Summary

- Most spaniels and pointers have a natural tendency to work back and forth on a scent line. You may have to deal with this problem through selection or training.

- The spaniel with an established reputation for blood tracking is the Wachtelhund from Germany.

- Many of the "versatile" breeds have separated into types with different working styles. Make sure that your tracking dog prospect has the traits you require.

- Versatile hunting breeds such as the Drahthaar are widely and effectively used in Europe to find wounded big game. They are ideal for the American bird hunter who wants a versatile blood tracking dog.

- Labrador Retrievers have an established reputation as off lead blood trackers in the American Deep South, in the UK and in France.

- The large size of the versatile hunting dog breeds is an advantage if the dog can be worked off lead. The large size becomes a disadvantage if a tracking leash is mandatory.

Chapter 6

Dog Breeds III: Curdogs and Cowdogs

When I began this book, I had heard of Texas but had little sense of how big Texas is…as a deer hunting state. The deer population and the deer kill in Texas is usually the largest of any state. Deer hunting in Texas is big, and Texas is one of the leading states in quality deer management. Quality Deer Management is a method of managing a deer herd to maximize the production of quality animals that live through their prime of life and produce quality offspring. Deer have great value in Texas, both aesthetic value and cash value. This concern for the animal has strengthened a tradition of using dogs to find wounded deer. This tradition is pure Texan, but in some ways it parallels the European tradition. More detail about this appears in Chapter 27 on "Regional Tracking Traditions."

Curs

To a Northeastern hunter the hunting ways of Texas seem to come from another planet. And much the same can be said of the dogs. Let's take the term "cur" or "curdog." Outside of Texas and the South, "cur" is not a complimentary word for a dog. It brings visions of gaunt, mangy garbage can raiders slinking along ten steps ahead of the dog warden. There is so much that we Yankees don't understand!

"Cur", south of the Mason Dixon and in the West, is an honorable term for a specific type of dog. Within curdom there are breeds, registries and field trials. If we had anything like British pride in our native dog breeding, we would have elevated these dogs as canine icons of our American heritage. The Southern Black Mouth Cur might be as well known as the Airedale Terrier or the Jack Russell. Only Louisiana and Texas have had the vision to honor native breeds as official state dogs, with the Catahoula Cur from Catahoula County, Louisiana, and the Lacy Dogs from Texas.

Most cur breeds had their origins as generic cattle and hog dogs adapted to a particular locality. The theories of their origins lie, for good part, in unproved legend, but the base was certainly stock dogs and guard dogs brought from Great Britain by 18th and 19th century settlers. Spanish guard dogs, Indian dogs and a dash of coyote possibly played a role as well. These dogs were expected to locate cattle and feral hogs in thick brush, tree coons and squirrels, guard the home place, and not expect any fancy food. The curs had to be at least as tough as the tough men who depended upon them. In a frontier environment a man-dominated form of natural selection operated;

the dog that was unintelligent, inattentive or incapable of meeting his master's expectations did not survive to reproduce.

The Mountain Curs and Leopard Curs of the Southeast have a different origin. These breeds were developed primarily as tree dogs, but some have proved to be good trackers of wounded big game.

The curs and their history are worthy of a book in themselves; DNA research may tell us more than we know now about their origin. For the blood tracking purposes of this book, we have to stay out of these fascinating thickets and focus on what curs are doing today.

The Catahoulas and the Southern Black Mouth Curs both have their roots in the borderlands of East Texas and Louisiana. Although their colors are very different, they have strong physical and psychological similarities because they were both used for the same type of cattle and wild hog work. They are big dogs; males can reach up to a hundred pounds. The larger curs are not as suitable for working on a leash. They have broad skulls, moderate sized drop ears, and powerful jaws. A typical Catahoula has a spotted, blue merle coat, very different from the tawny mountain lion color of the Southern Black Mouth Cur.

A dog is more than what it looks like, and it is in the mind of the Catahoulas and Black Mouths that their true character and value is to be found. They are highly intelligent, and their intelligence permits them to make distinctions. My own Southern Black Mouth Cur, Stone Apple Cleo, was quick to learn the difference between a wounded deer (of great importance to her master) and healthy deer (no more important to him than a cow). I could find a dead deer with her in the morning and then hunt coons at night. In the process of searching for a coon track, she would bump a healthy deer and ignore it completely. I have never had another dog learn these things so fast (color Fig. 8).

The problem with Cleo, and with most of these curs, is that they really lack the nose of a hound for ground scent. Under equal conditions of moisture and temperature, they will work a six-hour-old line but may fail on a twelve hour line. Working the wind or wind scenting is something else again. A dog that can air scent a small squirrel in a tree at 100 yards or more has no problem locating a dead deer from down wind at 200 yards.

Cleo had the misfortune to pass her career in the Northeast, where her deer searching chores were a bit curtailed by the regulations and customs of New York State. Curs handle very well, and a dog like Cleo would have been at her best working off lead as they do in Texas. In New York working off lead is both illegal and very dangerous for the dog. Still, Cleo found a number of deer for me on lead; these were deer that I probably would not have found with my Dachshunds. Cleo was my windy day and deep swamp dog. The following stories illustrate the value of using cur dogs in the Northeast far from their place of origin.

Cleo found her first deer near Woodstock up in the Catskill Mountains at the beginning of the bow season. The wind was roaring and the deer had

A Southern Black Mouth Cur, Cleo, with nose, eyes and ears all at work

been paunch shot 23 hours earlier. What little blood and scent had been there in the first place was long gone, swept off the ridge with the dry leaves. The young Dachshunds could not get a clue except when we showed them where blood drops had splattered here and there on rocks. After trying with the Dachshunds, we worked down wind with Cleo in a wide semi-circle below where the deer "should" have gone to bed down. Still nothing. Then, as we worked back to the barns where we had parked, Cleo's head went up, and she pulled hard into the wind, across the road to a patch of weeds between two farm buildings and not ten feet from the pavement. There lay the dead eight-pointer, where no one had dreamed he could be. There was a chained yard dog and an occupied house 50 yards away.

In another case, I decided to rely on Cleo's wind scenting abilities from the start. A doe had been shot 24 hours earlier by a bowhunter right at the edge of a large swamp. This swamp was not deep, only six to twelve inches, but it covered at least 40 acres. This would have been a tough call for a Dachshund or for any hound that needed to work a line of scent. There was a good breeze from the south.

Cleo and I waded a couple of long traverses across the swamp working farther down wind each time. Cleo was easy to read and when her nose went up I followed her to where the doe was lying dead and out of sight in a hollow on a little island. This would have been a tough deer to find by eye... or by following a line. The venison was in good shape but something had been nibbling the head a bit around the eyes. As we gutted out the deer, Cleo began barking tree out in the water. It was broad daylight; it should have been a squirrel, but what Cleo had was a lay-up coon. We left Mr. Coon in the tree, peering down at the guts that we were leaving for him.

Lacy Dogs

In all but five Texas counties it is permitted by law to work up to two dogs off lead in order to find wounded deer. Various breeds of curdogs, including Catahoulas and Southern Black Mouth Curs like Cleo, are used. In this group, we must also mention the smaller Lacy Dogs (also called Blue Lacys, Lacy Game Dogs) that have become the most widely used tracking dogs in Texas. The Lacy Dog is officially the State Dog of Texas, and its breed organization has remained entirely independent of the AKC.

The Lacy Dogs from Texas have many of the characteristics of the cur breeds, but their supporters do not consider them to be curs. In addition to "blue" coats ranging from light gun metal grey to dark charcoal, there are tri-colored Lacys, and "red" Lacys, which range from light cream to rust. They weigh from 30 to 50 pounds, and what is most distinctive is their yellow or orange eyes.

The Lacy Dogs were developed in Texas after the Civil War from the working dogs of the Lacy Family. They were multi-purpose dogs, tough, intelligent and responsive enough to perform any task from treeing bobcats to

Lacy Dog is Texas State Dog Breed. General, this Lacy is owned by Hugh McClellan.

Photo courtesy of Hugh Mc-Clellan of San Antonio, Texas

baying wild hogs. The early Lacy Dogs were extensively used to work tough range cattle. In all of these tasks they relied upon speed and agility to stay safe in dangerous situations. The modern Lacys are an outgrowth of the Texas land and culture, and this is what has endeared them to so many Texans today. Like many other breeds, from Labs to Dachshunds, Lacys are kept by many owners even if they do not work cattle or bay hogs or track wounded deer. They have become a Texas icon.

The Lacy Dog is at his best as an off-lead tracking dog. He combines ground scenting with wind scenting; and the wind always blows in Texas. Under tough, dry Texas conditions, the typical Lacy ranges back and forth on

Tila is a Lacy who tracks wounded deer for Chris Morris from Michigan.

the scent line, recognizing the right scent where it happens to have collected, in a clump of grass or at the foot of a bush. Off lead he works rather fast and when he finds a wounded deer that is still alive he bays it from the front in the best cowdog style. The Lacy is not a big, strong dog that crowds a deer and is quick to take hold. The Lacy bay style depends on intelligence and agility.

When called upon to blood track on a long leash up North, many of the Lacy qualities are wasted. They have to work more slowly than they would like. When tracking a bow-shot deer their typical swinging style, back and forth over the scent line, makes it difficult for their handler to see and read what little blood sign exists. *Are we dealing with a mortal wound or a high shoulder hit meaning that the deer will go on for many miles and ultimately survive?*

Lacys have the high intelligence and the responsiveness that is characteristic of the herding breeds. This means that the "typical" working style of the Lacy can be modified by training and by the environment in which it has to work. So beware. Generalizations about a breed can never be absolute. There are always exceptions to the rule. In Chapter 13 on off-lead tracking you will read more about Lacy scent work and intelligence.

The recent recognition coming to the Lacy Dogs is due in good part to the efforts of Marlo Ondrej, formerly Marlo Riley, of Helotes, Texas, near San Antonio. She has publicized Lacy Dog's work and organized tracking workshops to train handlers and dogs. Current information about Lacys can be found on the websites of the Lacy Game Dog Registry and the National Lacy Dog Registry.

The Lacy Dog is the most widely used tracking dog in Texas, and keep in mind that Texas has the biggest deer harvest of any state. Lacy trackers are also expanding across the states of the Deep South. Profiting from excellent promotion and a very active educational network, Lacys are well on the way to becoming one of the leading tracking breeds in the United States. Lucy, a Lacy owned and handled by Mike Lopez off lead, found 142 deer in a single tracking season (2015-16).

In Texas it is impossible to draw a line between curdogs and cowdogs. Many curs work cattle and others, called cowdogs by their owners, have considerable cur background. The methods used to find wounded deer with all these dogs are derived more from the methods of working livestock in brush country than from any European ideas.

To find and herd up cattle in the mesquite brush of Texas, cowdogs must use their noses on the ground and in the wind. When they find a steer, they stop him from running off by heading him, baying him from the front, until he turns back into the main herd. Many cowdogs readily and naturally adapt these tactics to wounded deer situations.

Working from the hit site, they pick up the scent where they can and take a direction. In the usual arid conditions common to Texas, the dog does not always work a continuous line of ground scent. He works the ground; he works the brush and he works the wind. The deer may be dead, but if he is alive, he will not go far before he turns to face his pursuer. Then the dog will bay him from the front as he would a cow, holding his attention until the handler can move close to get a clear, finishing shot. In this dry country, with poor scenting conditions, the method works best if the buck is not tracked and pushed a long way by the hunter before the dog is called.

The Dogs of Roy Hindes

No one better describes Texas cowdogs and how they track wounded deer than the master tracker Roy Hindes himself. Roy, sometimes known as "Little Roy," is the second generation of his family that has been doing this. The Hindes strain of Blue Dogs is not the only type used in Texas, but they represent the Texas tracking tradition at its best.

"The first blue cowdogs we ever had were given to my father, Roy Hindes, by Harry Sturges, a rancher friend, in 1936. Daddy was nine years old. They came from somewhere in east Texas. Daddy used them for several years to trail up, find and herd cattle here in the brush country of south Texas.

One day, when the dogs were four or five years old, the cowboys had a real bad fighting bull held up in a white brush thicket. They couldn't get close to him because the brush was so thick you couldn't see the ground under a horse and the bull would run at and try to hook anything that got close enough. Daddy finally climbed a tree and shot the bull in the base of the horn to make him run out of the thicket. The bull left the thicket in a run and when those

Roy Hindes' Jethro, a great tracking dog from South Texas. Note the tracking collar and antenna.

two dogs smelled the blood that was squirting out of his horn they just went nuts, barking right in his face. Daddy noticed their interest and enthusiasm in the blood trail and soon after that he put them on a wounded deer's trail and caught the deer. Daddy was fourteen or fifteen years old at the time. He trailed deer until he was seventy and could no longer go. Many of our friends, on neighboring ranches, have had a top blood dog at one time or another, but Daddy always had a good dog all of his life.

These dogs are bred to go to the front of a herd of cattle. Many of them do not make blood dogs, but they all work the lead of a herd. In thick brush you don't need a dog behind a herd, pushing cattle on ahead, faster and faster, while you try and keep up in brush so thick you can't see the ground. It's much easier and safer to have the dog in front of the herd, barking and drawing their attention and slowing them down while you bring up the rear. Daddy always thought this trait — the dogs wanting to be in front — was why it was so easy and natural for them to stop a deer and hold him bayed.

In the mid 1950s we bred our best cowdog to a top blue jip belonging to Jack Kingsbury from Crystal City Texas. Her name was Mitzi and she was a lead dog and deer dog just like ours. From this cross we got a cowdog named Caiman who fathered a dog we called Bull, who was one of the best we ever raised. He was good at trailing and herding cattle but he really shined as a hunting dog. He could kill a coon or a bobcat by himself, and real quick. He was good around kids, but all business on the trail.

Old Bull was the dog that introduced me to the thrills of chasing wounded deer. I learned at an early age the importance of trusting and having faith in a good dog. In 1964 we lost old Bull, when a snake bit and killed him. He was six years old and had recovered seventy-eight wounded deer in his lifetime. I still think of him and wonder, had he lived a full life, and with the use of the tracking collars and mobile telephones we use today, how many deer he could have caught. We have had many deer dogs since Bull died, and I know they are getting better, but Bull was ahead of his time.

In the mid 1960s we bred Bull to a bloodhound jip belonging to rancher and lawman friend Graves Peeler. From the cross we kept a red female puppy we named Mandy that made a wounded deer dog real quick. Unfortunately, she was poisoned at about four years of age and we lost her. But before she died she had a litter of puppies out of Bull, her own father. This produced a big, good looking blue dog for my uncle Bob Hindes that he called Shorty, who was a real good cowdog, hogdog and deerdog. Shorty was a big, scary kind of a dog around strangers but he loved kids. Bob's daughter used to ride him around the yard.

When Shorty was about two years old, he was hanging around the yard at my grandfather's ranch house. A hunter shot and wounded a deer about a mile up the river, and Shorty heard the shot and went to it. Shorty found the track and trailed the deer up and bayed him alive. The hunter went to him and killed the deer. That was the first deer Shorty ever caught. He had no training other than being along when jackrabbits were shot from a pickup, and being used as a cowdog. Daddy used to borrow old Shorty from Bob in the wintertime and catch wounded deer with him.

Now, six generations of good wounded deer and cowdogs have passed and I have Jethro, who at eight years of age has recovered a blackbuck, an axis deer, an eland, a mountain lion, and hundreds of deer for people all across south Texas. All my dogs are direct descendants of old Shorty.

When our puppies are old enough to follow us horseback and keep up, we take them along. The best ones love to chase rabbits and sometimes unwounded deer. When they try to run a deer we are able to run up on them horseback, jump down and whip them good with a doubled rope and they soon learn not to run un-wounded deer. Later, when they are older, they know when we are on horseback we hunt cattle and when we are afoot we hunt wounded deer, looking for blood.

Low humidity and persistent drought are always a problem for a dog smelling a track. But even in the semi-desert of south Texas the humidity goes up at night and a track always smells fresher the next morning at first light. For this reason when I get a call on a deer shot in late evening, I prefer to go early the next morning. This also gives a deer more time to fever and go to water.

Many of our dogs wind cattle and wounded deer. Some of them seem to have to be taught to trail. By that I mean we go back again and again putting them on the track. My dog Jethro can do both, but he does not concentrate on the wind, like some do. He, in the absence of grass and weeds to hold the scent, actually presses his nose on the dirt, sucking up dirt in the process, and sneezes frequently! About half the deer he recovers are found the day after they were shot. His slow and thorough sniffing is his best trait.

All of our best dogs have had the knack or reasoning to stay on the right track when the blood plays out. Last season I put him on three different deer that had been trailed by other people's "deer dogs". He found one alive and *we shot him in thirty minutes. He found one dead the next day. The other one he couldn't trail up. He was shot in the top of the back and was seen alive over a month later, before succumbing to his wound.*

I never use over two dogs on a deer or three dogs on cattle. Fewer dogs are more accountable for their behavior. My favorite deer to trail have a broken front leg. They don't bleed much and some deer lick the blood off a front leg, like a dog does, making them hard to trail up, but they trip on the hurt leg when they run and bay up quick. Broken hind legs bleed good, but a deer can really run with a broken hind leg. In the last two years my dogs have failed to recover one deer with a broken leg, only because the trail went under the neighbor's fence line and I called them off. I will travel many more miles to find a wounded deer when I find out there is bone on the trail.

When I arrive where a deer was shot, I unload the dogs, get a drink of water, visit a few minutes, and when the dogs leave on the trail, I take the hunter who shot the deer with me. I allow no one else to shoot over my dogs or even take a gun. But the shooter knows the lay of the land, the creeks (bucks use them like highways), windmills, etc. We follow not closer than one hundred yards behind the dogs. I don't want to be in the way if the dogs make a lose (have to work a check).

The dogs don't bark until they jump the deer up and run him. When he stops to fight the dogs, or "bays," the pitch of their bark changes from a running cry to a chop. Then I sneak slowly up on the deer fighting the baying dogs (if he sees me, he'll run again) to less than thirty steps and shoot him under the ear with a pistol. When he falls the dogs jump on him and I praise them and show them my satisfaction. Water is a reward and I take them to water as soon as possible. When they cool off I'll feed them the heart or liver. Then, when I get home I might let them in the house!"

Since this was written in 2003 a number of the Hindes family's dogs have passed on. Jethro died at a ripe old age, and his gifted son Jasper died of snake bite, ten days before the start of the 2005 season. Then Hoss, another Jethro son, was shot and killed by hunters as he crossed a property line onto another ranch where Roy's son-in-law had been given access permission. This caused "quite an uproar." Texas tracking dogs lead a tough and dangerous life; more of Jethro's sons carry on the work.

Roy's methods of using his dogs off lead are representative of the Texas tradition of using the cowdog breeds, in which tracking wounded deer is an extension of cattle work. The dog is asked to find a designated animal; the animal is now a wounded deer.

In the cold trailing part of the search the dog works silently at a slow pace and the handler stays in contact by sight or by GPS. If the deer is still alive and takes off from the wound bed a chase follows. Surprisingly for outsiders, the chase does not end with the cowdog pulling down the wounded deer. Most cowdogs have the "pull down" power to do this most of the time, but this is not the cowdog way. The function of the cowdog is to bay, not pull down the deer. The dog and the deer face off with the dog baying until the handler moves in to take the careful finishing shot. As Roy Hindes points out a dog that grabs the deer cannot bark and is more difficult to find. And in physical contact with a big aggressive buck, the dog is in greater danger.

Border Collies

The Border Collies were developed to herd sheep, not cattle, but we have included them in this chapter because their sheep work required them to be highly responsive and intelligent. Many dog specialists have found them to be the most intelligent and trainable of all the dog breeds.

Gary Neal, who uses Border Collies to find wounded deer in New York State finds that his dogs have a different sort of prey drive than the typical hound. He believes that they track more to please their handler than to get the game. Whatever the dogs' deepest tracking motivation may be, they don't lose focus while on long difficult calls, and they are very good about staying on the right deer.

The long soft coat of the Border Collie is certainly not ideal for work in burrs and briars. Snowballs will develop in wet snow. Spraying the dog with a horse grooming product like Cowboy Magic will reduce these problems.

Summary

- High intelligence and responsiveness are essential qualities in a good tracking dog. Some very good tracking dogs have come from breeds developed for working livestock.

- Curs and cowdogs are big dogs bred to be intelligent and responsive. They are especially valuable in circumstances where a dog can be worked off lead such as in Texas.

- Most curs have good but not great noses for working ground scent.

- Curs tend to be exceptionally good at working the wind to find wounded deer.

- Curs are tough dogs well suited for high temperatures and snake country.

Chapter 7

Dog Breeds IV:
Old Breeds With a New Mission

There seems to be no end to the sorts of dogs that are being used successfully to find wounded deer. Breeds, which were originally developed for quite different purposes, have ended up being used very successfully as blood trackers. In this chapter we will mention some of these dogs with different origins and working styles. An alert intelligence is the unifying characteristic within this selection of breeds.

Terriers

Terriers are bright, handy dogs that come in many different breeds and sizes. Within the terrier group and within each breed, there will be individuals with quite different interests and aptitudes. When the terrier breeds were developed, scenting and tracking were not the first priorities of the early breeders. The hunting terriers were selected for the use of all of their senses: eyes, ears and nose, to locate vermin, from rats to badgers and beyond. Very important in the terrier was a hot, aggressive temperament, friendly toward people but deadly to the furry unwanted. By their breeding terriers are not "naturals" for the task of tracking wounded big game. As a group, the terrier breeds are not going to display the scenting power and the persevering line sense of the scent hounds. If I were called in to trail a deer wounded the day before, with no visible blood to be seen, my first thought would not be, "Bring in a terrier."

For the hunter who tracks only for himself and a few friends, the case of the day old, difficult line is not going to arise very often. More often, there will be a need to follow a wounded deer's scent line that is only a few hours old. For this a trained terrier might be very useful. In the process of training, the terrier owner will be able to develop some idea, in advance, of how capable this dog is likely to be on the real thing.

German Jagdterrier

The German Jagdterrier is definitely a working terrier in its psychological makeup, but it is the one terrier that has been bred with tracking ability in mind. The Jagdterrier in Germany is expected to kill foxes underground, flush game above ground, and blood track. The German Jagdterrier Club organizes working tests for all these types of work.

The origins of the "Jagd" are to be found in the English terriers: fox terriers, Welsh terriers and in an old black and tan terrier that gives the modern German

Sage, a rough-coated Jagdterrier was used very successfully for tracking wounded wild hogs in Oklahoma.

Photo courtesy of Matt and Cheryl Napper

terrier its dark coloration. According to the Jagdterrier literature the breed dates back only to the 1920s. The hunting capabilities of the dog, including hardness and scenting ability, were developed by rigorous selection.

German Jagdterriers were brought to the United States after World War II and there are a number of active breeders here. Most of the pure Jagds in America are a bit too large for American underground game, but this is not a disadvantage for tracking. They are high energy dogs with enormous hunting desire and no fear of anything. They are suitable for someone who lives in a rural area and will hunt with them actively and regularly. This could mean squirrel hunting and coon hunting, or underground work, if the critters and their dens are sufficiently large. The aggressiveness of the Jagdterrier is combined with great agility, and this makes them valuable as part of a small pack working wild hogs or bear.

A Jagdterrier is not likely to work out for the bowhunter who wants a house dog to wait patiently at home for a few opportunities each year to track up a wounded deer. In the meantime Johann Jagdterrier will be hunting squirrels in the chandeliers.

As I have written before, you can't evaluate an individual dog by his breed category. I have seen Jagdterriers that are good, cold trackers, but they are not in the majority. Marc Niad in Westchester County, NY has a Jagdterrier bitch named Dakota that has developed into a focused tracker that successfully works old, cold lines.

In Europe dog people agree that the Jagdterrier is a capable tracker, but there is some question whether most these terriers can handle the older scent lines with the proficiency of a scent hound or a trained versatile hunting dog like the Drahthaar pointer. For a group of hunters on a deer lease in the South, a resident Jagdterrier could be valuable to track deer shot a few hours before. But the Jagdterrier should have one handler, and that handler had best be like a Jagdterrier himself — fast, tough and strong hearted.

Marc Niad's Dakota, a Jagdterrier, is an accomplished tracker who has found 60 deer and four bear.   *Photo courtesy of Marc Niad*

Jack Russell Terriers

We get quite a few inquiries about Jack Russell Terriers over the phone or by e-mail. Are they good tracking dogs? Should I train mine to find wounded deer?

Russells have recently acquired quite a reputation as tracking dogs. This is based, to a considerable degree, on the fact that they are used by professional hunters in Africa to find shot game for their bowhunting clients. If an antelope doesn't go down within sight, a few Russells are turned loose on the hot line. They quickly find the animal dead, or if alive, they hold it at bay so that it can be finished off.

Some of these African critters, like the big gemsbok, have long, lance-like horns that they can use with precision to skewer the attacking dogs. It's dangerous work for the terrier, and many of them are killed before they learn to have some caution. The Russell has a heart as big as his head, and is not by nature a cautious dog.

This use of Jack Russells works on the plains game of Africa. The animals are generally shot by bowhunters out of blinds as they come in to drink at water holes. The guides and the terriers are close by and ready to go. No doubt some of these terriers have good nose and line sense. But their work is very different from the use of cold-nosed tracking dogs in North America where they are used only when necessary and generally many hours after the deer, elk or bear has been shot. The question is: Does the wide use of Jack Russells on plains game in Africa prove that they are going to be useful over here where our conditions and hunting traditions are so different? I doubt it, and I have some experiences to back up my concerns.

About twenty years ago I owned a small, very good Jack Russell. Banner weighed eleven pounds, and I used him mainly for underground work on woodchucks, often called groundhogs. There were also some coons and a fox. One summer I took enough groundhogs to seriously reduce my dog feed bills.

I had plenty of fun with Banner until one night when I was coon hunting with my Black Mouth Cur. Banner had come along for exercise; he lagged behind a couple of hundred yards, investigating something. Then I heard him yelp, and a coyote gave his chattering laugh. When I rushed back to the spot, there was nothing to be seen but some of Banner's white hair on the ground. I searched for several days but never found a trace of him.

Anyway, before Banner disappeared he taught me quite a bit about the breed. I don't base my conclusions about any breed upon one individual dog, but Banner's underground skills helped me get to know a number of Jack Russell groundhog hunters, who used to come up to work the horse country near where I lived.

The area was full of groundhogs whose dens made the fields and pastures treacherous for horses and their red coated riders of the Millbrook Hunt. This was during the period when coyotes were just beginning to filter into the Mid-Hudson Valley area, and before these invaders largely cleaned out the groundhogs.

I saw a number of Russells work, and game they were. They would battle and dig under ground, and they had no quit. But they didn't seem to have much in the line of nose. After all, the breed had been developed in England primarily for underground work, with a little rat killing on the side. One of the problems of groundhog hunting was deciding which dens were occupied so we could send down a small dog to locate and work the chuck. If the groundhog could be located and harassed, he wouldn't be able to dig away. Then we could dig down to the spot with shovels so that bigger, stronger dogs could draw and kill the chuck.

The best dogs to show what dens had a chuck in them were the Dachshunds. My tracking Wirehaired Dachshunds excelled at this. They would come up to a den entrance that a Russell had checked out with little interest. With a finer nose the Dachshund could tell that the den was occupied, and then the fun would begin.

All this reinforced the impression that I had gained from trying to tree squirrels and coon hunt with Banner. It seemed to me that Jack Russells don't have such great noses for either air scenting or ground scenting. Certainly they have better eyesight than the Dachshunds; they could see a squirrel twitch high in a tree, but they had neither the nose nor the patience to work out an old, cold line.

We have stated repeatedly that the buyer of a young tracking dog prospect should not be guided exclusively by breed labels. This is especially true in the case of the Jack Russells. Breeders in Africa, and a few breeders in the United States, have bred selectively for tracking ability. If you love terriers, select the individual dog that shows the greatest desire to track. And search for a breeder with blood tracking experience.

Norwegian Elkhounds

In Norwegian " Elg" is the word for moose. Elkhounds were developed to hunt the European moose of Scandinavia rather than the animals that we call "elk" in North America. The Elkhound type goes back to prehistoric times in northern Europe, and there are a number of breeds working today in Scandinavia and Russia that fit into this general family of dogs. Norwegians refer to the Grey Elkhound, which is the most common, and also to a Black Elkhound, somewhat different in appearance and behavior patterns. There are many other representatives of these Nordic breeds, which include the Jämthund and the Karelian Bear Dog. Hunters who use these breeds will point out that there are significant differences between them, but their appearance and working styles have certain things in common.

These northern dogs have broad strong skulls and prick ears, and the tails curl rather tightly over the back. Their long, dense coats are protective against extreme cold. In behavior they are unlike scent hounds in that they are air scenters first and ground scenters second; they are locators more than they are line trackers, and in this sense they have behavior traits in common with the cur family discussed above. The Elkhound family of dogs also uses their eyes more than most scent hounds.

In Northern Europe Elkhounds are used to locate moose for the hunter, as well as to track any moose that is wounded and disappears. Most moose in Scandinavia are taken with the assistance of dogs who must handle well. When in hunting mode, one or two Elkhounds range out ahead the of the handler and accompanying hunters. Other hunters are posted in the surrounding area. When the Elkhound wind scents a moose he moves in barking and bays it if possible. Then the moose is shot while preoccupied by the bay dog. If the moose breaks away, it is hoped that the Elkhound will drive him into one of the posted hunters.

If a moose is wounded, the Elkhound is commonly used as a bandhund (tracking dog), working in a harness on a short, three meter tracking leash. Usually this does not involve an old, cold line.

Dogs of the Elkhound family should be adaptable to the American situation in which dogs may be used legally to track wounded big game. They should be most useful in the northern states and in the Canadian provinces; they would not be the best choice for tracking deer under moderate conditions where ground scenting on old lines is very important. I would like to use an Elkhound or a Karelian Bear Dog to track wounded bear. Bear leave a very heavy scent trail, and they go into deadfalls and the heaviest cover. On a bear trail it would be good to have a dog ahead of me that wind scents extremely well and also uses his eyes and ears to locate the bear before I crawl too close.

German Shepherds

German Shepherds are seldom used in Germany for tracking wounded deer and boar. This ancient activity is associated with the traditional German hunting breeds that we have already discussed. Americans, not as tied to tradition in their hunting, have discovered that the German Shepherd can be a very valuable tracking dog. This is a highly intelligent dog, not the greatest dog in the world for working ground scent, but excellent in wind scenting and scent discrimination.

The ancestors of the German Shepherds were generic sheep herding dogs. Some wolf blood was added in the 19th century; how much is a subject of dispute. The breed was stabilized in the 19th century, and since most German breeders were not interested in sheep herding, this role was played down, and guard dog work was emphasized. The dog was courageous, tough and adaptable, and his value was quickly recognized elsewhere in Europe and in North America.

You would have to go very far back in the pre-history of dogs to find common ancestry between the German Shepherds and modern sheep dogs. Despite the name of the breed the inherited behavior traits of the German Shepherd are most useful for searching, guarding, and alerting the individual handler as to what lies ahead. The German Shepherd is no longer a sheep herder.

John Engelken, a licensed guide who lives in Apulia Station, NY, has used a German Shepherd extensively for finding wounded whitetails in New York State, and wounded caribou and bear in northern Canada. He works his German Shepherd on a stiff leash, 40 feet long, and in many hunting situations he finds it to be more useful than his trained Bloodhound. The German Shepherd is much easier to handle; he will stop readily on command, and he works the wind extremely well. His superior intelligence and responsiveness are conducive to picking out the correct animal, the wounded animal. This German Shepherd has more than enough nose to deal with the ground scenting challenges that arise when a guide is working with clients, as this account by Engelken demonstrates:

> The dog led us out of the goldenrod field across a gravel road. We followed and then crossed a trout stream. The German Shepherd had taken us a half mile on a trail over 24 hours old. Forty yards downstream, the dog wanted to re-cross. Barely visible was the mostly submerged buck, antlers under water. When I exclaimed "There's your deer!" the hunter said it wasn't. He became a believer only when I waded out and lifted the rack from the water. (North American Whitetail, Feb. 2002, p. 21)

Fig. 1. Billy, owned by John and Jolanta Jeanneney, illustrates the FCI/Deutscher Teckelklub standard for the Wirehaired Dachshund.

Fig. 2. Josie was a conveniently small Bloodhound bitch trained and handled by John Engelken, a licensed guide in New York State. Josie and John also tracked under contract to outfitters in Illinois.

Photo courtesy of John Engelken

Fig. 3 (above). Vars is a very good Bavarian Mountain Hound imported from Poland. He is owned and handled by Dan Kendall, who tracks professionally in Georgia and Illinois. The above picture was taken by Dan when Vars was 9 months old.

Fig. 4 (below). Mirko is a Bavarian Mountain Hound imported from Germany by Ken Parker from Georgia.

Fig. 5 (left).
Frida is a very typical
Hanover Hound tracking
in Italy.
> *Photo courtesy*
> *of Serena Donnini*

Fig. 6 (below).
Carl is a multipurpose
Deutsch Drahthaar
tracking for Patrick Van-
Haverbeke from NY.

Fig. 7. For many years, Rosie, a yellow Labrador Retriever, has been one the top tracking dogs in Georgia. She is owned by JJ Scarborough.

Fig. 8. Cleo, a Southern Black Mouth Cur, was equally skilled at treeing squirrels and tracking wounded deer.

Fig. 9. Roy Hindes' Jethro bays a big Texas buck.

Photo courtesy of Roy Hindes

Fig. 10. Michael Schneider, a guide in British Columbia, found this moose with his Slovensky Kopov, a tracking hound breed from Slovakia.

Photo courtesy of Michael Schneider

Fig. 11 (above). A fine tracker of wounded deer, Mac is a Beagle-Bluetick Coonhound mix owned by Kirk Vaughan from Chapel Hill, NC.

Fig. 12 (below). Annie is a Kemmer Stock Mountain Cur owned by Randy Vick of Georgia. *Photo courtesy of Randy Vick*

Fig. 13 (right).
Seva is an eight-month-old Catahoula owned by Chris Rea from Mississippi.

Photo courtesy of Chris Rea

Fig. 14 (below).
Henry Holt's Wirehaired Dachshund Bear found this Illinois buck, but the coyotes got there first.

Photo courtesy of Henry Holt

Fig. 15. Eleven-year old Sabina swimming a beaver pond on the track of a wounded bear.

Fig. 16. Sabina with the buck that slashed her in fall 2004.

I would not question the value of a good German Shepherd for blood tracking. Of course, the natural aggressiveness and enterprise of a good German Shepherd does have to be controlled by serious obedience. I once judged a poorly trained German Shepherd in a Deer Search Certification Test. This dog had been exposed to attack guard dog (Schutzhund) training, but clearly the training had not been very thorough. In the process of working the test line, the dog left the line to lunge at each of the three judges. He did not pass, and he never made it as a tracking dog.

In the United States some breeders have dealt with potential problems of aggressiveness not by sound training but rather by breeding the aggressiveness out of their dogs over several generations. This has made German Shepherds more marketable as family pets, but such dogs have lost their usefulness for law enforcement and for tracking. Most German Shepherds in use by law enforcement agencies today are from European rather than American breeding.

Aggressiveness toward humans is not needed in a tracking dog; if not controlled through rigorous obedience training, it can be a serious liability. Critics of the American German Shepherd say that when he was bred to be a gentler, more easily managed family dog, other things were lost as well. They maintain that the incredible alertness and sensitivity of the original German Shepherd also disappeared.

It is not the purpose of this book to engage in this argument, but a prospective buyer should be aware that an abyss lies between the AKC show-oriented breeders and those involved with the breed for guard work, search and rescue, and law enforcement. The dogs even look different. The dog favored in American shows has extreme angulation of the rear legs. The hocks extend far beyond the dog's rear. The topline slopes more radically than in the European dogs. The very strong angulation produces a reaching, driving trot in the show ring, but critics of the type say that this is not a stable, durable structure for rough, athletic work.

Certainly there are fine and useful German Shepherds being produced in this country from American bloodlines. But this is a breed that has become deeply divided, with European authorities and many Americans turning away in disgust at what they see in the American show ring. Ask lots of questions when considering a German Shepherd for blood tracking. To explore the European alternatives to the American show type German Shepherd, consult the numerous breeders who advertise in Dog World magazine.

Belgian Shepherds

The Belgians have developed several closely related breeds of dogs that have a physical and psychological resemblance to the German Shepherd in its earlier forms. These Belgian Shepherds, also known as Belgian Sheepdogs, are a little smaller than the German Shepherd and much less angulated in the rear. They are a great favorite of law enforcement agencies in Western Europe, which is a testimony to their stability and alertness.

These four associated Belgian breeds are the Belgian Sheepdog or Groenendael (long black coat), the Belgian Turveren (long fawn to mahogany coat), the Belgian Malinois (with a brown, shorter coat), and the Belgian Laekenois (wire coat). From the standpoint of coat, the Malinois and the Laekenois are probably best suited for working in briars and burrs, but all of the four related breeds are well worth considering as an alternative to the German Shepherds. These breeds have the intelligence and air scenting abilities of German Shepherds, but they are largely free of some of the extremes introduced into German Shepherds by American show breeders.

When sheep herding in Belgium declined early in the 20th century some breeders of the native herding dogs shifted their attention to police work and tracking. They bred dogs to be strong in the character traits that are important in blood tracking. These Belgian breeds offer great possibilities for the person who wants a very intelligent and responsive tracking dog of medium size.

There is much more to selecting a tracking dog than settling upon a breed and then finding someone who has pups of this description. Blood tracking will not be fun, and you will not accomplish very much, if you do not have good material to work with. It is truly sad to be forced into a situation where you must either abandon the sport or get a new dog. Time spent on preliminary research is time well spent.

Summary

- Most working terriers have great intelligence and desire. Their most likely fault is a lack of patience and line sense.

- The German Jagdterrier was selectively bred to combine tracking ability with other terrier talents.

- The Elkhound family of breeds from Scandinavia was developed more as air scenting dogs than as cold-nosed ground trackers. They are most useful under very cold conditions.

- The German Shepherd breed in the United States has suffered severely at the hands of breeders interested exclusively in appearances and the trotting gait in a show ring. There are some fine tracking prospects out there, but select your breeder carefully.

- The Belgian Shepherd breeds offer great possibilities for the person who wants a very intelligent and responsive tracking dog of medium size.

- If you will be tracking very old scent lines, a scent hound may suit your needs better than the breeds discussed in this chapter.

Chapter 8

Puppy Training

Reinforcing Natural Instincts

Training a dog of decent ability to be a useful blood tracker is largely a matter of focusing and reinforcing the two instincts we have discussed: 1. prey drive as the motivation to find the game, and 2. cooperation that appears first as a desire to please the handler.

One of the underlying reasons why dogs fail in real searches, or fail in blood tracking tests and competitions, is that the two principles introduced above have been disregarded or unsuccessfully developed.

Part of the motivation to track wounded game scent is natural; it is an expression of the natural predatory instincts inherited by many dogs from their wolf ancestors. Wild canids know instinctively that injured prey species, identified by scent and sight, are the most likely to provide a meal. In a good tracking dog prospect the desire to follow a wounded deer is also instinctive. The task of the trainer is to stimulate and focus that instinct so that it becomes strong enough and enduring enough to keep the tracking dog on the wounded game trail for many miles if necessary. Not all wounded game bleed on the outside; in some cases the bleeding is all internal. In some cases the wounded animal that does not leave a blood trail is going to die and can be recovered with the assistance of trained tracking dog. So **the overall goal is to train a dog to follow a specific, individual deer.** I wish that they didn't call it blood tracking. Still blood is one of the scents that a dog tracks naturally. I train puppies in the early stages on deer blood that I dip from the chest cavities of the deer that I find. This blood has plenty of scent, and ten-week-old pups follow it with ease; they learn to love it. It is a better motivator in the early stages of training than a dragged piece of skin. At the end of the blood trails I like to have a piece of deer skin and pieces of liver and heart as a reward.

The tracking dog's desire to follow blood, for the sake of tracking it, can exist independently of any expected reward at the end of the line. Some puppies will be fascinated by a line of deer blood the first time they encounter it. But to sustain this drive, and to strengthen it for long, difficult tracking tasks as an adult, there is a need to enhance the tracking experience itself and to maximize the dog's satisfaction at the end of the line.

Encouraging the positive motivation to track is essential. Because the dog must take the initiative and not simply obey orders, methods of force training are not applicable here. Instead, the trainer must rely on the natural tracking instincts of the dog. These must be encouraged and then focused upon a highly specialized task. Your first goal in training is to have your dog realize that he loves to track and find game. Once this desire has come to the surface, other aspects of tracking training will fall into place with little difficulty.

Before we get down to the specifics of training, let's take a look at the "desire to please the handler." Put another way, it is a desire to cooperate with the handler. In training and in natural tracking, the handler will ask the dog to stay with an old, now invisible blood line, a day or more old, and to ignore smoking hot scent lines of healthy deer that have just crossed the old line. This is not an easy thing for a dog to do. At first, he will stay focused on the old line only because he understands that the handler wants him to do this. Gradually, he will learn that successful cooperation with his handler leads to a find. This brings mutual rejoicing, a chew on the deer and probably some warm venison. Compared to this, hot lines are an empty promise.

This desire to please the handler has a strong genetic basis, and I have seen it expressed strongly in American breeds such as the Southern Black Mouth Cur, which were developed as cow and hog dogs. The tendency to be attentive and responsive will vary from breed to breed and from individual to individual, but environmental factors are also tremendously important.

A dog that is neglected or treated too harshly will not live up to his potential. The more time spent with the dog the better, and the ideal is to have the dog really live with the handler and be a part of his daily life. Living together you learn to interpret one another. For example the dog learns what a question means. When I ask one of my dogs, "Do you want to go out?" with a questioning tone in my voice, the dog wags his tail in a certain way and moves toward the door. Later, when I ask, "Is that right?" when we are working a line, the dog recognizes the questioning tone in my voice and checks or corrects himself.

Companionship and communication are important factors in the development of a tracking dog. This is not to say that discipline should be absent in training for blood tracking. But keep in mind that positive reinforcement should play a much greater role than negative discipline. You should not use an electronic collar on a dog working a blood line!

Discipline does have its place in your relationship with your dog. For example when it comes to house breaking you do not treat him as an equal partner who can poop and pee where he wants! A dog must also learn that he does not have the option to come or not to come when you are hunting small game or when he is standing on a highway. For recall training in the field the conservative use of an electronic collar is justified.

Tracking is different. Here the dog rises in authority, frequently takes the initiative and may disagree with his handler about where the wounded deer went. The handler learns to trust his dog and accept his leadership in this particular case.

Getting to Know Your Puppy

As soon as your new puppy has adjusted to you and to his new home, you should begin tracking training. It's in your interest to start him young when his rapidly developing brain will be stimulated as discussed in Chapter 3.

There is really no way to reduce a training plan to something as simple as a cookbook recipe because individual dogs are so different. However, I do offer a sample training plan at the end of the chapter. This can be modified to your needs and situations, just as you would modify your cookbook recipe. Different dogs learn and mature psychologically at different rates.

Before you begin any serious tracking training, you must understand your puppy's temperament. This knowledge is very important for establishing a close relationship with your puppy and for adjusting your training style so that it will be most effective. Does you puppy have a soft or hard temperament? When we use these two terms we refer to the level of correction to which a dog responds. A "soft puppy" might drop his ears and put his tail between his legs when he is scolded. This kind of dog is usually very willing but may need a lot of encouragement. A "hard puppy" can take a correction easily and will bounce right back. This does not mean that one temperament is better than other; good tracking dogs cover the whole spectrum of temperaments.

The pup's reaction to discipline is always a consideration, but remember that most of your training will be done through positive reinforcement (praise and treats). Your tracking dog-to-be should grow up to be your enthusiastic working partner.

A puppy is not a factory-produced machine. You must establish a working bond with him as a unique individual. A secure puppyhood, in which the dog gets affection, attention and structured discipline, will greatly increase the odds of having a good tracking dog. Forming a close bond with your dog does not mean making the dog your social equal, who sits on a chair at your dining room table. Canine social psychology is hierarchical, not egalitarian. Be a fair and consistent trainer. Play with your puppy, give him attention and start basic obedience training in a friendly atmosphere. This will be a good foundation for a trusting relationship. As you begin to train him to track, make sure that he is having fun.

The most important thing is to understand the current mental growth level of your own dog. Did he get early conditioning from the breeder before you brought him? Your aim should be to give him exercises of increasing difficulty that are interesting and challenging but not beyond his capability at that time. Some puppies are very early starters and later have periods of slump and boredom. Be prepared for mental paralysis that comes later in adolescence. Other puppies take months to develop a love for and ability to track. And of course there are some that eventually show that they will never have the makings of a tracker.

The trainer must be realistic, and he should avoid being too rigid in his methods and expectations. Remember that you are developing a working partner, capable of making independent decisions about where a wounded deer went. If you attempt to cram the young dog into a highly structured "command and obey" training regimen, you will not have the best long-term results. Training for tracking, unlike some other types of training, has to be fun for the dog. You must foster his passion for later when he will need to track for long, dry miles, to swim cold creeks and plow through falling snow.

Psychological Preparation

This chapter concentrates on the aspects of training specifically related to blood tracking, but the general psychological foundation upon which this training is built is equally important. A dog's psychological stability and readiness to adapt to new situations is fundamental to his abilities as a tracker. In dogs a large component of their basic temperament is controlled by their genetics. Some of this will be expressed and can be tested in puppies at an early age as discussed in Chapter 3. Your puppy's early social environment and later experiences are also very important. These environmental factors are something that you can control once you have your dog. The best-bred puppies will turn sour if they are not properly socialized and exposed to a rich variety of situations.

Tracking dogs should be comfortable around strangers. When outsiders come to the house, the puppies should be introduced to them. Puppies should be taken to outdoor gatherings where they will be exposed to numerous people. Take them for a walk at an outdoors shopping mall. We like to take our young dogs to outdoor concerts. Your aim is to develop a dog that will not be disturbed by the presence of a strange hunter as you track his wounded deer. I have seen situations in which shy dogs, of otherwise good abilities, did not work well, or refused to work at all, because of the presence of an unfamiliar person.

Tracking dogs should be comfortable riding in any vehicle from your 4 X 4 to an open farm truck. For a Dachshund-sized tracker it is a plus if he will ride on a four wheeler or ATV. Your puppy is less likely to grow up to be a good traveler if he never rides in a vehicle except for trips to the vet. It is not pleasant if the young dog has nervous diarrhea in his travel crate on the way to track a deer. If he arrives in an anxious, unsettled emotional state, he will not concentrate well.

Tracking dogs should be accustomed to working in water, even if it is icy cold. Begin on a hot summer day by taking your pup for a walk along a stream or half dried up creek bed. Walk in the water; cross back and forth, and the pup will follow. Then, when the time comes, your tracking dog will swim through swamps and cross streams without a moment's hesitation. I have seen dogs quit, especially if they were Dachshunds, when the water came up over their bellies. The problem was not with the breed; the problem was their owners who had trained them as if blood tracking were something always done on a golf course.

If dogs are not introduced to darkness in the woods, they may be unsure of themselves when they are called upon to track at night. Begin by taking your puppy for walks at night while you are carrying a flashlight. Later, it will be beneficial to work him on training lines when it is dark and you have to carry a light.

Your dog will not become a reliable tracker, under any and all circumstances, unless he has been exposed to things outside the routine of his daily life. The presence of strangers, farm livestock or the barking of other dogs should not interrupt his focus on tracking when he is at work. Never pass up an opportunity to gently introduce him to potential distractions. If you carry your puppy up to sniff a horse or cow while he is safe in your arms, horses and cows will not be a serious distraction later on when the dog is tracking a wounded buck across a pasture.

Basic Obedience

This book stresses throughout that tracking wounded deer is not a "command and obey" operation. When actually tracking, your dog must use his own initiative and judgment.

This does not mean that obedience is unimportant in your daily life together. For his own safety a dog must come when called. He must sit and stay on command. Learning to heel off leash becomes very convenient.

Obedience training or yard training, should be conducted at the same age as training for tracking. The two are very different, and do not interfere with one another; one is not a prerequisite for the other. In most situations tracking training should begin at a young age, and it will usually progress faster than obedience training.

Motivating and Encouraging Your Puppy

For nose-oriented puppies from hunting bloodlines the motivation to track a blood line is genetically inherited and traces far back to the origins of the dog as a canine predator. Tracking comes naturally to a good puppy; as puppy trainers we shape their prey drive rather than create it. Try to operate within the puppy's attention span and offer strong verbal encouragement. The puppy should be helped to realize that tracking is the most important and fascinating thing that a dog can do. At the deer skin the puppy should be praised warmly and played with to the point that he feels that his find is the greatest emotional event of his puppy lifetime.

During the track itself I have seen handlers get carried away and fall into a pattern of chattering "Good dog! Good dog!" whether the dog is making good progress or just fooling around 30 feet off the line. If you talk too much, your words become meaningless; the dog tunes the handler out and communication is lost.

Some trainers respond to a decline of interest in their canine trainees by increasing the freshness of the lines and increasing the amount of blood. This seldom increases the level of canine enthusiasm, and it may actually make things worse. Dogs often become bored when we request them to do something uninteresting and unchallenging for an extended period of time. They pretend that they don't know what to do, and they make a fool of their handler. How interested would a child be if asked to follow a broad white stripe across the landscape, and if at the same time he were expected to ignore cool swimming holes, patches of wild strawberries and other delightful distractions? Would the child become more motivated if the guiding stripe were painted twice as wide? Dogs respond to an interesting challenge.

If your dog becomes bored with training lines laid with blood, another possible solution is to begin using tracking shoes in training. Especially after finding a few easy deer, some young dogs will tell you by their body language, "I don't like these phony blood trails any more. I want the real thing!" Tracking shoes (the German originators call them Fährtenschue) are one solution to this problem. Mounted on the tracking shoes are deer hoofs, which make the artificial blood trail more realistic. Tracking shoes are discussed in detail later on, and if you think that they might be useful for your young dog, "reach" ahead to Chapter 12. In recent years tracking shoes have become an extensively used training device in Europe and in North America.

Your emotional relationship with your puppy plays a big role in motivating him and much of this grows out of the time spent in affectionate play around the house. It really helps on the training line if the puppy wants to please you. For some character types, Labs and herding dogs for example, the desire to please may be even stronger than their "prey drive" to get the game. With all tracking dogs the relationship of dog and handler becomes very important. It grows into a strong emotional BOND. After you and your dog have tracked and found a real deer together, this bond will be the most important emotional tie in the dog's life. It may become rather important for you as well!

A Flexible Plan for Stages of Training

The order of training stages, described below, can be adjusted to the age and needs of your dog. But remember to also adjust the length and age of the training line so that it is appropriate for your dog's level of development.

1. Deer Liver Drags

Deer liver drags are the simplest and easiest introduction for a very young puppy. He can follow an enticing scent trail for ten feet to the piece of raw liver that is a delight to chew on. Working the pup on liver drags, at five to ten weeks of age, can provide the bridge between mental "conditioning" and training. At the beginning the pup won't seem to accomplish much, but as explained in Chapter 3, that rapidly growing little brain will be stimulated in all the right places.

The time of transition from mental conditioning to actual training will vary from puppy to puppy. The scent line is continuous and very attractive to the dog, especially if he has been given an opportunity to chew on the liver before the drag is made. If the puppy is put down on the line 30 minutes after the drag, there will be plenty of scent. At this very early stage a deer skin can also be used as a drag. This leaves a broad band of scent and may encourage loose, sloppy work if it is used in more advanced training.

The length of the first line can vary from 10 to 50 feet, depending on the size and maturity of the pup. Encountering his first right angle turn helps the puppy realize that he can check himself when he overshoots the corner and runs out of scent. At the age of seven weeks, most puppies will not be leash trained. A tracking leash is not really necessary at the beginning. Use your judgment as to whether it will be a distraction.

When the puppy tracks up to the liver and sinks his teeth into it, praise him enthusiastically. Your tone of voice is the most important thing. Since the liver is still attached to the drag cord, have a little tugging match with him. Let him chew off and swallow a few small pieces before you pick him up. In the first month of training liver drags can be extended up to 200 yards and aged up to four hours.

Once the puppy knows what he is looking for, his motivation will be high, and this will carry him through several checks at right angle turns. You will gradually be extending the liver drags to 50 yards or more as you see that he is gaining the attention span to handle this.

When you sense that it is appropriate, introduce the tracking leash of plastic clothes line or other light, low-friction material. Yard training to walk on a leash should have progressed far enough by this time so that the tracking leash will not be a distraction. The tracking leash will actually become a line of communication. If the pup overshoots a right angle or drifts off the line, a gentle twitch on the leash and a "Is that right?" in a questioning tone will ease him back into the task at hand.

During the liver drag phase, two-three sessions a week are fine and one is not a disaster, particularly if the weather is uncooperative. Avoid high heat and high winds.

2. Training With a Deer Foot Drag

Laying a training line by dragging a freshly thawed out deer foot on a cord works surprisingly well, and it is simple to set up. The handler drags a deer foot, cut off below the knee or hock, just as he would drag a piece of deer liver. Scent from the interdigital gland between the cloves of the hoof seems to be one of the odors that the puppy can pick up and follow after an aging period of an hour or so. When the pup finds the deer foot he can pick it up and march along proudly with it. This training procedure imprints the dog with the awareness that foot print scent is important for finding a deer. Blood is not the only thing that a tracking dog can follow!

3. Artificial Blood Trails

There does not have to be an abrupt change-over from liver drags to blood trails created with a dabber or squeeze bottle. Blend one phase of training into the next. There are differences that should be understood. A fresh blood trail, with wet drops of blood still glistening, does not work very well. Pups stop to lick it, and they forget about moving ahead to the prize at the end. It works best to wait until the blood has dried, even though it is less attractive than a liver drag of the same age. Wait until the blood is dry. This will range from 30 minutes to two hours.

The blood line does not offer the easy linear continuity of the liver drag. The dog must "reach" from one drop or dab of blood to the next. When the blood is to be found at intervals of a foot, this is not a problem. When the distance between drops or dabs is extended to a pace or a yard, the puppy has something new to learn. He will begin finding and interpreting scent as it will occur when he begins tracking the real thing.

Old, dried blood is not as exciting to a puppy as a fresher liver drag, but there are advantages. It is more realistic in that it approaches the scent line left by a wounded deer. It also lasts a long time. A drop of blood continues to give off microscopic scent particles for many hours. A hunter knows that a fox or coon track four hours old is an old track. In contrast a four hour blood trail is not at all old for a dog's nose. When you are working with a four-month-old pup, you should not hesitate to work him on a track that has aged overnight. You can begin to ask the puppy to track a line that obliges him to really concentrate. When you ask your puppy to work hard, do not ask him to work for too long or too far. The limiting factor at this age is not his nose; it is the processing power and attention span of his still-growing brain.

When you begin working blood lines, you should also have been conditioning him to be enthusiastic about the various scents of a deer: interdigital and tarsal gland scents as well as the smell of a deer skin. It's great if this has already occurred in the whelping box. At the end of the line place a deer tail or some other deer part. I find that a piece of thawed-out deer skin, hair and all, works best. Let him smell it, chew it and shake it, if he wishes. Dachshunds and Jagdterriers are more enthusiastic about this play than Labs and versatile pointing dogs. For the former a piece of skin is more fun than a deer leg.

Enhancing the prize at the end of the line with treats, such as pieces of raw deer heart, makes the tracking experience even more memorable for the puppy. Other sorts of meat will work, but raw venison parts relate directly to the tracking work. If you work your dog on an empty stomach, he will be especially eager to track on the next exercise.

4. Training With Tracking Shoes

Some trainers prefer to use tracking shoes from the very beginning of puppy training as the use of tracking shoes with mounted deer feet is another way of adding realism to a blood line. Details on the use of tracking shoes are to be found in Chapter 12.

These tracking shoes were designed and built by United Blood Trackers members, and they hold the entire deer leg. More information on tracking shoes is given in Chapter 12.

Training in the Woods

Usually your training has begun on lawns and nearby fields where the cover is not too heavy. As you and your dog progress, the limitations of this environment become evident. On a breezy day the scent is spread over many feet. You also realize that the dog remembers where the skin was placed last week. Dogs have a great memory for where things are or have been located. He may even be able to smell the old blood line. You need fresh ground and fresh adventures.

There is also the problem of marking the line. With surveyors' flags on the ground, the pup quickly learns to recognize that they mark the line. You want to train your dog to use his nose, not his eyes. Traveling to forests and woodlots makes it easier to mark the longer, more complicated blood trails you are now using. Wooden clothes pins, with six inches of surveyor's tape attached, can be clipped to branches at eye level.

In the woods wind will no longer be a problem, and now you will be training in the same types of places where you will actually be tracking when the hunting season comes. There will be the same distracting fresh scents of deer and turkeys. The distraction problem will get worse instead of better for several months, but you and your dog must start dealing with this, the greatest challenge that you will encounter.

Lay blood trails through bedding areas. If there is a field where deer come out to feed in late afternoon, lay your marked line through the trees along the perimeter. When you come to work the line at dusk the deer will leave the field producing the hot scent lines that will distract your dog as he follows the blood trail. You will learn how to read your dog as he reacts to the hot scent. Your dog will learn to get back on the old cold line. It may take a "Is that right?" It may take a stern "No!". Do not resort to an e-collar.

Tracking Leashes and Collars for Puppies

Selecting a tracking leash for a young, seven-week-old puppy is not complicated, but the leash must be adapted to the pup's age and size. At the very beginning you probably will not need a tracking leash at all. You can walk along with the pup, encouraging him as he tracks a very easy, fresh line. After two or three weeks of this, and after the puppy has some familiarity with an ordinary walking leash, the tracking leash should be introduced. A light tracking leash of 20 feet is a good idea for early training, even if the adult dog is going to be worked in a state where it is legal to let the dog work off lead when tracking wounded deer.

This tracking puppy does not notice the light plastic clothesline.

The first tracking leash should be as light and friction free as possible. For small breeds like Dachshunds 20 feet of plastic clothesline is a wonderful solution. The puppy will barely notice it in his enthusiasm to follow the blood. For pups of the larger breeds you may want to use a heavier material; new, braided cotton clothesline has the stiffness that will help prevent tangles. At any rate, your puppy, whatever his weight and strength, should begin working with a tracking leash shorter and lighter than what would be appropriate for that dog as an adult. For all dogs avoid the very limp nylon called parachute cord. This will tangle and hang up at every opportunity and distract your dog from tracking. We will have much more to say about leashes in the chapter on equipment.

As a pup gets bigger and faster, a leash and collar give the handler much more control. If the pup overshoots a turn and clearly is not going to correct himself, it is much easier to stop him on the lead, let him swing in an arc, and then let him go forward, with encouragement, when he crosses and recognizes the scent line. As much as possible, let the puppy solve his problem for himself. That's what he will have to do when tracking wounded game. If needed, guidance by slight tugs on the leash is preferable to actually picking up the puppy and carrying him back to the point of loss.

This early guidance is better done with a collar than a harness. The harness will work, but since the leash attachment is roughly at the middle of the dog, "steering" is more difficult than when the leash is attached to the front end of the dog at a collar. You do not need a special tracking collar until the puppy is nearing his adult size and the collar becomes a special cue to get serious.

Training Line Preparation

Materials for Laying Training Lines

The training procedures that we have just discussed require advanced planning. You will need deer blood and other deer parts for preparing the training lines. In addition you will need equipment, a leash and so forth suitable for the age and size of the dog you will be working with.

In most parts of North America it is not difficult to collect deer blood if you plan ahead. When deer hunting, carry several one-gallon Ziploc® bags and a half-pint plastic margarine tub. Ask your hunting friends to do the same. When a deer is shot, use the plastic tub to scoop the blood from the chest cavity into one of the gallon Ziploc® bags, seal it, and for insurance place the whole thing in the second bag. When a quart or so of blood leaks out of a plastic bag into your hunting coat, it does make a mess. Once back home, I like to pour the blood from the Ziploc® bag into half-pint plastic containers or bottles for freezing. On the cover of each tub I use an indelible marker pen to date the blood and list its source. The containers can be thawed-out individually and provide just the right amount of blood for a test or training line. If the blood is going to be applied on the line with a squeeze bottle, then it should be strained before it is frozen.

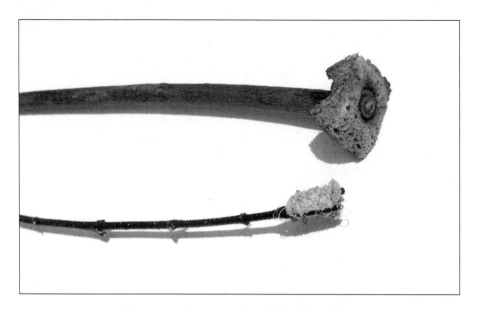

Above: Sponge on a stick for dabbing blood
Below: Sponge on a whippy branch for flicking blood droplets

When a deer is being field dressed, it is usually possible to collect blood and the heart and liver as well. Most hunters leave these organs in the woods, and if you see that this is their intention, you should pop them into another Ziploc® for future training sessions. As we have already discussed deer liver drags are very useful in motivating a puppy to follow his nose to a tasty chew on deer. This is a good way to get started. However, if you live in an area where liver flukes are a problem in deer, skip the liver part.

In general liver should not be fed in large quantities to dogs for health reasons; use it as a small, tasty reward. Dogs usually prefer deer heart to deer liver, but the heart does not leave as enduring a scent line when dragged; heart is more useful as a treat once you begin working on blood lines.

It is a good idea to slice the liver and heart into smaller pieces before you freeze it. But make sure that the pieces are big enough so that your dog can't wolf the whole thing down at once. Place the pieces in separate plastic bags so that you can thaw out only what you need. Your objective is to give the pup a tasty chew. You must have something that smells of deer to put at the end of the line. A deer leg can be used, but I prefer a piece of thawed out deer skin that your dog can grab and shake.

For laying out a blood line there are several different procedures. The dabbing and flicking method of laying a track requires a one-inch cube of cellulose sponge lashed to the end fork of a three-foot wand from a green, whippy branch. This is best for flicking, which gives you a continuous line of very fine droplets, which entices the pup to follow.

You can also attach a two inch square of sponge to one end of a heavier stick with a large headed screw and a washer. This works best for dabbing blood at each stride. The advantage of the sponge on a stick method is that you can use unstrained blood, which you carry in a small plastic bucket in one hand while you hold the stick in the other. This avoids wasting any of your tracking blood, which may be in short supply. If you screen out coagulated blood and food particles that would clog the fine spout of a squeeze bottle, then you end up throwing away a lot of gunk that would be perfectly good for laying a track. Of course you can avoid the whole problem by buying a $25 blender especially for the purpose.

In the sponge-on-a-stick method you redip the sponge every ten dabs of so, or whenever the sponge gets dry. Normally, you are dabbing at every stride, but you may want to flick or dab the blood at closer intervals in early training.

I find the squeeze bottle method faster and more efficient once the blood has been strained or broken up in the blender. With the bottle you can readily put up markers and place blood without setting down your equipment at each marking stop. As an alternative to the squeeze bottle some trainers simply use a soda bottle with a small hole bored in the plastic cap.

Sometimes trainers do not have access to deer blood that has been collected during the hunting season. There are alternatives. Deer are killed on highways all year round, and these deer can be a source of blood and a training hide, provided that there has been no decay. Highway departments are generally staffed by serious deer hunters, who will appreciate what you are doing and will give you a call when they pick up a suitable deer. Be sure to touch base with the local conservation officer. There are usually major legal complications if you are found in possession of an untagged deer, or deer parts, without official authorization.

In some cases cattle blood may be used as an alternative to deer blood, but this could lead to other complications. We have had some unsatisfactory experiences with cattle blood from a small slaughterhouse in New York State. There were several problems. First, since cattle blood can transmit disease the U.S. Department of Agriculture required considerable paper work authorizing its use. The federal veterinarian attending at this slaughterhouse was very patient and cooperative, but it is possible that the veterinarians in a larger, busier establishment would have no time for this sort of foolishness.

Another problem was that the gallon of cow blood, which we drew off,

Laboratory squeeze bottle with spout coming out of cap

coagulated into jelly almost immediately. Heparin, which is expensive, and potassium citrate, which is cheap, are both very effective to keep blood liquid and usable for laying out training lines. Potassium citrate can be purchased in large pharmacies and chemical supply houses without special permit or prescription. It seems odorless to humans, and dogs are certainly not repelled by it. You can also rely on a blender, but this is extra work.

Dogs will track cattle blood, but clearly they do not find it as appealing as deer blood. For Dachshunds, Beagles and Jagdterriers deer blood does produce the greatest animation and desire to follow at the beginning. Curs, Labs and pointing breeds tend to accept cattle blood better than the scent hounds.

If you prefer to train with tracking shoes, gather four deer feet from a harvested deer or a road kill.

Marking the Line

As you progress to longer and more complicated training lines with less blood, it will be necessary to place markers so that you know exactly where the dog should be working. In the woods wooden clothes pins with a strip of biodegradable marking tape knotted on at the hinge work very well. You can carry these clothespin markers in a shoulder bag. With one hand you clip the clothespins on twigs and branches while your other hand is free to squirt blood from your plastic squeeze bottle.

For both dog and trainer it is very useful to lay well-marked training lines in wooded areas where deer are plentiful. As the dog works the scent line, the handler will know the exact location of that line by the markers. If the dog is distracted by hot deer scent and leaves the marked line, the handler will know it. Moreover, the handler will learn how that particular dog expresses himself in body language when he goes off on a hot line. When the dog departs from the marked blood line for other, unknown reasons, the handler will learn to recognize the dog signs for this as well. Learning to read your tracking dog becomes very important when you are working a natural, wounded deer line with no visible blood.

As mentioned previously, in open country small, red surveyors' flags on wire stakes can be pressed down into the soil. But it does not take long for a smart, visually oriented dog like a Lab or a Black Mouth Cur to learn to follow these markers. Even scent hounds learn to read flags on the ground very quickly.

As your training lines get longer you should consider using a GPS to record the track that you have laid. A GPS will not always give you the necessary accuracy, especially if you are working under a dense forest canopy. Try it. Much preparation time can be saved for you if the GPS works in your situation.

It is a good idea to keep a record of each training track. This will help you evaluate your dog's progress and recognize his problems.

Patterns for Laying Early Training Lines

Most trainers put at least three 90-degree turns in a training line. These are more difficult for your dog than gradual curves. On a 90-degree turn, a dog has a tendency to overshoot. Then he must correct himself by working the "check" and regaining the scent. Dogs learn more by working such checks than by cruising along on straight lines.

At 90-degree turns, dogs tend to be "righties" or "lefties", that is they will always circle to the right or to the left. Most dogs are righties. Be sure to include both left and right angle turns on your training lines.

When a dog is well established in his training, you can try leaving deliberate gaps in the line of ten yards or more. The dog will have to learn to search or "reach" ahead to reestablish his contact with the line. You can set this up at a road crossing or a small stream as it would occur in natural blood tracking. A dog learns from encountering new problems and figuring out how to solve them. Try to build new lessons into your training lines, but don't make them too difficult for the young dog.

If possible, begin and end a training line along a road that passes through woods. Mark your starting and finish points with small streamers so that you can return to the right spot. Consider the prevailing wind direction and the distance because you don't want your dog to scent the training skin at the end of the line from his starting point. Your blood line can be laid as a broad inverted "U", but more than two right angles should be worked into it.

When you return to train your dog, you first place the skin at the end marker. You did not leave it when you laid the track so that it could be

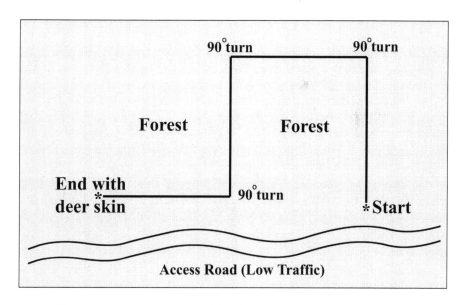

There are many variations of this basic layout of a training line.

destroyed by maggots or hungry coyotes. To avoid contaminating the area with drifting scent from the skin, carry it to the end point in a plastic garbage bag. Do not cross the training line as you do this. Then you drive back on the road to the beginning marker. When the dog has tracked over the line to the deer skin you praise him. As you carry the skin triumphantly back to the vehicle, which is only a few hundred yards away, more praise is in order.

The "Prey" at the End of the Training Line

A deer skin and edible treats at the end of the training line are the traditional means of motivating the dog. The tracking exercise may be over, but the dog will remember these treasures and track enthusiastically on the next training line. In Europe, where they have small roe deer, a complete, road-killed roe will often be used.

For Dachshunds, Jagdterriers or hunting hounds, the deer skin at the end always seems to turn them on. They grab it, shake it and chew on it. Other types of dogs may not show the same enthusiastic reaction. Cleo, my Southern Black Mouth Cur, was bred as a cowdog. Finding the skin was not a big deal for her. I have seen Labs act in the same indifferent way at the deer skin even though they did a good job of tracking. Their prey drive was not on the surface. For some dogs it is worth considering enhancements in addition to the deer skin and edible treats. A deer leg that can be thrown out for a few retrieves may be useful.

I think that we have something to learn from the very successful methods used to train military and police dogs used in detection work. The breeds most commonly used here are German Shepherds and Belgian Malinois (see Chapter 7). These working breeds tend to have a fascination, even an obsession, with a play object which they grab, retrieve and play with. In military and police training a rubber ball or "Kong" toy are used. When the dog in training finds explosive material or narcotics, his handler throws him the Kong to play with for about a minute. For some dogs this works extremely well.

For the dog that seems bored or unenthusiastic at the skin, the Kong approach may be useful. Try the Kong as a supplement to the skin that represents the deer. Place the Kong, or some other beloved object, under the skin. Of course to make this method work, you must first cultivate the dog's interest in the play object.

The Kong approach is for special training situations only. It isn't necessary or useful for most dogs.

Record Keeping

It is very useful to keep a record of your training tracks. This will permit you to recognize the progress that is being made and to identify where your dog needs to improve. If you need to describe your dog's training level to someone, it is good to support this with solid evidence. In Appendix H you will find a record keeping form, which has worked very well for us. Believe me, if you are training more than one dog, their work tends to blur together if there are no written records.

Sample Training Program for a 12-Week-Old Puppy

Until you develop a feel for working with your individual puppy, it may be useful to start a puppy with a standardized training program. This is a good way to start after your new puppy has adjusted himself to you and his new surroundings.

We are assuming that your puppy has already been introduced to short deer liver drags on the lawn. As you begin working blood, introduce a very light 20-foot tracking leash.

Week I

Exercise A. On a large lawn or nearby field with short grass lay 50 yards of blood drops or dabs at intervals of one foot. Include one right angle turn. At the end place a foot-square patch of thawed out deer skin or a tail. Include an edible treat, preferably from a deer. Age 30 minutes.

Exercise B. Use the same pattern as in A, but blood drops should be spaced farther apart. Leave the deer skin, or deer leg and also edible treats at the end. Age one hour.

Week II

Exercise A. Lay a 100 yard line, as you did in I B, in a pasture, mowed field or in open hardwoods. Age two hours.

Exercise B. Lay 150 yard line with markers at two right angle turns. Age four hours.

Week III

Begin working in the woods where there will be wildlife distractions.

Exercise A. Lay a 150-200 yard line with three right angle turns for the puppy to overshoot and correct himself. Age 8-10 hours.

Exercise B. Same as A but in a different location. Age overnight.

This sample exercise plan should be adjusted to the needs and progress of the puppy. For a year-old dog each stage should be made more challenging. Avoid training under windy conditions or high heat. At the end of three weeks you will have a good idea of how to extend the length, age and difficulty of the line.

This training plan works, but it's not the only way to train a puppy. There are trainers who believe that tracking shoes, or even a dragged deer leg, is best for their puppy. Use a method that you and your puppy are comfortable with, but avoid training with huge amounts of scent, such as would come from a dragged deer or a deer skin. Even at the beginning your puppy will be stimulated by a challenge he can deal with.

A satellite view of a 160-meter scent line prepared for puppies by dragging a deer neck. The track was recorded by using "My Tracks" app for Android phones. The starting point is marked as "A" and the end of line is marked as "B". This app has been discontinued.

Summary

- Develop a relationship in which your dog desires to work with you.

- Developing and shaping the dog's natural prey drive is the most fundamental part of training.

- Plan ahead and gather deer parts (blood, liver, heart, skin and legs) during hunting season when collection is easiest.

- Use a liver drag or lay out blood lines as soon as the puppies show an interest in these scents.

- Place a part of thawed-out deerskin, or other deer part, at the end of the line.

- As you undertake lines of more than a hundred feet, use a tracking leash for better control in early training. This is worthwhile even if your puppy is eventually going to work off lead.

- Talk to the dog on the training line and give lots of positive reinforcement when you are sure that the dog is right.

- Let him solve his own problems if possible.

- Adjust training exercises to the progress and maturity of the dog.

Chapter 9

Training Young Dogs: Problems & Solutions

Frequency of Training Sessions

When it comes to training for blood tracking, excessively frequent repetitions generate boredom. Repetition is essential in many trained canine activities such as retrieving, but in blood tracking the value of constant repetition is limited. In traditional blood tracking one relies much more on the initiative of the dog than upon his readiness to repeat the patterns of daily training drills. After the puppy introduction phase is over, most experienced Europeans maintain that one training session every week will produce faster, better results than daily drills. One eager American trainer, who had lots of spare time, gave her Dachshund bitch a blood line almost every day for two months. At the end of this time, the dog performed little better than when she began training. The handler did not have a tracking dog with which she felt confident to go on calls and search for real wounded deer.

The intensity and the rhythm of appropriate training should be determined by the characteristics of the breed and the character of the individual dog. Some dogs will respond to frequent training lines much better than others; there are no hard and fast rules. Highly trainable dogs like Labs or German Shepherds usually tolerate frequent repetition better than hounds. Experience does demonstrate clearly that the pace of training cannot be forced. If a dog seems to go stale for no good reason, back off and give him a mental rest. Haste makes waste.

Canine boredom is one of the greatest enemies of the tracking dog trainer. Challenging the dog's ability, within reason, is one of the best means of holding the attention of a tracking dog. Variety is also important. Don't set out training lines repeatedly in your back yard. Associate a training session with a ride in the car to strange, new woods. Boredom will kill your training efforts faster than the distractions of exciting new training sites.

A vacation, especially during a long, hot summer, is a relief for the dedicated trainer, as well.

Training in Varied Vegetation and Terrain

Scent holds differently in different types of vegetation. In an open pasture, swept by a light breeze, the scent trail for the dog will be thinner and more spread out than when the line is laid on a surface of dead leaves under the shelter of mature hardwoods. The handler should give the dog experience in working the scent line in different types of cover.

Ideally the dog should be exposed to different sorts of cover on the same training line, but this is not always possible. The variations are not always available. A more practical solution may be to change the type of training sites from lesson to lesson. The important thing is to prepare your dog to work well in whatever environmental situations are encountered on a natural call.

Training in Hot Summer Temperatures

Let's not assume that dogs are just like humans, and that they can take the heat like a tough outdoorsman. A dog does not sweat like we do. The dog sweats through his paws whereas we sweat all over and are cooled by evaporation. Yes, a dog pants, but this can't compare with the human cooling system. Then there is the matter of insulation: fur coats vs. T-shirts.

When we ask our dogs to work training lines in very hot weather, the dog may survive with his life, but it can be a very unpleasant canine experience. The memories of this are not going to promote enthusiasm about tracking in the future. Any value of the training experience is going to be vastly outweighed by the negative feelings associated.

It is not a disaster if our dogs take a summer vacation. They are not going to forget their skills. On the contrary, they are going to be fresher and sharper when cool weather comes back. We ask our dogs to track the real thing in hunting season when the temperatures are more suited to their physical construction. Agricultural damage shooting is an exception.

As discussed in Chapter 8, for puppies in their first six months, a short, 100 to 300 yard track once a week is adequate in summer. Put the scent down in the evening and run it at dawn. For a dog over a year old, who has tracked a few natural lines, there is really no good reason for running longer training lines if the temperature is over 75 degrees. Over the summer they won't forget what they have already learned.

Some of the background for these opinions comes from my experience running small training workshops one summer. Usually there were five or six dogs at each session. When the temperature rose above 80 degrees there would be a dramatic fall-off in enthusiasm and performance in most dogs. The Labs and the Wirehaired Dachshunds had to be urged to track. There was only one dog that didn't care about the heat. That was Cleo, my Southern Black Mouth Cur. Cleo's tough ancestors were developed in East Texas and Louisiana, where they allegedly lived on corn meal and road-killed armadillos. They were expected to work cattle and hawgs no matter how hot the weather. Perhaps this "natural selection" adjusted the thermostats of the tough southern working dogs. If you have a Black Mouth, Catahoula or a Blue Lacy, ignore this section!

In the South the early part of deer season coincides with some hot weather. To some degree a dog like a Lab can be conditioned to work better in this heat by exercising him for short periods in the heat of the day. Exercise is one thing; training is another. A dog will learn more from practice lines when he is not suffering as he works them.

Training During Northern Winters

During northern winters, when the landscape is covered with deep snow, we trackers yearn for bare ground. This is the time when we would like to be in the southern woods. What sort of training for tracking is possible during a tough northern winter?

Unless there is hard crusted snow that you can walk on, your best bet is to go to an area of broad, heavily used snowmobile trails. Lay your blood lines when there is no snowmobile activity, and work them when the temperature is above 20F. Experienced dogs can track when it is colder, but there is no point in stressing a young dog.

In some locations the plowed-out parking lot of a mall or school may offer possibilities. You have to do your training when there have been no vehicles present for several hours.

If you lay a trail in the fields or woods where there is enough snow to show your visible foot trail, most dogs won't learn very much about using their nose. They will find it easier to follow your footsteps by eye even if you have laid the blood well to the side.

With four to six inches of snow in the fields, you can produce a network of ruts with your truck. Then lay the blood down in these ruts, shifting the blood trail from one set of intersecting ruts to another. The dog will have to use his nose at the checks rather than cruising along continually in one tire rut.

Training After Dark

Once things are going reasonably well in the woods in daylight, you should try working the young dog occasionally at night. After all this is when you will be doing much of your real deer tracking. The woods are so different at night! Your headlamp casts strange shadows that your dog is not accustomed to. Scenting is generally better, but this also means that the smells of prowling wildlife have to be recognized and disregarded.

Tracking Accuracy

Sometimes dogs just take a lackadaisical approach to the line. They "drift" it, hit or miss, and because they have pretty good noses they manage to keep going in the right direction. This is not very satisfactory because a good tracking dog should be able to show you exactly where the deer passed, show you the occasional visible spot of blood, and give you an opportunity to judge where and how hard the deer has been hit. If you miss a bed in which the wounded animal has been lying, you may be missing some very important information. Encourage your dog to work closely by using older, more difficult lines.

Keep in mind that some dogs, such as Bloodhounds, with their exceptional noses, can follow a day old line from ten yards or more away. This is not necessarily an advantage if you wish to read blood sign and determine if an animal is mortally wounded.

In general, dogs will be more eager and alert in what they do when they are not stuffed with food. Work a dog lean and hungry; the interval of time since the last feeding depends on the age and disposition of the dog. You may be able to sharpen him up by leaving bits of food on the line. I find that dried deer liver, baked to a hard, rubbery consistency, works very well, and it is not very attractive to flies and ants. If you drop small bits of this liver every fifty to a hundred yards as you lay the blood line, you will find that most of it is still there several hours later when you work your dog. A hungry, greedy dog will soon figure out the new game and stay glued to the line as never before. It will encourage accuracy if you put a bit of liver ten yards after the 90 degree turns.

For older lines a variation of this technique is to put a bit of meat, perhaps an inch section of hot dog, into an old plastic film canister or a pill container. This will deter the skunks and coyotes to some degree. Rub a little of the treat on the outside of the film canister so that the dog will readily find it. The film canister will keep the yellow jackets and ants off the meat, and the dog will appreciate your help in opening the canister for him. This helps to make him realize that you work as a team on the scent line.

Avoiding Gun-Shyness

Wounded deer are found alive about ⅓ of the time, and in most states they are put down with a handgun or long gun. Therefore, the tracking dog should be unshaken by loud noises including gunfire. If a dog has never been exposed to gunfire in hunting, the blast of a heavy handgun is likely to come as a shock. A few nervous, fearful dogs will be gun-shy under any circumstances, but otherwise stable dogs can develop problems when precautions are not taken. It is very important for the young dog to associate gunfire with game and good things. You can imagine how inconvenient it is to have a dog refuse to continue tracking if the first shot at a wounded, bedded deer happens to miss. I have seen dogs that tucked their tails under their bellies and quit when they were exposed to shooting fifty yards away.

A tendency to develop gun-shyness is part of the genetically determined psychological character of the dog. Exposing five-week-old puppies to distant gunfire can help avoid problems later on, but this is the breeder's responsibility. Avoid nervous puppies, which are more likely to become gun-shy, but also try to condition dogs to accept what comes. Your young puppy should be exposed to reasonably loud noises like the beating of a cooking pot with a heavy spoon. Popping bubble wrap close by is the next step. Later, fire a .22 around the kennel, starting with .22 shorts and working up to .22 long rifle. Then take walks and fire a shotgun when the dog is not too close. Remember that handguns for deer, with their short barrels and added muzzle blast, are much more disturbing than a twelve-gauge shotgun.

What also works very well in training is a clapper, constructed out of two short boards connected at one end by a hinge. With this piece of home-made equipment you can make a big bang or a modest clap depending on your pup's stage of development. This gadget can be carried as you take walks afield with your pup, and it is just the thing for working up to firearm blasts.

If you have any worries that your dog may develop gun-shyness, consider buying a conditioning tape or CD from Master's Voice. The address is listed in the Appendix A.

I know of two different cases where gun-shyness has developed out of a bad experience with 4th of July fireworks. If your dog has to be around heavy blasts and concussion, you should be with him to calm and reassure him.

Gun-shyness and other problems of shyness or "spookiness" occur infrequently in otherwise well-bred dogs, but there is no excuse for them to happen at all. Pay attention to this psychological preparation as you train for tracking.

Excessive Possessiveness

For some young dogs enthusiasm and prey drive translate into excessive possessiveness and aggression toward any human, including their handler, who approaches them when they are on "their" deer skin. This can become a serious problem, and this form of aggression must be nipped in the bud. You do not want to have your tracking dog take a hunter's ear off when he rushes in to kiss his big buck.

If the puppy growls and shows his teeth at you, gently roll him over on his back and growl in return. He must learn that he is not the exclusive owner of the game he finds. He must share. Sometimes picking a puppy up by the scruff of the neck while growling, as his mother would do, is another option. Afterwards make it clear that you are proud to share the skin with him. Finding the skin must be a positive experience.

The lesson can be reinforced back at the house by giving the possessive puppy a rawhide chewy. Once he is enjoying himself with it, gently assert your dominance. Take the chewy away from him, give him a tasty treat and then return the chewy to him. Make him share! Dogs understand this dog language, and they do not resent it as a child would.

Finding the Time

Let's be realistic! For most trainers the problem is too little training rather than too much. I have met so many people who had a dog of fine promise that was never fulfilled. Such owners explain, regretfully, that they would like to train their dog but never can find the time. Other people, who are actually much busier, make the time to work with their dog. It is a matter of priorities.

In this modern world everyone has too much to do; the less important things always get pushed down to the bottom of the priority pile and are never done at all. Obviously, a tracking dog has to come after family and job, but if

No, it's not your deer. You have to learn to share.
Photo courtesy of Taylor Schulze

this dog also comes after getting a really big buck every year, after having an exceptional garden, after fishing, after bowling.... If this is the case, perhaps the prospective purchaser of a tracking dog prospect should reconsider. Rather than let a good dog waste his life behind the bars of his kennel or as a couch potato, it is better to find, or encourage the development of a dedicated local fanatic who has a dog that can be called in cases when a deer can't be found by eye-tracking.

Training Variations

In Chapters 8 and 9 we have presented a basic training method with artificially prepared lines that is widely used and certainly works, but keep in mind that this is not the only way to train a tracking dog. Excellent dogs have been trained by other methods or by a combination of methods. In the long run it will be clearer for most people if we present a brief overview of these alternative methods. It may make sense to introduce some of these, such as tracking a real wounded deer, into your own puppy training plan.

Following easy natural blood trails to a real kill is a great motivator for the young dog with sufficient self-confidence. We know of dogs in the Midwest that have been trained exclusively by this method. The dog in training experiences the excitement of trailing and finding the real thing. Nothing is lost if the deer is gutted in the field before the handler brings out the young dog for a training session.

Often it may seem convenient to put the dog down on the easy, very fresh line within a half hour of when the deer was shot. The problem is that this puts the dog in a big tunnel of air scent rather than on a line of ground scent. For the dog, there seems to be scent all over the place, and he can bounce around in this tunnel without much sense of direction. It is better to bring the dog in after all the deer and blood scent hanging in the air has drifted off a bit. This will encourage the dog to do clean work and follow the actual scent line on the ground.

On the other hand, it is not practical to leave a deer in place for a half a day or more for training on old, cold lines, the kind that come up in the real world of hunting. It takes some experience with lines a day or more old before the dog learns how much can be accomplished by close, careful nose work and unrelenting concentration. This sort of experience is best acquired when artificially laid blood trails are used.

In most Texas counties, blood tracking is legal and up to two dogs can be worked off lead to find wounded deer. Many Texas dogs are trained simply by letting them work on natural blood lines along with an experienced veteran.

In the states where the dog must stay on lead, a young dog can be introduced to tracking in a similar way by working him with a second handler behind the seasoned blood tracker.

These practices off lead and on lead are useful with some dogs, but they can be overdone to the point that an inexperienced dog becomes a "me-tooer", lacking the initiative to work difficult lines on his own.

Tracking as an Obedience Exercise

We should add that there is still another variation in training, which is used by certain versatile hunting dog trainers. These trainers believe that blood tracking, like any other sort of tracking, can be taught as an obedience exercise. In this approach the dogs actually begin by tracking a human scent line, and then later a transition is made to blood. The philosophy and the procedures used in this method are often in direct contradiction to those advocated in this book. To avoid confusing the reader with contradictory advice, the discussion of this highly structured method is presented separately in Appendix D.

Training a dog to track as an obedience exercise obviously works for certain dogs, and we do not seek to condemn it. Personally, I do not think this method is the best way to develop a dog whose primary role will be finding wounded deer, and after all, that is the focus of this book. However, this "structured discipline" approach obviously has its value for the trainer whose first priority is bird finding and retrieving, and who wishes in addition, to have a dog for tracking wounded deer if the need arises.

Many useful insights on training can be drawn from the numerous books written on man trailing with Bloodhounds or other breeds. However, wounded big game tracking is psychologically different for the dog particularly in the early motivating and training phases. Training for tracking wounded big game relies heavily on prey drive. This is not an important motivation in human tracking.

Many recent books on dog training are based on the theory of "Operant Conditioning" . We don't have to get involved in this here. Since most dogs are naturally motivated to track game and get to the "deer", clicker training and frequent treats, are not necessary. The dog learns very quickly that the "positive reinforcement" will come at the end of the scent line. The traditional training methods discussed in this book are compatible with modern training theories in that praise and rewards are used rather than negative punishment.

Summary

- Develop the dog's motivation to track. Everything depends on this.

- Whenever possible, have the puppy track easy deer that other hunters have shot and already found for themselves.

- Don't let the puppy become aggressively possessive at the deer skin. Nip the tendency in the bud.

- A blood trail is not like a human track. The blood scent remains for many hours.

- Usually a blood tracking session once or twice a week will produce better results than more frequent exercises. Don't overdo training and bore the dog.

- Prepare your dog to welcome, or at least tolerate, the sound of gunfire.

- Gently expose your pup to a wide variety of situations so that he will be psychologically prepared to take what comes when tracking the real thing.

- All dogs are not the same! Know your dog. Adjust your training schedule and methods to his needs.

Chapter 10

Working With Dogs Through Adolescence

It may seem strange to bump into this chapter on adolescence sandwiched between several chapters focused on training. Actually it is right in the middle of training that you will have to deal with this mental change in your dog. As you continue training your dog at increasingly advanced levels, you may encounter a disappointing downturn in performance. Relax! Do not despair. In all likelihood you have run into this temporary psychological phenomenon known as "adolescence".

How should you react when a fine young dog goes sour? You have been pleased with his tracking work on advanced artificial lines, and he has done surprisingly well in finding real deer in that first season when he was still a puppy, not yet a year old. All of a sudden he can't focus on anything. He is distracted by a butterfly or a mouse. Sometimes he doesn't want to track at all. In the 21st century psychologists understand adolescence much better than they did in the 1960s. The first advice they give us today is "patience". Let's look at an example of canine adolescence.

I first encountered canine adolescence in Clary, who was to become the best dog I have ever owned. Clary von Moosbach was a Wirehaired Dachshund who became my do-everything dog. She just knew intuitively what I wanted her to do. It could be hunting pheasants one day or rabbits the next. She would tree coons at night and leave rabbits and deer alone. She never tracked a wounded deer until I started her on this when she was four years old. Then she put together all the skills she had learned hunting other types of game; she became an expert on cold tracks and staying on the right line.

What was Clary like in adolescence? In her case this unsettled period came between 12 and 18 months. For six months after her first birthday she was close to zero. She would quit a rabbit trail after 50 yards and begin hunting mice. She was incapable of remembering that certain types of game ran up a tree. She couldn't do anything right.

I had started to think about finding a pet home for Clary, but then she emerged from her fog of confusion. She became the dog that made hundreds of Americans aware that the right kind of Dachshund is a practical hunter.

Andy Bensing had a similar experience with his Wirehaired Dachshund Eibe:

> I had great expectations when I got off the plane with my newest Wire-haired Dachshund puppy. I had waited a year for this repeat breeding. My new puppy, Eibe, was a full sister to a very precocious 6 month old bitch that I had first seen in Germany on an apprentice judging assignment the year before.

I began blood tracking training with Eibe right away and by the age of 8 months she was doing 800 meter overnight lines with no trouble and could not have been doing any better. She was all the dog I could have hoped for. Then, like a light switch, for the next 12 months there was almost nothing. I would lay training lines every few weeks to check, but she was terrible, with little or no interest in following the blood line. I tried everything to no avail during that time to build drive for the blood line. I tracked her hungry for food, went back to easy drags, put caged critters at the end for her to bark at, nothing worked during that time. To keep her nose well connected to her brain I spent that summer after she was a year old having her chase 4 or 5 rabbits per day since blood tracking training seemed to be a waste of time.

In the fall of 2008, Eibe was almost 1½ years old but I did not even consider putting her on a real blood trail that season unless I already had visually marked the natural line and was using the line only as a training exercise. After that hunting season, at about 20 months of age, things finally started to turn around and begin to improve with Eibe's training. Her focus and desire for the blood line began to come back and I could again see glimpses of the brilliance she showed up until 8 months of age. It was difficult waiting out what is often called "that adolescent period". As the months piled up during that period of time I have to admit I began to doubt if she would ever turn back around. I bought two other dogs during that time to hedge my bets just in case she didn't.

To understand canine adolescence better, it helps to recall what we were like as adolescents ourselves. In 6th grade I distinguished myself as the spitball artist of the class. I spent a third of that year in the detention room looking out the window, watching the squirrels play. I suppose it was in this room that I was "imprinted" for squirrel hunting later on. That was a good thing. But looking back on 6th grade 65 years later I believe that some firm, "sit/ stay" lessons would have been good for me. Learning that I had to sit still and not jabber would have been a calming experience for me, and it would not have stressed my powers of concentration too much. Leaving me in the detention room "kennel" was probably not the best solution, but there was little scientific understanding of adolescence in 1948.

The big breakthroughs in understanding what goes on in the human teenage brain began in the 1970s after the development of functional magnetic resonance imaging equipment or fMRI. This was a specialized version of the MRI machine that was being used to take pictures of soft tissue abnormalities such as cancerous tumors deep within the body. By monitoring minute differences of oxygenated blood flow in various parts of the brain, the fMRI could determine which parts are involved in various human activities, and how these parts were linked together by the circuitry of brain neurons.

With fMRI it became possible to learn what parts of the human brain were most active as specific mental tasks and operating decisions were performed.

It was then realized that in humans the adolescent brain and the mature, adult brain might appear similar, but they were significantly different in how they operated. Brain development and mental capacity were not completed by age ten as had been previously supposed. Actually the brain's functions, its capabilities in matters of judgment and decision-making, were not at their peak until the mid-twenties.

Now what does all this human research have to do with the problems of adolescent dogs and other mammals? More than might be suspected. An article was published in the top scientific journal, *Science*, showing that even mice demonstrate some parallels between human and animal brain development. Researchers found that adolescent mice actually **regressed** temporarily in their capacity to avoid mild electric shocks from a moving object. There were brain circuitry changes that explained this. For a dog trainer, who has seen an adolescent dog incapable of doing what it had "mastered" two months earlier, this certainly sounds familiar.

It seems that we are now on the threshold of a new type of research on the function of canine brains. We are not sure of how closely the canine research will parallel the established research that has been done on humans, but we do know this: The components of the dog brain, and the connecting circuitries are much the same as those in the brains of humans. However, the relative size and importance of the brain components are quite different. For example, the olfactory bulb in the dog brain is much larger than the equivalent area in humans. Surprise! Surprise! It's not our fault that we are so pathetically weak in our ability to use our noses. Even if we did have a big nose like "Old Deer Finder", we wouldn't have the brain power to process the olfactory information that the nose brought in.

On the other hand, the frontal lobe of our brains is proportionally larger than that of other mammals. The neuroscientist Elkhanon Goldberg refers to this as the "executive brain". The frontal lobe, and its prefrontal cortex, receive and coordinate information coming in from other parts of the brain. It's this part of the brain that makes decisions, tunes out irrelevant distractions and reins in impulses.

Dogs have frontal lobes too, but theirs are much smaller than ours, and the functions are more limited. Dogs never become as good at reasoning and planning as we humans. Despite real differences between dogs and humans, in this aspect of brain function through the frontal lobes, it seems very likely that there are some parallels when it comes to adolescent development.

At this time in 2016 most of the MRI based research on adolescence has focused on humans, not on dogs. Neuroscientists have followed the gradually maturing brain functions of teenagers, and they have established that one of the underlying reasons for more mature judgment and responsible behavior is based on a growing efficiency of the "executive brain", the frontal lobes. The neural circuits linking this area to other parts of the brain change; they become better organized and extensive. An insulation of these connections, a grey substance called myelin, also increases so that messages go back and forth more swiftly and effectively from the frontal lobes to other parts of the brain.

In the early stages of human adolescence it was found that decision-making was so poorly managed by the "executive brain" that tasks were often delegated to parts of the brain that couldn't handle them very well at all. With growing maturity the "executive brain" delegated decisions to the rest of the brain in a more adult-like pattern. This was reflected in such things as a reduction of teenage driving accidents per mile.

At this time it seems likely, but has not actually been proved, that similar changes are taking place in the frontal lobes of adolescent dogs. It hasn't been scientifically proved yet, but we do know that the adolescent tracking dog has some of the same general tendencies as the "mixed-up" teenager. The adolescent tracking dog frequently loses focus; he is easily distracted and when he gets to a tough check he often fails to persevere. He is not very good at deciding, on his own, whether he is dealing with a back track, a gap in the scent line or a sudden change in its direction. Staying on the right line, distinguishing the scent of one deer from another is often very difficult.

There is much more to adolescent brain changes than what I have sketched here, but more detail would not necessarily make the important point more clear. The research of the neuroscientists does have practical value for us as dog handlers. It gives us a basis for rethinking some of our old ideas about raising and training dogs:

1. Have we been too quick to cull young dogs in the past? I remember when I was shopping around for a Southern Black Mouth Cur puppy as a tracking dog prospect, a man called me up from Florida and tried to sell me one of his pups. To establish his credentials, he told me that he had "culled" over the years a pick-up load of his young dogs that weren't showing him much. I wonder how many pups in that pick-up load would have turned out to be good dogs in the longer run.

2. Can we use stern discipline to force an adolescent dog to shape up and think about the bad moves he is making as he blunders on a tough scent line? *"The damn dog looks like he is full grown, but he acts like he has no brain at all"*. Well, to tell the truth his brain isn't worth much for tracking at this particular time. He is no good at making the independent decisions that a good tracking dog must make. We have to be patient.

3. What can you do with a screwed up adolescent dog? Leave him in the kennel or ignore him until he grows out of his condition? During the adolescent period the dog can learn useful things, even though he is incapable of making much progress in blood tracking. This is the time to continue with structured training: command and obey stuff like "sit/stay" and "heel". Response from a distance to "Come" can be perfected, probably with a little gentle persuasion from an e-collar. Like a teenager, your adolescent dog needs structure, clear rules combined with affection. During adolescence you can lay the basis for

future responsive work and a working partnership by cultivating the bond between yourself and your dog.

The problems of canine adolescence are not inevitable, and the timing of its occurrence varies with the individual. It can begin at any time from nine to 12 months. I have also owned and observed pups that acted like little grown-ups right from the beginning; they never wavered. These adolescent "straight arrows" did not always turn out to be the best in the long run.

Adolescence seems to have a pattern that varies from breed to breed. The Hanover Hound and the Bavarian Mountain Hound are generally recognized to be slow developers with a prolonged adolescence that may continue until they are three years old. Many Dachshunds of European hunting bloodlines seem to have a definite but short-lived adolescence. Usually they are in and out in less than six months. However, I had a German import, Lucy, who tracked like a little machine until she was eight months old; then she blew sky high and did not come back to earth until she was nearly three. Every generalization has its exceptions! Looking backward, I think that Lucy would have had fewer problems if I had known more about managing her.

Recently we raised a male and a female Dachshunds to the age of one year before we sold them as trackers. Luna and Volt were almost exactly the same age, and they were close companions. In tracking training Luna was slightly better than Volt, but both were doing excellent work on 24 hour lines. They were both excellent prospects from strong tracking parentages! At the age of one Luna fell apart. She remained a warm and responsive young bitch, but temporarily she showed no interest in tracking. After several months Luna recovered her old aptitudes, and she had an excellent first tracking season.

At the same time Volt, Luna's male counterpart, continued to progress, doing more and more difficult work and showing no signs of adolescence. He also had an excellent first tracking season.

Patrice Stoquert, a French forester, has had extensive experience first with Wirehaired Dachshunds and later with Labs of British breeding. Patrice believes that problems of adolescence are greater in Dachshunds than in Labs.

To return to the starting point of this chapter, we are at the beginning of a new era in the practice of dog training. In the past most writers of books and articles have dealt with the subject in terms of two categories: puppies and mature dogs. It was assumed that the dog's brain was fully formed by the end of the puppy stage. After that, training was a matter of teaching, working with the fully formed mental equipment that was already there.

In the future those who work with dogs will become more and more aware of how and why the mental capabilities of dogs continue to grow over a much longer period than was previously realized. Training programs will reflect this understanding. The structure of firm but gentle "command and obey" training will be retained during the phase of adolescence, but command and obey will no longer be an end in itself. In certain human/dog activities (tracking is one of these) the slow-to-mature judgment of the dog, as informed by his special sensory gifts, will be valued as unique and valuable. Man and dog will be bonded into a working team that combines the best qualities of each. The old model of the commander and the robot will be restricted to certain types of artificial field trials.

Summary

- Canine adolescence involves changes in the way the brain functions. It can have a major impact upon behavior.

- The age, length and severity of adolescence varies from one breed to another.

- During a dog's adolescent period, the objectives of training should be adjusted accordingly.

- Patience, gentle, structured discipline and affection are required.

- The potential of a tracking dog cannot be evaluated during adolescence.

Chapter 11

Advanced Training for Blood Tracking

There is no substitute for practical field experience to train a dog in the finer points of blood tracking. Recognizing and working a backtrack, or following a particular wounded deer by its individual body and interdigital scent, are higher levels of the art. These are not easily taught by working artificial blood lines or by tracking easy, natural blood trails of deer shot by your friends. Still, much value comes out of formal training, not only for the inexperienced dog, but for his handler as well. The training experience forges dog and handler into a working team that will be far more effective than an untrained dog and an inexperienced handler that do not work together.

Bonding

As training progresses you will ask your dog to track wounded deer in favorable situations or in cases where the deer has already been found by the hunter. At this time a bond will begin to develop between you and your dog with a power never experienced before. Finding the game, praising the good work, gutting the deer, sharing tidbits of heart or belly meat cement the human/dog partnership in an amazing way.

Back in the house, the young tracking dog begins to follow you from room to room, waiting at your feet and hoping for the next deer call. Mature dogs respond to the team experience of finding a deer with similar emotions.

The story of one of our own brood bitches, Keena, is a good example of what can happen:

Keena was trained as a tracking dog and did good work on a number of calls before she met Dan Hardin, a graduate student and dedicated bowhunter. Dan was drawn into tracking when another of our dogs found a difficult buck for him. Dan later got his New York State tracking license, took a few calls with me, and then began to take calls on his own with our Keena. Usually Dan picked up and returned Keena to our house, but sometimes after a long, night call she would spend the night down at Dan's. Keena and Dan bonded as they found a number of deer together.

The power of that bond between Dan and Keena soon became apparent. Keena remained affectionate with us in our home, but the people who fed and cared for her on a daily basis ranked far lower in her esteem than did Dan. At any time of the year when Dan drove up our long driveway, Keena would begin to whine and wag her tail. She could recognize the sound of his car when it was still 100 yards away. When Dan arrived it was total bliss.

A bond like this deserves respect. Dogs like Keena will work hard and well with their human partner. Needless to say, Keena has now gone to live with Dan on a permanent basis. The BOND must be respected.

Keena's story demonstrates why a busy man, who buys a "trained dog" cannot buy the important working bond that was developing with the original trainer. The new buyer must recreate it, and this takes time, dedication and natural tracking experience.

Check Work

As we have explained earlier, for training purposes checks are created by making right angle turns in the artificial blood line. It is natural for the dog moving along a straight section to overshoot the corner. The dog may go a yard, or twenty yards, before reacting to the mistake by checking back to search for the line. Usually, he will swing around in a circle until he reconnects with the line. Dogs tend to be left handed or right handed, meaning in this case, that they have a preference for swinging to the right or to the left.

When a dog overshoots, you hope that he will recognize his mistake and correct himself. If the self-correction does not occur, ask the dog if he is right. The words themselves will mean little, but the dog will quickly recognize the questioning inflection in your voice and respond to it by checking back. If the dog persists in continuing straight ahead, then stop the dog, scold him mildly and take him back to a known point of blood before the corner. Encourage him to pay attention and turn at the corner, which he should now recognize. To facilitate this you should have laid blood more heavily right after the angle. In doing this, you are training the dog to work a check more than you are attempting to replicate a natural line.

Dogs quickly learn that the blood line is artificial because there are too many things missing like deer body scent and interdigital scent, which we cannot reproduce in a realistic way. The whole pattern of distribution of scent particles is very different on an artificial line from what occurs naturally. Nonetheless, dogs do make the transition easily from "faked" training bloodlines to the real thing.

The patterns of verbal communication, which you establish in training, will serve you well in the field. In both cases reporting blood that you see with praise and enthusiasm will reinforce the dog. The heavily inflected words of the question, "Is that right?" will lead the dog to consider whether he is still on the right line. Often he will turn back to the point of loss and give you a sheepish look when you ask him if he is sure of himself.

As much as possible allow the dog to make the move of correction himself instead of taking over and leading him back to a known point. For practical blood tracking in the woods, you need a dog that relies on his own nose and brain for guidance when no human knows where to find the scent line. Constant corrections may train a dog to stay close to the line and thus score well in tests and competitions. However, when you are out on a live line, and the deer has milled around in intersecting loops, you need a confident, self-reliant dog able to take charge and use his great skills to discover the line leading out of this mess. I once had a tracking dog, Max, who as a young dog would come back to me, place his paws on my knee and ask with his eyes "What should I do now?" This kind of dog is not the best one to have when scenting conditions are poor, and there are natural gaps in the line. Max eventually gained the self-confidence to solve his own tracking problems.

In the real world of natural tracking, checks can be very difficult. The tracking dog may have to search an area of more than a 100 yard radius to find the spot where the deer exited from a series of loops in his trail. Sometimes there are scentless gaps in a natural line, and the dog must "reach" to recover the scent line. In such situations the tracking dog must go into a "search" mode and work for many minutes to figure out the confusing mess and get going again.

A good dog will learn through experience to go into the "search" mode when necessary, but his development can be accelerated through training on artificially laid scent lines that loop around, have 20 yard breaks or backtracks. The handler may give his dog some assistance at first by leading him in circles and using the encouraging command "Search" or "Where is it?". But as much as possible let the dog make his own moves and figure things out for himself. Encouraging him with your voice will help to keep him focused on the task.

Advanced Check Work Exercises

Not everyone will have the time and the motivation to train a dog beyond basic check work. Advanced training involves preparing the dog to deal with such things as backtracks, situations where there are "dead spots" in the scent line, and cases when the wounded deer has milled around leaving a confusing jumble of looping tracks. Over a period of years an intelligent, well-handled dog can learn to deal with such problems through experience on natural tracks.

However, advanced training can speed up this learning process. In advanced check work training, scent lines are set up to create tracking problems for the dog to solve. At first the handler can give some guidance with strategic tugs on the tracking leash, enthusiastic praise when the dog makes the right moves, and a questioning "Is that right?" when he is not moving in a productive way. As the tracking dog becomes more familiar with this sort of problem solving, less and less guidance will be necessary.

Artificial backtracks are usually set up at the right angle in a training line. The line is extended beyond the corner for 20 yards or so, and then blood is dripped back over the same track. At first the backtrack should be in the form of an inverted narrow V. Later the V can be tightened up into a proper backtrack that comes back over itself. The same technique can be used with tracking shoes. The first few times that the tracking dog trainee encounters this, he should be encouraged to circle where the line seems to end until he cuts into the track and gets going again. With experience he will learn to recognize a backtrack and work back on it the way he came.

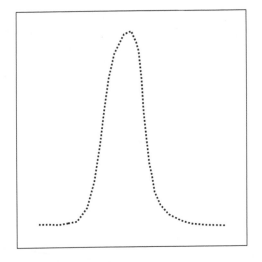

*First stage in
backtrack training*

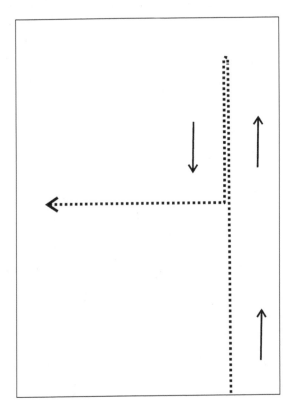

*Backtrack problem
in advanced form*

The dead spot, where there is no wounded deer scent, occurs frequently in natural tracking. In training it is created by eliminating blood drops or tracking shoe scent for 10 or 20 yards of the line. The track layer should walk a large loop around the break in the scent line so that the tracking dog does not use human scent to bridge the dead spot. If tracking shoes are used they should be taken off where the dead spot begins and put on again where the line continues.

For the tracking dog this scent gap is confusing. In the beginning the dead spot seems to have the same scent pattern as the backtrack, but now the dog must "reach" ahead, across the dead spot. This usually involves some exploratory circling. With training, dogs learn to recognize the subtle scent differences between the end of a backtrack and a natural break in the line due to an absence of scent.

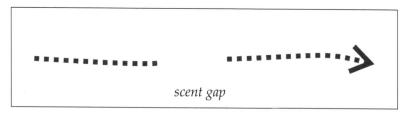

scent gap

The dog can also be trained to more efficiently find the exit track from a place where the wounded deer has milled about in a small area. The solution is for the dog to circle around the mess and recognize, by scent, the deer's line of departure. As in dealing with the two previous tracking problems, the dog must be encouraged to systematically search the area in widening circles. As discussed earlier, dogs have a remarkable capacity to remember where things are located spatially. Using the information their noses bring to them, they can remember where the wounded deer scent is, and where it is not, much better than humans could do, relying on their eyes.

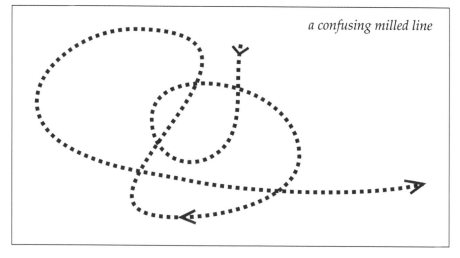

a confusing milled line

Once a dog has learned the basics of tracking, there is little point in repeating the same old patterns of training tracks over and over again. In advanced training, each track that you lay for your dog should have a specific instructional purpose. This may involve strengthening a weakness or improving his efficiency in working difficult checks.

Blind Lines as a Reality Check

Trainers may consciously guide their dogs a bit at the beginning of training; later they may find themselves doing the same thing unconsciously when there are markers or visible blood to show them where the line is. It is so easy! When the dog is on the line, you let him move freely. At a right angle turn, if he begins to overshoot the line, you hold him back and let him swing until he crosses the line again to the left or right. Dogs read us better than we read them. Even if you let the leash drag free at the critical parts of a training line, responsive dogs often sense what you want them to do. In these circumstances it is instructive, for both dog and handler, to work a blind line.

On a blind line the identifying markers are placed on the opposite side of the tree so that the handler cannot see them as he approaches. He cannot guide the dog because he does not know, himself, where the line goes. This simulates the psychological situation of a natural blood line, which no one is able to follow by eyetracking.

A blind line can be a reality check for a handler, who believes his dog has mastered blood tracking. Have a friend lay a blind line for you. He will be able to keep track of the markers on the other side of the trees and rescue you and your dog if you get too far off the line. If you can easily "forget", and your woods have no prominent features, you can also lay out a blind line for yourself. Put up a few "just-in-case" markers on the backs of trees, "forget" what you have done and run the line with your dog the next day. In forgetting, you will be surprised at how much you can learn. Modern GPS equipment can also be used for marking a blind line.

Hot Lines

To a blood tracker a hot line is a fresh scent line, usually the scent line of a healthy deer. At night in deer country, the old, cold lines, which we track with our dogs, are crisscrossed with steaming hot lines that can drive an inexperienced dog to distraction. The problem was discussed in greater depth in the chapter on general field techniques.

Training on artificial blood lines will seldom eliminate totally the problems that young dogs encounter with hot lines as they track their first wounded deer. After training they may be able to recognize that it is a sin to leave the old blood line for a hot track, but this does not mean that they will resist such a sin when they are tempted. But training will at least make correction easier when the young dog goes astray while tracking a real wounded deer. Your dog will understand what he has done wrong, and why you, the handler, are disappointed. The prospects of improving behavior will be excellent, and the dog will soon realize that only the old blood line leads to the recovery of a real deer and to the rewards that come with it.

In training the dog must clearly understand that he should track blood scent, must know that he can track it, and must be convinced that blood tracking is supremely important in the mind of his handler. Once this is established, the time is right for confronting hot lines. The same principle applies if you are using the tracking shoes as mentioned earlier.

One training method is to lay a well-marked trail inside the woods around a field where deer are known to come out to feed an hour or so before dark. Lay the track in the morning and return with your dog at dusk. As you and your dog approach, the deer will cross the scent line as they move back into the trees. You will recognize the hot lines by reading your dog's reaction. The head will come up and the tempo of tail beat will accelerate; there may be whines or barks. The dog will begin tracking faster and pulling harder as he leaves the blood line for the hot line. The expressions of excitement that you see will be the same hot line indicators that you will read on future occasions when the circumstances will be less clear.

Scold the dog, lead him back to the correct line and wait until his excitement subsides. Resist all temptation to use a switch or worse yet a shocking collar. Only positive reinforcement for doing the right thing will be effective. After a few minutes start again on the trail with lots of praise for positive performance.

Normally, the trainer does not have to try very hard to create hot line set-ups for his dog. Deer are almost everywhere, and a trail laid across deer runs and through bedding areas will involve hot lines, especially if the line is worked early or late in the day.

The hardest part, and the most important part, of training a "blood tracking" dog comes in teaching the dog to concentrate on the right scent line despite distractions of other game.

Working Speed

Most young dogs in training try to work the scent line too fast. The best time to adjust their speed to a practical rate is right from the start. Even if you are training in level, open hardwoods, ask yourself what speed you would prefer if tracking over slippery rocks on a steep mountainside. How fast would you want to move if it were essential that you see most of the blood sign yourself? Particularly in bowhunting it is important to determine how seriously the wounded deer is hit.

Various steps can be taken to help slow the puppy down so that he will be ready to dig old, cold scent out of the grass roots when the time comes for this. Even if you plan to track with your dog off lead, it is very helpful to start with some work on a tracking leash. For this purpose I like to use 20 feet of plastic clothesline, which is light and almost friction free. The pup will not be distracted by it, but the trainer will have some control when he needs it.

It goes without saying that all dogs should be trained not to pull ahead when they walk with their trainer on a short leash. Especially with a pup of a large breed, it is essential to teach the meaning of "whoa" and "slowly". One of the best ways to accomplish this is to reverse your line of travel every time the dog lunges ahead.

Usually it is easier to deal with the excessive speed problem if the dog wears a wide, leather tracking collar rather than a conventional dog harness. By flipping the leash down between the dog's legs so that he straddles it, you can pull his head down into the track and at the same time exert steady pressure against the back of his neck. There will be no pressure on his windpipe, and he will not choke and cough.

Another way of slowing down a young dog is to loop a half hitch over his loins just ahead of the hind quarters. When the pup pulls in his enthusiasm, the tracking leash will pinch him.

Yet another way to slow a dog down is to work him on older training lines that will challenge him a bit. We don't have enough respect for a young dog's nose. A four-month-old pup may lack the mental maturity to process and interpret what he smells, but his ability to recognize the scent is already operational. He can smell a drop of blood that is many hours old.

Many trainers reason, "He's just a pup. I'll give him a training line a half hour old, or perhaps even an hour." When the pup is brought in to track a fresh line of blood and the air is still, he actually encounters a big "tunnel" of scent rather than a scent line on the ground. Because there is scent everywhere in this tunnel he doesn't pay any special attention to the blood line, even if it is clearly visible to his handler.

If there is a breeze, scent particles from the blood will have drifted downwind for 25 yards or more. There will be a wide swath of blood scent, and the puppy will run in "S" Curves downwind of the actual blood drops.

The best way to get a pup to work slowly, and close to the line, is to give him one that is considerably older and colder. Your four-month-old pup should be able to work a line that is six, twelve or even twenty-four hours old. Remember that a line ages faster in the daytime than at night. The more challenging, older trail will hold the pup's attention better and force him to stay on the line and "dig for it" a little.

Keep in mind that a blood trail laid out for training is very different from a game animal's track. Each blood drop stays in place and continues to give off scent particles for days. A day-old trail of blood drops, a yard apart, is a whole lot easier than a day old coon track. Unless the conditions are very good the scent particles left by the coon will have largely blown away or burned off after half a day. If you are using tracking shoes, remember that the interdigital scent from the hoofs does not last as long as blood.

Age and maturity also play a role in slowing down a dog's working style. We have encountered countless cases in which a dog that tended to race as a puppy settled down with age and became a much slower, close-working tracker. Be patient. Time is on your side.

Wind, Rain and Darkness

If you are an experienced bird hunter or deer hunter, you are already in the habit of thinking about wind direction. When you place the hide at the end of your training line, consider whether you want the dog to "wind" it before the dog reaches the end of the line. The scent of a hide placed two hundred yards upwind from where you began your blood line may well pull a dog right to it. You cannot reprimand a dog for air scenting his way to the hide, and you will confuse the dog if you scold him for leaving the line because you do not realize that he is air scenting. When the dog raises his head and moves purposefully into the wind, you must think of what he might be doing. He may be attracted to a bedded deer, an old carcass or a gut pile. Always give the dog the benefit of reasonable doubt. If you reprimand him for relying upon his curiosity and intelligence, you may end up weakening the dog's initiative. This can make the difference between a plodding drudge and a great dog.

When working a blood line, wind direction makes a difference. A cross wind, which has blown for several hours, will end up sweeping scent particles from the blood and depositing them as far as ten yards down wind. Don't be concerned if your dog works off the line for good reason. For him headwinds and tailwinds along the line are easier to work.

There is no need to abandon a training line before you use it, just because the wind has blown hard, or because rain and snow have fallen on the line. You will be amazed at how little effect an inch of rain or snow has upon the scent to be tracked. The blood may be diluted, spread out and invisible to your eye, but this does not affect the dog. The blood is still giving off scent. Working a rained-out line is a good confidence builder for a handler.

Certain precautions should be taken. Avoid actually laying a line while it is raining hard. Such a line will not hold up as well as a line that dried before the rain came. For unknown reasons, blood laid on snow, which then melts away, becomes very difficult to track.

Much of a deer tracker's work is done at night, and nighttime is a good time to work a young dog on a training line. Use the same lights that you would use on a live deer call. Stumps and rocks have a different look in the glare of a light at night; you may find that your dog is spooky at first, but with exposure, he will become accustomed to the darkness in which he will be tracking many wounded deer.

Working Several Dogs on the Same Training Line

Marking and laying a training blood line is not very exciting. As a matter of fact, it can become such a chore that some would-be trainers never get around to doing it. There are ways to reduce the drudgery. Frequently, we work one dog on the line at 12 hours and another more advanced dog at 24 or 36 hours. If the second dog notices that he has a used line, he does not complain, and he gives no sign of "me-tooing" on the scent of the first dog. Each of the two dogs seems to encounter his own problems, and each makes his own mistakes in different places. Usually working two or three dogs on the same line will save you a lot of time. See if it works for you. In one case I was training Tommy, an experienced dog, on a 40-hour-old line in preparation for a blood tracking test. In this one case I did find that Tommy was misled by the mistakes of another dog that had worked the line at 20 hours.

Two trainers can each host training sessions on alternate weekends, laying out marked lines or blind lines for one another. Mutual support keeps interest up in this most tedious aspect of serious training.

In certain situations a dog that lacks enthusiasm for his work can be stimulated by working him with another dog at the same time. Let the indifferent dog lead and have a more enthusiastic dog follow a tracking leash length behind. Out of competitiveness or jealousy the lead dog will work harder to get the tracking work done ahead of the dog in the rear. Keep the dogs separated at the skin. They will be jealous of one another, and this is an excellent occasion for a serious dog fight. This motivation method is a bit extreme, and it should not be done on a routine basis.

Working Two Dogs Together When Tracking a Wounded Deer

If the right sort of calm, experienced back-up dog is available, it can be useful to work your dog on the easier sections of a real wounded deer's trail. The experienced dog can be used to start the line, and to come in to work out a difficult check after the less experienced dog has had a fair chance to solve it on his own. Avoid any situation in which the beginner dog is tempted to follow the experienced veteran instead of doing his own nose work. Working a real line can heighten a dog's enthusiasm for tracking, especially if the call culminates in jumping the wounded deer from its bed and following the fresh line. This scenario is likely to develop with leg-hit deer. The real danger of taking two dogs on a call is that it can weaken or destroy self-reliance in the less experienced of the two. Use this tactic with discretion. A variation of this training method is used extensively in Texas where both dogs are worked off lead.

Using an experienced dog as a back-up does limit your risks when you are breaking in a young dog on natural lines. The story of Alec and Sabina in Chapter 1 is a good example.

Turning on the Prey Drive

I have spoken with many dog buyers who were thinking of a tracking dog as a pure specialist in wounded deer tracking. Deer hunting is their own primary hunting interest, and they see little point in getting their dog involved in hunting other types of game that might prove to be distractions when tracking. Sometimes such an approach works because a dog can be exercised by "roading" with an ATV or by other means. In other situations exposure to different types of hunting situations can actually spark hunting desire or what the dog psychologists refer to as prey drive. Two recent and related cases taught me a lesson.

The first case involved a little Dachshund bitch that we had sold as a 12-week-old puppy with the guarantee. "Return the dog and we'll refund your money if she doesn't live up to your expectations as a tracking dog." After about a year and a half, the purchaser said he wanted to return her. She was lackadaisical, lacked desire, and didn't measure up to a very nice male that he had bought, who was related to some of our dogs.

The bitch came back, about 20% overweight, and she tracked a training line about as indifferently as her former owner had described it. She knew what to do, but didn't try very hard if things got tough. Otherwise, she was well trained with nice house manners and a friendly attitude. Her former owner makes his living as professional dog trainer, but his specialty is companion dogs and problem dogs, not hunting dogs. He had treated her as the type of dog that he understands very well. She spent her time in his fenced yard, in his house, and on training blood lines.

When I worked "Miss Indifferent" on a training blood line myself, I had to agree. Despite her early promise, this bitch just didn't seem to have the desire to do anything that required much enterprise. She was not a dog to dig scent out of the grass roots.

To help get her weight down we began putting her into our 11 acre running enclosure with Rip, our Beagle. Rip was a good gundog type of hound, who did clean work, ran medium speed and had a good mouth, which he used correctly. At first Miss Indifferent had all she could do to keep up. She was like a low, dark shadow, struggling along behind Rip with her tongue hanging out. As the extra pounds began to melt away, she moved up so that she ran on his shoulder, and even began to pick a few checks on her own. We heard her trail bark kick in loud and strong. It was clear that she enjoyed her new work.

The real surprise came when I took her out to work another training blood line. It was about 600 yards and aged about 12 hours. Now she was screaming with anticipation as I put the tracking collar and lead on her. She worked with the focus and desire that had been missing. It seemed that all the rabbit running had somehow flipped her "prey drive switch". She was a different dog.

My experience with Miss Indifferent was confirmed by another case. The professional dog trainer who had returned her to us, under the terms of the guarantee, had a grandson of my best tracking dog. I liked the working style of this dog, but the trainer, who is a perfectionist, wanted to see more drive and enthusiasm in tracking. He took the dog down to an acquaintance with a fenced running ground for starting Beagles. He left him there with four young Beagles for two weeks. His Dachshund had the opportunity to chase cottontails day and night, and there was a dog house, food and water when these things took his fancy. I can't say that this Spartan boot camp transformed the dog into a great rabbit hound, but it did put new desire into his tracking work. The trainer wrote:

"Not only did the starter pen time help his hunting instincts awaken,
but another payoff came this morning when I ran him on a 20 hour line that

I laid yesterday....This was a real challenging line that I laid to find out ex-
actly where we stood in preparation for the NATC tracking shoe test we hope
to take in June. Well, at the risk of sounding too bold, let me just say that he
was phenomenal!"

The dog went on to gain a Prize I with 100 points at the tracking test.

A strong dose of work on small game is not the solution to the motivations of every dog. But in the right circumstances, it may make a decisive difference.

Orders of Priority in Training Versatile Hunting Dogs

Some hounds should probably be maintained as wounded deer specialists only; it depends on the individual hound and the hound's aptitude to make distinctions between one task and another. With hounds it is always safest to begin first with blood tracking training. In the case of Dachshunds, we like to introduce rabbit trailing off lead after they are well-started in working blood lines. Most of the time this works, and the rabbit trailing teaches them to solve problems with their noses. However, for the very high strung or hyperactive Dachshund puppy, rabbit work can be counter-productive; it can produce a wild, flighty puppy that will not settle down and work a check intelligently and with deliberation.

The versatile hunting dogs that point, such as the Kurzhaars and Drahthaars, present a more delicate problem. These dogs are used both to track wounded deer by ground scent and to locate birds by air scent. Usually the bird finding work is more important to the owner than the occasional blood tracking tasks that may arise. The bird hunter may wisely prefer to introduce blood tracking *after* the dog has learned to locate birds by wind-scenting and to point them from a safe distance so that the birds will hold. If the dog has a strong tendency to search for birds by tracking, he will find fewer of them. With a highly developed desire to track birds, the dog will have a tendency to move in too close before he detects them and goes on point. As a result birds will be bumped out of range rather than pointed and held for the gun.

There is no simple cookbook answer to this problem. The trainer of a versatile pointing dog must consider his own hunting priorities and also the balance of natural instincts within the individual dog. In some gifted versatile Pointers there will be little problem in moving back and forth from ground scenting to air scenting modes of work. With other dogs there may be some conflict between the two. A dog trained first to find birds on the wind, may end up having a greater tendency to swing back and forth on a wounded deer line. This will not prevent him from being a useful dog to find wounded deer, but it is not ideal.

The versatile pointing dog, as developed by Europeans, has many varied tasks to learn. For Drahthaars the problem of having the JGV blood tracking test at the end of the training curriculum contributes to the lack of interest that some of these dogs show toward an old, cold blood line. They have already been imprinted on other things, and sometimes their genetically based tracking drive is much weaker than their drive to find birds.

Some dogs, and they are not all versatile pointing dogs, need a more structured training program in tracking to compensate for their lack of enthusiasm.

If you are new to the game of blood tracking, it is worthwhile to have an experienced handler help you evaluate your dog and develop the best training strategy for that particular dog. Marty Ryan of the Verein Deutsch Drahthaar/USA has developed a training program for blood tracking that is very different from the traditional system. It is described and discussed in Appendix D.

With dogs used for flushing, such as Spaniels and Labs, it would seem that the earliest introduction to blood tracking would be preferable. Again, the trainer has to use his wisdom and intuition; there are no absolutes in such matters. A truly gifted and versatile dog is not dependent on any special training sequence to realize its potential. The best tracking dog I ever owned was Clary, a Wirehaired Dachshund. Clary could run rabbits, but when pheasant hunting in similar cover, she readily understood what was needed and would go into her quartering, spaniel mode. At night she treed raccoons, and ignored rabbits. Clary was never asked to track a wounded deer until she was four years old, but she adapted readily to slow, painstaking work on very old, cold lines. She was a natural.

It is tempting to conclude from all these complex uncertainties that it is simplest and safest to train a dog for just one thing—tracking wounded big game. This is an illusion if it means that the blood tracking specialist will lie around, getting fat and out of condition during most of the year. It is a mistake if it means that the specialist-tracking dog has no opportunity to work in close cooperation with his handler except during deer season.

Training Older Dogs

This chapter has focused on the training of younger dogs for the simple reason that most handlers will acquire a puppy for the purpose of blood tracking. Of course, this is not always the case; a dog between two and eight years old can develop into an excellent tracker. Clary von Moosbach, my best tracking dog ever, saw her first blood line and tracked her first wounded deer when she was four years old. However, at this age she already had considerable hunting experience, and she knew how to use her nose.

In most cases it is impractical to introduce a dog older than eight years to blood tracking. A tracking dog is formed even more by practical field experience than by formal training. The formal training is important, but it cannot, by itself, produce a tracking dog that demonstrates his full potential. After you invest the time in formal training and add the years when the finer points are learned through practical experience on real wounded deer, there is not much time left to enjoy an accomplished, finished dog. At twelve or thirteen physical or mental weakness compel most dogs to retire.

If a middle-aged dog has been a "brush-wise" hunting dog and knows how to use his nose, this dog will have a real head start over the green, young dog. The potential of this older dog may be greater than that of a green dog, who has never done anything.

Avoid buying a mature dog that is for sale because he is already running deer. You don't want a dog that is going to run hot deer lines any more than the seller does. A confirmed deer chaser will be a lot harder to keep on the old, cold line of a wounded deer than a dog that has never been seriously involved with deer in the first place. He will be much more difficult to train than a young dog with no bad habits.

Tracking dogs should perceive healthy deer in the woods as non-game to be ignored. A deer should not become game to be tracked unless it is wounded. Dogs that come to blood tracking with a lack of interest in healthy deer will not become deer chasers when they are asked to track a "designated" wounded deer. Initially, there may be a short period of confusion concerning healthy deer, but this is easy to straighten out. The bonding and discipline of a dog and handler who have hunted other game will certainly carry over into the new activity of tracking wounded deer, both on the training level and when tracking the real thing.

The same Clary, mentioned above, was versatile enough to hunt rabbits and pheasants by day and raccoons at night. She would quickly sense the game that was being hunted and adjust her working style accordingly. When she was four, and I first began to track wounded deer with her, she did chase several deer, which she bumped when hunting off lead. This ended within a week after a few verbal reprimands. Later I often saw Clary in the moonlight searching for coon scent where deer had just been feeding. The deer were not a distraction.

Hagar, a NAVHDA Drahthaar ("German" Wirehaired Pointer) owned by Ralph Williams, was an exceptional bird dog, who worked weekends pointing and retrieving pheasants at exclusive, private shooting clubs. When Hagar was being tested for blood tracking performance, he pointed a grouse on the test line, settled down and then finished tracking the blood line with the best possible score of 100. Hagar remained a disciplined, handler-responsive dog on the pheasant preserves. Tracking wounded deer did not change this, although he encountered many deer while working birds.

In the case of Clary and Hagar, their previous training, and their awareness of healthy deer as "non-game" actually made them more effective blood trackers.

Physical and Psychological Conditioning

Hagar and Clary, the two dogs mentioned in the section above, were involved in other hunting activities in addition to blood tracking. This made it easy to keep them physically and mentally sharp because there were so many different aspects of their work to be practiced and polished. Hagar, the versatile pointing dog practiced water work and retrieving, even in the hottest weather. Clary, the Dachshund, was prepared for AKC field trials, which are run on cottontails, and she won a good many of these. Both dogs used their noses and their muscles on a year round basis. Cowdogs and "hawg dogs" have similar advantages. They work all year around and conditioning takes care of itself.

There is a problem, however, for the specialist—a dog who is never asked to do anything else but track wounded deer. If the specialized blood tracker lolls around in his kennel between hunting seasons, he gets soft and puts on weight. His attitude and his hunting desire may deteriorate as well. This dog needs physical and mental exercise, and it is very difficult to provide this by means of practice blood lines when the real lines are not available. It would require a great many artificial blood lines to keep a dog fit, if these were his only exercise. These lines would take many hours for the handler/trainer to lay out. Also, this could very well bore the dog and is no way to maintain his enthusiasm and mental sharpness.

Long hikes, off lead, are a good means of conditioning if the tracking dog handles well and does not take off on his own. For larger dogs, "roading", that is running the dog in a harness with a long lead, can be part of the solution. This can be done from horseback, from an ATV or some other type of vehicle on farm and logging roads where there is no traffic. These techniques are used effectively by competitive bird dog handlers. But just exercising a tracking dog's heart, lungs and legs is not enough. He needs to use his nose; he needs to revitalize all that sophisticated neuron circuitry that runs from the nose, to and through the brain.

You may have observed that a Beagle, brought out after a long lay-off, will fumble on what should be an easy rabbit. After a few days of concentration on rabbit scent, the hound's nose will be working much better. The same thing can be observed in tracking dogs.

Practically speaking, we humans have no "nose" at all, so it is hard for us to imagine that a dog uses a great deal of nervous energy in using his nose at high performance levels. The tracking dog really gets tired on a tough natural line, but this is not a matter of muscular fatigue. It is much more a nervous or mental burnout.

Try taking your dog on a leash for a half-mile walk in the woods on a warm day. This will not be much stress on the dog. Then work the dog on a difficult training line for the same distance. The dog will probably not travel as fast, but he will pant and show that he is putting out considerable effort. It is not the pace that is tiring him. In part, it is the mental effort of focusing the whole scenting system, nose and brain, on the scent line. A good tracking Dachshund can track an easy line all day long, but on difficult lines, which require intense concentration, I have observed a burn-out and decline in effectiveness after two or three hours.

André Brun, a Norwegian guide who specializes in blood tracking, makes the point that the tracking dog is rapidly and continuously passing scent-laden air samples over the olfactory surfaces of its nasal passages. This rapid and controlled sniffing and exhaling of air through the nose is hard work. There is much that we humans do not understand about the world of scent, but we can observe that an effective dog is working hard even when the difficulty of the track requires him to move at a slow walking pace. Whether he tracks for 200 yards or for four miles, the dog will give a better performance if he comes to the track physically and mentally fit.

With Dachshunds we have found that running cottontail rabbits in the off-season is a good way of keeping mature dogs in working condition. The more experienced Dachshunds understand that rabbits are recreation, and they are not tempted to fool around with them when wearing the tracking collar and lead. When these dogs were younger there were a few "misunderstandings", to be sure, when they left a tough deer line for a rabbit. These mistakes were easy for a handler to recognize. The dogs soon got over any interest in cottontails when there were more important things to be done.

My Southern Black Mouth Cur had no problems being a coon dog, squirrel dog and wounded deer dog, all at the same time. I could hunt coons with her one night and track a deer the next. She always understood her designated task. Tree dog activities were a way of keeping her in shape through much of the year.

Certainly an intelligent scent hound, bird dog, or herding dog can do multiple tasks, all year around, to maintain physical and mental conditioning. Such a tracking dog stays healthy and works well into his senior years, when his acquired experience makes him especially valuable. Some dogs are bred to be versatile, but introducing varied, year-round scenting activities will improve almost any dog in the long run.

Summary

- Set up training lines with problems for the dog to solve.

- Lay training lines where there will be distractions of healthy deer and other wildlife.

- Encourage your dog to slow down to a convenient speed.

- Work the dog on training lines in the dark and under difficult conditions.

- Middle aged dogs that have learned to use their noses in other types of hunting or searching can readily be trained to find wounded deer.

- The blood tracking dog does not have to be a narrow specialist. For most breeds other types of hunting are compatible with and even enhance tracking capability.

Chapter 12

Training After the First Season of Live Tracking

A loss of interest in tracking after the first season occurs frequently, and often it is simply an indication that the dog is passing through the adolescent phase of his psychological development. But there can be a more enduring problem. Dogs that have been in on some finds, or have found deer on their own, may lose all interest in working artificially prepared blood lines afterwards. Of course, they know a fake when they smell one. It is probably not as much the thawed blood as the absence of other things that should go with the blood: body scent, the pattern of scent particles, the odor of disturbed ground cover. Handlers become frustrated when their dogs, who have been finding wounded deer successfully in the woods, fail miserably in a tracking test because they do not even attempt to track. The introduction of the "tracking shoes" (Fährtenschuhe) as a means of laying tracks makes the scent lines more realistic and more attractive to the dog.

Fährtenschuhe (Tracking Shoes, Scent Shoes)

One European method of training, involving the use of tracking shoe has spread widely in North America and it merits our serious attention. The German word for these tracking shoe is Fährtenschuh, pronounced in German as "Fair-ten-shoe". Probably it is safer for us, as Americans, to call them tracking or scent shoes. In simplest terms the tracking shoes are a pair of sandals to which deer feet are attached. This footwear is used to simulate the scent and the ground disturbance left by a walking deer.

The tracking shoe, strapped to the soles of the tracklayer's boots, leaves the scent of the attached deer hooves, including scent from the interdigital glands, as the tracklayer moves through the woods. A very small amount of deer blood, is dripped or trampled into the track, especially at the beginning of the line.

The tracking shoes cannot fully replicate the scent of a real deer. For example, there is no body scent or tarsal gland scent. Unquestionably, an important role is played by scent from the interdigital glands, which are found on all four feet. The slit-like openings of these glands are located on top of the foot where the two parts of the hoof come together so there is no direct contact of the gland openings with the ground. However, the abundant waxy substance from the glands, sort of a "toe jam", seems to scent the area surrounding the track. The dog does not necessarily work from hoof print to hoof print.

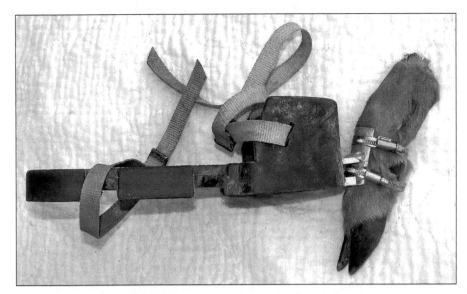

The Waidwerk tracking shoe (Fährtenschuh) holds the deer foot with hose clamps mounted at the back of the rubber and aluminum base.

For some reason, the tracking shoes are amazingly effective in motivating a dog to focus on the training line. The enthusiasm, working style, and body language of the dog are very much like what one sees when a dog works a real wounded deer. The track is easier to prepare, and clearly more realistic than a line of dripped or dabbed deer blood.

German tracking authorities maintain that it is the associated ground disturbance that makes the tracking shoe so effective. I am not persuaded that this is a sufficient explanation because I have laid lines in a dry summer woods underlain with hard, sun-baked clay. Very little ground disturbance could have occurred, and yet my tracking dog was able to work a 26-hour line without difficulty. I suspect that she was smelling the general track area permeated by interdigital scent.

Tracking shoes have been in use for well over a century in Europe, but their use is now more widespread than ever before. Lars Haugaard, a forest ranger and professional tracker who uses Bavarians in Denmark, explained that he uses scent shoes exclusively when he trains his hounds on artificial lines. They are especially valuable in training a dog to pay attention to the individual scent of a particular deer when there is no blood.

Some of the current models of tracking shoes are a vast improvement over the crude earlier versions that have been used. I especially like the model made by Waidwerk, which can be sent to you directly from Germany by Leroi Jagdt und Sport GMBH (See Appendix A). The Waidwerk tracking shoe has a flexible polyurethane sole and heel cup which makes it much easier to walk in rough terrain. It fastens to any hunting boot with nylon straps. The deer hooves are fastened to the tracking shoe behind the heel by means of hose clamps mounted on sophisticated aluminum welding. In the United States tracking shoes are currently available through the online store at unitedbloodtrackers.org.

The best way to use the tracking shoe is to carry a small bottle of deer blood with you as you lay the track. At the beginning and then at intervals of about two hundred yards make a small circle of spattered blood and trample it with the deer hooves attached to your tracking shoes.

In normal training circumstances much less blood is used with the scent shoes than would be appropriate with the dripping or dabbing method. The standard amount of blood for the conventional German 1000-meter test is 250 ml of blood and for Fährtenschuh Test 100 ml, which is less than half that amount. As you introduce your dog to this kind of track, you can use more than the normal amount of blood at first to ease the transition.

The tracking shoes (I am tempted to call them toe jammers), can be stored in a plastic bag in the freezer, with feet attached, between track layings. The same pair of hooves will stay effective, despite repeated freezings and thawings if not completely dried out or decayed.

For someone who becomes seriously involved in training tracking dogs, it may make sense to use the tracking shoes exclusively after the very young puppy stage. Personally, I find that it takes less time to lay a training line with this method. It holds the dog's interest, and it is very effective in training for the real thing. The results have overcome my early skepticism, and I am now relying heavily upon my "toe jammers". Since the publication of the second edition of *Tracking Dogs for Finding Wounded Deer* in 2006, the use of tracking shoes has really caught on and is very widespread among serious trackers on both sides of the Atlantic.

Raymond Holohan's Buck Shock Tracking Shoes come in a size suitable for women.

In the previous chapters on training to track, the use of tracking shoes for puppies was mentioned but not fully explained for simplicity's sake. Tracking shoes are not essential for puppies, but they can be useful. I recently got a report of a seven-month-old Dachshund puppy that tracked closely and found a deer on a natural, 40-hour line without visible blood. It is unlikely that the pup would have accomplished this if it had not had very early training with tracking shoes.

German trainers of the renowned Hanover Hounds take the natural track approach to the ultimate level. Their traditional method is to train the "Hannoverscher" on the scent lines of naturally moving deer that have been observed by the trainer. This method is very time consuming and requires almost monastic dedication. The final results are impressive, but most likely this approach will not appeal to many Americans.

Let's not forget that excellent tracking dogs have been trained by the conventional method of laying a blood line as described in Chapter 8. You don't have to begin training by making an expensive purchase of the tracking shoes.

American Perspectives on Other European Training Methods

We Americans can learn from many aspects of European tracking, but we should also keep in mind that European game, customs and circumstances are different from our own. One of the most useful training techniques to come to our shores from Europe is Fährtenschuh work as described above. Another is training for Verweisen, a word the Germans use to describe the dog's action of showing, pointing out, to the handler sign that may be important.

Training for Verweisen is accomplished by putting bits of meat along the artificial line and warmly praising the dog when he stops to check them out. Traditionally the Germans use bits of lung tissue for this. Praising the dog whenever he indicates a good blood spot on a sparse, artificially laid blood line, or on a natural track, will reinforce this training.

For a long time to come, many American dogs will do most of their learning on the job after they have completed no more than basic training. Some dogs have begun service right out of boot camp and have concluded their careers by participating in over 300 calls and finding over 100 deer. Few European dogs ever get this volume of opportunity, with much of it coming from challenging cases during bow season.

By all means give your dog formal training, but remember that training alone, even if it is very sophisticated training, cannot take the place of hands-on, nose-on experience with wounded deer.

There are other differences between the North American and European approach to blood tracking. East of the Atlantic handlers and test judges like to see a dog work very briskly if scenting conditions permit. We Americans, who track many deer during the archery seasons, have to contend with certain problems unique to bowhunting. A slower, more precise dog is preferable when tracking a bowshot deer. As explained earlier in this chapter, it is important for Americans to "read" all the blood sign in the case of a bowshot deer. Therefore, unlike the Europeans we must encourage tracking at a speed that makes possible a thorough observation of the trail. This is not so important when the deer has been hit by a high-power rifle. Bowhunting is still uncommon in Europe, but its popularity is growing.

European Off-Lead Methods; Pre-GPS

Before the invention of GPS instruments the Germans developed two remarkable off-lead methods of using a highly trained dog to guide the handler to a wounded or dead animal. These methods, Totverbellen and Totverweisen, could be used in parts of the United States where dogs are allowed to search freely.

Both of these German "T" words refer to a means of announcing the location of dead game that the dog has found; they do not involve the tracking process itself. Training for blood tracking is a separate operation that normally comes first. In German hunting language, Totverbellen literally means barking at death or the kill. In Totverbellen the dog tracks off lead and announces that he has found the kill by barking so that the handler can locate him.

Verweisen means "to indicate" or "to direct". In Totverweisen the dog finds the dead animal, returns to the handler, indicates the find and leads the handler to the kill.

Bringsel attached to collar

Totverbellen training begins by teaching the dog to "speak" on command. A common way to do this is to show food at the dog's kennel gate and then withhold it until the dog barks in frustration. At that point the dog is praised and given its food. Soon the dog learns to bark on command and then is commanded to bark at a fresh deer skin in order to receive a reward. It is then sent out to a deer skin, placed at progressively longer distances, and always rewarded. Finally this training is extended to a freshly killed deer.

In Totverweisen the handler sends out the dog to track down and find the wounded deer while the hunter sits down and, according to tradition, smokes his pipe. The dog wears a Bringsel or short leather strap hanging down from his collar. When he finds the deer he flips the Bringsel up into his mouth and carries it back to the handler as an indication that the deer has been found. The handler then snaps on the leash, and the dog leads him to the dead game.

Totverweisen training is begun only after the dog has been force trained to retrieve. The Bringsel training is an extension of this retriever training. Totverweisen training begins by having the dog retrieve a Bock (retrieving buck) that has been placed on a deer carcass or skin. The Bock consists of a broomstick-sized dowel with four smaller, shorter dowels protruding from the ends at right angles to hold it off the ground. The Bock is thus easy for the dog to pick up. As in Totverbellen training, the dog is sent out for longer and longer distances to retrieve the Bock, which is placed on the carcass or skin. A short blood line is laid out to guide the dog, who continues to indicate his find by returning with the Bock. In the last stage of training, a heavy strap is attached to the collar so that it dangles almost to the ground. The dog goes out to the skin or carcass, but this time there is no Bock. The dog is frantic to retrieve something. After a few tries, he grabs the strap hanging from his collar, returns to his handler and receives lavish praise. At this point, it is an easy transition to have the dog flipping the shorter Bringsel up into his mouth to indicate the find.

There are some variations in the training methods used for both Totverbellen and Totverweisen. Training must be adapted to the temperament of the dog. Some dogs learn with great ease to bark when they find the game. Other dogs, with different genetics, may be so hard to train for Totverbellen that it is not worth the trouble.

Totverweisen with the Bringsel is most often used for the versatile hunting dog breeds like Drahthaars and Kurzhaars. These dogs are force trained to retrieve anyway for their upland bird and waterfowl work. It is not a big step to move on to Totverweisen once the dog will reliably retrieve under any circumstances.

Both off lead methods, Totverbellen and Totverweisen, make the most sense for big, powerful dogs with the capability to bay or pull down the wounded animal if it is still alive.

Since the development of the electronic tracking collar, Totverbellen and Totverweisen are less of a practical necessity than was once the case in off lead situations. The GPS collar and receiver accomplish the same purpose in locating their dog quickly when the game has been found. GPS tracking equipment is now used extensively in Europe and in the parts of North America where off lead tracking is legal.

No doubt there are some handlers who see modern electronic gadgets as interfering with the traditional and natural relationship of handler and dog. Totverbellen and Totverweisen are a means of avoiding modern technology and also the $700 plus price of electronic tracking equipment.

Reflections on Training Methods

All dogs are not the same; for this and other reasons there are many different valid ways to train a dog for blood tracking. Excellent dogs have been developed simply by working a dog on multiple natural lines of real wounded deer. Some of these might be easy 50-yard tracks to a dead deer. Others might be so long and challenging that they are beyond the young dog's line sense and attention span. Dogs with great natural abilities have been successfully trained by simply dragging a deer skin through the woods and later asking the dog to track it. This method has many disadvantages, but it can work. We all know some humans who have done amazingly well with little or no quality education.

At the other end of the spectrum there are some handlers who use the intricate, progressive steps used by those who train dogs to track human beings, a situation in which prey drive plays a very small role in the dog's original motivation. Some dogs that have little natural desire to track wild game can be trained in this way. This can work for "versatile pointing dogs" that are not quite as versatile as they should be. See Appendix D.

Trainers, like dogs, are not all the same. The trainer and handler can have many different motivations. He may be primarily interested in training a dog to pass a test and acquire a title. Or the motivation may come primarily out of his ethical consciousness and the practical necessity to conserve good venison or find trophy antlers for a client. Tracking with a dog does not have to be a passion, but for some it does become a passion as will be discussed in Chapter 21.

Darren Doran in New Jersey is an outstanding trainer and tracking dog handler. The following quotation from Darren illustrates how innovative and meticulous his training lines have become. Not everyone will find the time to train with Darren's methods, but this extra effort can be worth it when you have a very talented dog.

> So I decided that for my next line I would try to make it as close to a real hunting track as I could. In New Jersey you are allowed to bait deer, and most of my tracks start in a bait pile. I have a spot in a natural county park, which holds a lot of deer that are not hunted. I train here frequently, and I decided that I would place bait in the park in two spots. After the deer started feeding there I would start a training line at one bait pile and track through to the second about 300 yds before the line ended. After about two weeks I had the deer cleaning up about 25 lbs of corn every two days or so.

I had a trail camera out at what was going to be my hit site and photos confirmed that deer were there regularly, and at any time of day. Mornings and evenings were the best, just like in hunting season. I also had raccoons visiting the corn at night as well.

I decided that Friday after work I would pack in another 25 lbs of corn and the materials needed to make the training line. I dumped the corn and put on my tracking shoes. This line was going to mimic a bow shot deer from a high tree stand with a pass-through the liver and gut. I brought an old half of an arrow and put it in a plastic bag, poured blood on it and let the fletchings soak it up. I put a wad of hair at the hit site and dropped in the arrow. I was going to walk out of the hit site for 30 yards and then put down a small squirt of blood every third time that my right foot hit the ground. After the 30 yard mark there would be no more blood on the line. I tried to walk out so that I wasn't on a deer run but there were tracks everywhere. I wanted to make it as evident as possible that Theo was taking the line and not just any deer leaving the bait. One thing I want to mention is that all my training materials used on a training track come from the same deer. The feet, blood, hair, and skin and not only that I only use materials that come from a deer that has been shot and run before it dies. I don't use road kills or deer that die instantly from a gunshot.

I believe a deer that has been shot and is going to die smells differently to a dog or predator than a healthy one. I see a difference in my dogs tracking style on a deer that we find as opposed to one that is hit high in the back or shoulder. I want my training lines to be as close to real thing as possible.

Summary

- The German scent shoes (Fährtenschuhe) can be a very effective means of training puppies and mature dogs.

- It is useful to train your dog to indicate wounded deer sign.

- A GPS collar is a simple, non-traditional way to locate an off-lead dog that has found the deer.

Chapter 13

Working Dogs Off Lead

There is a deep divide in American hunting traditions. In most of the United States outside of the Deep South and Texas, the idea of allowing tracking dogs to work off lead is politically unthinkable as of 2016. If the early advocates of legalizing the use of tracking dogs had insisted that the dogs should be released to bay and stop a live wounded deer, they would have accomplished nothing. We would still be in the pre-1975 era when little could be done, legally, in those cases when a wounded animal could not be eye-tracked.

In the 1970s Tom Scott did advocate releasing dogs after a successful experiment on the Crane Naval Ammunition Depot in Indiana. Scott got nowhere when he tried to convince the Indiana DNR to extend the procedure to the state as a whole. Indiana did eventually legalize the use of **leashed** tracking dogs, but they were required to work on leash at all times no matter what the circumstances.

As will be more thoroughly discussed in Chapter 27, the histories of deer hunting have been very different in the Deep South and in Texas. In each of these areas, attitudes about the use of dogs in deer hunting have very different roots. In the South dogs were and still are used to drive deer to the hunter's gun. This is becoming more and more restricted today because it is incompatible with quality deer management on private properties. Nonetheless, the use of tracking dogs off lead for the specific situation of recovering wounded deer does not clash with traditionally held views about deer hunting, as has been the case in the North.

There are advantages, as well as disadvantages, in working a dog off lead. The most important positive feature of working the dog off lead is that a higher percentage of wounded deer will be recovered. In the "leash at all times" areas of most of the country, the recovery rate will seldom rise above 33% unless the handler turns down many tracks that are uncertain and might, or might not, result in a find.

If dogs can be worked off lead, the recovery rate will be substantially greater, at least 50%, and sometimes more than that depending on the cover and terrain. Some of the wounded deer bayed and dispatched by the handler would actually have a good chance of surviving. For an example, a deer hit high in the back above the spine can walk all day and keep away from a leashed dog. With such an injury this deer cannot run very well. He will be stopped by a "bay dog" working off lead. The same is true for broken leg hits. If the coyotes are not too aggressive, a three legged deer can make it in the South where there is little snow in winter.

Big, strong breeds are usually better bay dogs, but they have another advantage. They are less enticing to the coyotes that are always present in deer country and are certainly more aggressive after dark. A Dachshund is not a good candidate for off-lead work at night.

One disadvantage of working off lead is that it allows the handler to see and interpret much less blood sign from the wounded animal. This can be a significant factor in bowhunting seasons. However, at Tara Plantation in Mississippi, as described in Chapter 24, almost all the deer are shot by bowhunters. The Tara guides work their tracking Labs off lead and do very well.

For working off lead, southern style, it is very important to have a calm, intelligent dog that handles well and is responsive to the handler. This is one reason why the right sort of Labs are so popular as tracking dogs in the South. A big-running, competition bred coonhound would not be a good choice.

No one in the North, "Leashed Tracking Dog Land", can equal the recovery rates achieved by dedicated off-lead trackers like JJ Scarborough and Mike Lopez, whose stories follow in this chapter. But the dangerous risks to the off lead tracking dog are very real. Use of the Garmin Astro and Alpha collars is helpful, but this does not solve all the problems

First there is the risk of crossing busy roads and highways. JJ Scarborough lost a gifted young Drahthaar that was killed by a vehicle as he was tracking a wounded deer. To be sure, small dogs like Dachshunds are less visible to vehicle drivers than 80-pound Drahthaars, but no dog is completely safe when tracking off lead.

As a bay dog, a large, Lab-sized breed is obviously more qualified than a small dog. But baying a big, heavy-antlered buck is dangerous for any dog, particularly if we are dealing with a younger, inexperienced dog that has not learned to keep his distance. An antler tine in the abdomen will require expensive surgery, and the dog will be laid up for at least a month. A lung puncture will probably kill the dog.

A very aggressive dog that tries to close in and grab the buck is the type most likely to be injured. He may get way with this a few times, but eventually he will be gored. The most effective bay dog stays out about 20 feet from the deer and barks until handler and hunter arrive. And of course it is much safer to shoot the wounded deer, if the bay dog is not jumping around, close to the animal.

Coyotes are a real problem for small dogs working off lead. A Dachshund has no chance against two or three coyotes that are homing in on the same deer. Off lead work is for big dogs. As a long time handler of Dachshunds I believe that these small dogs make a lot of sense for the North. If I were tracking off lead in the South, I would work with a much bigger breed.

JJ Scarborough and his tracking Lab Rosie are fine examples of off-lead work at its best. JJ is a professional forester, operating out of Macon, Georgia, and his position allows him to take a great number of calls during Georgia's very long deer hunting season.

Rosie is a yellow Lab bred by a backyard breeder in Macon. The sire was reputedly an English Lab. The dam was out of field breeding. Sound, practical stuff, but nothing distinguished. Rosie is an accomplished retriever able to handle multiple blind retrieves with ease, but what she loves best is tracking wounded deer. She doesn't particularly like artificial blood trails or command and obey retriever training. According to JJ "She enjoys (natural) tracking much more because she is able to take charge and doesn't have to be structured like during retriever training."

The following account by JJ of his experiences with Rosie is a wonderful guide for Southern off-lead trackers.

JJ Scarborough from Macon, GA, and his super talented tracking Lab Rosie

For the first 4½ years she worked exclusively on lead. On lead she recovered the deer about 40% of the time and about 1/3 of the deer that were recovered were live recoveries. After that she has worked both on and off lead. The last three years have been almost exclusively off lead when highways and property lines will allow. Off lead she has recovered about 60% of the deer with about half of them live recoveries.

I have worked her on lead at the beginning of old tracks, but I prefer to let her work off lead any time conditions are difficult. I know she can work them out better without me and the lead.

When she bays, 10 or 11 yards is the distance she likes to stay away from a standing deer in fairly open woods. When the woods are thick or the deer is weak or lying down she will be closer. She will grab a swimming deer by the tail if she is able to catch it. I've seen her drown a weak buck. She has grabbed and killed some does, weak bucks, and hogs on land when she could tell they were really weak. She runs silent on track, squeals in high pitch when she sees fleeing game, and chop barks when animals turn to face her. She will eat from the tail end of the deer any time she is left alone with a find for very long.

JJ and Rosie have had some bad experiences:

This year was the first year she was injured while baying. A big boar hog cut her just before deer season this year. Three different deer got her with antlers this year. The first two got her with two tines each that were flesh wounds in the right ham and butt area. The last one went between her ribs on the right side and punctured her lung. The lung didn't collapse. It really bothered me and the vets but didn't slow her down at all. She even swam in 2 ponds and caught the deer about ¾ of mile after it hit her. I know that she has been run over many times by deer and hogs without getting hurt. They don't usually catch her unless it's real thick.

We lost her for almost 14 hours when she pulled away from another handler on lead. She got the lead hung up while baying over half a mile away. I owe Ken Parker and A.J. Niette, who tag teamed to re-track the deer and find her. She was sitting on top of the deer with water running on both sides when we found her.

Her oldest continuous track with recovery was 47 hours and 472 yards. She has had two deer hit by automobiles while we were tracking them. The longest track ending in recovery was 4.25 miles. She tracked one over 6 miles on lead that got away. She recovered six in one day in 2010. I have dispatched deer that she bayed that had only one front hoof shot and hanging from below the dew claws when we found her.

Rosie's numbers lifetime (at age ten) are as of February 10, 2016: 1064 calls and 510 recoveries, of which 261 were live recoveries. Only deer, hogs and bear are included in these numbers.

Lucy, a Lacy Dog owned and handled by Mike Lopez off lead, found 101 deer in 2014-2015 and 140 deer in 2015-2016 season.

Mike Lopez, who lives in Georgia, is a friend of JJ Scarborough. Mike is a passionate tracker, who ranges out across the Gulf States tracking wounded deer off lead with Lucy, his Lacy:

While tracking off leash, the handler has to have a bond with his dog, to trust her to go out and determine, by herself, which deer is wounded. The handler has to know that no matter how far out the dog is, no matter how old the track, no matter what things are out there, his dog will stay on the right deer.

If the handler and dog don't have a special bond, off-leash tracking is not feasible. Because of our bond I am the only person Lucy will track for. When she comes in to check on me and sees me, she whips around and runs back to the track and continues. The only exception is if she has jumped the deer and is trying to stop it, or has it bayed up.

Texas Off-Lead Tracking

As discussed in Chapters 6 and 24, the use of dogs off lead in Texas has origins that grow out of their use as cow dogs. Up to two dogs may be used off lead at the same time. The traditional training method is to let a beginner dog work with an experienced veteran. Little leashed work is done in the majority of the Texas counties west of the eastern Gulf counties. As of 2016 the use of tracking dogs was still illegal in five counties of southeastern Texas.

When I visited Roy Hindes in south Texas during 2002 his veteran "Blue Dogs", out of his old family breeding, worked slowly and carefully off lead on old, cold lines. The wind was always blowing and the exposed soil, between the patches of prickly pear cactus, was hard, dry clay. A tracking dog had to pick his way carefully, finding scent here and there where there was low vegetation to collect it. The handler had to deal with mesquite and impenetrable whitebrush. In that country the off-lead methods being used seemed to make a lot of sense!

Tracking Collars and GPS

Dogs were used off lead in the South and Texas long before there was any fancy electronic paraphernalia. A dog bell would have been considered High Tech! But certainly developments like the Wildlife Materials tracking collars and the Garmin Astro and Alpha made off-lead tracking more efficient and less risky. The tracking collars with transmitters require line-of-sight communication between collar and a receiver with a somewhat bulky antenna. The Garmin collars and Sport Dog GPS collars rely on satellite communication for location, but the dog/handler communication is still by radio and does not work out of a canyon.

The European Approach to Off-Lead Tracking

The Europeans have been tracking wounded game with dogs for centuries and methods have become standardized in practice. The tracking dog starts the track on lead, and if a wounded animal is jumped from its bed the dog is then released to chase, bay and stop its flight. Today tracking dogs in Europe are almost always equipped with some sort of satellite-dependent tracking collar.

Training Dogs for Off-Lead Tracking

There are several ways to train a dog for off-lead tracking. As previously described, the older, traditional method in Texas has been to work the beginner dog off-lead with an experienced off-lead tracking dog while actually trailing a wounded deer. Of course not all Texans have access to an experienced dog.

In the South, east of Texas, the training method described above by JJ Scarborough is widely used and works very well. In training, and on the first live wounded deer trails, the dog is worked on a long lead. This gives the handler more control to guide or correct the dog, when needed.

As the dog becomes more experienced, he is released on the line. If the scent line, at the start, is very old or difficult, the tracking dog may be kept on lead until it is clear that he has the right scent and is making progress.

Randy Vick (right) and Annie with a big Georgia buck she found. Annie is a Kemmer Mountain Cur who works on lead and off lead where it is safe to do so. Mountain curs were developed as squirrel dogs, but Annie prefers wounded deer.

Summary

- In most of Texas and in the Deep South the use of tracking dogs off lead is legal and widespread.

- Working tracking dogs off lead elsewhere in the USA is politically and legally impossible.

- The percentage of deer recoveries rises to above 50% if the dogs can be released.

- The use of GPS collars has made off-lead tracking even more effective.

- When dogs working off lead catch up to and bay antlered bucks, they can be injured.

- Many of the training techniques used to develop leashed tracking dogs have an application in training dogs that will eventually work off lead.

Chapter 14

Special Tracking Situations I:
Wounds in the Body Cavity

The art and science of tracking wounded deer does not end with the training preparation we have just reviewed. The tactics to be used when tracking real wounded animals are also very important. A good blood tracker realizes that deer behave differently depending on the location of the wound. When actually tracking a specific deer, it is not very useful to think about wounded deer in general. Depending on the wound and the individual deer, the prospects for survival or death vary enormously. The kind of trail the wounded deer leaves will also be a reflection of how it was wounded. The dog handler may be able to get reliable information in advance on how and where the deer was wounded, but when he begins to track the deer, he should always verify this information for himself. He must be as tactful as possible in the process. Generally, bowhunters can give more reliable information than firearms hunters because they are closer to the game, and often they see the arrow enter the deer. However, even the most experienced bowhunters sometimes have to admit later that their arrow actually entered higher, or farther back, than seemed to be the case.

In this chapter we will discuss various types or categories of wounding hits within the deer's body cavity. In some cases broadheads can produce results quite different than those of a slug or a bullet that strikes in the same place. This is especially true in chest shots. To make the explanations simpler to follow, we have treated chest shots under separate archery and firearm headings.

In connection with each type of wound, we will review the "sign" or evidence for that sort of wound, the possible behavior and survivability of a deer hit in this way, and finally the best techniques for finding such a deer. This sounds simple, clear and straightforward. Always keep in mind, however, that deer don't read hunting books; they sometimes do what is unexpected or untypical, and a good tracker will keep his mind open to a broad range of possibilities.

Even in the case of bowhunting, it is difficult to recall shot placement and even more difficult to predict the results of the shot. In bowhunting, where the lethal damage is localized in the immediate area cut by the broadhead, a difference of a quarter of an inch up or down, forward or backward, can create entirely different situations. It can be the difference between a severed major artery and a non-lethal wound that slices a few small blood vessels.

Even organ hits cannot be summed up in a simple generalization of what will happen and when. For example, two broadheads passing through different parts of a lung can produce either a quick kill or a non-lethal wound. When a beginner gets into this new subject, he should not worry about all these fine points and distinctions. The basics must come first, but he should be aware that things can be complicated and unpredictable.

In blood tracking with a dog after the hunter's search has failed, we are less likely to get simple, straightforward situations than would be the case in ordinary hunting. Cases where a tracking dog is called in are generally difficult ones in which the deer did not do what was expected. This chapter contains more detail than most beginners will need to start tracking. Beginning trackers may choose, for now, to look only at the "Summary" of this chapter. It is designed to give the essentials of the subject without loading the reader down with technical details. After some field experience it will be easy to absorb the rest.

Let's consider all of the types of wounded deer cases that actually occur in the field. I would set them up into seven broad categories:

1. chest wounds
2. stomach, liver and intestinal wounds
3. wounds to the legs that break the supporting bones
4. flesh wounds not involving vital organs or the bones
5. wounds temporarily or permanently damaging the spine
6. neck wounds
7. head wounds including damage to the jaws

In this chapter we will deal only with wounds of the first two categories listed above. In the next chapter we will deal with the five other types of wounds.

Chest Wounds: Archery
Overview

Deer are tough! When I began my blood tracking career, it was difficult for me to imagine a deer going very far with an arrow passing deeply into or through its chest. When, in my lively imagination, I applied such a wounding scenario to myself, I could sense that hemorrhage would be turning out the lights after a few minutes at the most. What has been hammered into me ever since, through many miles of tracking, is that deer are incomparably tougher than human beings. When I began tracking wounded deer, I undoubtedly gave up too soon on certain calls because I underestimated the enormous vitality of the animal that I had been called to track and find.

For obvious reasons, trackers do not have to worry much about heart shots; the heart is an ideal target, but it is also a small target. The practical hunter is more likely to think of the heart/lung area, and in fact more deer will die from shots in the lungs than in the heart.

If you track often during bow season, you will be called in cases when the deer is hit in the lungs or when the lungs have been missed by a narrow margin. Such cases will be rare when you work with shotgun and rifle hunters. It is possible for a broadhead to pass completely through the chest, narrowly missing major veins and arteries, and not produce a fatal wound. When this type of pass-through occurs, you and your dog are likely to be called to help. On the other hand, a rifle bullet or shotgun slug does much more lethal damage when striking the chest in a similar place with a similar trajectory. Hydrostatic shock creates a broad corridor of damage. Hunters who make chest hits with their rifles and slug guns will usually find their own deer without much tracking effort.

The traditional wisdom of deer hunting maintains that the hunter should "always wait" no matter how the deer has been wounded. This is certainly a good rule for gut shots, but it should not be the rule for dealing with most other types of wounds. The sooner the handler and his dog can get to chest or leg shots the better. Reasons for this will be presented in this and the next chapter. The experience of military combat medicine clearly demonstrates that wounded humans have the best chances of survival when they are not forced to walk, and the same most likely applies to deer.

From the viewpoint of the handler, deer wounded in the chest during bow season present the most frequent and important challenges. Therefore, we will consider these cases first.

Signs of Chest Wounds

Shots in the heart, or the big veins and arteries coming out of the top of the heart, do not always produce a great deal of blood on the ground. However, there is generally enough blood for eye-tracking, and heart-shot deer never go very far anyway. Two hundred yards is the maximum and most heart-shot deer go less than a hundred yards. Only once out of a 1000 plus calls, was I asked to track a heart shot deer. In this case the broadhead cut heart muscle but did not slices into the chambers of the heart. We do not need to concern ourselves with heart shots here. To the tracker lung shots are much more significant.

The classic indication of a lung hit is frothy blood on the arrow and in the blood trail. There are many tiny bubbles the size of #9 shot (.08 inch). You may see occasional bubbles in blood from other parts of a deer, but they will be larger (BB size) and not as numerous. After a good shot, the bowhunter will often see abundant bubbly lung blood on the trail; usually this leads right to the dead deer. The handler of the tracking dog is much less likely to see these classic signs of a lethal lung shot because he and his dog are called in only for those unusual cases when something went wrong, cases in which the deer did *not* bleed on the outside and did not collapse after a desperate dash of a hundred yards.

In bowhunting the lung-shot cases for which a tracking dog is needed will generally involve very little external blood, or even no blood at all. A pass-through chest shot may seal almost immediately because the deer's chest muscles are stretched as the arrow penetrated. As the muscles slide back across the wound after the shot, they effectively seal the opening in the chest. You may see no blood at all, or only a round, frothy splatter blown from the nostrils. Sometimes your diagnosis of a lung shot will have to be based only upon what the hunter can tell you about how he saw the arrow fletching disappear into the deer.

Larry Gohlke is a handler/tracker from Neshkoro, Wisconsin with extensive experience. In October 2000 he shared this story:

"I was called by Randy Marks to look for a doe that had been (standing) broadside, shot at 30 yards with a Bear head and no insert. The shot was a pass-through and the arrow smelled like meat. There was absolutely no blood. Since Randy is about the best tracker I know, I figured that I would take Lolly, my tracking dog, for a walk, find no blood, and head for home. Turns out the shot went through both lungs and the doe fawn was dead in a corn field about 200 yards away. There was almost no blood under the deer and no blood trail. This goes against everything I would have guessed."

I have also found that double lunged deer seldom go over 200 yards.

Physical Characteristics of Chest Wounds in Bowhunting

A review of the chest anatomy of deer is essential if we are to understand the problems that arise in tracking. Note that the heart and the major blood vessels coming out of the heart are located low and to the front of the chest cavity. Blood is pumped from the right side of the heart up into the lungs to be oxygenated; then it flows back into the left side of the heart from which it is pumped out through the arteries into every muscle and organ of the deer. Broadheads that slice into this major plumbing at the top of the heart and the front of the lungs kill quickly. You will seldom be called to track a deer that was shot low and forward in the chest just behind the forelegs.

The lower and forward parts of the lungs have a much heavier concentration of large blood vessels than the portions located higher and to the rear. A shot to one or both lungs, placed low and forward, is going to kill the deer, whether it is a broadhead, a bullet or a shotgun slug that does the job. If only one lung is damaged, and the wound is higher and farther back, problems begin. A broadhead cutting into the pink spongy tissue (alveolar tissue) of the lung, high and to the rear, will slice the microscopic blood vessels or capillaries and some medium sized vessels as well, but there may not be enough bleeding, internally or externally, to kill the deer.

The damaged lung will probably collapse and cease functioning, but this is not too serious if the other lung is intact. Deer, like humans, can function reasonably well on one lung. In addition, the smaller blood vessels in the damaged lung tend to constrict due to lack of oxygen when the lung collapses. Blood flow through this lung is greatly reduced, and therefore, major

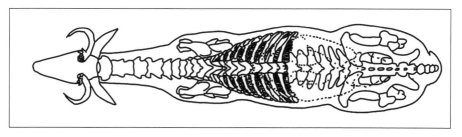

Top view of deer showing lung placement and V-shaped structure of rib cage

hemorrhage fails to occur. One lung hits are not necessarily killing shots. This distinction is less important for firearm hunters because of the greater tissue damage produced by bullets and slugs.

Hunters should always try to take out both lungs, collapsing them both and making it impossible for the deer to breath. In bowhunting this is not as easy as it sounds because most shots are taken from tree stands with the hunter looking down on the deer. Viewed from above the lungs do not present such an easy target. They are "suspended" in the chest, lying side by side like two large, fat sunfish separated from one another by a few inches of mostly non-vital space. When shooting downward at a steep angle at a broadside deer, it is easy to shoot over the near side lung and hit the far side lung too high to kill the deer.

When shots are in the chest area, the difference between the work of arrows, on one hand, and bullets and slugs on the other hand, is most apparent. The arrow does not produce hydrostatic shock like the slug and bullet. If the arrow passes all the way through the chest, does not hit the food pipe (esophagus), and does not hit anything else important enough to bring death within a half-hour, then the chances that the animal will survive are quite good. Broadheads cut cleanly and do not pull in hair and other material that might contaminate the wound. The broadhead is not sterile, but the deer's healing (immune) system can generally deal with the small amount of infection that develops. Slugs and bullets, on the other hand, produce a broad corridor of damage. In many cases they completely destroy the natural vacuum within the chest cavity causing both lungs to collapse. They also carry hair into the wound, which causes serious infection to the rare deer that does not die quickly.

Head-On Shots into the Front of the Chest

Every bowhunter education course stresses that frontal shots into the chest should not be taken. Unfortunately, when no other shot presents itself, even experienced bowhunters can forget the lesson. Visually, the deer's chest appears from the front as a solid blocky target a bit like our own. The reality is quite different. The deer's rib cage comes to a point in front like the bow of a ship, but this V-shaped structure is hidden by muscle tissue. If the arrow does not penetrate almost exactly into the small opening at the center of the chest, it strikes the ribs at a narrow angle and is deflected backward without ever penetrating the chest cavity. It is likely to pass between the rib cage and the shoulder blade or the next bone down (*humerus*), cutting muscle tissue and producing a heavy blood trail because all of the bleeding is external. The deer will lose serious amounts of blood, but normally the flow slackens before the point of no return is reached. From an archer's eye view, this looks like an excellent chest shot, but this is an illusion. Unless the arrow passes through the small "window" at the front of the chest, it is seldom fatal.

Normally I receive about one call a year that fits this description. These calls are hard to screen on the telephone because there is no way of being certain whether the broadhead passed inside or along the outside of the chest. You really have to go and check each case. You will probably be able to track much farther than the bowhunter, verifying the trail with occasional drops of blood. If the deer remains strong, you now know the probable explanation.

In the fall of 2000, I tracked a large buck with a distinctive rack that had been shot from the front. The buck went almost straight up a small, but very steep mountain. The hunter was certain that it could not go far with such a massive hemorrhage. The deer lay down after reaching the top, rested and then went on without bleeding. Two weeks later the buck was observed in the same area. It was moving well.

Bowshots to the chest, taken when the deer is quartering toward the hunter, are similar in that they will often be deflected along the outside of the rib cage. Generally bleeding will be heavy at first, but the wound will seldom be fatal. Like the shots taken directly from the front, these front-quartering shots can be difficult to diagnose with certainty over the phone.

Finding Chest-Shot Deer

Deer shot by bowhunters often have little awareness of what has happened. They are in shock, feel weakness and sense that something is wrong. They will try to return to a secure spot, and this may involve circling back to a place close to where they were shot. In any case, they will try to remain in their home territory or return to it. A rutting buck roaming out of his territory in search for does is likely to take off in a straight line for his home turf immediately after being hit. The chest-hit deer that does not drop quickly may travel a long way.

At first, it may be difficult to understand how bowshots to the best target area of the deer produce difficulties and a low percentage of finds for the handlers and tracking dogs called in on the tough ones. This is something that the tracker will have to learn to live with. He may turn down some calls, but there are numerous chest-shot cases about which he can never be sure on the basis of what he hears in a conversation with the hunter. The hunter's description is useful, but it can seldom be a reliable substitute for checking out the situation in the woods where it took place.

The most important thing is to talk extensively with the hunter, prior to taking the call, about such things as the angle of the shot. If the hunter can describe to you the position of the deer and where he saw the arrow strike, then you should be able to determine, through reconstruction, where the arrow probably exited, and through which organs the arrow passed. The hunter may assure you that he shot through both lungs. If this were actually the case, the hunter would not have needed to call you in the first place.

If the hunter reports that the arrow entered the deer's chest halfway down from the topline of the deer, the chances are fairly good that you can accomplish something; if he says that the arrow is a third of the way down

The photo above was taken by tracker Rob Miller of Michigan. It clearly shows how difficult it can be for a hunter to know whether he has made a lethal chest shot or has shot too high. The buck in Rob's photo first took a broadhead in the top of the chest, well within the area that most hunters consider to be the kill zone. The hunter was sure that the deer was dead. The deer was tracked for 1.5 miles, but the tracking dog could not catch up to it. Two weeks later the same buck was shot by the hunter's friend while it was chasing a doe. The second arrow, which penetrated lower and farther back, did the job. The first arrow was still in the top of the rib cage with 13 inches of penetration.

Photo courtesy of Robert Miller

from the top, prospects are less bright. Hunters know that the chest cavity begins under the spinal column, but they do not realize how far this part of the spine lies beneath the apparent topline of the deer. Above the spine itself are the spinous processes, prongs about five inches long, that come up from the chest (thoracic) vertebrae. These prongs angle slightly to the rear, but they add about four inches total height to the deer above the spine. Above this, there is the winter hair along the back. This long, coarse hair pushes the apparent topline even higher above the spine and the chest cavity. When hair and the prongs are taken into consideration, the top of the chest cavity and the lungs begin a good one third of the way down from what we see as the top of the deer.

Any shot, taken at an angle into the rib cage, can be deflected so that it never enters into the vitals of the chest cavity. Shots that angle forward into the chest from an entry point in back of the rib cage are much better. Such a shot will certainly kill the deer, and it will be easy for the dog to track.

Frequently you will get the report of a deer shot high in the back, at a steep downward angle into the chest. It turns out that there is little blood because

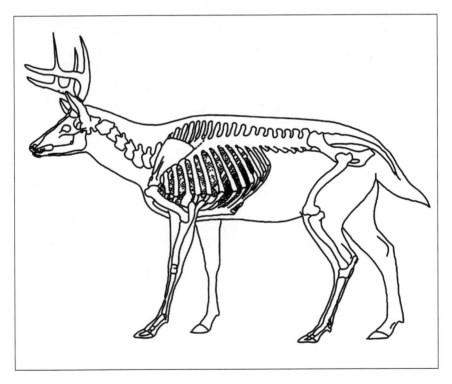

The lungs begin a good one third of the way down from what we see as the top of the deer.

there is no exit wound. Such a shot should never have been taken, but this is a situation that you cannot control as a tracking dog handler. In such cases it is very important to inquire about penetration. How much of the shaft and fletching were visible outside of the deer?

Sometimes you will hear that the penetration was poor; all but 8 or 10 inches of the arrow were sticking out of the deer as it took off. Generally, these poor penetrations develop because the shot was taken when the deer was too close, and the arrow was still in flex and fishtailing as it struck. The arrow slapped into the deer at an angle rather than striking directly. On these poorly penetrating shots there is very little that can be done. Gently, try to make the hunter see the error in his ways. He shot because he knew that he could not miss the deer. He hit the deer, but he missed everything that was vital.

A more promising variation of this steep angle chest shot is one in which the arrow gets almost to the bottom of the deer, but does not exit. If the arrow is well forward, there is a good chance that serious damage was done even though the broadhead did not quite cut through at the bottom, and even though there is little or no blood on the outside. If your dog can track such a deer by interdigital scent and the few blood droplets or smears available, you may find the deer dead. Sometimes you will track to a place where the broadhead worked out the bottom of the brisket releasing all of the blood pooled inside. Suddenly you will have a broad band of blood leading to a dead deer.

> Some years ago I took a call in Columbia County, New York. A bowhunter, for whom I had tracked and found deer before, reported that he had shot a deer down into the chest at a steep angle as the buck passed him. There was good penetration, but no exit wound, and absolutely no blood. Because I knew the hunter and had confidence in his ability to recognize a killing shot, I took the call.
>
> It was very difficult to get started because many deer had passed later on the same trail taken by the wounded buck. We made several false starts of two hundred yards in one direction before circling back and picking up another line going in the opposite direction. On this one, my Dachshund Max seemed more positive, but the trail was obviously difficult. Again, we went about two hundred yards, and suddenly there was a heavy blood trail. Within 50 yards we found the buck dead. Working back and forth with each stride, the broadhead had finally cut its way out of the bottom of the chest. By this time the buck's chest had filled up with blood; it had energy left to go only a few more yards before it collapsed.

Mechanical heads, with cutting blades that expand as the arrow enters the deer, can also produce inadequate penetration. This is especially likely to happen when the arrow is shot from a tree stand, enters high behind the shoulder and penetrates downward towards the lung area. Because of the cutting angle of the deployed blades, and because they are cutting such a broad swath through bone and tissue, all the arrow's energy may be used up before the vital zone is reached. Mechanical heads work best when they are shot with heavy arrows and high poundage bows; they are least effective when they are used with light arrows that lose momentum rapidly after the resistance of the deer is encountered. Another problem with the mechanicals is that almost all cutting ceases once the arrow has stopped moving through the deer. The folding blades then "float" and do not continue to cut back and forth as does a fixed-blade broadhead. I probably would not have found the "Columbia County buck" described above if the hunter had used a mechanical broadhead.

There is no easy and simple advice to give concerning chest wounds in bow season. When you talk to the hunter, try to reconstruct the angle of the shot as accurately as possible. Many of these shots will have damaged and collapsed only one lung. These one-lung hits are never a sure bet, as we have seen, but usually they are worth trying. The odds improve greatly if the arrow entered the deer lower than the midline. Generally, the lower and farther forward the entry, the better are the chances. The greatest concentration of large pulmonary vessels is low and forward in the lungs. In an unknown percentage of cases, bowshot deer do survive wounds to one lung.

On one call my dog and I arrived late in the afternoon, about eight hours after the buck had been shot. All the classic signs of a lung hit were present. In the first hundred yards from the point of impact there were drops of blood that still showed fine bubbles no larger than number nine shot (.08 inch). A few of these were even present on the arrow. Smears of blood on the right side of the trail up to a height of 24 inches suggested that the deer had an exit wound about two feet above its hooves. The hunter confirmed that this must be the exit wound since he had shot the deer from the left side. The blood trail dwindled rapidly to a drop every hundred yards or so, which was the reason that Arnold had called me in the first place. It was easy enough for the dog however, and we tracked about 600 yards to the deer's bed. We heard the deer depart in the dense undergrowth, and a few drops of blood in the bed confirmed that we had jumped the right deer. To shorten a long story we pushed this deer, "which had to be dead," hard for over two miles. We never got close to it.

This scenario has happened many times since. Often hunters have called back to report seeing the deer again alive and well a few days later. Trail cameras reveal the same thing. Hunters have reported a buddy taking the deer with the same wound later during gun season. One bowhunter even shot the same deer again later in the fall.

In 1977, I organized a research team of biologists that examined 51 deer that were shot in an intensive, one-day bow hunt at the Howland Island Waterfowl Refuge in Cayuga County, New York. Deer were brought to the check station gutted, but with chest cavities intact ahead of the diaphragms. Out of the 51 deer, one doe, a year and seven months old, had clearly survived an arrow wound in one lung while she was a fawn. She was in good health and weighed 101 pounds, normal for her age and the area. The sample size is not large enough to constitute "scientific proof" concerning deer survival, but there is certainly enough anecdotal evidence to justify some serious research. There needs to be a careful examination of the theory held by some wildlife biologists that a breach of the vacuum in the chest cavity inevitably produces collapse of both lungs. A large hole in the chest wall may well produce lung collapse, but some deer can certainly survive the sealed or semi-sealed chest wounds produced in bow hunting.

Remember that not all pass-through shots reported as lung shots actually involve the lungs. There is such a thing as being too far forward. I can think of a case a few years back when I tracked a bear that had been shot low behind the foreleg the day before. In this case what applies to bear applies to deer. The bear had been angling away and unfortunately, the bowhunter did not think three-dimensionally and adjust his point of aim to the rear. The arrow angled through the very front of the chest, ahead of the heart and lungs, and exited from the brisket on the far side. There was no visible blood, except for a few smears on saplings, but there was plenty of scent; the bear was easy to track. It kept going, and we never came to a bed or any evidence of a hot bear scent.

When you commit yourself to a call on a chest shot deer during bow season, take into consideration the fact that it will be difficult to track because the arrow wound is likely to have closed and to be high on the deer. If scenting conditions are poor, it may be wiser to wait until they improve at the end of the day.

The first blood from a deer hit high may be some distance from where the shot was taken. It takes some time for the blood to drip down off the side of the deer onto the ground. You may be able to verify the line for a while by blood on the ground, but then, as bleeding slows, the last traces of blood will probably be smears on brush or saplings above ground level. Be sure to look for them. If the dog tracks and shows you some blood sign for several hundred yards, it is a good assumption that he can take you farther even if you have no absolute proof that he is right. It is not unusual to go a half mile without visible blood. The dog works on interdigital gland scent and other scent molecules.

When I become convinced that the deer being tracked is not going to bed down, I like to pick up the dog on a positive note. If possible, I like to find one last drop to show the hunter and prove to him that we have been tracking the deer that he wounded. The best place to find this last trace of blood is where the deer went under or over a fence, or stretched while crossing a stone wall.

When you go out on a deer track that involves a chest hit ahead of the diaphragm, it is useful to have some sense of the odds of finding the deer. A general rule on these chest hits is that if the arrow is no longer in the deer, and the deer has been able to live a half-hour and travel over a half-mile, it has an excellent chance of survival. Don't bet big sums of money on it; I can think of a few cases when this rule did not apply, but it may be useful in helping you to make a decision on when to pick up the dog.

In tracking wounded deer, especially in the case of a chest shot, you will become very frustrated if you allow yourself to believe that anything but a tagged deer means failure. The questions you must ask yourself are: "Did the

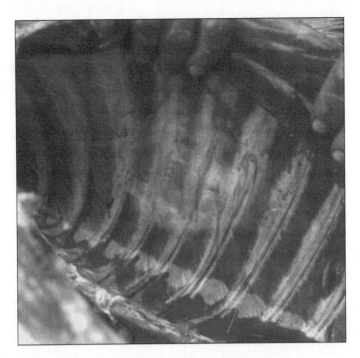

Scar on chest wall of Howland Island doe

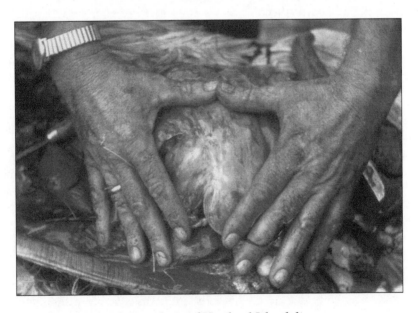

Scar on lung of Howland Island doe

dog work well? Did the dog take a verifiable line farther than the hunter? Did you come up with convincing evidence that the deer was still alive, strong and capable of staying ahead of you indefinitely?"

What bothers hunters most is leaving a deer to suffer, die and be wasted in the woods. Of course, they would like to find the deer that they shot, but if they become convinced that the deer is strong and probably will recover, this is the next best thing. You and your tracking dog can do a successful tracking job, even though the deer is not found and tagged.

Chest Wounds Made by Firearms
Overview

It must be very rare that an appropriate rifle bullet or shotgun slug enters the chest cavity and does not end up killing the deer. There is massive damage inside, and the external wounds, especially the exit wound, are likely to stay open and disrupt breathing. Usually there will be the same heavy bleeding, and often the same frothy lung blood that are typical of bow-shot deer. When things go according to plan there is no need to think about a tracking dog. This subject is discussed in a later chapter.

One of the biggest problems for the tracker in rifle or gun season involves determining that a valid chest hit is involved. You don't want to spend hours searching for a deer that was merely grazed or perhaps missed altogether. Hunters attempting to find wounded game should think positively, but positive thinking can slip easily into wishful thinking. Every hunter wants to believe that he hit where he aimed, and he usually aimed at the chest. If the bullet actually missed the heart-lung area, it is most likely that it went high and grazed the back. It is especially easy to shoot high with open sights.

Beware of the hunter who says, "I hit him right in the chest, and he dropped like a ton of bricks." Deer hit in the chest rarely drop on the spot. They may stagger, stumble, make a few jumps, and collapse, but they will not drop instantly unless the central nervous system is temporarily or permanently knocked out. Instant knockdowns are discussed in the high back wound section of the following chapter.

In assessing the possibilities of a chest shot, the handler should use all that he knows about the possible alternatives. Many head on "chest shots" actually turn out to be wounds that broke the shoulder blade or the humerus, which is the heavy leg bone directly beneath the shoulder blade. These leg-hit situations are also discussed in the next chapter.

Grazing shots, which do superficial damage, are another possibility, particularly with frontal shots. In quartering away shots, the hunter may not aim far enough back to shoot diagonally through the heart-lung area. He may rake the front shoulder instead. One giveaway in such shots is a larger than normal quantity of hair that has been cut by the slug. Another indication of the same thing is hair still attached to flakes of skin, which were scuffed off as the slug plowed along the surface.

Signs of Chest Wounds

Deer hunting books often show illustrations of how chest shot deer react by lunging straight forward. Richard B. Smith in his excellent book *Tracking Wounded Deer* points out that deer sometimes have no immediate reaction to a lethal chest shot. I have taken lung shots myself, which put the deer down within 25 yards. Yet, these deer gave no detectable sign that they had been wounded. They just trotted or ran off. The tail usually stayed down if it was already down when the shot was fired.

At other times the reactions of deer do confirm the hunter's hopes that he has made a good shot. Deer, which are already spooked and have their tails up, are likely to clap their tails down, but there are exceptions to this. Some chest-shot deer may lunge straight forward or upward in the best classic form. Other deer stagger visibly, but do not go down until they have run for several hundred yards.

Usually a valid chest shot will produce ample blood on the ground, and the hunter will find his own deer. However, in shotgun and rifle hunting it can happen that the high chest shot produces lethal bleeding that pools in the chest cavity and never spills out on the ground.

It may seem strange that a slug wound does not always bleed from surface tissue at the entry and exit, but I have seen this happen. In one case, the torn up shoulder muscle produced by the exiting 12 gauge slug made a wound too big to cover with my hand, and yet this button buck traveled over half a mile and left only two nickel-sized drops of visible blood and a splatter of bloody foam blown from his nose.

If there is no blood on the outside, even 200 yards can be a long way in heavy cover. A lack of tracking blood may result when a high power rifle bullet fails to expand. Modern high power rifle bullets are certainly very reliable. However, in my rather limited experience with rifle bullets in chest shot situations there have been at least two cases in which .30 caliber rifle bullets did not expand and passed right through leaving pencil-sized entry and exit holes. The weight and design of the bullet used in these two cases seemed to be a reasonable choice for deer-sized game.

When small caliber, centerfire cartridges from .243, and smaller are used, there can be problems because there is a small exit wound or no exit at all. If the bullet placement is not very good, the tracker will be called, and he is in for a difficult time. The deer may go a long way, and it will be hard for the dog to follow.

Physical Characteristics of Chest Wounds

When a deer is hit in the chest with an appropriate deer load, there is a great deal of damage to organ tissue surrounding the path of the slug or bullets. This is due to hydrostatic shock, which is not an important factor in bowhunting. Survival of the deer is highly unlikely, and deer will not go as far as they would with an arrow wound in the same place.

Finding Chest-Shot Deer: Firearms

Deer, wounded in the chest in no-blood situations, are hard to track, but there is usually something for dogs to follow. This may be the interdigital scent of the individual deer, the body scent of the wounded deer, or the invisible blood droplets exhaled in the deer's breath.

If the line is old or conditions are poor, it is often possible to work the dog downwind from the heavy cover in which the dead deer is suspected to be lying. Dogs vary in their abilities to do this, but I have had good dogs "wind" a dead deer at 200 yards, and I am sure that this is not the limit. If you see your dog raise his head and pull strongly into the wind, it is always worth investigating. Your dog may lead you to some old gut piles, but you will also pull off some "miraculous" finds.

Gut Shots: Stomach, Liver, Kidney and Intestines
Overview

The general and loose term "gut shot", as used by hunters, is usually applied to the whole area of the animal's body cavity in back of the diaphragm, which separates the heart lung area from the other organs behind it. The diaphragm is an all-important dividing point between two very different types of wounds that require very different strategies for finding the deer. When hit in the stomach, liver, kidney or intestines, deer are almost always doomed to death, although the results are not immediate. Finding the deer is largely a matter of time, patience and not making mistakes.

Signs of a Gut Shot: Archery and Firearms

Gut shots often occur because the deer takes a step as the bullet or arrow speeds toward the chest. Generally the animal hunches up as it is struck.

Deer hit in the stomach or intestines usually bleed very little externally. Certainly, the seriousness of the wound can't be judged by the amount of blood that is left on the ground. Most of the bleeding will be internal; this internal bleeding empties the arteries and veins as effectively as external bleeding, and it has the same lethal effect.

Blood from the stomach and intestines is usually dark red and muddy looking. It may contain fragments of food particles, grass, browse, acorns, corn, etc., and it may be quite watery from digestive fluids. If the wound was made by an arrow, and the arrow was recovered, much can be learned from it about how the deer was wounded. If you talk to the hunter by telephone, ask him about this evidence, but if he reports nothing, ask the hunter to bring the arrow along with him. Sometimes the obvious has been overlooked. Tiny flecks of food material are usually stuck in the angles of the broadhead and around the base of the fletching. An arrow that has passed through the stomach will also have a distinctive "cow barn" smell. Cows and deer are both ruminants, eat some of the same food, and have similar types of stomach bacteria breaking it down during the digestion process.

The blood line, which is visible to the hunter or dog handler tracking a stomach-hit deer, will often be misleading. Most of the blood will be bright red and will not fit the description of stomach or gut blood. This bright blood actually comes from the outside layers of the deer and not from the digestive organs. However, it requires only one drop of dark blood among a 100 bright ones to confirm that you are tracking a stomach-shot deer that will surely die, a deer that will suffer and then be wasted if you give up too soon.

Physical Characteristics of Gut Shots

Technically speaking, a deer's long stomach system has four sections; the first and largest of these is the rumen, where 40% of the nutritional value of the deer's feed is absorbed. The other three sections of the stomach and the small intestines also absorb nutrition but to a lesser degree. These highly absorptive areas of the gastrointestinal tract have the highest density of blood vessels, and a broadhead that does damage here kills the most quickly. Within the wall of the rumen itself there are many, tree-like branchings of blood vessels. If the

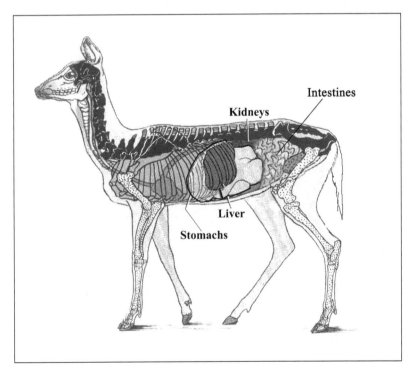

Digestive system of a deer. Note placement of rumen partly inside the rib cage. The liver lies along side the stomach.

main branches are severed, the deer dies quickly, often within half an hour. If the arrow passes between the main branches of blood vessels and cuts only fine capillaries, death may come after 12 or 24 hours, or even longer. Likewise, an arrow cutting into the blood vessel-rich first section of the small intestine can kill very quickly.

Veterinarians have observed that in cattle a hole high in the rumen is not necessarily fatal because the contents of the rumen do not drain into the abdominal cavity. The wall of the cow's stomach can heal itself. It is possible that the same thing can happen sometimes in a deer that is shot high in the rumen.

An arrow placed farther back beneath the loin, and cutting through the large bowel or intestine, has little immediate effect on the strength and viability of the deer. There are fewer blood vessels here as this large gut is mainly a holding place for waste to be excreted. These are the worst types of gut shots, from every standpoint, and we call them "peritonitis hits". Death comes very slowly from blood poisoning as body wastes seep into the blood supply from the damaged large intestine.

The blood trails from stomach-shot deer have a peculiar characteristic that the dog tracker should understand: the drops or splatters of blood from the inside of the deer are turned on and off as if by a faucet. What happens is that the deer's perforated stomach rotates as it travels along. When the arrow wound in the stomach lines up with the arrow wound in the outside layer of the deer, dark blood from the stomach spills out onto the ground. When the stomach turns slightly and the openings move out of alignment, leakage to the outside is abruptly sealed off and there is no blood to track. There may be just a very few drops of normal-colored, red blood. It is at one of the "turn-off points", with no gut blood to be seen, that the hunter often loses the track and resorts to the tracking dog.

In these cases it does not seem to make much difference to the tracking dog whether there is visible blood or not. At all times there is plenty of scent coming down from the wound. The dog continues tracking with a confidence that the handler should share.

Liver wounds are usually associated with stomach wounds. Because of the location of the liver beside and behind the stomach, an arrow, slug or bullet passing through the liver has a good chance of passing through the stomach as well. In such cases the liver wound will usually be the more immediate cause of death. Liver wounds kill very quickly because such large volumes of blood pass through the liver. However, all sections of the liver are not equally vulnerable. If the major artery entering or the major vein exiting the liver is severed, death is almost immediate. However, the onset of death will be much slower if the broadhead passed through one of the lobes of the liver four or five inches from the major plumbing. I have tracked several deer that went over a mile, without being pushed, after the liver had been perforated by an arrow or slug.

The indication of a liver hit is very dark blood. A wound to the liver may produce little or no external bleeding because fat, the stomach or the intestines block the wound. However, steady internal bleeding without clotting is certain to occur, and we have never heard of a deer lasting more than six hours with a liver hit.

One of my best learning experiences occurred when I was asked to track a deer, which had been shot in the liver with a 12 gauge shotgun slug. A friend had first taken the call with his very promising, but still inexperienced, young Wirehaired Dachshund. Waldie, the young bitch, had tracked the deer out of a swamp, across a field, through a passageway in a stone wall and across a road into a cluster of spruce trees next to a house. There the trail seemed to end. The hunter even inquired at the house about whether someone had picked up the deer.

I was invited to give it a try with Clary, Waldie's dam, and a much more experienced tracker. Clary trailed from the last dark liver blood up to the house, just as her daughter had done. At the dead end she made several small circles and headed back across the road and through the same opening in the stone wall. This time she passed through on the opposite side of the opening and headed down across the field by another route. At the edge of the swamp, I saw one pinhead-sized drop of blood on an alder branch. We tracked over a mile, seeing no more blood, and I sensed growing doubts on the part of the hunter. Clary was positive. Finally we climbed up a long hill and there at the top lay the six-pointer, dead.

The slug had passed through the center of the larger lobe of the liver. The buck had not been pushed, but the last thing that buck had done was climb a long, steep hill.

Kidney wounds and damage to the renal arteries that supply the kidneys are fairly rare, but the tracker should always remember that they do occur. A shot high in the loin just behind the rib cage might be a "peritonitis hit" offering poor prospects, or it might be a kidney hit, which will kill the deer quickly. Enough blood passes through the kidneys via the renal arteries and the renal veins so that a wound in this area will result in a lethal loss of blood. There is enough blood volume and pressure in the renal arteries to produce a spray of blood on weeds and brush as the deer passes.

A hunter and a tracker are not able to predict the timetable of events after a deer has been wounded in the gastro-intestinal system. But if the deer eventually survives, it is certainly a rare case; the tracker should be very persistent.

Finding Gut-Shot Deer

It is almost always to the advantage of the tracker to wait as long as possible when there are strong indications of a stomach hit. This is also the case with hits to the intestines. Wounds to the small intestines, which are involved in digestion, generally kill as quickly as stomach wounds because there are many small blood vessels there. As we have stated above, placement of the shot by the hunter can usually be determined by the behavior of the deer at the shot (hunching), by the scent on the arrow, and by the special character of the blood sign observed.

Eight hours might be the ideal length of time to wait since stomach-hit deer are generally easy for the dog to follow even though there is little visible blood. However, almost always there are other factors to be taken into

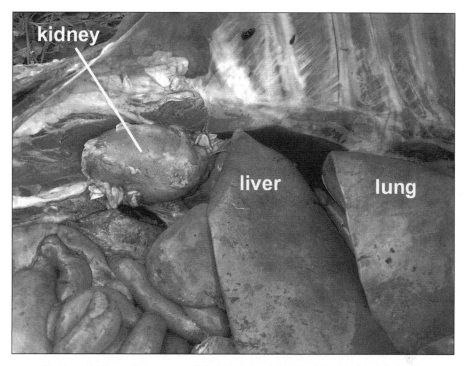

Photo of kidney (fat removed) just below spine and just behind last rib.

consideration in deciding when to begin tracking. Is the weather so warm that the deer is likely to spoil if it is actually dead? Eight hours in bow season, if the temperature is above seventy, can be too long a time. Are there coyotes in the area? A night's work by a family pack of coyotes will leave very little venison for the hunter (color Fig. 14). In heavily hunted areas, is there a strong likelihood that someone else will find the deer?

Finally, there are weather conditions. The eyetracker has to consider whether rain or snow is predicted. The tracker with an experienced dog should be less concerned about precipitation. A light to moderate rain will wash away all visible traces of blood, but it will actually enhance the scent for the dog. If the tracker can trust the dog to follow the wound scent and ignore healthy deer, there is not much to be concerned about, unless there is a long, torrential downpour. Likewise, snow actually seems to preserve the scent. Four inches of wet snow is certainly not a problem. Six or eight inches of snow will be difficult, as will very dry, dusty snow that goes up the sniffing dog's nose.

As in most cases in which a tracker and dog are called in to track a wounded deer, getting started on a gut-shot deer is usually the hardest part. Often the hunter will have tracked some distance by eye, and he will have pushed the deer up out of its bed because he did not wait long enough. There

One night's work by coyotes
Photo courtesy of Gary Huber

will usually be blood in the wound bed but no blood trail at all leaving the bed in which the deer spent several hours. As in the case of chest shots, it is almost always worthwhile to go back to the hit site and move from there to where the hunter first saw blood. The hunter's point of loss will generally be a difficult place to start because this area has been crisscrossed with the scent of deer blood that was on his boots. Be careful that the dog does not follow the path that the hunter took as he gave up and left the area. There is usually a reason why the hunter lost the line at a particular point. If the line ends abruptly, it may be because the deer backtracked over its own trail.

If the dog has worked several hundred yards of good line with visible blood, he will know what he is searching for and may be able to carry on past the point of loss as if by psychological momentum. If this does not work, the dog will recognize the scent again as you work together in circles around the contaminated area.

About 80% of the time, the tracker who has allowed sufficient time to elapse, will conclude the search by tracking into a dead deer. Even if the deer is still alive, it can often be approached closely enough for a finishing shot. The deer is sick and doesn't want to move. However, if the hunter or the tracker moves too much in trying for the absolutely perfect shot, the deer may take off. Once adrenaline is pumping again the deer can go a mile or two more. We have seen this happen many times.

If the arrow has ranged far enough forward to perforate the stomach, the bleeding and leaking of other body fluids will be mostly internal and there will be little blood on the trail. If the gods of the hunt are with you, and the broadhead cuts the kidneys or renal arteries, the deer will die quickly, and there is a good chance that blood will have sprayed out under pressure. In this case the tracking dog is usually not needed. But when the arrow has passed through the large intestine high in front of the pelvis, the odds of recovering the deer are poor because the deer is likely to live for several days. These peritonitis hits are a real challenge to the tracking dog's ability and to the handler's persistence and technique.

Needed, first of all, is a very intelligent and experienced dog that is capable of recognizing a specific deer by the individual scent, which comes in part from the interdigital glands high between the cloves of the deer's hoofs. Once it has become clear that the deer will not weaken for many hours, the strategy should be to push the deer gently into good bedding cover, "park" it there, and check back a full day later. If coyotes are numerous, there is always a chance that they will find the deer first.

Alternatively, the dog and handler can stay continuously in contact with the deer, eating and sleeping on the trail if need be. We can imagine situations where dedicated handlers would make this sort of commitment if they had the time available.

Another last resort for finding gut-shot deer is to check ponds, streams and any bodies of water in the area where the deer was lost. Gut-shot deer become dehydrated, and we often find them dead next to the water, or in the water where they went for their last drink. Water does not seem to have the same degree of attraction for deer with other types of wounds. But if you know that the deer has been gut shot, keep water uppermost in your mind. Carefully search all water surfaces for a gray-brown bulge of the deer's side. Deer with their winter coats always float, but the head and hindquarters hang down and most of the deer is not visible.

Summary

- Evaluate chest shot calls carefully and do not expect to always find the deer.

- There is nothing to be gained by waiting to track on a chest shot. The fresher the wound, the more likely that the deer will bleed internally and externally.

- An arrow recovered after a pass-through shot can provide useful information. Ask the hunter what is on the arrow and how it smells.

- Be alerted to a gut shot by even a small percentage of dark blood. Most of the blood may come from the outside layers of the deer.

- Gut shots are the easiest to track, but wait at least four hours before beginning. If coyotes and weather permit, eight hours is better.

- Bow-shot deer sometimes survive chest shots, but very few survive gut shots.

- Gut-shot deer are likely to go to water.

Chapter 15

Special Tracking Situations II: Wounds Outside The Body Cavity

Many deer that are reported by the hunter to be wounded in the chest actually turn out to be wounded outside the body cavity. Leg wounds and high back hits usually make up the majority of these cases. In this chapter we will examine these two cases and, in addition, the head and neck shots that have not proved immediately fatal. You should be able to recognize the signs of different "outside-the-body" hits and know the best tactics for recovering these deer, if this is possible.

Leg Wounds: Archery and Firearms

Overview

When deer are wounded in the fleshy parts of their legs, they can be expected to recover, even though they may leave a strong blood trail at the beginning. When the leg bones are shattered by a bullet or slug, or even by a broadhead, the situation is very different. These deer are likely to lose the affected leg and heal up as a three-legged deer, but the long-term prospects for such a deer are poor, particularly in areas of heavy snows. These handicapped deer cannot feed as efficiently, and they have difficulty escaping from coyotes and other predators. There are exceptions, but according to Glenn Cole, who was New York State's Region 3 Wildlife Manager for many years, few three-legged deer with old wounds show up at Highway Check Stations. This suggests that most of them do not survive the winter after they lost their leg. It is better to track down these deer and kill them as humanely as possible rather than let them face a lingering death or a very difficult life.

Signs of Leg Wounds

Often a deer, whose leg is broken and swinging, will be reported as having been shot in the chest. However, there are a number of signs clearly indicating that a leg has been hit in such a way that it can no longer support the deer's weight. After the deer is shot, it will often stumble and fall once or twice when it attempts to run. After a fall or two, the deer departs rapidly on three legs. This is an entirely different case from the instantaneous collapse that occurs when the spinal column has been damaged or shocked.

The exact spot of terrain where the deer was struck by the hunter's projectile should be carefully checked. If the bone has been hit, it is usually possible to find some bone fragments on the ground at the point of impact or in the first few hundred yards of the trail. Often, these fragments will be described as "pieces of rib" but they invariably turn out to be leg bones.

If you are really serious, it is a good idea to collect samples of the major bones and familiarize yourself with their contours. Then in many cases, you will be able to match fragments with your sample bones. It took me a long time to realize that the presence of leg bone chips does not always mean that the leg was broken; assume a broken leg until you see evidence that the deer is moving on all four.

On a leg hit the hair at the hit site will be much shorter than what would be produced by a body hit. The blood itself will be bright and difficult to distinguish in color from blood flowing out of a flesh wound. However, it will often be distributed in many small droplets, and more reliably, a leg that is broken and swinging will leave bloody drag marks over branches and logs that lie across the trail. In dry, loose leaves, there will be drag marks if the wound is high enough so that the deer cannot hold up its leg.

On soft ground, or in sand, another sure indication is that the track made by the hoof print on the side opposite the damaged leg will be deeper, and the tips of the hooves will be abnormally spread because of the unusual weight being carried.

Physical Characteristics of Leg Wounds

A deer with smashed leg bones will bleed heavily for a quarter or a half mile, and then the bleeding will greatly diminish or stop altogether when the deer halts. Much of this bleeding comes as a steady dripping from the exposed marrow ends rather than from blood vessels supplying the leg muscles. If the deer can stop, stand and cease its exertions, this blood flow from the marrow will begin to clot up. There is considerable difference from one individual deer to another in how fast this clotting takes place. Mud packed in the wound or freezing of the end of the broken bone will also stop the bleeding in very cold weather. We have seen a few exceptions, but generally, the leg below a broken bone loses its blood supply and eventually sloughs off.

Tactics for Recovering Deer with Broken Legs

Absolutely nothing is to be gained from waiting before tracking a deer that has been wounded in the leg. The problem is that many hunters, unaware of exactly what has happened, track a short distance and then decide to wait and "let the deer stiffen up". When they do begin tracking again and move the deer from its resting place, they find that they have little or no blood to follow. In this case, if the hunters know that a tracking dog and handler are available, they are likely to call for assistance.

As a handler/tracker, you should be able to determine quickly from your questioning of the hunter by telephone, or later from your own observation,

It required four miles of pursuit with a leashed tracking dog before this buck ran out of blood.

whether a leg hit is involved. Track such deer as soon as possible after they have been wounded, particularly in very cold weather when the wound may freeze solid. The strategy is to cold track the deer to where it has stopped and then to get it moving again. Leg-hit deer are often reluctant to lie down, so frequently there will be no bed. Once you are certain that you have jumped the right deer, you should push it hard for at least a half mile. If heavy bleeding resumes, you can probably walk the deer down, although it may well require four miles or more at a fast pace to accomplish this. The deer will bleed out steadily from the exposed marrow until it is too weak to go farther. If the leg wound does not begin to bleed again, it is best to back off since there is little prospect of catching up to the deer.

The dog and handler can track far faster than the unaided hunter tracking by eye, and this speed puts pressure on the deer and keeps it bleeding. You may only see a nickel-sized drop every ten feet or so, but more blood is being lost in fine droplets as the broken leg works back and forth. It is an easy track for the dog to follow, and rarely is the deer lost because the dog loses the trail.

If large streams or lakes are approached, it is better to ease up and avoid driving the deer to water. Deer learn from being chased by coyotes and free-running dogs that water is a final resort of escape.

Young, leg-hit deer will sometimes give up after a very short time. A seasoned adult is a very different animal with enormous toughness and stamina. A mature deer, especially a tough old buck, will go full power, up and down hill, almost until the end. Once the deer allows you to approach within fifty or a hundred yards before it gets up, the end is very near and not in doubt.

High Back Wounds

Overview

High back hits fall into two broad categories. If the backbone is broken or the spinal cord is damaged, the blood tracker will never be called. Such a deer drops instantly, stays put and dies almost immediately. A somewhat higher shot above the spine can produce identical immediate symptoms and yet have a very different result. After collapsing as if struck by a great hammer, the deer regains consciousness and coordination, stumbles to its feet and is gone, usually forever. As a dog handler and blood tracker, you will be called in on the shots above the spine that stunned but did not kill the deer. Usually these will be cases where firearms rather than bows were employed. Be wary of cases where the deer has gone down instantaneously.

A hunter called and told me a story that was at once funny and sad. It more than sums up all the other tales of woe that we hear each season. The hunter in southeastern New York asked me to come and find his deer. He had shot his buck, and thought that he had killed it instantly—it dropped and did not move. The first thing the hunter did was to take a photo to preserve the moment. He rested his sling-equipped shotgun in the forks of the buck's antlers. As he stepped back with his camera to take the photo, the buck shuddered, lurched to its feet and took off. The hunter never found his shotgun and never found his deer.

Another story shows that there are exceptions to most of the rules about wounded deer, including the rule that you never catch up to deer hit high in the back.

Once I was asked by a Conservation Officer to track a deer that had been wounded out of season. The deer carcass was needed as evidence to prosecute the case. After tracking the buck for 200 yards, I saw enough blood sign to decide that the deer was hit high above the shoulder. It seemed very unlikely that we would ever see the deer. The Officer said, "Well, let's give it a try anyway". After a half mile of difficult tracking with no visible blood, we came up on the buck very much alive in the middle of a rhododendron thicket. He was wounded exactly as the evidence had indicated. I saw hair fly as two handgun shots hit the deer. The deer took off, and we never caught up to him again. The regulation .38 caliber solid bullets did not do much of a job.

Signs of a High Back Hit

After the shot, another clue that you are dealing with a high, grazing back shot is a large amount of deer hair on the ground at the point of impact. There may be as much as a small handful. A bullet or slug that hits the deer squarely cuts only a small amount of hair.

High blood smears on weeds and brush are another giveaway, although the eye tracker, concentrating upon what is on the ground, will often miss this. The average buck in New York is only about 34 inches at the shoulder so be concerned if there are smears above 28 inches in height. However, don't base all your judgment upon one piece of evidence. I remember tracking and catching up to a deer that left one waist-high blood smear near the beginning of the trail. It turned out that the deer was wounded just above the front hoof. The deer was jumping when it left the high smear on a bush.

Physical Characteristics of High Back Hits

High back hits may temporarily, or permanently, paralyze the central nervous system. The spinal cord, which runs through the holes of the spinal vertebrae, receives a massive jolt from the high-energy slug or bullet passing in close proximity. If the projectile hits or passes close to one of the prongs (*spinous processes*) that stick up from the chest vertebrae, this readily transmits shock to the spinal cord that runs inside the vertebrae. The deer may stay down a few seconds, a few minutes or forever. However, if it gets back on its feet and regains its coordination, it is generally impossible to catch up to it.

Above the spine there is enough muscle tissue to produce considerable bleeding, but ordinarily this bleeding does not continue long enough to kill the deer. With damaged back muscles, the deer may not run well, but it will

Waist-high blood smear from doe. She dropped instantly and was later tracked for six miles. She probably recovered.

keep walking with little difficulty. There are exceptions. In the fall of 1996, I tracked a deer that had been shot across the loins above the spine and was very dead. A mechanical broadhead with wide cantilever cutting blades had produced enough external hemorrhage to kill the deer. The only reason I was called in was because four inches of snow had covered the blood line.

Shots that pass closely beneath the spine can produce the same temporary paralysis as an above the spine shot. Here, the large dorsal aorta artery that runs along beneath the spine will probably be ruptured by the same impact. The deer will be dead of hemorrhage before it can get back on its feet. Deer shot with firearms directly below the spine do not have to be tracked.

What are reported as high chest shots often do not enter the chest cavity at all and are actually well above the spine. As discussed in the last chapter, many hunters do not realize that the length of the *spinous processes* and the length of the hair along the deer's topline can make the top of the deer appear to be six inches or more above the actual level of the spine. Arrows shot into the upper ribs may be deflected horizontally into the spine, seldom killing the deer. An arrow shaft, sticking out high and horizontally from the deer, indicates that this has happened.

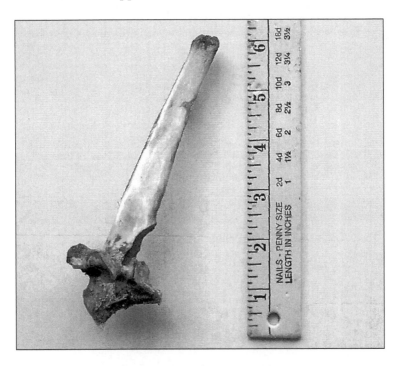

One of the spinous processes projecting upward from the spinal vertebrae

Tactics for Dealing With High Back Shots

There is no perfect strategy for dealing with high back shots. The best policy is to screen these calls carefully on the basis of clear evidence before you drive a long distance to track the deer. The best indicators are the instant knockdown and the high blood smears. Often the hunter will miss critical evidence, and you will not be aware of the true location of the hit until you have tracked several hundred yards. Once you are there, the best policy is to continue, pointing out sign to the hunter until it is clear to him that this deer is strong and will survive.

Head Shots, Jaw Shots: Firearms

Overview

There are hunters, particularly riflemen, who love head shots. "Clean kill or clean miss," they say. "You don't spoil any meat." But anyone who has worked very much with wounded deer will condemn the head shots. The question is not necessarily a matter of marksmanship because deer often move their heads quickly and unpredictably as the shot is squeezed off. The result is not always a clean miss; it can mean a smashed jaw and a deer unable to eat or drink. Any injury that damages a deer's teeth and its ability to browse and chew, is a mortal injury for that deer. It will not be a quick, clean death, but rather a slow lingering one from starvation.

The deer's brain, which is about the size of your clenched fist, makes up a small percentage of the deer's total head volume. The rest of the deer's head may not be essential to maintain life from moment to moment, but without a nose, mouth and teeth in good working order, there can be no long-term survival.

Signs of a Jaw Injury

Injuries to the head are easy to identify once you know what to look for. There may be reports of the deer's unsupported jaw hanging down. At the location where the deer was shot there are likely to be small fragments of bone and teeth. This is one of the reasons why it is so important to go back to the original point of impact when you begin to track.

Generally, there is not sufficient bleeding to permit eye tracking at a practical speed after the first few hundred yards. However, a deer with a mouth wound will, from time to time, shake its head in pain as it travels. This produces ropey strands of saliva tinged with blood, which are shaken out at a 90-degree angle to the trail. At the deer's bed, blood and saliva will lie outside of the indentation formed by the body of the bedded deer.

Methods of Tracking and Taking a Jaw-Shot Deer

A jaw-shot deer is doomed, but catching up to it and ending its misery is not easy unless the deer is a fawn. In places such as big swamps with heavy cover it may be impossible.

Once you are certain that you are dealing with an ultimately lethal head shot, do not attempt to track at night. Move the deer into some dense holding cover and "park" it until daylight. When you have good visibility, try to push the deer into open hardwoods or fields and hedgerows, where a careful long-range shot is possible on the slowly moving deer. In many cases, the hanging lower jaw is a certain means of identifying the right deer.

Neck Shots

Overview

The general rule with neck shots is that either the hunter gets the deer very quickly or he does not get it at all. The heavy vertebrae of the neck are highly vulnerable to a slug or bullet, and a broadhead, striking in the same place, may get through and sever the spinal cord. Below the spinal column in the neck lie major blood vessels: the branching carotid artery and the jugular vein. If these are severed, there will be no need for a track-

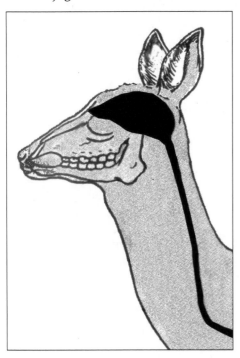

The brain is a small part of a deer's head.

ing dog. There will be a solid six inch-wide path of blood to where the deer collapses. However, for bowhunters the neck is not a good target. If the spinal cord and the major blood vessels are not disrupted, the deer is likely to keep going and soon will stop bleeding.

Signs of a Neck Hit

Even on the less serious neck hits there is usually quite a bit of visible blood. The hunter should be able to track by eye for at least 300 yards. Some of the blood he sees will be high on brush and branches, and generally, there will be blood spots on both sides of the trail. When there is no more visible blood, the tracking dog should be able to follow for at least another half mile. Blood smears on brush and occasionally a drop of blood on the ground will confirm the line.

Usually there will be little internal bleeding on the neck shots you are called upon to track. What you see on the outside is the sum total of what the deer has lost. Since a deer's neck is narrow and an arrow usually passes completely through, there will be no further damage from an arrowhead working about. Because of this same narrowness of the neck, a bullet or slug will pass through with minimal expansion if no bone is encountered. The wound channel and the shock will normally be less than in a chest hit.

Physical Characteristics of Neck Wounds

As explained above, breaks of the spinal cord and wounds to major blood vessels, the carotid arteries and the jugular vein, are swiftly lethal affairs. Especially when a carotid artery is cut, the brain is starved for blood and oxygen, and the deer loses consciousness. Beyond these major conduits, there are not many good places to hit a deer in the neck. Of course a high velocity rifle bullet striking almost anywhere in the neck may still generate enough shock and damage to anchor the deer for a second shot. But a shotgun slug, particularly if it passes through the fleshy area above the vertebrae and ahead of the shoulders, will not accomplish very much. For a bowhunter, the situation is even worse. If he misses those narrow, lethal targets in the neck, there are no acceptable secondary targets. Cutting the esophagus or food pipe will not kill the deer for a very long time. If his broadhead cuts the windpipe or trachea, he may realize what has happened because he hears whistling and wheezing. Unfortunately, if the deer does die eventually, only the crows and coyotes will be there to enjoy it.

Most non-lethal neck wounds are simple pass-throughs in the fleshy tissue above the spine. As a handler, you should explain to hunters that these low percentage shots should be avoided.

Tactics for Doing the Best You Can on Neck Shots

It is hard for a tracker to find a deer that has been shot in the neck. If possible, turn down such calls. Usually you will be able to track much farther than the hunter, but you are not likely to come up with the deer. Again, we must go over the exceptions. If the broadhead has stayed in the deer's neck and is situated close to major blood vessels, take the call. As the deer moves, the arrow will work back and forth. Sooner rather than later, it may cut far enough to create a sudden hemorrhage and death to the deer. Near the top of a deer's neck there are two tendons that hold up the head and neck. If both tendons are severed the deer is in serious difficulty, and it is possible to walk it down. This situation occurs rarely.

Muscle Wounds: Archery and Firearms

Overview

Various flesh wounds or muscle wounds occur in deer hunting, but if no bones are broken, the deer has a good chance of survival. An adult deer's toughness and recuperative power are vastly greater than that of a human being. Deer often show a remarkable capacity to stop bleeding a few minutes after sustaining serious tissue damage. This does vary from deer to deer; some deer will bleed to death from a wound that will have little effect on another deer. There has been research to suggest that during the rut bucks have the highest level of clotting factors in their blood.

Muscle Wounds and Blood Sign

Muscle blood is generally bright red, and there will be a lot of it on the ground because all of the bleeding is on the outside. The color and length of hair cut by the broadhead, slug or bullet help to identify the site of the wound on the deer. The placement of smears of blood on weeds and brush is also important. Blood that has spurted out under pressure indicates that an artery has been cut. The odds of finding the deer greatly improve when the larger arteries are involved.

Inexperienced hunters, who see dinner plate-sized pools of blood, are certain that this guarantees that the deer lies dead somewhere over the next ridge. Such a quantity of blood from the ham of an adult deer guarantees very little in itself. A lot of blood may flow out from the smaller veins and capillaries of a deer's thigh, but if the bleeding stops, there will seldom be enough blood loss to kill the deer. You will find that the bleeding from muscle wounds clots up before an adult deer is in serious jeopardy.

Trackers will never be called in on cases where the deer has been hit in the femoral artery. The femoral artery is a high volume, high pressure blood pipe that feeds the massive thigh muscles of the deer. It runs through the muscle close behind the thighbone or femur, hence its name. When the femoral artery is cut, blood loss is so rapid that the deer goes down within 100 yards.

The femoral artery should never be an intentional target; it is scarcely more than half an inch in diameter when filled with blood, and it is a difficult target. The femoral artery can be ruptured by a slug or bullet that plows through adjacent tissue. In bowhunting, a miss of the femoral artery by a mere quarter of an inch produces a muscle wound that it is unlikely to produce more than exercise for the tracker and the hunter.

Tactics for Dealing with Muscle Wounds

Practically speaking, the first task of the tracker is to determine if the deer has been hit only in muscle tissue, or whether the external muscle bleeding is masking more serious bleeding from the deer's internal organs. Generally, you must track an adult deer to a wound bed to determine its condition. A cold bed with little blood suggests that the deer was strong enough to leave voluntarily. If you find that the deer has stopped bleeding, is moving well and jumping fences, you are usually safe in deciding that the deer will survive.

In a few cases deer with massive muscle wounds can be recovered by tracking the deer to its wound bed and then pushing it hard. The tracking dog will follow the deer much faster than you can track it by eye. If the deer begins bleeding again, or if it is very weak, you have a chance of catching up to it. This is often worth a try, but you should base your decision upon how closely the deer allowed you to approach before it left the bed.

In the Deep South and Texas where dogs are allowed to work off lead, muscle-shot deer can frequently be run down and   "bayed up" with an efficiency impossible in the North.

Fawns, young deer that were born the previous spring, are much easier to recover when they have muscle wounds. Sometimes the tracker and dog can walk right up to them, or the fawns will quit after moving out a hundred yards from their bed.

Once a deer has lived through a winter and has matured, it becomes a very different animal. Adult deer do not quit. A tough old buck is like a truck; it goes up hill, down hill, wherever it wants to go as long as there is gas in the tank. Only when it is totally out of gas, does it collapse, and generally this happens suddenly. A mere muscle wound is unlikely to reduce it to this point.

Most of your calls involving muscle shots will be calls in which you evaluate the situation by tracking several hundred yards beyond the point of hunter's loss, or beyond the first wound bed, to determine that the deer will probably be all right. The hunter is generally more relieved than disappointed. Your work did not lead to a find, but certainly, you did not fail. Working as a team, you and your dog did all that was possible.

What Does the Amount of Blood on the Ground Tell Us?

To sum up the subject of blood sign in muscle hits, the amount of blood is much less significant than the type of blood and its placement. For example, the amount of external bleeding on a muscle-shot deer may appear to be identical to what was seen in another case where the deer was recovered dead after a modest distance. In making comparisons about real blood loss, both internal and external bleeding must be added together. Let's face it, such calculations are impossible for a hunter to do under field conditions. Bright muscle blood on the ground does not tell us very much.

Particularly when a big buck is involved, many hunters will greatly exaggerate the volume of external blood loss. Actually, it does not take much blood to make a very good blood trail. In training your dog you will discover that it is easy to lay a visible blood trail for over a half mile with only a half pint of blood. With a pint (half a quart), you could produce quite a few good-sized pools of blood in the track. Yet a pint of blood is the amount that a deer-sized human loses when donating blood. The drawing of this pint of blood from our own bodies when we donate at the Blood Bank has little effect upon us.

I have had a few hunters on the phone report "gallons" of blood on the ground. When I got to the hit site, the amount was much less, of course. For your own estimates, it helps to know how much blood is actually in a deer, and how much blood loss must occur before the deer reaches the point of no return. A whitetail, weighing 150 pounds on the hoof, has in its whole circulatory system about eight pints of blood, which is four quarts or one gallon. The deer has to lose more than a third of this amount, roughly 2¾ pints before blood pressure falls to a point where irreversible shock sets in. The deer then slips into a coma, and all its vital processes spiral downward.

Tell your hunters who have shot "big bucks" that it will take more than a quart and a half of blood loss to put their deer down. This is a lot of blood.

There is another useful thing to know about the amount of blood to be seen on the trail. A deer dying from internal or external bleeding, or a combination of both, will gradually stop losing blood as death approaches. For the last 200 yards before it goes down for good, there may be no visible blood on the trail at all, but there will still be scent for your dog to follow. When visible blood ends, it is not the time to quit! At this stage, it is likely that the deer's blood pressure has fallen to the point where there is no external bleeding. It will not go much farther.

Deer in the final stages of collapse due to blood loss are still capable of a final burst of energy. The handler should remain alert and cautious.

What Does the Hair at the Hit Site Tell Us?

Most of the white hair on a deer comes from the hindquarters or the lower half of the deer; the belly hair is very coarse; the long white hair is finer on the inside of the thighs and the hind end. Of course, the underside of the tail is white. There is a patch of shorter white hair at the deer's throat. The brown hair of a deer is located on the back and sides, the forelegs and the outside of the thighs and the rear legs. Hair on the forelegs is shorter than body hair. The brisket or sternum, the bottom of the deer's chest, will have dark, rather short hair, which is slightly kinky. It is unlike any other hair on the deer.

The brown body hair gives rise to some confusion because the lower two thirds of each "brown" body hair are actually light gray or beige. Sometimes in poor light, these hairs are reported to be white.

It is generally possible to recognize hairs cut at the entry from those cut as the arrow, slug or bullet exited. Some of the hairs at the exit will be matted with blood or tissue. Putting this information together with the known angle of the shot permits a reconstruction of the trajectory through the deer.

There is no way to give precise descriptions of the color and length of hair on each part of "the average" deer's body. The hair patterns vary from sub-species to sub-species and cannot be applied to all North American whitetails in the same way. For example, the South Texas whitetail is lighter in color and very different from the whitetail of the Northeast. In addition, hair grows throughout the fall hunting seasons. The coat of a deer on October 1 is much shorter than it will be on December 1. If you wish to do a precise analysis of hair sign, the best thing is to make a hair sample booklet for your particular locality and stage of the hunting season.

The amount of hair found at the hit site can be a valuable indication of how the deer was hit. If a firearms hunter reports a fist full of hair, it is an indication that he has raked or grazed the deer. As mentioned above, this is often seen on a high back shot. A slug or bullet hitting squarely will cut some hair but a much smaller amount.

Some of the hair may be adhering to a tiny patch of outer skin; this is another sign of a grazing hit, but most hunters will not notice this and recognize that it is significant. It is worthwhile checking to make sure that the slug did not hit a branch on the way in to the target. Too many hunters fail to inspect the hit site carefully, and some do not check it at all because they do not realize its importance.

Large amount of deer hair produced by a high, grazing shot.

Detail of photograph above showing flake of outer skin with hair, which is another indication of a grazing shot.

Summary

- Begin tracking deer with broken legs as quickly as possible and keep them moving.

- If a hunter reports that the deer went down instantly at the shot, it usually means a high back shot.

- If a deer gets back on its feet after a high back shot, it is unlikely that you can catch up to it with a leashed tracking dog.

- On neck shot calls, you either get the deer right away or you don't get it at all.

- Broken jaw shots are always killers in the end, but it is difficult to get close to the deer. Track jaw-shot deer in the daytime when you have a chance for a long shot.

- Muscle wounds, which cannot be tracked by eye, seldom kill the deer. These deer should be kept moving until their condition has been established.

- Fawns quit sooner than adult deer.

- The color and placement of blood has much more significance than the amount of blood that you see.

- A large amount of hair at the hit site suggests a grazing shot.

- Always check for blood smears above the ground as well as for blood drops on the ground.

Chapter 16

Tracking Wounded Bears

This book is about tracking wounded deer, but in certain parts of the country an occasional call may come in to track wounded black bear. Such a call requires some adjustments, but it should not present a problem for a dog proficient at tracking wounded deer. A guide, who is specialized in bear hunting over bait, might have more occasions to track a bear. In any case, it is not necessary to track bears with a bears-only specialist. Most dogs experienced in tracking wounded deer readily make the transition.

Some of us in Deer Search and the United Blood Trackers have tracked a number of bears with Dachshunds. Most of these Dachshunds had never tracked anything but wounded deer, but they started off willingly on a wounded bear line once they understood that this is what the handler wanted them to do. The Dachshunds gave us some funny looks at the beginning, and their shoulder hackles came up as they began their work. They sensed from the scent that a bear is something big and nasty, even if they had never seen one. On their first bear line, they showed some caution for the first 100 yards. When they warmed to the task, they forgot about being worried. If the bear was jumped alive, they were raring to go on the hot line.

Bears often leave a poor blood trail for the eye tracker. The fat of the bear tends to close the arrow or bullet wound, and the heavy coat absorbs much of the blood. In the more difficult cases, much of the blood that the unassisted hunter sees will be smeared on saplings and branches rather than dripped on the ground.

Bears can be hard to track by eye, but they are easy for a dog because the body and pad scent of the bear is overwhelmingly strong. I was called upon to track a bear 48 hours after it had been wounded with a 30-06 rifle. When I saw the evidence, I strongly suspected a grazing high leg or shoulder hit that had not broken bone. We tracked over a half mile of visible blood trail and through a deadfall area where the hunter had stopped tracking. My Dachshund Sabina was able to continue with little difficulty for over three miles of typical Catskill mountain terrain, forested with hardwoods and hemlocks. A few, widely scattered smears of blood on saplings indicated that we were on the right track. The bear just kept going, and we never caught up to it. The probabilities are very high that this bear survived.

I hope to see a bear killed cleanly, but when a bear is wounded, I do love to track it. I was in the middle of a beaver swamp one fall, trying to track a wounded buck, when a good call came in on my cell phone. It was a bear call; the bear had been shot with a bow a little too far back.

I track wounded deer at night most of the time, but I draw the line on bears after dark. Since it was already late afternoon, and the call was more than a hundred miles away, the hunter and I agreed to meet in the morning. When I began tracking, the line was 28 hours old. The hunter, Anthony Lamonaca, had done an amazing job of tracking that bear up Mombacus Mountain in the Catskills on the faintest drops and smears of blood. Finally, after about a half mile, he had run out of line. The bear had gone up through a blowdown area where a tornado had passed through. It was up and down through deadfalls, with lots of thick mountain laurel to crawl through. We had to track again, over most of the half mile of extremely sparse blood trail, before we could get to the point of loss. This was in the middle of a mess of downed trees, which looked like a war zone. By the way, as New York Law requires, I was using a tracking leash, thirty feet of stiff mountain climbing rope. It never got hung up.

Even though the blood drops and smears had completely stopped, there was no shortage of scent, and Sabina kept going without difficulty. We had no way of knowing if the bear was dead or alive. Probably, we went only another 200 yards, but it seemed liked a long way in that dense cover. Sabina was tracking along a slight trace of a path, still going up, when I saw her raise her nose into the wind. She pulled off at right angles into the wind with her head high. We went about 50 yards through the thickest laurel I had ever seen, and there was the bear, dead. Dead was fine with me. In the first excitement, it looked as big as a Volkswagen; much later on the scale it was a dressed 318 pounds, which is still a big bear. Sabina jumped right in and grabbed some fur, but once she realized the bear was dead, she did not care for the smell much.

Sabina was content to watch as we gutted the bear and started to drag it down the mountain. When she finds a deer, we have to tie her up to keep her away from the work that has to be done. We never would have moved that bear up a mountain, and as it was, it took the rest of the day to get it down the mountain and out to a four-wheeler. Even though the bear was not fat, it was like a 300-pound sack of jelly. Its head was big and heavy ($20^3/_8$", Pope & Young), and we struggled to lift it over every log or deadfall we encountered.

Under normal conditions the strength of bear footprint scent more than compensates for the lack of blood that is associated with many wounded bear tracks. However, there are some complicating factors. This overwhelmingly strong footprint scent does not stand up well to rainfall. When there is blood on the ground, rain merely dilutes it so that we humans cannot see it, but dogs can still smell it. However, if there is no blood on the ground to begin with, the dog will probably have problems with the rained-out footprint scent.

My own dogs have also had some difficulty distinguishing one bear scent from another. One time during bow season Sabina tracked what was

The author, Sabina and Frank Lamonaca with Frank's bear

obviously a bear for almost a half mile. Then she gave me a long look, which said, "This can't be right."

She readily followed me back to the hit site, and after some searching took a line out in a different direction. This time we found the bear dead at 250 yards, 43 hours after the shot.

In the right situation, a small tracking dog can be ideal for recovering a bear, and yet most of us in Deer Search, who have been tracking wounded bear, have come up with less than 20 percent of the bears we track. We find a much higher percentage of deer. One reason appears to be that a mortally wounded bear usually does not travel as far as a comparably wounded deer before it beds down. Therefore, the mortally wounded bear is more often found by the hunters, themselves. Even if there is no blood trail, a thorough area search has a good chance of turning up that bear unless the cover is exceptionally dense.

Another factor that contributes to a relatively low recovery rate in bears is the bear's anatomy. Compared to deer, bear have a proportionately smaller vital area, and it is lower in the body. The heart and lungs occupy a smaller part of the forward end of the body. Farther back, the stomach and intestines also occupy proportionately less space in a bear than in a ruminant like a deer that must process large quantities of bulky food. In other words, in comparing deer and bear, it is somewhat more likely that a bear, with its hairy, bulky outline, will be superficially wounded. Hunters do not aim low enough. This is especially true in bowhunting.

Most of the "difficult" bears that a tracking dog is called upon to track, when all else has failed, will not be mortally wounded. It is the handler's task to find out just what happened. If we track a bear and determine that it is strong and traveling well the next day, we believe that we have accomplished something. The bear is not wasted, and we have the satisfaction of knowing it will be there for next year.

Wounded bears generally do not go as far as deer hit in a similar way. In addition, wounded bears should not be tracked at night like deer. Good light is important; since a wounded black bear in thick cover on a dark night is not easy to see unless it is very close. Black bears, unlike grizzlies, will probably not be aggressive to humans even if wounded. Gary Alt, a noted bear biologist from Pennsylvania, advised me not to worry about aggressive black bears. Alt is no armchair theorist either, having taken rectal temperatures of sleeping bears in their winter dens! Still there is a difference between black bear attitudes toward people and toward dogs.

Bears swat dogs more freely. I spoke to Buddy Potter, an old bear hunter in the Florida "Big Bend" country. He had just lost six big Plott hounds, his whole pack, to a bear in one season. The bear, apparently one individual, had taken to doubling back and ambushing the dogs, one at a time, with a skull crushing bite.

We should not count on wounded bears being polite to our tracking dogs, even if the great majority are fearful of man. Nuisance bears in "no bear hunting" areas are certainly not always respectful of human beings. Where a leash must be used, it hampers the dog's mobility; the handler must be alert and ready to give quick assistance. Even though I carry a .44 magnum handgun, I prefer to have a calm, experienced hunter right behind me to my left or right. Armed with a 12-gauge pump shotgun loaded with slugs, his job is to stop the bear before the bear stops the dog.

Breeds of Dogs for Finding Wounded Bear

Much depends on the terrain, the cover and whether or not the dogs will be worked on a tracking leash. If for legal reasons the dog must be kept on a leash, there is no advantage in having a dog larger than a hunting Dachshund or a German Jagdterrier. The small ones can climb just about anywhere that a man or wounded bear will go. A small dog is easier to handle on the long leash in briars and blowdowns. Their small size makes them very handy to put on an ATV as you drive in on logging roads to the place where the bear was shot. In situations where the dog may legally be released on bear, as in British Columbia, I would probably prefer a 70 pound dog fitted with a GPS collar. The much smaller Jagdterriers with their great courage and agility would also be a good choice. An extremely good nose is less important than intelligence because the tracking dog must stay on the correct animal. You do not want a hound that will strike the first hot track and leave the country on it. A big game hound, particularly an old Plott or Bluetick bitch that has lost speed, could be useful. Generally, the cur breeds, particularly the ones that work cattle like the Southern Black Mouth Curs, handle very well. These curs are very intelligent... intelligent enough to stay on the right animal... intelligent enough not to get themselves killed unnecessarily.

The late Henri Parceaud of Chibougamou, Quebec, was a guide and outfitter who used French Griffons Nivernais as his hounds for running and treeing bear. His French ancestry probably had something to do with his choice of this wiry-coated breed. For his clients who hunted over bait from tree stands, Parceaud used an entirely different breed. He preferred European Wirehaired Dachshunds to the big powerful Griffons for tracking through the dense black spruce to the bears his clients had shot. Today (2016) European Wirehaired Dachshunds have become a popular breed for tracking wounded bear in Quebec.

Those who will have only occasional opportunities to track wounded bear should find that their regular wounded deer dog will work very well. There are, however, a few dogs who are very competent wounded deer trackers, and yet want nothing to do with bears. The wounded bear specialist does not need a dog with a Bloodhound class nose, and he should keep in mind that courage, intelligence and responsiveness are the most important factors to consider.

Breed labels are not an absolute guarantee when selecting a dog to track wounded bear. I can remember coon hunting as a boy with two big Redbone Coonhounds. We ran into a bear one moonlight night, and the two hounds came in to us with their tails between their legs. You would not expect this from Redbones. Such anecdotes do not prove anything about the various breeds; dogs must be judged as individuals. Of course, the chances for a good one may be greater in one breed than in another. There are cowards in every

Andy Bensing and Arno with their first bear find.
Photo courtesy of Andy Bensing

breed of dog. These should not be used for tracking or allowed to reproduce. Fear, or at least the tendency to be intimidated, has a strong genetic basis.

The complete book on tracking wounded bears remains to be written. The subject warrants much more attention than it has received; most bear hunters seem unaware of what a tracking dog can accomplish. If they do not find the bear themselves, they assume that nothing can be done.

In some states such as New Jersey, there is strong public opposition to bear hunting, but nuisance bears, which have entered houses or killed livestock, still have to be shot. In March 2002 a bear threatened a house-holder in Sparta, New Jersey, to the point that police officers came and shot it. The wounded bear escaped and according to press reports, "nearly two dozen police officers and state officials" spent two days unsuccessfully looking for it. The bear was probably no threat to society, but it would have been better public relations if an accurate report could have been made of the wounded bear's status, dead or alive. If a tracking dog and handler had been called in, it would have been an easy matter to either find the dead bear, shoot it if mortally wounded and still alive, or determine that it was alive and recovering.

Subsequently, the New Jersey Division of Fish and Wildlife did call me down to help check out the status of two other aggressive bears that had been shot. One bear was difficult to track without blood on wind-swept, bare rock after 24 hours, but we worked the wind and swept the area. At least we were able to say, with some confidence, that the bear was not seriously wounded. Later on this bear was live trapped in good condition.

We tracked the other bear for over a mile and found two beds that it had left voluntarily. It did not seem likely that this bear was seriously wounded either. Subsequently, the New Jersey Division of Fish and Wildlife bought two Black Mouth Curs to deal with bear problems.

Information on tracking wounded grizzly bears is beyond the scope of this book. It is a challenging subject. Research on grizzlies should be undertaken by a team of biologists, who never track the same animal together. It is essential that someone survive to write the report.

Summary

- Wounded bears leave little visible blood, but their strong scent makes them easy to track.

- Bears should not be tracked at night when visibility is poor.

- When similar wounds are involved, bears usually do not travel as far as deer.

- Most dogs that track wounded deer will track wounded bear without any specialized training.

Chapter 17

Tracking Wounded Moose and Elk

Finding wounded deer and bear with leashed tracking dogs has been my passion for more than 39 years in New York State. Since my origins are French, it was natural for me to become curious about what was going on in French Canada. Over the last five years hunters and outfitters of the Province of Quebec have been using leashed tracking dogs more and more to find deer, bear and moose that left no blood trail. I gave a tracking workshop in Quebec, participated in another and made some friends. In September of 2009 Alain Ridel of Mont Carmel invited me to come up with one of my own dogs to track with him in the early bow/crossbow season. I also tracked with Philippe Rainaud, an experienced tracker who had come over with his Dachshund from France.

We did our tracking in the Gaspé Region south of the St. Lawrence River. For much of the ten days we hunted and tracked out of an evaporator house in a big sugar bush, where we could look down Lac de l'Est (East Lake) right into Maine. The language of my friends may have been French, but the game, cover and terrain were very similar to that of the moose country just to the south. We actually tracked one moose that came within 100 meters of the border before he veered north. I'm glad he decided not to become an illegal immigrant.

According to Simon Lemay, a French Canadian outfitter, one of the important differences between moose and deer hunting is that there is a short time limit for finding wounded moose that run off after the shot. You can't just wait and find them the next morning as in the time-honored American tradition. A moose weighs between 800 and 1200 pounds on the hoof. The huge body mass, with all its natural heat, is well insulated by a coat almost as long and dense as a bear's. The rumen of a moose, where the first stage of digestion takes place, is proportionally much larger than in a deer. Moose fill this stomach with what deer hunters would call coarse, low quality browse. Moose have to eat a lot of this, and the bacteria-aided digestive system, which processes the browse, generates heat. Even after a moose is shot and killed this heat generation continues; the heat escapes slowly because of the large body mass and the insulating coat.

Simon Lemay maintains that he has to find a moose within five hours of its death to be sure that the meat will still be good. Alain Ridel and I had the experience of finding one moose that had been shot 14 hours earlier. The meat seemed all right when the animal was gutted where we found him, but the hunter, who is a professional butcher, told me later that it was inedible when they got it out of the woods the next morning. The outdoor temperature was running about 40 degrees F.

My romp in Quebec taught me that tracking wounded moose by eye is not an easy task. During hunting season the moose are no longer feeding on aquatic vegetation in wet areas that make for simple tracking of hoof marks. And you don't get much of a blood trail from a wounded moose, just as in the case of a wounded bear, because that heavy coat soaks up so much of the blood before it reaches the ground. The blood sign that you do see is generally wiped off on tree trunks and branches well off the ground.

From a dog's point of nose, a moose is easy to track. We are dealing with a big animal and lots of body scent. However, this scent does not seem to be as individualized as in the whitetail. Probably this is because moose lack well-defined interdigital glands between the cloves of their hooves. Depending on the moose you look at, or the authority you read, they either have no interdigital glands or they have glands that are barely visible. I could not find interdigital glands on the moose I observed in Quebec.

Clearly interdigital gland scent doesn't play a major role in identifying a particular moose; in the whitetail, on the other hand, these glands are much more important. Fortunately, moose are more solitary and their density in a given area is usually lower than is the case with whitetails. For the dog, identifying and staying on the right moose line is not too difficult.

From a handler's standpoint closely following a dog that is following a moose is not so easy; it's strenuous exercise. In all parts of Canada and in the United States where tracking dogs for wounded moose are legal, the handler is required by law to keep control of the dog on a long leash; this means that you have to go where the dog goes. Long legged moose stride with ease over the dead branches and dense young growth of the black spruce cutovers, but for a man this means stepping over, wriggling under or ramming through the same thick stuff. A big alder swamp, with the branches sticking out at a 45 degree angle, is another trial for short-legged humans, but a moose is built to deal with this.

This leads us to another point. When you work a tracking dog on a leash, there is no particular advantage in having a big, powerful dog that can pull you through the thickets a whole lot faster than you want to go. Many of the trackers in Quebec were using the same type of European Wirehaired Dachshunds that have become popular for tracking wounded deer in the United States. They were also using leashes made of the light, 4 mm polyethylene cord discussed in the equipment chapter.

At the time of this writing the trackers in Quebec do have one major problem that we do not have in the moose hunting areas of the United States. In Quebec it is illegal to carry a firearm, or any other weapon, when tracking wounded big game with a dog. This means that if the wounded moose, deer or bear is found alive, the tracker and his dog must withdraw while the hunter goes back to his vehicle for a gun or bow to put down his game. This delay is inconvenient, but the no firearms rule also creates a danger for both dog and handler. Are you going to stop a half ton of charging moose with a hunting knife? If you have been tracking for a while, you learn that moose, bear and even deer do charge on occasion. Even if mortally wounded, an adrenaline surge can give them enormous power at the last moment.

The lack of quick, efficient communication between trackers and hunters is a problem in Quebec, as it would no doubt be just across the border in northern Maine. Cell phone coverage is not very good in moose country, and then getting to the hunter over miles of rough logging roads takes time... time that really counts when a moose is down and body heat is threatening to spoil the meat. Clearly the Canadian guides and outfitters, who are in close contact with their clients in the woods, are in the best position to use a tracking dog to find a wounded or dead moose quickly. When the use of leashed tracking dogs finally catches on in northern Maine, it will be the guides and outfitters who are able use them most efficiently to find moose shot by their clients.

This brings up the delicate subject of why the use of leashed tracking dogs has been much slower to catch on in Maine the way it has in Quebec. Why has the use of leashed tracking dogs to find moose been so useful in Quebec and of little interest just to the south in Maine where it is also legal? Up in Quebec during three years (2009-2011) trackers took 610 calls for wounded moose and recovered 234 of them, a recovery rate of 38%. The great majority of the moose not found survived their less than mortal wounds.

Alain Ridel's Wirehaired Dachshund Théo with a recovered moose

We have to wonder. How many tons of moose meat will go to waste in Maine each year before most guides and hunters see the point of using a leashed tracking dog?

In recent years Susanne Hamilton in southeastern Maine has begun to modify the skepticism about tracking dogs. In 2015 her tracking Dachshunds, Buster and Meggie, found 31 deer, three bear and a moose on 73 calls. This accomplishment was well publicized. Most of the animals not found did not have mortal wounds. Susanne's example is changing the Maine mentality and it has inspired a number of other trackers in New England. Sooner or later the guides and outfitters in northern Maine will try the crazy idea of using a leashed tracking for finding wounded moose for their clients.

Elsewhere in North America the history of leashed tracking dogs for finding wounded moose is well underway. Independent of the Quebec example, Michael Schneider used a large Slovensky Kopov in British Columbia, and in 2010 Tim Nichols found his first moose in Vermont with Bruno, his Bavarian Mountain Hound. In Wyoming outfitter Justin Richins has used Remi, his Dachshund, to find a Shiras moose that his guides could not track.

The use of leashed dogs to track wounded elk is also being accepted. Species wise, the North American Elk is a larger version of the European Red Deer. As in Europe tracking dogs are proving to be very successful in finding them even in the arid conditions of the Rocky Mountain States. Elk do not have interdigital glands, but in the words of one tracker, "They are pretty stinky, and not hard to track even if there is no blood".

One problem is that the elk is much more a herd animal than the moose. When a wounded elk travels with a dozen healthy elk, it can be extremely difficult for the dog to pick out the right scent line and recognize the point where the wounded animal leaves the herd.

In the Rocky Mountain states outfitters are a driving force in legalizing the use of tracking dogs. An outfitter in New Mexico told me, "Our rifle and bowhunting clients were losing a certain percentage of elk. This had been accepted. Now we realize that something can be done about this."

Summary

- The value of leashed tracking dogs to find wounded moose has been clearly established in Quebec.

- Moose meat spoils quickly if the dead animal is not quickly found and gutted. A tracking dog can speed up the search and save the meat.

- The scent of elk is less individualized than that of deer. They do not have interdigital glands.

Chapter 18

Putting Down Live Wounded Deer

In 2003, when I wrote the first edition, this seemed to be a simple subject. Only two pages were directly devoted to it. But through conversations with hunters in various states and through more of my own experiences, I have come to realize that the subject is more complex than it seemed at first writing. In this third edition of *Tracking Dogs for Finding Wounded Deer* we are devoting a whole new chapter to the issue.

Ethics, Administration and Politics

There is an important ethical dimension of the problem faced by a tracker who approaches a wounded deer, still alive, but almost certain to die because of its injuries. This situation occurs about ⅓ of the time.

No ethical hunter or tracker wants to prolong animal suffering if there is a clear and decisive way to end it. The first moments after an animal is shot probably do not produce much pain. Shock serves as a temporary anesthetic. According to two surviving GIs of World War II, describing their experiences of taking a bullet through a lung, they felt immediate fear when they realized the implications of the injury they had just received. They went into shock; they felt confusion and drowsiness, but they did not feel pain for some time. The pain itself did not set in until at least a half hour later, and then it was alleviated by painkillers when the medics came.

A wounded deer does not have the benefits of morphine. If mortally wounded, it usually dies within the shock period. However, in the case of a smashed shoulder or a stomach shot, the deer can survive for hours or even days. Nature, in the form of wild predation or starvation, is certainly cruel, but we, as human predators, have the capacity to be more humane than coyotes.

Unfortunately, the tracking regulations for many states were written with the assumption that other considerations should be given priority over the ethical dimension. For example, the original Michigan regulations stated: It is unlawful to make use of a dog in hunting deer except that a dog may be used to locate a down or mortally wounded deer if the dog is kept on a leash and none of the persons in attendance possesses a firearm or bow and arrow. If the tracking is done at night, artificial lights ordinarily carried in the hand may be used. Fortunately the original regulation has now been modified.

In the real world of tracking there is of course no reliable way of knowing in advance whether a deer is mortally wounded or not. The hunter is usually convinced that he has killed his deer, but only tracking the deer and observing its actions will lead to a reliable conclusion about whether the deer is destined to live or die. Wisconsin, Indiana and Michigan all have or had similar regulations restricting the carrying of firearms and bows while tracking. The official assumption was that live, potentially dangerous deer would never be encountered.

New York State, in contrast, provides that only you (the handler) may carry a firearm or longbow while tracking big game. However, if it is daytime (sunrise to sunset) and the hunting season is still open, the hunter may also carry a firearm or longbow.... S/he may only use a firearm or longbow lawful during the season and location where the hunt occurred. In the Northeast, Vermont, New Hampshire and Maine closely follow the New York model.

Maryland regulations present a middle-of-the-road position, allowing the use of firearms only during legal hunting hours. During legal hunting hours Illinois allows the use of archery equipment during bow season and legal firearms during the gun seasons.

Back in 1987, when these matters were being discussed by leaders of Deer Search and officials of New York's DEC, the humanitarian issue carried considerable weight. For 11 years there had been an experimental tracking program in the state under the aegis of a "scientific collector's license", and the DEC was clearly aware that live wounded animals would be encountered in the field. The option of leaving them to a lingering death did not seem attractive at that time, especially when anti-hunters were stressing the "inhumanity" of hunting.

The reasoning that took place in some other states, after the New York regulations were in place, has yet to be publicized. We do know that in the upper Midwest the DNRs wanted to limit complications and administrative costs. They did not opt for a mandatory notification of a conservation officer before each deer call. Also these agencies did not put in place any requirements for tracking licenses or a handler exam on legalities, techniques and safety precautions. In Wisconsin, Michigan, Indiana, Illinois and Ohio any licensed hunter with a dog can track a wounded deer. This barebones system is very cheap to administer, but it also gives the DNRs no handles for supervision and control. In Wisconsin, Michigan and Indiana eliminating bows and firearms entirely promised to head off potential problems, and to prevent wounded deer tracking from being used as a cover for jacklighting and other forms of poaching. In the long run the no weapons provisions will certainly create serious problems of another sort. It is only a matter of time before someone is killed or gravely injured.

In Wisconsin, which was the pioneer state in the Midwest for legalizing leashed tracking, there was a special consideration that no doubt helped to tilt the balance against the use of firearms by handlers. Native Americans in that state had petitioned the DNR to restore their aboriginal rights to "jack" deer with a light. They pointed out that their ancestors had taken deer from canoes at night by means of bows and birch bark torches. It was politically very difficult to say "no" to Native American demands for firearm and flashlight for deer hunting, and yet say "yes" to others who wanted to use firearm and flashlight to put down wounded deer.

This chapter is not a legal treatise. It would not be very useful to go through a detailed, state by state analysis of the laws and regulation as they pertain to ending the suffering of a wounded deer. The spectrum of regulations extends from the New York State model, which was created after long discussion, and with ethical consideration emerging as paramount, to the Wisconsin model where the writers of the regulation believed that they were constrained by non-ethical factors that they could not ignore. We can explore the real life situations that can and have arisen under different systems of regulation. Almost certainly many of the regulations will change, and the reader must keep up to date through regular consultation with state DNRs.

Handler Safety

Since I wrote the first edition of this book I had an experience that gave me new insights into the problems of dispatching a wounded deer. This involves the handler safety issue which was not stressed enough in the first edition. My new experience involved wounded deer #210; I had gone a long time without any serious incidents. Way back in 1976, the third deer that I had ever tracked had charged my dog; that buck had been shot before he did any damage. My experience with my second aggressive deer was more serious.

On December 20, 2004 I found myself in the unusual position of tracking my own wounded buck. It was a hundred yard shot with my muzzleloader, but I had a broadside shot, and I could tell the placement was good because of the reaction of the deer. However, at the hit site there was absolutely no sign of blood, hair or bone. I circled the area many times and could find no trace of a blood trail. Strange things happen. Unwilling to admit the possibility that I had missed, I went home, notified DEC Law Enforcement and got my tracking dog Sabina. I took along a handheld tracking light, and my handgun with its scope sight and lighted cross hairs. I had shot many wounded deer with this rig, but it proved to be a stupid choice on this occasion. In the emergency situation that was to develop, this was like having no firearm at all.

At the hit site Sabina immediately signaled to me that the deer had been wounded. We were off together into the darkening woods as the light snowfall intensified.

We did not see blood for nearly six hundred yards and then jumped the buck shortly afterwards. I could see that one shoulder was broken, but he seemed very strong. I was to learn later that my sabot bullet had broken the heavy humerus bone that angles downward and to the rear from the point of the shoulder blade. This had absorbed enough energy so that the bullet skidded along the outside of the rib cage and never penetrated into the chest cavity.

The buck went a long way, over two miles; we saw him several times fairly close in the snowy darkness. I had learned from experience that when wounded deer knowingly let you approach closely three times, they are not long for this world. But this little buck was special. He had no preconceived notions; he was tough, and he was mad. He needed to do something about this dark, fox-sized creature, this little dog that followed him relentlessly wherever he went.

We were crossing a field when the buck charged out of the darkness. He must have been lying down, but once on his feet he could move fast, and he rolled Sabina with his antlers. It happened too quickly for me to be able to shoot. I had shot many deer with my scoped handgun, but this was with someone holding a powerful light and illuminating the deer. Now I found it impossible to hold the light, aim the handgun and hold the leash all at once. Still, we continued; Sabina was as focused and steady as ever.

The second encounter was more serious. We came on the deer standing at bay. He was magnificent and the magic of the moment transformed his little six point antlers to Pope and Young dimensions. I was trying to pick him up in the useless handgun scope, while holding the leash and light, when he charged. He hit Sabina and then he hit me. His contact with me was head-on and hard enough so that he knocked one antler off against my jaw and chest. I did not feel a thing, but opened my eyes to see his antler lying on the ground a foot from my face. Sabina was there, licking my cheek, and she had a gash in her side. I could not see how serious the wound was, but Sabina seemed ready to go. I put the antler in my hunting coat, and we began tracking again. In about 150 yards we came to a country road. It was not clear whether the deer had crossed or doubled back, and Sabina seemed a bit disoriented.

Now was not the time to risk her again. There were lights of a farmhouse down the road, and we walked down so I could make a phone call. It turned out that I was a mile from where I thought I was and on an entirely different road. The householder kindly drove us home in his pick-up.

I showed my wife Jolanta the bloody antler and explained that we were just coming home for reinforcements. Since Sabina, as always, was ready to eat her supper, we concluded that she had no serious internal injuries. She wagged her tail even though she had a bloody five-inch gash from her spine down the side of her flank. We had been very lucky.

I called two good friends with tracking licenses to come and help me finish the tracking job. I had a bite to eat myself, and I noticed that my jaw was out of alignment so that I could not chew my food. Nothing was broken or dislocated, and after a couple of days everything went back to normal. I had caught a lower tine on my chest, but it had slid along my heavy nylon coat instead of penetrating. A long bruise developed, and the next day I realized that the shock of the impact had cracked a rib in back next to my spine. I could press the bruise in front and feel a sharp pain on the same rib in the rear. My *injuries were minor. Sabina was less lucky, and spent the next day being sutured at the vet's. It could have been much, much worse.*

This is a good story, and I could not resist the impulse to include some of the colorful detail. Still, the most important lesson is that an experienced tracker, one who has even dared to write a book, can still make serious mistakes. Let's analyze those mistakes, because that is the most important part of the story.

First of all, don't track alone, especially at night. The hunter or some competent person should be with you; a cell phone should be carried if service exists in that area.

You do need a firearm, and this firearm should be readily accessible and equipped for fast sighting on the target. I had given lots of old man's excuses for using that scope with lighted cross hairs on my handgun, but it was not usable in that emergency situation. It was like having no firearm at all. This second aggressive deer experience pushed me into a new investigation of recent technology. In the "Equipment" chapter I will discuss various firearms and better fast sighting alternatives, such as laser sights.

Never underestimate the power of a deer fueled with its final surge of adrenaline. After Sabina was gored by the buck, we tracked no more than 200 yards to a road. It was then that I decided that Sabina had enough and went to the farmhouse. When I returned two hours later with another tracking dog and two licensed friends, the buck had made it only 100 yards farther. As we approached he ran heavily across a small field before collapsing. A 12 gauge slug ended it. We had been dealing with a tired and weak deer when he charged, but he never quit. You have to respect an animal like that (color Fig. 16).

Larry Gohlke is an experienced Wisconsin tracker who had another dangerous experience in his home state. He was tracking in daylight when he was charged by a wounded buck that in his estimation weighed 200 pounds. He could not carry a firearm or even a bow in Wisconsin, but fortunately Larry is six feet four and weighed even more than the buck; somehow he was able to grasp the antlers and hold on to the buck until the hunter caught up and was able to dispatch the deer with a knife. A smaller man, who knew less about deer, would have been seriously injured in such an encounter.

There is no way that the human risks of tracking wounded deer can be entirely eliminated, even if the use of some sort of weapon is made legal. Dangerous situations can develop quickly and without warning. Those in the tracking party must be aware that a deer is a powerful animal that can become aggressive when pressed. At night all those accompanying the tracking dog and handler must have a reliable light so that everyone is aware of the whereabouts of everyone else. Two-way radios and cell phones can also make injuries more manageable.

Alternatives to Firearms

There are some expedients that are better than nothing in situations where a weapon is forbidden. A noose can be fashioned out of a tracking leash, the deer can be "lassoed" and then snubbed to a tree to immobilize him. My own two experiences with aggressive deer would have offered no opportunity for such cowboy stunts, but I know some Midwest trackers who have done this successfully more than once.

An army surplus bayonet or a replica spearhead, mounted on a three to four foot shaft, can be very useful when the need arises, but plan in advance and don't try to do this when you are by yourself at night. The expert guides and handlers at Tara Plantation in Mississippi sometime use this short spear technique. Since many of those Tara bucks are eligible for the Pope and Young record book, there are reasons not to shoot a firearm.

Using a spear is certainly not the best solution for putting down a wounded deer, but it is better than getting in close with a hunting knife. Whoever carries the spear must be careful to keep the heavy leather sheath on the head until the weapon is ready to be used. In some states, under some interpretations, even the short spear may be illegal. Check with your DNR.

Today specialized spears with a multi-sectioned shaft are commercially available. Check the equipment chapter.

Pope and Young Regulations for the Record Book

When a handler is making a decision to finish off a large antlered buck with a firearm during bow season, he should be aware that his bullet may make the deer ineligible for the record book. For example, the Pope and Young Club maintains a record book for bowhunters who take trophy deer with antlers scoring above a certain minimum. Pope and Young's fair chase rules for bowhunters do not allow for the use of a firearm.

The Pope and Young regulations on the use of tracking dogs are detailed:

1. The dog must meet all local requirements concerning training and/or licensing.
2. The use is limited to one dog.
3. The dog must be on a leash and in the control of the handler the entire time of the search and recovery with the hunter present.
4. The recovery must be completed within 48 hours of the initial shot.
5. The dog may be used to recover a big game animal. If the animal is found alive, the use of a tracking dog must be abandoned immediately.
The final determination of eligibility for entry of all animals found alive and later taken will be at the Records Committee's discretion.

There are some problems with these regulations. Regulation 3 requires that the dog be on a leash at all times. How is this applied in the southern states where off-lead tracking work is legal and customary?

Regulation 5 states that use of the tracking dog must be abandoned if the animal is found alive. This actually happens with about 1/3 of the finds. If the wounded animal takes off, without leaving a blood trail, is it practical to stop using the tracking dog in this situation?

Elsewhere Pope and Young makes it clear that a wounded animal, still alive, cannot be put down with a firearm. Finishing off the animal must be done with a bow or other traditional equipment.

The Argument for Permitting the Use of Firearms

As the use of dogs to track wounded deer becomes more established in the United States, it will be recognized eventually that the careful and prudent use of a firearm is the only safe and humane means of ending the suffering of a wounded deer.

Throughout Europe the use of firearms to finish off wounded deer tracked by a dog is legally recognized, but night work is usually avoided. European trackers work in daylight. For one thing they do not have a counterpart of our carcass-devouring coyotes, and night hunting with an artificial light is taboo.

North America presents a unique situation because traditional coon hunting has legitimized night hunting with a light for certain types of game. Today, no one considers that a coon hunter, with his hounds and a .22 or shotgun, is likely to be a poacher. There is usually a state restriction that he may not carry a high-power rifle or a shotgun loaded with shells with shot larger than #4. Of course if a hunter wanted to jack deer while "tracking", it would be a very easy matter to discard shells loaded with buckshot or slugs in the event that a law enforcement officer appeared.

In some states it has recently been made legal to shoot coyotes after dark with a powerful light and a high-powered rifle even though it is illegal to put down a wounded deer with a firearm at night. Anyone, who has actually tracked wounded deer with a dog on a long leash, knows that this practice does not create an effective situation for illegally shooting healthy deer at night. Yet the assumption persists in some official quarters that a tracking dog handler, carrying a firearm is more prone to illegal activity than a coon hunter or a coyote hunter.

Many years of using firearms on wounded deer have passed uneventfully in New York and Vermont, where the handler licensing requirement and the provision that the conservation officer must be notified before a deer call is taken, have probably contributed to the clean records there. In New York administrative costs for licensing and law enforcement notification were less than anticipated, due in part to improvements in communications technology.

The risk of using a firearm at night to put down a wounded deer is probably greatest for the hunters and others in the tracking party. It is absolutely essential that everyone present carries a flashlight, and that the flashlight must be turned on. Handler education is needed on this very important point. Shooting is usually done at less than 25 yards and at a downward angle, so there is little danger of a shot carrying a long distance into unseen houses or livestock.

The North American hunting experience and legal precedents create a sound basis for reevaluating existing prohibitions on the use of firearms, day or night, when tracking. But we have learned that such issues pass very slowly through the four millstones of tradition, reason, practicality and political expediency.

Summary

- Hunting ethics and humanitarian concerns are an important aspect of wounded deer tracking.

- Hunters' reports are not a reliable basis for deciding whether a deer will be found dead.

- Current state regulations vary widely in wisdom and practicality as they apply to putting down wounded deer.

- Wounded bucks can inflict serious injury to both tracking dogs and handlers.

- Firearms offer the safest and most humane means of finishing off a wounded deer.

- If any shooting is to be done at night, all members of the tracking party must have powerful flashlights that are turned on.

- In situations where firearms or bows are prohibited, alternative methods exist to put down wounded deer.

Chapter 19

Equipment for Tracking

To track wounded big game you do not have to invest heavily in expensive equipment. Your dog and the way he is cared for, trained and handled in the field is vastly more important than the amount of money you invest in things that you can wear or carry with you on a deer call. I began my first season with little more than a collar, a long leash, and a six-cell flashlight. Equipment is something that you should acquire gradually as the need for certain items actually arises in your particular case.

Now after 40 years of tracking, my collection of equipment has expanded considerably. Here is a list of the basic equipment that I take with me now on a call. Not everyone will need the same items, but the list below will help you get organized. Most of these items are discussed in detail later in this chapter.

1. Leash and collar (or harness) for the dog. Short leash for going to the hit site and six foot length of chain for attaching the dog as the game is gutted.
2. A tracking light, mounted on a helmet or cap, for you as handler. Several smaller, hand-held flashlights for the hunter and his friends who may have nothing better than a penlight. Spare bulbs.
3. Firearm or other means of putting down live, wounded deer
4. Marking tape (biodegradable) for marking verifiable points on the scent line.
5. Eye protection if you don't wear glasses.
6. Clothing and footwear appropriate for the vegetation and terrain you will be tracking in.
7. Flame orange vest and cap for firearms season.
8. Sharp hunting knife and Ziploc® bags for carrying blood, heart and liver.
9. Pen with waterproof ink and string for hunter who forgot these items for tagging the deer.
10. Cell phone or GPS for recording tracking and establishing location. Magnetic compass as a backup.
11. Special fanny pack or hunting coat to store and carry equipment.
12. Small first aid kit.

Collars, Harnesses and Leashes

Most basic to your needs are the tracking collar and the tracking leash. You will not be going for a stroll in the park when you take your dog on a deer call. Your dog will probably be dragging a leash through heavy, entangling vegetation. You will need a suitable collar and leash that will be used only for

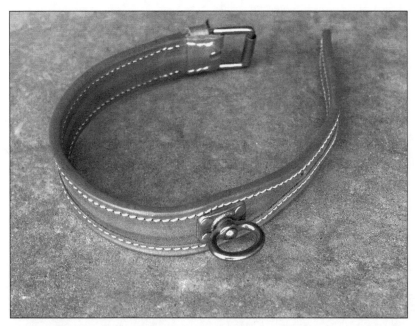

A wide leather collar with a brass swivel for attaching the tracking leash.

A Wirehaired Dachshund equipped with Ruffwear Web Master harness and a tracking leash made out of a climbing rope.

the purpose of blood tracking. Your dog knows that when you put on your hunting boots something good is going to happen. In a similar way, he will know that when you put on the special collar and leash at the hit site, a very special activity is going to begin. Dogs are very alert to cues, and experienced tracking dogs will usually whine or bark with enthusiasm as soon as they see this equipment.

Any wide collar will do as a tracking collar. It needs to be at least an inch and a half wide because it will be transmitting the weight and drag of the tracking leash to the bearing surface of the dog's neck. The Germans manufacture wide, quality leather collars especially for the purpose with a brass ring post for attaching the leash. These collars come in various sizes from small Dachshund to large Drahthaar/Lab size. German tracking collars are available from several German firms such as Leroi GmbH (www.leroi.de/de) and Sicherheit für Alle GmbH (www.sfa-bodoband.de). In the United States tracking collars and other blood tracking equipment are available through the United Blood Trackers website, www.unitedbloodtrackers.org.

All manufacturers and vendors of equipment mentioned in this chapter are listed alphabetically in Appendix A.

Some handlers prefer a tracking harness to the collar, and this is a matter of personal preference. Control, especially with an inexperienced dog, is better with a collar. On the other hand, a dog that pulls hard will not choke when a harness is used. For small dogs a harness is much more convenient than a collar for mounting a Garmin Astro type transmitter for location purposes. Several brands and models of harnesses are blood trackers' favorites: Niggeloh, and Ruffwear Front Rage and Web Master.

The leash attached to the collar is even more important. You will be spending a lot of time working with that leash, and you must select a leash material that works well in the vegetation of your area. For me, in New York State, a stiff, 30 foot leash of mountain climbing rope works best. Almost every deer call takes me into abandoned fields full of goldenrod, which entangles any leash material that is flexible.

However, when I worked with tracking dogs in the black spruce country of Quebec, I realized that my theories about stiff tracking leashes did not apply there at all. The trackers in Quebec use long leashes of a light flexible 4 mm marine cord used by commercial fisherman. This orange marine cord has very low friction, and 50 feet (roughly 15 meters) of it in a leash creates few problems and many advantages. In a thick cutover the handler can drop the leash, run around an obstructions and grab the leash again before the tracking dog gets away.

When the dog is working a difficult check, the 50-foot leash makes it easier for the handler to stand in one spot. He does not have to follow the dog and contaminate the area with human scent.

Many American trackers are coming to realize that the marine cord leash works for them in their kind of country. The marine cord is cheap, and the leashes are very easy to set up. Such a leash will wear out in a season or two, but they are inexpensive and easy to replace. Try the marine cord leashes first. If you experience too many hang-ups, then try a leash of mountain climbing rope.

For those of us who can't use the flexible marine cord leashes, mountain climbing rope is the solution at the other extreme. Mountain climbers use a special rope made up of a nylon stranded core covered by a tough, tightly braided synthetic sheathing. The tighter and harder this rope is, the better. For Lab-sized dogs, I prefer the 11 mm diameter. This is quite stiff and gives you something substantial to get your hands on. For a smaller dog, under 30 pounds, a diameter of 8 to 9.5 mm is lighter and less tiring for him to drag along. Look for a rope with a braided nylon or polyester sheathing over a stranded core. Static or rappelling rope is stiffer and more suitable for work in heavy cover.

Outfits like Eastern Mountains Sports (EMS) normally sell suitable mountain climbing rope by the foot off a spool at their retail stores. You can review a wide variety of ropes on the web site of backcountrygear.com based in Oregon, but they sell in lengths of 150 feet or more, which will cost around $175.00 and suffice for five tracking leashes.

BioThane® is a plastic leash material used by a number of companies that produce tracking leashes in various lengths and colors. It come in widths from 3/8 inch to one inch. BioThane seems to generate more friction in thick cover than the round cords and ropes we have discussed. I have found that this can be a problem when working with smaller, lighter dogs with less pulling power. In cold weather the friction can be reduced by coating the tracking leash with ski wax, but I would recommend BioThane® only for tracking dogs over 35 pounds.

Once you have the leash material, you must turn it into a tracking leash. Nylon ropes should be heated at the ends with a match to prevent any unraveling. A brass or chromed bolt snap can be "served" on one end with thirty pound braided fishing line as is done with maritime cordage. A neat wrapping of the fishing line secures the tight loop of rope that holds the snap. This serving and wrapping can be given a couple of coats of polyurethane varnish, which lasts a very long time. A less elegant wrap can be done with electricians' tape.

The 4 mm marine cord is even simpler to work with. The end of the cord is looped around the snap and then pushed back into the hollow cord for several inches. Then the connection can be sealed with glue or spar varnish.

The German leather tracking leashes certainly work very well in the brush-free, park-like surroundings of the traditional German forest, but I find them to be a nightmare in the briars, brush and deadfalls that we encounter here in North America. They are constantly whipping around saplings and debris, so that you have to stop to untangle things.

Leather is a nice, natural material, but in the experience of many Americans, it is really not the best material available for our tracking purposes today. The leather leash, particularly in the smaller widths and lighter weights appropriate for smaller dogs, is not very stiff and it generates considerable friction when wet. It will tangle more than a tracking lead made of appropriate synthetic materials. Today, even in Germany, most of the serious handlers, those who take many calls, are using leashes made of synthetic materials. Traditionalists turn away in disgust.

The tracking experts in Germany insist that the dog should go to the tracking site on a regular short leash that is different from the tracking leash. I have always followed this advice. A bright fabric or plastic leash, easily seen on dead leaves, has worked best for me. The short leashes have a magical way of getting left behind in the excitement of starting to track. Meddlesome fingers of brush pull leashes out of game pockets. For me, just being more careful has never been a sufficient solution. If you are ever absent-minded yourself, I recommend a cheap, hunter orange lead, which your companions will probably pick up as they follow behind you.

When you find your deer, it will generally be necessary to tie your dog up, because he will want to "help" you gut the deer. If you tie the dog up with your good tracking lead you may find that he has chewed right through it while you were preoccupied. After some bad experiences I began carrying a six foot length of light chain with a snap on each end. At the gutting site I take off the tracking leash, loop and snap one end of the chain around a small tree and snap the other end to my dog's collar.

As mentioned in the first chapter on training, young puppies may be distracted by the weight and drag of a heavy leash that they will pull willingly as they become older and stronger. Plastic clothesline is a marvelous temporary solution. The 4 mm marine cord is also suitable. Don't invest very much in a puppy leash because the pup will so rapidly outgrow it.

Lights

In Chapter 1 we have already discussed the real advantages of tracking at night. In night work you are very dependent upon a serviceable light that will stay bright for at least four hours. The coyotes don't wait, and the days of always waiting until morning to track are long gone.

The old lights, powered by lead/acid gel cell batteries and using filament light bulbs, have been supplanted by smaller, more efficient lights using LED (light emitting diode) bulbs and compact lithium/ion batteries. The LEDs last much longer and produce more light for the same amount of battery energy. These LED bulbs are paired with lithium/ion batteries that are smaller and lighter. Nite Lite is now selling LED lights which give you more and longer lasting light than their older halogen bulb, gel-cell-powered models.

The old fashioned Nitelite coonhunter's light with rechargeable 6 volt gel cell, spotlight, hard hat and cold weather cap

The Laser Torch lights, with a powerful, low weight lithium battery, are excellent for night work in thick cover.

I am particularly impressed with the products of Laser Torch, which have the advantage of using a small, but very powerful lithium battery which is mounted directly on a bump cap. There are no wires leading down to a battery pack in your pocket or on your belt. You pop the bump cap on your head, and you are ready to track all night with no worries. Unlike old fashioned bulbs, the new LEDs don't burn out for many thousands of hours. The lithium battery is easy to recharge and has a built-in cut-off to prevent damaging overcharges. This battery is rated for 800 recharges.

I used the Laser Torch II from 2012 to 2015 and was very pleased. My only criticism, then, was that the powerful light was tightly focused into a very narrow beam. This was fine for spotting a wounded deer at a distance and for shooting it. However, the tight beam was not the best for spotting blood along the track. A "diffuser" that lights up a broader area has been introduced, and this should eliminate the problem of an overly tight beam when actually tracking.

The evolution of LED lights is advancing so rapidly in that by the time your read this chapter even more efficient tracking lights may be available. Cree is a leading LED manufacturing company and they produce a number of different models of high output LEDs that are widely used in headlamps and flashlights. They do not actually make flashlights, even though some companies will describe their product as a "Cree flashlight." This refers to the LED inside the flashlight. In 2012 Cree released a much more efficient XM-L2 LED. Prices of LED lights have gone down, and if you want to stay up to date, you need to do your own research. Here are the features to look for:

- efficient LED light bulb,
- rechargeable lithium ion battery,
- maximum illuminating power of 500 to 1000 lumens,
- adjustable light intensity,
- provision for light diffusion beside the tightly focused beam,
- provision to mount the light on a cloth cap or plastic bump cap (Do not rely on a head strap mount that will not stay in place in heavy cover.)

If you really get hooked on blood tracking and find yourself tracking for many hunters, you will need to have on hand two or three "hunters' lights". The typical hunter comes out with you on a call with a penlight or something not much better. He will be happier and much more useful if he is using a decent light and is not falling down in the woods. If there is to be any shooting of the wounded deer at night by the handler, it is imperative that everyone present has a turned-on light that indicates his location.

It has long been known that the white gasoline lanterns of the type manufactured by Coleman are excellent for tracking at night by eye. Blood is much more visible because the white light of the lantern makes it stand out so clearly. However, when you are tracking with a dog this is not the equipment to bring along or allow anyone else to use. In my experience, the fumes from the gasoline lantern overwhelm the deer and blood scent. I have had an excellent tracking dog reduced to helplessness when a burning gasoline lantern was being carried in the area where she was working.

One last point on lights. If you are using light from the pre-LED era, come equipped with spare bulbs for all of the lights you will be using. Burnouts are difficult to predict, but usually they occur at the most inopportune times. To fix a light or replace a bulb you need another light. For this purpose carry a small light yourself.

I will never forget the night on Long Island when all the lights in our party mysteriously failed at once, for one reason or another, within a half hour. Fortunately, the deer was all but dead when we found it. Murphy's Law applies when it comes to lights. And never take a deer call in the afternoon without carrying a light in your coat or pack. Many times you will find your tracking adventure continuing into darkness.

Marking Tape

A number of years passed before I saw the value of marking tape. Today I would not be without it to mark the trail my dog is following. Often, a difficult scent line will be temporarily lost. It saves an enormous amount of time if the handler can go, with assurance, back to a point where the dog was definitely on the line.

Flame orange, plastic surveyor's tape, tied on branches at eye level is the most visible. The trouble is that this tape remains in the woods for several years as a confusing eyesore. Today we use biodegradable flagging that comes in similar rolls. You may not find the same blaze colors as in plastic tapes, but the red and orange are bright enough. Actually, this tape takes about six months to degrade to the point of falling to the ground. Still it is much better than plastic tape when it comes to landowner and public relations. Biodegradable flagging is available from CSP Forestry. In Europe white toilet tissue is the standard marker. The disadvantage is that it is often difficult to hang it at eye level where it is most visible. In the daytime tissue on the ground works fairly well, and the Europeans do not track at night as we do.

There are extraordinary situations when you, or a replacement handler, are returning to a point to resume tracking. If you do this at night, the exact location of the line may be hard to find. The patented Cyalume tubes of flexible plastic will give off a chemically produced light for 4 or 12 hours depending on the size. Cyalume tubes are widely available in outdoor stores. GPS coordinates accomplish the same thing!

Eye and Ear Protection

If you do not have to wear corrective eyeglasses, make sure to wear protective glasses or some other device to save your eyes. In daylight, you may be able to see and dodge thorny branches. At night, sooner or later, one of those thorns will get you, scratching a cornea, embedding in your eyeball or even puncturing it. If you are reduced to monocular vision, things will never be the same. Certainly your relish for thorny brush, the thicker the better, will dwindle to zero.

In most situations protective goggles won't work. You will be sweating and steaming to the point that you will not be able to see your dog, let alone a deer, through your goggles. Glasses, optical or non-optical are a more practical solution, but they must stay put as branches brush across your face. An elastic head strap, fastened to the bows of your glasses may be your best solution whether or not you need prescription lenses.

Hearing protection is also something to consider. The blast of sound from a high power handgun does not do your ears any good. You can carry protective earplugs in a little rubber case on a cord around your neck. Most often when you must put down a deer, there will be sufficient time to put in your earplugs first. North Safety Products manufactures an excellent model, Sonic Ear-Valvs®, which attenuates harmful, high-level noises, yet allows passage of normal background sounds and warning signals at ordinary volume. North retails its products through companies like Cabela's, but you can buy directly from North's online store.

Outer Clothing

The outer shell is the most critical if you will be tracking in a thorny environment. If you take a lot of calls and have to go where your dog goes, then you will realize that Cordura® nylon is a great product. This high-performance fabric is two times more durable than standard nylon.

I would begin with heavy nylon chaps, zippered at the bottoms so that you can pull them on over your boots when you arrive to track a deer in tough cover. I like a product now made by Stone Creek Hounds and Hunting Supplies in Pennsylvania. They are producing the very tough Cordura nylon chaps formerly manufactured by John Wick in Missouri. These chaps have a waterproof membrane beneath the 1000 denier Cordura® nylon exterior, which will keep you dry in the rain or when wading through wet brush. In wearing my Wick chaps for 20 years, I have saved at least 20 pairs of heavy pants, and yet they look almost new. Stone Creek Chaps should do as well.

Next in importance, after chaps, is a hunting coat that will allow you to bull through briars. Often I turn and walk through the briars backwards. In order to fully appreciate the joys of tracking in thorns and briars, imagine yourself as a running back, rolling out of the clinging hands of a tackle. A canvas hunting coat, or one of those suave, wax-finished British shooting coats will take on a delightful, distressed patina... before it falls apart. If you are into tracking for the long haul, forget your image and buy a Cordura® nylon hunting coat to go along with your chaps. Stone Creek is a good source for a briar coat.

Heavy Cordura® fabric is a great product to turn thorns and briars, but it does have its limitations in the prickly pear cactus country of the Southwest. The very fine spines of "pear" go right through the weave of heavy nylon.

Leather chaps would turn the spines, but dogs and handlers in Texas prefer to avoid the problem and pick their way with care.

In no case should you wear a coat of any color remotely resembling the color of a deer. Carry a flame orange vest and wear it in daytime during the firearms seasons.

While on the subject of protective clothing for handlers, we should not overlook our dogs. This makes me think of Max, a good tracking Dachshund, whose wire coat was on the soft side. He would pick up burrs badly. After one long, successful search and pursuit he was so scratched all over by briars that he was sick for several days. I fitted out Max with a flame orange Cordura® nylon vest sold for bird dogs as a "Tummy Protector". At first wearing, Max was humiliated, but he soon learned to wear the vest as his uniform and badge of pride. For tracking dogs with soft coats these vests can be purchased at www.gundogsupply.com and other online dog supply stores.

Footwear

For fording small streams, and for support and protection I prefer footwear at least 10 inches high. If the terrain is flat, I want boots that are going to be light and fast; in mountains I prefer something heavier with cleated soles that bite through wet leaves to a firmer base beneath.

Streams, swamps and land flooded by beavers will be encountered frequently in most whitetail habitat. If the weather is fairly mild, it is just too much trouble to wear boots that will keep you dry in every situation. Make up your mind to get wet. Since you will be on the move, a little water seeping in over the tops of your boots will refresh more than it chills. As the weather grows colder, you may want to take some precautions when you know that you are going to be tracking in a wet area. Rubber hip boots are heavy, and you will regret wearing them if the deer you are tracking unexpectedly turns to the upland ridges.

The best and most versatile boots for wet or dry situations are made for coonhunters by Stone Creek. Their "Frog Legs" are 16" Lacrosse rubber boots firmly attached by Stone Creek to nylon uppers that reach to the top of the thigh. You will find them light and comfortable if the deer turns out to be a ridge runner. On the other hand, you will stay dry if you wade for an hour in a beaver swamp. These are not boots for all-day trout fishing, but they are durable and ideal for wet country.

Clothing Beneath the Outer Shell

Your experience with your own climate and season will guide your choices here, but keep in mind that your clothing requirements, while tracking, are very different from those of a deer hunter, who stands still or moves very slowly. When you are tracking, you are almost constantly on the move, and sometimes you are moving as fast as your legs and lungs can carry you. Exercise and excitement will keep you warm. In almost any weather, you are more likely to be too warm than too cold.

You will sweat a lot; if you are wearing a cotton tee shirt under a cotton flannel shirt, your skin will be wet and therefore clammy cold while the deer is being gutted. For underwear the synthetic materials, especially Coolmax® and Thermax®, will serve you much better. For the active sport of tracking you will find that they are well worth the extra cost. Cabela's and L.L. Bean are among the many suppliers of Thermax® underwear.

For an outer shirt, wool is preferred, but make sure that it has buttons or a zipper. If you can't open your shirt in strenuous situations, you may cook in your own body heat.

Hats and Gloves

Unless your partner really enjoys picking thorns out of your head, you will need protective headgear. There is nothing worse than a knit wool hat, which is snatched off your head by every over-hanging branch. A billed cap of hard fabric or leather is much better, if the brush is not too bad. A boonie hat with a chinstrap is best for bulling through the briars. During firearms season, all headgear should be flame orange.

If you are tracking with a headlight at night, you will need at least two different hats with brackets upon which to mount your light. In warm weather, the light plastic bump cap sold by Laser Torch and several other manufacturers will be the coolest. It rides on the head, supported by an inside band and crossover straps. This gives good air circulation all around. As the weather gets colder, one option is to add the liner, which looks like a baby bonnet. You may prefer the twill or corduroy caps with an integral bracket for your headlight.

Handling a tracking dog on a leash can be tough on the hands. There is the constant friction of the cord on your palm, and then the briars that rip and tear. In late season cold can be a factor. Obviously gloves are needed. But what kind of gloves? Full-finger gloves are a nuisance when you are clipping leashes on and off, and they make you clumsy if you have to shoot. Specialized shooting gloves are not durable enough to last long while holding the tracking leash. I have found the best solution to be "carpenter's gloves as sold by Duluth Trading Post. These have the thumb and two finger tips open plus reinforced palms. They also provide the finger conductivity necessary to operate cell phone and GPS equipment.

Organizing Your Gear

As a deer tracker you will need to bring along many small items, which might be easy to lose in the general jumble of your gear. When you need a replacement light bulb or your Ziploc® bags and dipper, you should be able to lay hands on them with a minimum of fumbling.

The solution I like best is a sturdy vest with numerous pockets. Filson makes good ones that will last a lifetime. Keep all your support equipment in the vest, and then you do not have to run around gathering it, piece by piece, each time you go out on a call.

A fanny pack is an alternative solution that some prefer. If you have to go where your leashed dog takes you, avoid a backpack. You don't want even a small rucksack up on your shoulders while crawling on your hands and knees through dense underbrush or slipping under the strands of a barbed wire fence.

Speaking of organization, you will need a large container, such as a 16 x 16 x 24 plastic storage box, to keep all your clothing and gear together. I also like to have an open milk crate with air circulation for gear and clothing that need to dry out.

Equipment for Hunter Support

I am not thinking of a medical first aid kit, although this is always good to have in your vehicle, if not in your gadgets vest. The list presented here deals with the items that a hunter normally should have and would have with him in normal circumstances. But just this one time, he has forgotten to bring what he needs with him as you search for his deer. Remember, a man who has shot a deer, and has yet to find it, is a man under real stress. He should be forgiven for minor lapses. Of course, you should ask him if he has remembered to bring his deer tags, and you may have to provide him with a decent light since he lent his own to his brother-in-law last week. Beyond this you should carry these items: (1) a small hunting knife to gut the deer (knives are sometimes forgotten or turn out to be so dull that the back of the blade cuts better), (2) a pen with water-resistant ink for filling out deer tags, (3) string for attaching the tag to the deer, (4) a strap for dragging out the deer.

Many new hunters know very little about getting a deer out of the woods. They assume that you just grab the antlers and pull. This doesn't work too well if the deer is a spike buck or a doe. It is far more efficient to use a ten-foot nylon strap two or three inches wide. Make a noose in one end, place this around the deer's neck and bring the forelegs up under the noose and between the antlers or the ears. Tie the other end of the strap to a stout stick of wood and several men can pull at once. If there is only one man to do the pulling, he can put the broad strap over his shoulder and lift an average-sized deer partially off the ground. With the neck and the forward part of the shoulder off the ground there is much less friction, and the deer will skid out easily.

Handguns and Long Guns

Carrying a handgun to put down live, but seriously wounded deer, is both a humane act and a safety measure. Unfortunately, the wildlife officials in Wisconsin and Indiana drafted a "no firearms rule" when wounded deer are tracked with dogs. Michigan has modified its original no firearms rule. In the Canadian provinces where tracking is legal, firearms are generally prohibited

Thompson Center Contender (.44mag) with laser sight mounted on scope

Remington 870 (12 gauge) with folding stock and laser sight mounted beneath 21 inch barrel

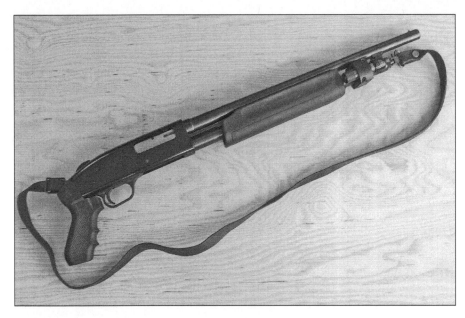

Mossberg 500C (20 gauge) with pistol grip and 18 ½ inch barrel

Shoulder holster for Thompson Center Contender. This rig accommodates a scope mount.

when a tracking dog is present. Sooner or later, a tracking dog or a handler, will be injured or killed as a result of the firearms prohibitions. The words below are written for those who are, or will be permitted in the future, to use a handgun or other firearm.

Depending on the season and the circumstances, between 25% and 50% of the wounded deer tracked and found will still be alive. They can be finished off with a knife, but this is dangerous for the inexperienced. They can also be left to suffer until they die, provided that coyotes do not find them first. Obviously, this is not an acceptable solution.

For several reasons, a handgun of sufficient power is needed to permanently stop a deer, even if the bullet placement is not perfect. Live, wounded deer are often found lying down in thick cover. It is difficult to get the perfect shot you would like to have.

There is another factor. A wounded deer, pumped full of adrenaline, may not be afraid of your dog. It may even be aggressive to a human. Everyone who has tracked seriously for any length of time has had an incident. About one percent of the deer that you confront will charge a leashed dog. It tends to happen at night, particularly when a deer has a broken leg. Suddenly and from nowhere, a buck is right there in your dog's face. Fueled by adrenaline, this deer has enormous power, at least for a few moments. As explained in the previous chapter, he can kill your dog; he may try to kill you.

A .357 Magnum is considered excessive for police work, but it is certainly not excessive for a wounded deer; it is the acceptable minimum. I have been with law enforcement officers when they finished off deer with their .38 revolvers or 9mm automatics. The deer did not seem to notice the first shots that hit them; it took many shots to finish the job. A deer has vastly more vitality than a human of equal size. Personally, I prefer a .44 Magnum, but for a man with small hands, or for a woman, something with less recoil is a better choice.

Revolvers are the handguns of choice; they offer simplicity, reliability and multiple shots, if needed. The single shot Thompson Center pistols—the Contender and the newer Encore—offer a wide range of calibers and they are extremely accurate. However, you should not be taking long shots so varmint rifle accuracy is not needed. If a deer or a bear makes unfriendly moves toward your dog, you may well wish for more than one quick shot. Smith and Wesson has bought out Thompson Center and discontinued much of the TC line. A selection of barrels is available at E. Arthur Brown Co.

The sights on your handgun are as important as the handgun itself. You will not be shooting from the hip. Except in emergency situations with an aggressive animal, you will be taking deliberate shots. However, you will often be shooting in poor light or at night.

As long as your eyes are good enough to give you a clear sighting picture with iron sights, these are recommended. They are reliable and durable. There are several manufacturers of sighting systems that use fiber optics or tritium. When properly aligned on the target the shooter sees the bright dot of the front sight between the two illuminated dots on either side of the rear sight notch.

Suitable sights of this type are manufactured by TruGlo and Williams Gun Sight Company. You will appreciate them in poorly lighted or dark conditions.

A low power handgun scope with lighted cross hairs is fine for older eyes if there is all the time in the world to take deliberate aim. As described in Chapter 18, there are times when situations develop on very short notice.

The lighted cross hairs are useful for deliberate shooting at night, but you must turn down the intensity to a very low level in order to see your target. The same problem arises with the red dot optical sights produced by various manufacturers. In these sights the red dot brightness is adjustable over a considerable range, but they are not designed for night shooting. Even at the lowest intensity setting, the target is not visible beyond the brightness of the red dot.

Holographic sights on a handgun are faster than a scope, and they are actually less bulky and awkward than they appear; I have met trackers who use them. Bushnell is a leading manufacturer. You may have to search to find a holster suitable for a handgun equipped with a holographic sight.

Where legal, a laser sight is best for fast shooting because it projects the laser spot directly on the target. This is almost never legal as a sight for deer hunting, but as a night shooting tool to put down deer it should come under the same category as a powerful flashlight, which also uses projected light. Check with Law Enforcement of your own state DNR to learn how they interpret this. Laser sights are available through Cabela's and other mail order firms.

A light, single shot slug gun, even in 20 gauge, gives adequate stopping power if needed. Shotgun adaptations of the fiber optic handgun sight discussed above are available from the same sources. As extra insurance, a laser sight can be mounted beneath the barrel.

If you are willing to carry a little more weight, a reliable pump shotgun, such as the Remington 870, with a short barrel (18 to 21 inches) and a folding stock can be carried. With a good sling I have found this rig to be quite manageable even in thick cover and blowdowns. My 12 gauge 870 weighs only 7¼ pounds when stripped down for tracking. New regulations may make folding stocks illegal.

An even lighter pump gun rig, weighing 5½ pounds, is the Mossberg 500C in 20 gauge with an 18½ inch barrel and tactical pistol grip instead of a stock. This is excellent with a laser sight. Again this may become an illegal weapon.

Slings for various types of shotguns are a matter of personal preference. You will be carrying your shotgun slung across one shoulder so some sort of rubberized, inside gripping surface on the sling should work well for you.

The barrel of your long gun will hang up much less if the forward sling swivel is attached near the muzzle rather than at the front of the fore end. With this arrangement the muzzle will ride below the level of your shoulder so that it doesn't catch on grapevines and tree branches.

In open terrain a scoped rifle of an appropriate caliber could be useful. In Germany where the forests are well groomed, this is the standard equipment for a tracker taking a call. I suspect that the rifle is less than ideal in the blocks

Left: Guide Barry Grantham with short spear he uses to dispatch deer at Tara Plantation. Right: Close-up of spear used as alternative to a firearm.

of dense young growth, which are a part of every managed forest. In the rough wooded areas where I track in the Northeast, I have very seldom felt the need for a long range rifle and powerful optics. I would wish for one only if I were tracking a jaw-shot deer that would be unlikely to tire and give me a close shot.

Carrying a handgun safely, securely and conveniently is not as easy as it sounds. For handguns a shoulder holster works much better than one worn on the hip. A big handgun in a shoulder holster is accessible, and yet it is not flopping around if you have to get down on your hands and knees to crawl under brush. The holster is secured by the broad strap over one shoulder and held down close to your body in a fixed position by the lower strap, which attaches to the belt or to a hammer loop. Leather, because of its stiffness, holds its form and is much easier to put on. Until I graduated to leather, I often got so tangled up putting on my nylon holster that I needed help from someone else. This was not the best way to establish an image of competence!

Avoid carrying your handgun in a hip holster if you have to follow your leashed dog wherever he goes. At hip level, your handgun is exposed to vines and snags much more than if it were carried higher and were protected by your jacket. If your handgun in a hip holster is really secure against snatching branches and driving rain, it will also be difficult to get to it when you need it. A rough deer track is a good occasion to lose a handgun with all the risks, costs and possible legal problems that can be involved. Hip holsters have contributed to all the lost handgun cases that I know about.

As discussed in Chapter 18, some states, such as Wisconsin and Indiana, currently forbid the carrying of either a bow or a firearm when a leashed tracking dog is used. A spearhead, mounted on a three or four foot shaft, is a useful substitute, if your DNR will accept this. Wisconsin specifically forbids any weapon, Indiana specifies only that firearms and bows are illegal. Michigan has modified it firearms legislation, and this will be discussed in Chapter 27.

The spear is used to put down deer at Tara Plantation in Mississippi, and such a spear has been used in certain hunting applications in Europe for centuries. A collapsible spear for putting down game at close quarters is for sale at the United Blood Tracker's website. The forged spearhead mounts on a shaft, constructed of 16 ½ inch sections of aluminum alloy attached together with snap pins.

Lassoing a wounded deer and snubbing it to a tree may be necessary. If you have a tracking leash of appropriate stiffness, you can fashion a workable lasso on the spot when you need it so there is no need to purchase a special rope for this purpose.

Summary

Most essential items to carry:

- Tracking leash and designated collar or harness

- Flame orange vest and cap for daytime gun season

- Powerful, rechargeable flashlight or headlamp

- Some legal means of dispatching a deer

- Eye protection

- Marking tape

Sources of equipment listed in Appendix A.

Chapter 20

Hi-Tech Equipment for Tracking

Since I wrote about electronic technology for tracking, back in 2006, the changes have been overwhelming. What I write now in 2016 may well be out of date next year. In this chapter we'll talk about the usefulness of certain electronic devices and general methods for using them. We will not get into deep discussions about different models or specific instructions.

It should be kept in mind that all electronic devices may fail when you need them most. Always carry a magnetic compass as a back-up.

Cell Phones and Smartphones

In most parts of the "lower 48" the radio has been replaced by the cell phone in all but wilderness areas. When you come out on a distant road at 2 AM and you are miles from the vehicles, it's great to be able to call your wife to come and pick you up!

Cell phones may be very simple when used mainly to communicate with others. But in the recent years cell phones have been converted into small-sized multifunctional devices that are very "smart". Their many capabilities have a lot to offer to trackers and hunters.

- Texting is very popular, and often this is how the communication is conducted between a hunter and handler.

- Smartphones are equipped with a camera and a hunter can send pictures of blood signs to a handler, who can evaluate the situation visually even though he is not there in person. Sometimes a hunter is able to capture a video of a deer's behavior and share it with the handler.

- An instantaneous access to the web allows a hunter with a smartphone to find a tracker quickly, for example, by going to find-a-tracker page on the United Blood Trackers website or a Facebook group that connects hunters with handlers.

- Smartphones have built-in GPS, and for navigation and tracking a handler has plenty of apps to choose from depending on his phone operating system. Thanks to GPS no phone signal is needed to see your current location or mark points. Some apps provide all the functionality of expensive handheld units at a fraction of the cost.

- Trimble GPS Hunt Pro is a popular app which allows viewing unlimited topographic maps in the United States and Canada, marking waypoints and recording your tracks. You can see your track's stats, including mileage, speed and elevation. The Blood Trailing option allows you to mark blood. Some other features include access to weather data like the current humidity, heat index, dew point, wind chill, wind speed and direction.

- GPS Kit and MotionX-GPS are excellent apps for the iPhone only. With MotionX-GPS you can record a scent track, and when you run your dog on it, you see the dog's path and how closely it follows the original track. On the other hand, the unique feature of the GPS Kit is called "Squawk", which allows you to connect with other users running the app and determine their position and direction of travel.

- Voice recognition allows you to record and save your "notes" before and after tracking quickly and efficiently.

However, during the tracking itself some hunters get carried away with cell phones. They are constantly chatting with their friends and giving a blow by blow report on what's happening. More than once I've had a cell phone hunter not see a deer on the jump from the wound bed. In hunting, and in tracking, the first priority is paying attention. Help your hunter to understand this.

Some trackers will find the cell phone apps are all they need. Others will find that more sophisticated GPS models are worth the extra money and complexity of operation.

Radio Tracking Collars (Telemetry)

A radio tracking collar is a special dog collar carrying a small radio transmitter operating on a specific frequency. The handler equipped with a receiver and somewhat bulky antenna can pick up these signals from miles away if there is not a hill obstructing the signal. The receiver is designed to show the direction from which the collar signal is coming.

After the development of GPS collars the electronic tracking collars became obsolete for most dog applications. However, they can still be very useful and many trackers continue to use them. The biggest advantage that radio telemetry tracking collars have over the Garmin Astro GPS is better range. They are also available at attractive prices second hand, since coon hunters used them extensively.

The greatest shortcoming of these transmitters is that they transmit to the handler the direction to the dog, but not the distance. This means that the handler must move to the left or right far enough to get a new angle and triangulate. It works, but it is not as efficient as the Garmin GPS.

GPS Tracking Collars

The Garmin Astro and Alpha, and similar devices, carry GPS technology a step farther. This equipment is designed to let you keep track of your dog, and it has replaced the "old fashioned" radio collar that is still used for long term research on wildlife movements.

In the Garmin Astro arrangement both dog and handler carry a GPS receiver. The dog wears a GPS unit on his collar and the handler carries another unit with a screen, similar in appearance to the regular Garmin GPS units we use for forest navigation and tracking.

The dog's unit picks up signals from the satellite and calculates its own location. The dog's GPS unit then sends a radio message to the handler's GPS unit, which has established his location as well by means of the satellite. With the locations of the dog's unit and the handler's unit "known", the system then calculates the location of the dog relative to the handler's location. This is displayed on the handler's GPS screen in terms of direction, distance and a small diagram.

Keep in mind that the communication between dog and handler is by direct radio signal not satellite. This means that you cannot locate your dog if he is on the other side of a mountain.

The applications are greatest when the dog works off lead as in the Deep South and in Texas. The handler knows how to go directly to his dog if it has stopped on the dead deer or is baying it. If there are no high ridges it makes losing a dog unlikely. But there are always the gators!

In the "always on lead states" the Garmin Astro is not such a bad idea either. Dogs do get away from us up north, despite our best intentions and efforts.

The experience of Michigan's Bill Yoder and his young Dachshund Daryl illustrates the point. This occurred in the days before GPS technology, and it would not have happened if the tracking team had been equipped with something like the Garmin Astro.

Bill and Daryl were tracking a wounded deer along a steep river bank. The footing was difficult, and for just a moment Bill dropped the leash to grab a tree. Daryl took off! Without an electronic tracking collar and not even the owner's name and phone number plate on the dog, the tracking team was in trouble. Daryl simply disappeared, and all Bill's efforts to find him were unsuccessful. It seemed likely that the ever present coyotes had done their work. Finally Bill drove sorrowfully home to Michigan.

Twelve days later Daryl miraculously appeared in a woman's backyard; she responded to a newspaper ad that Bill had posted. Bill arrived to find his dog starved down to almost half his original weight. The moral of the tale is that some sort of locating system would have spared the tracking team great stress. Even an ID collar on the dog might have helped.

The sequel to this adventure is off the main point, but it is just too good a story to drop in the middle. There was to be no rest after the joyful reunion. The outfitter, for whom Bill had been tracking, announced that he had lost a magnificent buck 48 hours earlier. They had eye-tracked and searched in vain. Could Daryl give it a try? Half-starved Daryl did track that old, cold line and find the buck in less than two hours!

Don't conclude from this tale that all dogs can survive anything. Take precautions not to lose them. Daryl was exceptionally tough for a pup nine months old. An ordeal that would have ruined many young dogs did not faze Daryl. This same dog had been charged and pinned by the first deer he ever tracked; he had continued tracking to come up with it for the hunter. Daryl knew that tracking was his job.

The Garmin Alpha for Dogs Working Off Lead

In 2011 Garmin Ltd. acquired Tri-Tronics, a major manufacturer of electronic or remote collars for dog training. One offspring of this union was the Garmin Alpha, which combined all of the features of the Astro, just reviewed, plus the capability to give the dog an electric "stimulation". The Garmin Alpha is not cheap, but it is a great safety feature for the South. When an off-lead tracking dog is on a deer and headed for a major highway, the handler has the means to stop him, perhaps saving his life. Experienced tracking dogs are not cheap either, and then there is the matter of the deep feelings that we have for our tracking dogs.

Use of GPS in Real Tracking

Andy Bensing has mastered the use of GPS on the track better than anyone else I've observed. After almost every call he reconstructs on his computer screen the path that he and his dog took in tracking the wounded deer. This is an ideal way of analyzing and recording his dog's work and understanding better any mistakes that were made.

Andy explains:

Besides the obvious use, getting you back to your truck in unfamiliar terrain, I have found the use of GPS while tracking wounded deer has enhanced my overall enjoyment of tracking as well as making me a more efficient and better educated tracker. Below is an example of a call I took in Harford County, Maryland. This buck was spine shocked on the first arrow hit and flopped around for 15 minutes after which the hunter was able to get another arrow through the deer from the front but did not see where the second arrow hit. The deer fell again and eventually got up and stumbled away. The hunter was able to track the deer for 350 meters to the point of loss.

We started tracking the deer 7 hours after the hit. As it turned out, this deer was not mortally wounded and was not recoverable with a leashed dog.

I will show you how my GPS helped me to determine that more efficiently.

I carry my GPS on all tracking calls and I record waypoints along the way to both record the events of the track, for later analysis back home on my desktop and to use in the field while in pursuit of the deer. Here is the list of the 9 custom waypoints preprogrammed into my unit for easy retrieval: Parking spot, Hit site, Hunter's point of loss, Sign (blood, bone, etc.), Wound bed, Live jump of wounded deer, Hot line / live jump of wrong deer, Pick up (if I take my dog back to restart at a confirmed spot) and Dead deer (my favorite).

A. Hunter's point of loss
B. Dog jumped deer
C. Fresh blood indicated correct deer
D. First backtrack
E. First visual contact with deer
F. Second backtrack
G. Hairpin turn after passing through original wound bed

Marking the above waypoints along the trail combined with being able to see the shape and size of the trail on my GPS allows me to much more efficiently evaluate what is going on in the field in real time. Most importantly seeing the pattern of a trail in itself tells a lot. For example, I have great trust in my dog, but if I have not seen any sign for 500 meters and I look at my GPS and see the path has been a very straight line, I can be almost 100% sure we are still on the correct line. I have found severely wounded deer most often go in a very straight line heading usually back to a core bedding area. On the map you can see that after the shot this deer's path was basically a straight line for 650 meters to a point where he bedded. The little dog leg in that path was the deer skirting the edge of a deep swamp but otherwise he went absolutely straight. If that deer had been mortally wounded he would have been found dead in his bed in a straight line from the hit site.

When we jumped the deer without seeing him, he ran off and started making a big circle 500 meters in diameter. We did not see his wound bed but a small drop of fresh blood, which was indicated by my dog, confirmed it was the correct deer. While making that circle you can see that he also put two small, 75 meter back tracks in his path and ran right back along a portion of his original trail from right after he was shot actually running right down the trail we originally jumped him on. After that he hooked a hard hairpin turn left out of the circle and kept on going.

When I look at the map the biggest thing that jumps out at me from having looked at similar patterns in the past is the size of the circle. 500 meters across! Typically, deer in bad condition that you have a decent chance of catching up to make relatively small circles. Sometimes as small as 50 meters or less in heavy cover. This was a big circle and had a couple of backtracks thrown in as well. Notice that both backtracks have the same pattern. This is typical. I often see, when reviewing the GPS map, that a specific deer uses the same evasive move over and over again.

The large diameter circle, the unknown second hit, the first hit being a spine shock hit for sure, seeing the deer halfway through the circle but way ahead of us in apparent decent condition, not allowing us to get close enough again to see him, and the lack of much blood in the first place all added up to an easy decision to quit the trail as this was not a mortally wounded deer recoverable for a leashed tracking dog. From my use of GPS over the years and from analysis of the maps on my PC at home afterwards, I am able to more quickly determine when to give up the chase. This saves a lot of wear and tear on me and my dog and has not changed my recovery rate.

Two other very useful aspects of GPS use not demonstrated on the above example are being able to easily get back to a known spot of sign to restart your dog and keeping track of how far the wounded deer has traveled, either on a cold trail or as a jumped deer.

And lastly, although it doesn't help you find wounded deer any easier, I like to make a nice keepsake for my scrapbook of deer I find. I overlay the GPS map on Google Earth like you see above and combine it on a page with a photo of my dog and me with the deer.

Use of GPS in Training and Testing

The most obvious value of the GPS involves its use when tracking real wounded deer. However, it can also be useful as a marking and verification device when laying and tracking artificial lines. There is no need to put up markers, and this can be useful when you are setting up a line in a public park. More than once I've had a "do-gooder" take down my surveyor's tape markers before I could work my dog.

When you put out your blood line or tracking shoe scent line, turn on and carry you GPS as you go. (Under a dense forest canopy this may not work.) Then when you work your dog on the line with the GPS collar, the second recorded track will indicate how closely the dog worked, and where he went astray.

This GPS method of training has the advantage of giving you a "blind line". You won't be unconsciously guiding your dog, unless you consult your GPS as you are tracking. You won't know exactly where you put the turns, and your dog will have to show you.

Below is an example of the use of GPS tracks to show the blood line (dark) and the tracking dog's work (light). The occasion was a North American Teckel Club 1000 meter test. I was handling Gilda, the dog that was being tested. Judge Andy Bensing laid and recorded the track on his GPS, and subsequently the dog's work was recorded in another color. As you can see Gilda worked most of the line flawlessly, but she was distracted at one point and departed

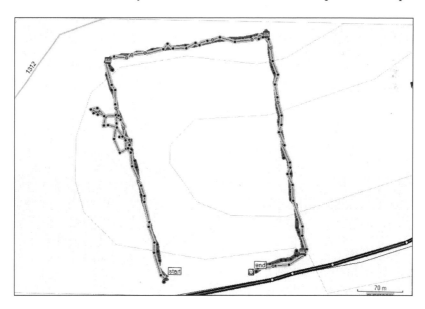

from the blood line significantly. This dropped her performance down from a Prize I to a Prize II, 90 points.

Action Video Cameras

The compact GoPro video camera is another technological innovation, which is having a growing role in the training of dogs and the recording their work on the real thing. This video camera can be mounted on the dog or upon the handler's head or chest. The videos produced are high resolution, and very useful for analyzing what happens as a dog works. It would be an ideal tool for teaching a beginner how to handle and read a dog. The models and prices of GoPro cameras will certainly evolve rapidly. For current information go to Gopro.com.

Pivothead's Video Recording Eyewear (www.pivothead.com) is an attractive alternative to the helmet-mounted camera. The tiny camera is located in the middle of a pair of glasses, right between your eyes. It records exactly what you are looking at. Pivothead glasses come in various frame styles, each with multiple lens choices.

Conclusion

An inestimable benefit of using some sort of tracking device is peace of mind. A hunting dog off lead is always at risk, and a dog tracking a wounded deer far from the handler can get into all kinds of dangerous situations. In the south there are snakes and alligators; the dog can get hung up in a fence, be attacked by coyotes or javelinas, or even be shot by an irate landowner. When your canine tracking partner is out of sight and out of hearing, there is no way to help. For hours the handler can be left with nothing but anxiety.

Summary

- Radio tracking collars send a directional radio signal that allows you to pinpoint the direction of your dog but not his exact location. They have a much higher range than GPS based collars.

- GPS based tracking devices are extremely useful for tracking and training.

- Electronic devices do fail, so carry an old-fashioned magnetic compass as a backup.

- The Garmin Alpha is very useful where dogs are worked off lead.

- All Garmin GPS device are dependent on radio transmission between dog and handler.

Chapter 21

The Makings of a Good Handler

In previous chapters we have focused on dogs and deer, but the larger picture of blood tracking involves more than this. Handlers, like their dogs, must be highly motivated to be effective. Let's look at the factors that motivate handlers. Furthermore, handlers, who are usually hunters themselves, must be able to link up with and communicate effectively with hunters. A discussion of the ways to accomplish this forms the second part of this chapter.

Handlers and Their Motivations

Blood tracking with a trained dog can be pursued on many different levels. Some deer hunters may simply wish to have a dog available to find or check out the status of any deer that might be wounded by their immediate hunting party. This is a modest, but admirable project. It is particularly appropriate for a hunter who desires a versatile dog that can also perform other tasks such as pointing and retrieving game birds, hunting squirrels and raccoons, or finding cattle or wild hogs in thick brush. A small group of hunters should not be producing a lot of wounded deer to track, but even if the dog tracks a wounded deer once a year, he should be able to do a decent job and find a good percentage of the deer that are mortally wounded and recoverable. An intelligent dog, who has a close rapport with his handler, can accomplish a great deal, especially if the lines he is asked to track are not too old and difficult. The owner who develops modest but solid skills in his dog, and then works within his own circle will always play a significant role in reducing the total number of deer that are wounded and lost.

Many hunters get involved in blood tracking in the beginning simply because they want to track wounded deer for themselves and their friends. Later some of them realize that they have been drawn in more deeply than they had ever anticipated. They realize that their dog will never reach his full potential as a tracker of wounded deer unless he is given more experience than comes from tracking a deer or two each year. No one would expect a pointing dog or a retriever to perform on a high level if he were given formal training only, and then was taken out to hunt only once or twice a year. The desire of handlers to excel with their dogs is compatible with their desire to help fellow hunters, to reduce animal suffering and to prevent the waste of venison.

In my own experience, which is primarily with Dachshunds, I would say that formal training on artificial blood lines and deer that have already been found takes a dog only about 25% of the way to his full potential. The rest comes from taking one "natural" call after another. Only in this way does a dog learn just how hard he has to "dig" for the scent under the leaves and in the grass roots to move an old, cold line. Through experience dogs learn to handle difficult backtracks and sort out a check when the deer has milled around and around in a thicket. A dog can be instructed to work the artificial blood line and ignore healthy deer, but the lesson is never really solid until the dog has learned that only a wounded deer can be found or overtaken.

Partly because they want to have the best tracking dog possible, and partly because they love to track, some handlers find themselves drawn into taking 20-30 or more calls a season. Some handlers have taken over a 100 calls in a season. They are willing to sacrifice some of their own hunting; they track a lot at night, and they don't get a great deal of sleep.

An altruistic desire to help fellow hunters is certainly a motivating factor for many of us. Humanitarian and conservation concerns are also very real. However, in themselves these factors are not enough to explain why, for certain handlers, tracking becomes an addiction.

The simple drive to make more money cannot explain the phenomenon. In New York and certain other states of the Northeast it is legally forbidden, at the present time, to accept monetary payment for tracking unless one has a Guide's License. Other states have no such restrictions, and there can be real financial incentives to track for a stranger. But in any case, tracking wounded deer for pay will never make you rich.

In Texas, hunting for trophy bucks on private ranches is a sport for which hunters are willing to pay substantial sums of money. In this system, there is also money to be made by the professional handlers willing to drive long distances with their dogs to find big-racked, costly bucks for clients. Roy Hindes, one of the very best Texas trackers said, "I sure like the money, but even if I didn't get paid I still would do a lot of tracking".

We could place the individual, who occasionally tracks a wounded deer with his trained dog at one end of the spectrum. At the other end, we find the professional handlers, who are on the road or in the field with their tracking dogs most of the deer season.

Somewhere in the middle are the licensed guides, who keep a tracking dog to find deer shot by their clients. The services of the dog are but one of a number of services that they offer to the hunters who hire them.

Especially in the South, the deer lease has become an institution, and variations of the tradition are spreading to other parts of the United States. In the South, ten to thirty hunters will form a partnership that leases deer hunting rights from a large landowner, such as a timber or paper company. In many parts of the South, it is becoming difficult to find a place to hunt if you are not a member of a deer lease.

Often the deer lease includes a clubhouse or at least some sort of shelter used for cooking meals and telling stories in bad weather. Deer hunting is more of a social sport here than in the agricultural sections of the North. Whitetails are often too abundant in much of the South; the seasons are long and the limits are generous. Many deer will be shot on a large hunting lease, and invariably some of these will travel a distance after the shot. In the dense southern cover they can be hard for anyone to find, and the southern hunting tradition does not place as much emphasis on finding your own deer for yourself as is true in Yankee Land. It is considered good, ethical practice to bring in a tracking dog if a deer is shot and not readily found by the hunter.

Some deer lease associations already have a member or an employee with a tracking dog. Frequently, we have inquiries from members of deer leases who are considering whether a tracking dog would be feasible for them. In most deer lease situations, it makes a lot of sense to have an experienced handler with his own dog appropriate to the terrain and the seriousness of snake problems.

Incidentally, this sort of arrangement is mandatory in many of the states of the German Federal Republic and in parts of Scandinavia. In these legal jurisdictions it is not legal to hunt big game unless a tracking dog is available and on call. Most Americans would not be too happy about this sort of legislative coercion. We would prefer to leave such matters to people's judgment, ethical concerns and enlightened self-interest.

Dedicated handlers can be found working their dogs in many different kinds of situations. There is the lone tracker who distributes business cards and tracks for personal satisfaction. There are also those who track within the framework of a deer lease or a larger tracking organization like Deer Search Inc. Whether they call themselves amateurs or professionals, they stay involved in the activity because they have a good tracking dog. It is just too embarrassing and no fun at all to flounder around with an incompetent dog.

The most dedicated trackers do have certain things in common. It may be useful for you to consider this "profile" of the promising handler prospect. Applying the profile to yourself may help you decide if and how deeply you really want to get involved in blood tracking. Don't be too concerned if you fail to fit the profile perfectly. I have seen some notable exceptions.

Some common traits are matters of temperament and physical ability. A good handler is usually a stubborn individual, who like his dog, hates to quit. He has pride in his dog and pride in his own ability. He will not cave in to laziness and indifference when he and his dog have their reputations on the line. Many difficult deer are found when the search is extended a half hour beyond the point of hopelessness.

The successful handler should have good color vision. If a drop of water is indistinguishable from a drop of blood, if squirrel poop looks pretty much like deer blood, then you are in trouble. It will be difficult for you to work with an inexperienced dog unless you have a good tracking assistant; women are rarely colorblind.

Handlers usually start and get hooked between the ages of 35 and 50. My French mentor, Hubert Stoquert, said many years ago that blood tracking was a young man's sport. Now that I am in my eighties I am beginning to understand the wisdom of his words. The infirmities of age may finally undo you. At best, you will have to make a greater effort to stay in shape and keep your weight down. "The hills get steeper." On the other hand, the prospect of another tracking season is a splendid incentive to walk, jog and not eat too much.

The lower age threshold for active handlers is above 30. Many teenagers like to go along on a few calls, but few young people are ready to get involved until they are in their mid-thirties. When young people are dating, few are willing to pay the price that comes with saying, "Honey, I know it's Saturday night, but I just got a deer call." Later, a heavy mortgage, two jobs, and young kids need a lot of attention. By the age of ten, boys and girls are physically capable of going along on many calls; then tracking has the potential of becoming an activity for the whole family. At any age, a tracker needs an exceptionally patient spouse.

The best handlers, the tracking addicts, generally turn out to have been involved with dogs from their youth. Many of them did a lot of coon hunting with hounds as teenagers. These coonhunters, by the way, are comfortable working in the nighttime woods, and that is a big plus in deer finding work. If any adult approaches me about getting a tracking dog, and he or she has never had a dog, then I am suspicious in a friendly way. How could this person have stayed away from dogs for so long?

A cold, rainy night in an alder swamp offers an opportunity for the real handler prospects to sort themselves out from the faint-hearted and the impatient. Even if you come up with the deer, the joys of snaking it out through all those wet alder branches, leaning out at 45 degrees, will give the handler-to-be something to think about. If he comes back for a second deer call, he will probably be a good one.

Most outstanding male handlers are, or have been dedicated deer hunters with the patience to wait on stand for many hours. They are fascinated by deer, and they have a good sense of how deer act, wounded or unwounded. Finding a wounded deer has already become a very strong motivation, an overwhelming drive.

The best long-term handlers are truly determined to come up with a dog that can do the job; if an individual dog, or one particular breed fails, they turn to another. Sometimes this may mean finding a new home for the failed prospect. For some aspiring handlers and their families, this can be a painful decision to make. Watch out for the dog owner who calls up and says, "I have this nice Lab (or Dachshund or Shih Tzu), and I want to have something for him to do." If a person is so focused on an individual dog that his interest begins and ends with that dog, then his motivation will not carry him very far. If the dog happens to have talent, he may train him and take a few calls. If the dog has no interest, he is gone forever.

If you look at the numbers, it is clear that more men than women are drawn to tracking wounded deer. Women handlers are less likely to be deer hunters. For them the strongest motivation seems to be dog related. They bond with their dog and love the intuitive teamwork in a worthy cause.

To summarize, successful handlers take pride in what their tracking dogs can do. They know that an outstanding dog gets that way partly because of natural talent, but even more by going out on many deer calls. They realize that a dog that tracks one or two wounded deer a season will never develop to his full potential, even though he has received good basic training in the beginning.

The most dedicated handlers, with great dogs, take all the good deer calls that their job and family obligations permit. When they hunt in the daytime, they track at night. They do not get a whole lot of sleep. The following interchange between Greg Accardo in Louisiana and Andy Bensing in Pennsylvania reveals the depth of their passion for tracking. Greg wrote:

> This experience with blood tracking has changed me. I don't know about the rest of you in the UBT, but I can honestly say, this dog thing has changed my life. Instead of sitting in a bow stand for hours, I sit at home waiting for the phone to ring. Instead of spending the off-season working with hunting gear, I work with my dog. Do I miss the hunting? I don't think so because my passion has shifted. Is that a good thing or bad thing? I guess it depends on the individual. This I do know; after all the deer I've killed in my life time, maybe close to 200, nothing tops the feeling of excitement I get working with my dog and finding that deer and watching her act like she's conquered the world. The final question is, will I ever hunt again with as much drive and passion as before? I don't know. All I do know is I've found my new passion, and I'm not ready to trade it for something else.

Andy, who had to go out of his own state of Pennsylvania to track, responded:

> Darn Greg, you almost brought a tear to my eye. But all kidding aside, I feel the same way. I have been sitting in my tree stand many times and even at the most productive last hour of light if the phone vibrates with a track-ing call, I take it in the stand and have left the stand with light left to get to the call that much sooner. My desire to hunt is still there but not nearly as much as it used to be. It has definitely been replaced with my desire to track. It sounds ridiculous but this year I feel the urge to make a few less than per-fect shots on purpose to give my new pup a better line than just a 50 yard slam dunk! I won't do it on purpose, of course, but there is no doubt where that kind of twisted, crazy thinking comes from. A passion for blood track-ing!!!! It is infectious. The other day I canceled 5 sales appointments in the afternoon when I got a call in the AM to go tracking here in PA where it is normally illegal. The hunter had gotten special permission from his buddy, the local game warden, and I just could not resist the opportunity. I risked a ton of sales just to go track. If that is not a sign of addiction, I do not know what is! I think we must all be a little nuts.

Women as Handlers

The overwhelming passion to track wounded big game with a canine partner is not restricted to men. The intuitive woman who loves dogs and knows how to read them has the potential to become a very proficient handler. Tracking wounded big game does not have to be a male-dominated activity, and over the years a number of talented women trackers have proved it. In recent years in northern New England Susanne Hamilton, Lindsay Ware and Joanne Greer have been tracking deer, bear and moose; they are on call day or night and combine tracking with their jobs.

The passion to find big game with their dogs drives them, just as it drives male trackers. Tracks of several miles, through brush and beaver swamps, do not deter them. The ordinary woman might be reluctant to go out in the woods at night with men they don't know. The very professional attitude of these dedicated women trackers, who are armed, precludes any male attempts to get "affectionate".

Susanne explains how she and Lindsay Ware tracked a leg-hit deer for about ¾ mile.

Then I stopped Meggie, my tracking Dachshund, to have a "talk" with my hunters... I told them that we needed to see a lot more blood if we were going to continue much longer... so far we had been pushing it for about a quarter mile with only occasional drops of blood.

We had all agreed that we'd go a bit farther when that doe opened up. Things looked rather encouraging, when after a mile and a half, we jumped her twice and I got a shot into her while she was in a lake... I believe this opened her up even more. However, she then took off straight into a horrid, horrid swamp.... (one of those that consists of floaty cushions, that you slip off of). We hoped that it wasn't going to be deeper than waist high. To stop her from going, I aimed another long shot and we all saw the deer drop again. It was 30 degrees; it was COLD!!

Lindsay, one of hunters and I worked out way through treacherous swells and waist high water until we came to the island, where we had seen the doe last. We had hoped that hitting her again would stop her, but she was a fighter.... and she got just out of sight. We marked the swamp grass and slowly worked our way back out. Our thighs were stinging, and we were hoping desperately that the next hole wouldn't be the one that's over our heads.

Then we walked a mile through the woods to a main road where one of the hunters friends came to pick us up... Lindsay and I got into second sets of clothes. We were dry, but we were both still shaking, and we just knew that we were going to get wet a second time.

Then we went to pick up a canoe and drove in the truck around the lake to the other side. We put the canoe into the water, and started paddling at midnight out on this beautiful lake. The surface was like glass and the moon was bright.

We paddled up to the swamp, and found the mouth of the swamp river. We expected that it would take us about another 100 yards to where we had last lost sight of the doe. When we were about 30 yards from the river opening Lindsay said "I think I just saw some eyes..... there she is"!! Unbelievably, she had actually spotted the doe. I handed Meggie to Lindsay, and we quietly paddled into the swamp. When the eyes shined at me at about 15 yards, I took a head shot, which put her instantly out of her misery.

Sad for this deer to suffer so long, but we were ecstatic to have finished a job (from a canoe and in dry clothes). We ended up floating her back to camp where a very excited hunter finally got to lay hands on the deer.

Few people, male or female, could experience this passion and dedication to drive and track all night. Where does it come from? I would like to think that it has deep roots in human genetic history.

The Spouse of the Tracker

Behind every good handler there is usually a good spouse; this is not a paraphrase of the old cliché. If one of the partners is negative to the whole time-consuming activity, it can literally lead to divorce.

A spouse, and usually this means a wife, must share the handler's conviction that tracking wounded deer is a responsibility requiring professional attitude. When a physician has a call, he or she goes. When a firefighter has a call, he or she goes. When a tracker gets a good call, which he cannot pass off to another competent person, he goes. Appearance at the hit site, ASAP, is not quite so essential for the tracker, but once committed, he stays on the line until the job is done. He either finds the animal, or determines, in his experienced judgment, that it is not "findable". A deer call is open ended. Promises should not be made: "I'll be back for supper" or "I'll be back at 11 PM". Not every woman can handle this; not every male spouse can handle this either.

It works better if tracking wounded deer becomes an established activity before marriage. Then both partners know what they are getting into, and both know that sometimes the marriage will be temporarily "suspended". After all, deer season does not last forever. In any case, if you decide to take up blood tracking in a serious way, discuss the step with your spouse and the whole family before liftoff.

It is a rare and beautiful thing when a couple takes calls together. It can work, but it is not as easy as it sounds. Some of the good marital principles of equality must be adjusted a bit, and this may be difficult. In the woods on a deer call, one member of the human team is dominant over the other. The dominant partner is the one handling the tracking dog, or the most skilled tracking dog, if there are two. The experienced tracking dog knows more

Jolanta and John Jeanneney with the deer they recovered together.

about the situation than anyone else present, and his handler is in the best position to make decisions on the basis of what the dog tells him.

Spouses can work together, and the example of Fred and Barbara Schmidt proves this. They took some calls independently, but most of their calls were taken together. Over the years they found many deer out on the eastern end of Long Island. Fred was quite a few years older than Barbara. He developed a heart condition, but this did not weaken his will to take deer calls with his wife. Fred left this world at the end of a deer call that the two took together. Back at the highway, at the end of a deer call, Fred said that he felt weak and he sat down. Then he died right there, with his wife beside him and his Dachshund licking his face. Is there a better way to go?

Communicating With Hunters

If you want to start taking some deer calls outside of your immediate circle of friends, you will find that the grapevine or word of mouth network among hunters will generate some work for your dog. If you are ready to take on even more activity, have some tracking cards, similar to business cards, printed up. Leave them in diners, sporting goods stores or wherever hunters congregate. I think it works best if you have four or five different names and phone numbers on the same card. In this way, one tracker can cover for another or refer calls. This takes the pressure off any one individual. I certainly do not enjoy turning a hunter down when I have something else pressing to be done. Don't distribute so many cards that your reach exceeds your grasp. If hunters can never get a dog and handler when they need one, they will turn sour and stop calling.

Leashed Tracking Dog Service for wounded deer and bear

John Jeanneney	no fee, day or night, mark point of loss
Licensed NYSDEC	
Home (518) 872-1779	
Cell (518) 265-0070	
www.born-to-track.com	

Above is a copy of a card I have been using in Albany County.

Tim Nichols, the first Vermont tracker, hatched the idea of using magnetic signs on the doors of his pickup truck. I was one of several who followed his lead on this. These signs stir up a lot of interest. They identify your vehicle while you are tracking, and in parking lots it is a way of opening conversations and making new friends. Be sure to have a supply of your tracking cards in your glove compartment.

A magnetic, removable sign on a pickup truck

Volunteer organizations like Deer Search have a dispatching system to put hunters in contact with available handlers. This is an excellent arrangement, but effective dispatching does require planning and coordination. In Deer Search's Founding Chapter, which is strongest in the Hudson Valley area of New York, members and volunteers take turns, on a daily basis, to answer calls that come in from hunters. The Deer Search telephone connection is moved around from house to house by call forwarding. The two other New York Chapters use a different and more automated system. Hunters who need help leave their messages on a central recording machine. When a handler is free to take a call, he taps into the list of messages and selects one that is from his general area. Both systems work well, but the problem is that a hunter with a wounded deer to find is not a patient man. He wants to talk to someone immediately and begin the search with a tracking dog more quickly than is possible for handlers who have jobs and families.

The Deer Search system in New York for dispatching handlers, training new people and informing the public is largely responsible for making New York's tracking program a respected success. Deer Search Inc. was developed in the 1970s and 80s, and has always been dependent upon the support of dedicated volunteers. In the 90s, Deer Search, like all volunteer organizations from fire departments to Emergency Medical Services, began to experience problems in recruiting volunteers from the next generation. There were many reasons for this, 70-hour work weeks, and a greater desire to put oneself and one's family first were certainly part of it.

Georgia Outdoor News prints and posts online a list of Georgia trackers available to take deer calls and also posts this information on their web site at www.gon.com as "Dial-A-Tracking Dog". The names and phone numbers of each tracker are presented under the name of the county in which they operate. This is a good model that other state based outdoor publications might follow.

In the 21st century it may well be that simpler, less time-consuming organizations will fit needs better in other states. People, who want to track wounded deer but have limited time and patience for meetings and committee work, may find that the Internet and cell phones provide the communications needed to keep handlers aware of one another. With a cell phone and Internet network, hunters can be referred to a handler who can help them. Social media such as Facebook and Twitter have been playing a rapidly increasing role in connecting hunters to handlers but also in connecting handlers with other handlers for education, exchange of information and support. At the beginning of 2016 there are a number of Facebook groups dedicated to tracking wounded game with dogs such as United Blood Trackers, Mississippi Blood Trailing Network, Alabama Blood Trailing Network, Blood Trackers, Blood Tracking Dogs International, American Blood Tracker, Game Recovery & Blood Tracking Dogs, and the list is growing almost daily.

UBT *"Find a Tracker"*

United Blood Trackers is a national trackers' organization, which was founded in 2005. UBT's emphasis is on education and promotion, but it also offers a new means of bringing hunters and handlers together via the Internet. A hunter can go the UBT web site www.unitedbloodtrackers.org, click on the "Find a Tracker" page and then click again on the state where he is hunting. A list of UBT trackers there comes up with their locations. Another click and you have their phone numbers and details of their service.

Cash

The outlay in time, gasoline and vehicle wear and tear can be considerable if a handler takes numerous deer calls each year. In some parts of the United States, handlers with experienced dogs charge a flat fee, or a fee plus travel expenses. This is especially the case in Texas, where deer management and deer hunting are a real industry upon which many millions of dollars are spent.

For example, on many of the big ranches of south Texas trophy quality bucks are not harvested until they are four and a half years or older. At this point, they are trophies indeed. Hunters, who can afford it, are ready to pay $20,000 and more for bucks that are in the 160+ Boone and Crocket class. Payment is due to the rancher not only when the deer is shot and killed. There is an unwritten rule that you pay for a deer wounded, just as you would pay for one that ends up in your trophy room. A low percentage of deer are wounded under these circumstances, but Texas is a big place. When I was in south Texas with tracker Roy Hindes, I could well understand why a wealthy corporate executive was willing to pay Roy very well to drive 100 miles, each way, to find a buck in the 165-inch class. With a really good dog, and a reputation to match, tracking deer in Texas can be a very profitable alternative to more ordinary forms of work.

On deer leases and hunting preserves in the Southeast, paid employees sometimes handle the tracking dog along with their other responsibilities. No doubt, they enjoy this more than hanging tree stands and sweeping out the clubhouse.

At the other extreme from the Texas model is the example of New York State and some other states in the Northeast. In New York handlers are legally forbidden to charge a fee for tracking wounded deer unless they have a Guide's License. Since blood tracking was legalized in New York the great majority of handlers have not been licensed guides. They have considered themselves volunteers serving their communities and fellow hunters in a spirit not unlike that of volunteer fire fighters.

To cover the substantial costs of driving to the site where a hunter has lost a deer, they accept donations, which are paid by the hunter to an organization such as one of the Deer Search chapters. The chapter then pays the dog handlers for the mileage driven. For many years, this payment was 30 cents a mile, which was certainly not an inflated sum. Recently this has been adjusted upward to reflect higher energy costs. Deer Search handlers, themselves, pay for the other associated costs for equipment and dog maintenance.

Deer Search does offer another significant benefit to its members. The chapters pay for a liability insurance policy, which gives a 2 million dollar liability coverage to members engaged in Deer Search activities such as tracking. If a $500,000 Black Angus bull is shot while standing behind a wounded buck at night, then the Deer Search handler is protected in a liability suit. As of 2016 there has never been an insurance claim.

Fire departments have successfully integrated both volunteers and paid professionals within their organizations, but this arrangement has not been easy to achieve within Deer Search. Licensed Guides in New York have stayed independent of that organization. Some of these Licensed Guides have acquired the additional Leashed Tracking Dog License, which authorizes them to track wounded deer. They do this either as part of their regular service to their hunter clients, or they take outside deer calls for an agreed upon fee.

The decline of involvement in volunteer community service, as described above, may be reflected by a growing interest in tracking for pay. Certainly, we are not seeing the "Leisure Society" that social scientists were predicting in the 1980s. More and more, the individual wishes to justify every waking hour with added income. The national trend is likely to be toward the Texas model with tracking done more and more on a cash basis.

Summary

- Tracking wounded big game can be undertaken with varying levels of intensity and time commitment.

- Tracking can become "addictive".

- For many it becomes much more than a source of cash income.

- Be sure that a commitment to tracking is compatible with such priorities as your family and job.

- If a handler advertises his services well, he will have no difficulty in getting all the calls he wants.

Chapter 22

Working With the Hunter

The Telephone Interview

The telephone conversation between hunter and tracking dog handler is the critical link that makes a tracking service effective. If you take more than a very few deer calls, you must screen them so that you do not waste your time in situations where you and your dog can be of no help. In earlier chapters the point has been stressed that not all deer reported as wounded are actually mortally wounded or recoverable. Especially in the case of bowhunting, a majority of the deer hit and not recovered by the hunter will survive. This means that a handler and tracking dog will be invited to go on many wild goose chases in which there is no chance of actually finding the deer.

An extreme example of this developed when I was asked by a bowhunter to track a deer whose tail had been shot off. In another case a gun hunter was very determined that I should come out and track his buck because it had snorted after the shot. There was no blood, no hair and no reaction of the deer to suggest that it had been hit.

Screening deer calls by asking the right questions is an essential part of being a successful handler who works with hunters beyond his own close circle of friends. You might take a dubious call to give peace of mind to a friend, but probably you do not have the time to drive 100 miles round trip when the chances are next to nil that you can come up with the deer. To make a good decision you have to gather as much information as possible, and this means communicating effectively. To do this you need to understand the state of mind of a hunter who has just shot a deer and is unable to find it. The less experienced the hunter and the bigger the rack of antlers on the buck, the more emotionally upset he is likely to be. If you have hunted yourself, you can empathize with the hunter and realize that he will not be at his calm, rational best when he talks to you. Practical powers of positive thinking may well have been transformed, under the stress of the situation, into the wildest, ill-founded optimism. You must be tactful and sympathetic, but at the same time, you must try to find out what actually happened when the deer was shot. The hunter may make an honest exaggeration of some evidence he saw such as the amount of blood. And what is more important, he may omit critical details because he does not realize that they are important.

When a hunter telephones, you should find out where he is calling from and then ask him to describe what happened when he shot the deer, and what evidence he found afterwards that the deer was hard hit. Explain to him, right up front, that you and your dog cannot help hunters in every situation, but that you probably will be able to give him some helpful advice.

Hunters are usually eager to talk, and they will provide some useful information right away. Put this together with your follow-up questions. When you are done talking, he should have given answers to the questions listed below. Of course, the information may not come out in any particular order, and the answers to some questions may simply be unavailable.

The types of wounds reported in bow season are quite different from those encountered in firearms seasons. For the two types of hunting, you will have to find answers to different sets of questions. I am including here a list of such questions for each of the two broad categories of hunting. In this chapter, we will not dwell on why each question is useful. That information has already been covered in the two chapters on "Special Tracking Situations".

Questions for Bowhunters

1. Where did you hit the deer and from what angle?

Most bow-shot deer are shot from tree stands. Therefore, the arrow seldom passes through the deer in a horizontal plane. Usually the arrow angles down into the deer, and if the site is fairly flat the steepness of that angle depends on the height from which the arrow was released and the distance from the hunter's tree to the deer. The position in which the deer presented itself is also an essential piece of information. Was the deer broadside, quartering toward the hunter or quartering away? This data will help develop a working hypothesis of what organs lay in the arrow's trajectory, and what the damage is likely to be. Light carbon arrows shot from modern compound bows may travel over 220 feet per second (150 mph). This is fast enough so that the hunter may not have seen the arrow disappear into the deer.

2. How much penetration occurred?

Ideally, the arrow shot from a tree stand should pass completely through the deer, exiting on the far side at a lower level than it entered. In the real world a "pass through" is not always achieved. Insufficient penetration may occur when a deer is shot at very close range and the arrow is still in flex when it enters the deer. Recently more and more bow hunters have begun using mechanical or expandable broadheads. The blades open up to cut a wider swath through the deer but this requires more kinetic energy than does a conventional broadhead. Mechanical broadheads work most effectively with heavy weight arrows and high poundage bows. Unfortunately, many hunters do not realize this. Sometimes an archer sees the arrow protruding, but more frequently, he can determine the degree of penetration if he finds the broken arrow. Arrows sticking out of deer, whether they are made of wood, aluminum or carbon, usually break off against trees. The break point generally occurs on the arrow shaft at the point where it protrudes out of the deer. By comparing the broken, fletching end of the arrow to another arrow in the quiver, it is a simple matter to determine the depth of penetration.

3. What did you find on the arrow itself?

This question is useful if the arrow passed though the deer largely intact and the hunter found it. Digested bits of food on the arrow indicate that the stomach or intestines were cut. Sometimes these fragments are not very obvious, and they are missed unless you ask specific questions. Ask the hunter to check very closely around the angles of the broadhead and along the base of the fletching. The hunter should also smell the fresh arrow because this will give an accurate indication of where the arrow has been. Women seem to have a better sense of smell for this than men. Especially if a hunter is a smoker, I will ask him to have his wife check it out. There may be fat or grease on the arrow shaft. In the case of a buck, this can be significant. Usually bucks are not as fat as does, and what fat they have is carried high on the rib cage. Fat on the arrow suggests a high hit in the case of a buck, but this is not a certain indication, and it should be balanced with other evidence.

4. What did the blood look like, how much was there, and what was the pattern and placement?

In previous chapters we discussed the different types of wound blood (lung, gut, etc.), and inquiries should be made about this. Remember that blood from the muscles on the outside of the deer frequently masks organ blood, which has flowed out in much smaller amounts and is quite different in appearance. Usually, you can't get much useful information over the phone about the nature of the blood that was seen. Questions about the amounts of blood lead to very different sorts of reports. Few hunters have an accurate basis for comparison. To some a half pint of blood on the ground looks like very serious hemorrhage. It is easy to exaggerate amounts in the honest, post-shot excitement of the hunt. As the two chapters on "Special Tracking Situations" suggested, the amount of blood on the ground is usually not very significant anyway. If there really was a huge amount of external bleeding, the hunter would have quickly found the deer himself, and he never would have called you. Internal bleeding is just as fatal as the external sort, but it is much more difficult to evaluate. In practice, the pattern and placement of the blood is usually more significant than the amount. Was the blood spraying out under arterial pressure, or was it flowing and dripping straight down from the wound? Was there blood on both sides of the trail? Smears of blood on weeds and saplings are very important because they enable you to estimate how high in the body the deer was hit.

5. What kind of hair was at the hit site?

Hair can offer valuable clues about where and how the arrow entered and exited from the deer. Sometimes an arrow alters its trajectory after it is in the deer. A shot that should have gone through the lower part of the lungs may be deflected by bone so that it exits from the white hair area of the belly. It is important for the hunter to report white hair and brown hair, and this is sometimes not as simple as it should be. The brown, deer color of body hair is actually restricted to the outermost part of each hair, about a third of an inch. The rest of the hair is a light, beige gray. At dusk, the beige gray can appear almost white. Many times on the phone, hunters have reported that they had white hair, although they were actually talking about brown-tipped hair from the upper body. Ask, "Was it really chalk white or was it a light gray?"

6. What were the reactions of the deer when the arrow entered?

In bowhunting, a razor sharp broadhead sometimes passes right through the deer's chest and the deer keeps on feeding. There is no reaction at all. An unfortunate shot to the stomach, liver or intestines is likely to provoke the animal to hunch its back and move away slowly when it does not know the source of danger. Usually a deer, with its tail raised in alarm, will clap it down at the shot. If the tail is down when the deer is hit hard, it normally will stay down. Jumped from cover where it has taken refuge after being hit, a seriously wounded deer normally will not show the white of its tail. I have seen exceptions to all of these rules, but they are rare. You should think of probabilities, not absolute certainties when you are talking with your hunter.

7. How far did you follow the deer?

On many productive deer calls, the hunter reports that he lost the blood trail after a 100 or 200 yards. A deer can be bleeding to death internally, but very little blood has dripped down on the outside. This happens often, and this is why a tracking dog is so useful. What gives me pause, when I am talking to a hunter, is the report that the deer was tracked for miles before the blood sign stopped. Unless you are dealing with a gut shot, or a broken leg (unusual in bowhunting), this is an unpromising indication. If a large blood vessel had been severed by the broadhead, the deer would not have been able to go that far before collapsing. If smaller blood vessels in the neck, shoulders or hams were cut, they finally clotted up, and the deer had the resources to continue. Generally a chest-hit deer that goes a half mile or lives a half hour is unlikely to die. This rule is useful, but not absolute. If the arrow is still in the deer, a conventional broadhead may work back and forth, and finally cut a large vessel, which brings death. A mechanical broadhead will not do this. The cutting blades float once the arrow stops, and little further cutting occurs.

8. What broadhead were you using?

 The probabilities of finding the deer are lower if the head was a large bladed mechanical. When the mechanicals penetrate well, they kill the deer quickly and there is no need for the tracking dog. The problem is that mechanicals often lose their kinetic energy too quickly, and fail to penetrate far enough.

Questions for Rifle and Gun Hunters

For rifle and gun hunters the same set of questions is useful, but the emphasis is different and the significance of the answers varies. For example, the rifle hunter probably will not be able to give you as accurate a report about where he hit the deer.

1. Where did you hit the deer and from what angle?

The question is worth answering, but chances are the hunter will not be able to reply with certainty. If he took a running shot or shot through a screen of brush, the range of possibilities is very broad. The hunter may have no idea of where he hit the deer and may realize that he should not have taken the shot at all. If the hunter aimed for the neck, or worse for the head, the likelihood is that he either killed the deer on the spot (Then he wouldn't have called you!) or he created a situation in which the deer would be very difficult to recover. As discussed previously, there is much non-vital, fleshy tissue in the neck.

A head shot, which goes slightly astray, may break the jaw. Such deer are doomed in the end, but catching up to them is very difficult. If the hunter had only a head-on, frontal shot and yielded to temptation and took it, he should have killed the deer if the bullet entered the rib cage. The chief remaining options are a broken shoulder or a low brisket shot. A leashed tracking dog can do a good job on these, but he cannot catch up to a deer with a superficial shoulder muscle shot even though there is heavy bleeding at the outset.

2. What cartridge and bullet were you using?

A hunter can seldom be sure of how much penetration occurred, and with the high energy of standard deer cartridges and shotgun slugs, this is not an important consideration. Penetration problems arise with the smaller calibers, particularly when they are used with light varmint bullets. You should ask what sort of cartridge and bullet the hunter was using. It may be more than pure coincidence that I have had more deer calls involving the .243 than with any other rifle cartridge. With correct placement of an appropriate bullet, the .243 is quite adequate for shooting whitetails. A light .243 varmint bullet, however, can blow up on the outside of a deer's ribs. Even if the ammunition choice and the marksmanship are impeccable, other things can go wrong. If the deer moves at the critical instant, the shot, which is slightly off target, wounds but does not kill. With a heavier caliber like the 30-06 the same shot would not produce a problem.

I was once called upon to track a doe that had been shot with .357 Magnum handgun. Despite it formidable name, the .357 Magnum is actually a marginal deer cartridge. There was almost no blood, and the tracking was very difficult. We found the doe dead with a pencil-sized hole in the rib cage. The bullet placement was good, but there was no exit wound. We were lucky to find this deer. At some point, you, as a handler, will have to draw the line on tracking deer that are shot with legal, but inadequate firepower. During the 2001 season, I turned down two calls to track deer that had been shot with rifles from a tree stand. In both cases the bullets went in high behind the shoulder and penetrated down into the deer. One hunter used a .222 and one a .223, which is slightly more powerful. There was no blood and probably no exit wound. These deer were likely to die, but there was little hope of tracking them. When deer and fresh scent are everywhere, it is very tough to get the dog started on the right deer if there is no blood at all.

3. What did you see at the hit site?

In gun hunting, unlike bowhunting, you will very rarely find the projectile itself, but if the hunter goes to the hit site, he will often find important evidence of the bullet's or slug's work. There will be hair, tissue and possibly bone fragments. These are often described by the hunter as "pieces of rib", but usually they turn out to be fragments of leg bone. You should suspect a broken leg, and deer injured in this way should be tracked as soon as possible for the reasons reviewed in Chapter 15. Ask the hunter what kind of hair he saw and in what quantity. You do not want to take a long drive to track a deer that was merely grazed by a slug or bullet. The hunter may have thought that lots of hair is a promising sign, or he simply may not have noticed. Then, of course, there is always the possibility that wind blew the hair away.

If there is no other evidence to clarify the situation, you are within your rights to ask the hunter to go back to the exact point where the deer was shot and report to you everything that he sees. Very often hunters call from the woods on their cell phones so this is easily done. Ask the hunter to put up markers so that an hour is not wasted later searching in the dark for the hit site where you will start the dog.

4. What did the blood trail look like?

The hunter will have much to say about how much blood there was on the trail. Often the amount of blood and its significance will be greatly exaggerated in his mind. It is hard to start the dog if you have no blood at all, but the amount of blood is not very useful for evaluating the prospects of finding the deer. A muscle wound can produce a great deal of blood, but if the blood clots, and there is no internal bleeding, the deer is likely to survive. If the blood does not clot, the hunter finds the deer for himself and has no need to call you.

The hunter may report "pieces of meat" on the trail, but these are much more likely to be blood clots that have formed and then broken loose. As in bow hunting, the amount of blood on the outside is not a very reliable indicator of whether the deer is recoverable unless you also know where the deer was hit. The height of blood smears on brush will help you determine this, if the hunter noticed and can describe it. Firearm hunters who have lung hits (fine bubbles in the blood) are unlikely to be calling you, although this does not apply to bowhunters.

The most important thing is to identify deer that have been gut shot. These deer are high priority, but weather and coyotes permitting, they should be given as much time as possible.

5. What was the reaction of the deer at the shot?

Sometimes a mortally wounded deer reacts very little, but on the whole, answers to your questions about deer reaction will be useful. The background for interpreting these reactions is given in Chapters 14 and 15. If the deer goes down instantly at the shot, it cannot mean a broken spine; in this case, the hunter would not be calling you. An instant knockdown strongly suggests a shot above the spine that has temporarily stunned the deer. A shot beneath the spine that knocks the deer down is very likely to rupture the large dorsal aorta, and this is quickly fatal. A leg or shoulder hit deer will probably go down, but the drop will not be instantaneous. Only when the deer tries to run and puts weight on its leg, will it stumble and fall once or twice. A deer hit too far back in the abdomen will probably hunch its back. Deer, well hit in the chest, may stumble or sag, but they will almost never go down immediately. As a tracker, you need not concern yourself very much about heart-shot cases in which the deer generally leaps upward.

6. How far was it possible to track the deer?

Distance, in itself, will not tell you much, but it is very useful to know what the deer did as it traveled. Did it bed down and then leave the bed voluntarily? This is not a good sign. If the deer allowed the hunters to approach quite closely, and then left the bed running low with the tail down, then there is likely to be something seriously wrong with it. It may be necessary to remind the hunter that large and numerous spots of blood do not necessarily mean that the deer has lain down. It is more likely that it stopped for a moment. When a deer lies down, the blood is usually smeared and matted into the ground cover.

7. What is the coyote situation?

As I write this in 2016, I find that many hunters are still unaware of the high risk that coyotes may destroy their deer. This level of risk varies from one locality to another, but the hunter should be reminded that coyotes don't wait, especially after dark. Gut shots in late afternoon should not be worked right away, but if coyotes are numerous, more is to be lost than gained by waiting until morning to track.

Evaluating the prospects of finding a wounded deer by means of a telephone conversation is not as clear and decisive a process as I have made it sound. There are cases in which you just cannot be sure about how seriously a deer has been wounded. In these situations, you generally end up going out on the call. If you have limited time and more than one request to track, you usually take the most promising one.

If you think too much about your percentage rate of recoveries, and turn down all calls except those that seem certain to produce a dead deer, then some deer that you and your dog could have found will be left dead in the woods.

On the phone you have to be respectful of the stressed hunter on the other end of the line. He may not agree with your own conclusions because most of his experience has been with well-hit deer that died quickly. If he saw that a certain quantity of blood spilled out of a deer that went in just a few hundred yards, it is easy for him to conclude that such a quantity of blood on the ground always means that the deer will not go far. On the other hand, as a handler/ tracker you know that you are dealing with a small and special minority of all the deer shot in hunting season. In the cases of the wounded deer that you are called upon to track, something went wrong. You are dealing with special situation deer, and your understanding may not mesh too well with that of the self-proclaimed "deer expert", who may have tagged twenty deer, but who has never had a real problem.

We have seen that some hunters will grasp at straws, particularly if it is a big buck that they have lost. Once they realize that they cannot find the deer on their own, they may expect that a tracking dog will perform any miracle needed. You must gently explain to them that catching up to or finding the deer depends, above all, on how the deer was hit.

If you are reading this in a Southern state or in Texas, you may wonder why I seem rather conservative in my expectations of what a tracking dog can accomplish. I am writing this book from the perspective of a handler who necessarily works his tracking dog at all times on a leash. When Roy Hindes showed me how cowdogs track deer in Texas, I realized that his dogs, working off lead, found and bayed live, wounded deer much more quickly than we can do with leashed dogs in the Northeast or the Midwest. Quite a few situations certainly arise in Texas and the South in which deer, weakened, but not mortally wounded, are recovered by big dogs working free. If the same deer were tracked up North by a dog on a leash, they might escape and live.

If you are a Southerner or a Texan, you must make your own adjustments to what you read in this book. You should also realize that there is a need for another book written by and for Southerners and/or Texans. On a continent as wide and diverse as North America there can be no such thing as one definitive book. I hope that this book gets the ball rolling and leads to others.

There are certain general questions that a handler should ask a hunter before he takes a call. He should make sure, in a tactful way, that the deer was legally shot and can be legally tagged. The landowner situation can be very sticky. There is no such thing as a fundamental right of pursuit that allows a hunter or tracker to follow a wounded animal wherever it goes. On privately owned property in North America, the rights of private property come first. Therefore, you should inquire as to whether the deer is likely to stay on the land where the hunter has permission. If a deer was shot 100 yards from a property line and goes onto the land of a neighbor, you will be out of luck if the hunter does not acquire the necessary permission in advance. Hunters tend to underestimate the distance that their deer may travel.

In some of the Northeastern states, there is specific information that the holder of a leashed tracking dog license must gather from the hunter and report to the Law Enforcement Office before he takes a call. This creates extra work for the Law Enforcement Dispatcher, but it strongly discourages violators from calling a dog and handler to give him a "cover" as he drags out an illegally shot deer. These special questions, which must be asked of the hunter in New York State, are not of universal interest so we have placed them in Appendix G, which contains the Leashed Tracking Dog License regulations for that state.

This chapter has been written to show that tracking wounded deer involves more than simply training and using dogs. Handlers tend to be a strong race of loners, but to have a real impact on the crippling loss problem they must recruit other handlers and cooperate with them. It is also essential that hunters be able to reach handlers and communicate with them well. This is not too difficult since handlers are usually hunters themselves.

Working With the Hunter on the Track

When you meet the hunter, ask him to sign this Tracking Report Form confirming that he has permission from the property owner. You should have begun filling in the other information that you will need for your tracking records. If there is ever a question about landowner permission having been given, you will have evidence that the hunter gave you false information This will take you off the hook as the tracker, if complaints are filed or arrests are made.

Put the hunter at ease with friendly conversation. If he will be carrying a firearm to put down the deer, explain that he should not have a shell in the chamber. Guns have a way of going off all by themselves when a big buck jumps up.

Explain that the hunter, and anyone else in the tracking party, must stay behind you and your dog. Later, if you get into thick cover, direct the hunter to move to where there is better visibility, usually on higher ground, and have him move on a parallel course to your own. The tracker is the one who must follow the leashed dog everywhere the deer went through the thick stuff. Often the tracker will not see the deer when it gets up.

TRACKING REPORT

HUNTER'S NAME ⎯⎯⎯⎯⎯⎯⎯⎯⎯⎯⎯⎯ TELEPHONE No. ⎯⎯⎯⎯⎯⎯⎯⎯

ADDRESS ⎯⎯⎯⎯⎯⎯⎯⎯⎯⎯⎯⎯⎯⎯⎯⎯⎯⎯⎯⎯⎯

BACK TAG No. ⎯⎯⎯⎯⎯⎯⎯⎯⎯

DATE & HOUR DEER WAS WOUNDED ⎯⎯⎯⎯⎯⎯⎯⎯⎯⎯

LAND OWNER'S NAME ⎯⎯⎯⎯⎯⎯⎯⎯⎯⎯⎯

LAND LOCATION ⎯⎯⎯⎯⎯⎯⎯⎯⎯⎯⎯

HUNTING OR TRACKING PERMISSION   YES ⎯⎯   No ⎯⎯

| HUNTER'S SIGNATURE | ⎯⎯⎯⎯⎯⎯⎯⎯⎯⎯ |

(I Certify That the Above Information Is Correct)

DOG'S NAME ⎯⎯⎯⎯⎯⎯⎯⎯⎯⎯⎯⎯

DOG'S BREED ⎯⎯⎯⎯⎯⎯⎯⎯⎯⎯⎯⎯

DOG HANDLER'S NAME ⎯⎯⎯⎯⎯⎯⎯⎯⎯⎯⎯

DESCRIPTION OF DEER ⎯⎯⎯⎯⎯⎯⎯⎯⎯⎯⎯

DESCRIPTION OF WOUND BY HUNTER ⎯⎯⎯⎯⎯⎯⎯⎯⎯⎯⎯⎯⎯

DESCRIPTION OF WOUND AND BLOOD TRAIL ⎯⎯⎯⎯⎯⎯⎯⎯⎯⎯⎯⎯⎯

TIME ELAPSED BEFORE TRAILING WITH DOG ⎯⎯⎯⎯⎯⎯⎯⎯⎯⎯⎯

WEATHER CONDITIONS ⎯⎯⎯⎯⎯⎯⎯⎯⎯⎯⎯⎯⎯⎯⎯

ESTIMATED DISTANCE DEER WAS TRAILED BY HUNTER ⎯⎯⎯⎯⎯⎯⎯⎯⎯

ESTIMATED DISTANCE DEER WAS TRACKED BY DOG ⎯⎯⎯⎯⎯⎯⎯⎯⎯

CIRCUMSTANCES WHICH ENDED TRACKING OF DEER ⎯⎯⎯⎯⎯⎯⎯⎯⎯⎯⎯⎯⎯⎯

COMMENTS ⎯⎯⎯⎯⎯⎯⎯⎯⎯⎯⎯⎯⎯⎯⎯⎯⎯⎯⎯

Hunting Equipment:
Bow ⎯⎯   Draw Weight ⎯⎯⎯   **Deer Recovered: Yes** ⎯⎯ **No** ⎯⎯
Shotgun ⎯⎯   Gauge ⎯⎯⎯   Buck ⎯⎯   Doe ⎯⎯
Rifle ⎯⎯   Caliber ⎯⎯⎯   Description Of Deer Found ⎯⎯⎯⎯⎯
Handgun ⎯⎯   Caliber ⎯⎯⎯   ⎯⎯⎯⎯⎯⎯⎯⎯⎯⎯⎯

NAME OF DOG WHICH FOUND THE DEER ⎯⎯⎯⎯⎯⎯⎯⎯⎯⎯⎯⎯⎯

SUBMITTED BY: ⎯⎯⎯⎯⎯⎯⎯⎯   DONATION $⎯⎯⎯⎯   MILEAGE ⎯⎯⎯⎯

WITNESSED BY: ⎯⎯⎯⎯⎯⎯⎯⎯ | **HUNTER'S SIGNATURE** | ⎯⎯⎯⎯⎯

(I Certify That The Above Information Is Correct)

Updated October 1997 / Printed 02/24/15

It is very important for everyone in the tracking party to realize that they cannot roam around looking for sign on their own. If they do so that will track up the scent line and make things harder for the dog.

At night everyone in the tracking party must have a light and have it turned on before any shooting occurs.

Particularly if the tracker is a young man or a woman, some hunters may try to take over and direct the operation. It must be made very clear that the tracker is the person in charge, and that if the hunter can't accept this, the tracker and dog will go home. This is necessary for efficiency and safety.

On the other hand be aware that the hunter may be upset because he wounded a deer. Don't make him feel like a guilty fool that had to call someone else in to clean up his mess. Let the hunter participate in the search instead of being a helpless bystander. One good way to do this is to give him a role of biodegradable marking tape. While you are reading the dog, the hunter can be putting up strips of tape on branches at eye-level. This can be useful if the dog loses the line, and you need to go back to visible blood and restart. Once the deer is up and moving ahead, there is a fresh scent line, and tape is no longer necessary.

If it becomes very clear that the deer is not "gettable", let the hunter participate in making the decision to quit. Review with him what evidence you have seen on the track. Explain what all this sign and deer behavior means, in your own experience. Usually the hunter will want to quit sooner than the tracker, but in any case, try not to let him feel that the decision to stop was imposed upon him.

If possible pick up the dog on a drop of visible blood, so there can be no doubt that you were tracking the right deer.

Summary

- It is essential to screen your calls and select those in which the deer is seriously wounded. There are few certainties.

- Hunters, who have wounded and lost a deer, are not in a "normal" state of mind. Be tactful. Don't lecture or preach.

- During your telephone interview, ask questions to draw out information.

- Be wary of instant knockdowns.

- Be wary of reports of large amounts of hair.

- Be wary of calls where the deer has been tracked for over a half mile with dwindling amounts of blood and no signs of weakness or serious injury. This does not apply to gut shots or leg hits.

- Make sure that the deer can be legally tagged.

- Make sure that you and the hunter have permission to enter all private property that may be involved.

- Involve the hunter in the search so that he doesn't feel like a guilty bystander. Make him a part of your decision-making process.

Chapter 23

The Tracking Dog in the Family

In writing the first edition of this book it never occurred to me that a chapter like this would be necessary. There are excellent books that deal with dog care, house training and socialization, and it hardly seemed appropriate to include this basic material in a rather specialized book. Many long phone conversations and e-mail exchanges with people new to tracking dogs have made me realize that much needs to be said about fitting a dedicated tracking dog into a family setting. It was easy to explain that a great deal is lost if a tracking dog spends his days in a kennel and has little social contact with his handler. But it became evident that everything would not automatically take care of itself, after the tracking dog moved in with the family and the other animals that are part of the household.

Working Dog Temperament

There is a Grand Canyon of non-communication between the companion dog and the hunting dog worlds; this is unfortunate. Hunting dogs are different from the show and pet-bred dogs that most dog behavior specialists know and write about. If we generalize about high level tracking dogs, they have a certain tendency in common. Underlying the desirable, laid-back temperament, there is a will of steel. It takes will and desire to stay focused on a difficult line for hours and to stand up to wounded big game that can kill. With experience and success, tracking dogs develop very strong egos. They are proud of their work and purpose, and they identify with what they do. Particularly in male dogs this can translate into a certain stubbornness, and a conviction that lesser beings in the household, especially other dogs and cats, should know their subordinate place.

In most modern dog breeds that were once bred for a specific working purpose the tendency to strong personalities was deliberately eliminated through selection of breeding stock. For example, in the breeds that were originally developed for police and guard work, the tough, strong-willed dogs were not used for breeding show and companion dogs. A breeder of show or pet dogs knew that it would be dangerous to sell puppies of the original type to an uninformed public that was looking for a lovable "Disney dog", one that would not require a firm structure of discipline. Most American-bred German Shepherds and Dobermans are warm, friendly dogs that fit easily into a suburban household with kids, cats and visiting neighbors. They come close to what the puppy buyer hoped for, in part because they no longer have the working dog temperament of their ancestors.

But law enforcement trainers cannot use these dogs. They say that they have been "calmed down", or less kindly "dumbed down" to meet the expectations of the suburban puppy market. Trainers for law enforcement have learned that you cannot shape and control aggressiveness and inquisitiveness if these traits are no longer inherent in the dog. Today most law enforcement dogs come from Eastern Europe where breeding objectives are different.

Some of the same issues of tough-mindedness come into play when a future handler considers buying a tracking dog prospect. We get many calls from bowhunters who are looking for a family dog that will be good with the kids, loll around in front of the TV and in the backyard, until the call comes in to track a deer. They expect that the dog will track one or two wounded deer a year for their family and friends. Most of these prospective owners do recognize that the dog will need some training to track and to stay on the right deer. But they don't understand that training of a tracking dog must be more comprehensive than this.

Teaching a Strong-Willed Dog His Place

A dog is a hierarchical creature, most comfortable when he knows who his leader is and what the leader's rules are. If the dog has intelligent flexibility, he will understand that he works as a partner in tracking, but that he is not an equal partner when he considers marking a table leg. True bonding of dog and handler is not damaged by discipline. Bonding is actually enhanced because the dog is most comfortable in a world with known rules and limits. Because we love our dogs so much, it is easy for some to assume that they are four-legged versions of people akin to us. Actually, the difference between dogs and people is one of the things that attracts us to them. Could we ever find a human friend who was as loyal, uncritical and forgiving as our dog?

A puppy doesn't know who he is; he goes with the flow. He may be excitable, playful and yappy, but he senses that he is subordinate to any dog or person more mature than he is. His pride and ego will come later, and it is best that the disciplinary structure be firmly in place before this happens.

As the puppy matures into adolescence he will seek to place himself in the social hierarchy of the household. His place will be somewhere near the bottom, but infants and toddlers can be bullied a bit. The canine adolescent, especially if he is a male, may growl and snap at a young child that crawls up to him as he gnaws upon a rawhide chewy. This same young dog would not dream of trying this on a senior dog of his own size or larger. This is where the human master and the mistress of the household must intervene sternly and promptly. Any human of the household, regardless of age, is not to be "put in its place" by a dog. All humans are under the protection of the master and mistress of the household. They are not fair game for upstart dogs out to improve their status through intimidation.

One of our own experiences impressed upon us the necessity of having the heads of the family enforce their rules upon uppity canines on the make. We sold a very good young male puppy into a situation where he was to be a family dog and blood tracker. One of the young sons, the product of a previous marriage, was somewhat timid and unsure of himself. He was the only one of the children that Gusto tried to intimidate.

Gusto recognized his opportunity to climb, and he got away with it… for a while. The human parents did not nip the problem in the bud by demonstrating in clear, physical terms, that all their children inherited the human, social superiority of the parents.

The problem was resolved, but in a way that was unfortunate, especially for us. Gusto was castrated. We had written into the sales contract that we would retain breeding rights on Gusto for our own bitches. By the time we realized that neutering might be an option, the crisis was full-blown, and we gave our consent to the operation.

Gusto never worked out for his owner, who never got around to tracking. He was sold in middle age to a serious tracker, and found his share of deer.

Behavior in the House

The puppy must also learn from the beginning to respect the rules concerning physical objects. He cannot follow his every whim, grabbing this and grabbing that. He must learn what "NO" means, and re-enforcement of this must be so consistent that he never forgets. Gloves and shoes are not rawhide chews. A puppy learns this quickly and by adolescence he will understand that all personal items from socks to books are off limits. If he is bored and left alone with possibilities for mischief, he will still give into temptation. That is why he should go into his crate if he is unsupervised. He is not a child perceiving confinement as prison. A crate is the puppy's den and place of security where he knows that he will not get into trouble. All of this is not irrelevant to tracking. A good relationship with his handler, in which he clearly knows what to expect in a consistent world, will make him desire to please and be part of a working team.

If you, as handler, are new to this, you may find it useful to go with your dog to an obedience class. It is a great way to expose him to different dogs, people and situations. I have found that dogs become more eager to learn something if they see other dogs doing it successfully and being praised for it. At first the presence of other dogs may serve as a distraction, but soon your dog's observation of other dogs performing becomes a positive reinforcement.

Avoid Raising Two Young Dogs at the Same Time

House and yard training of a young dog is easier if he recognizes that you are his most important social contact. The necessary bonding will be more difficult if the young dog has a constant playmate of the same age. You will seldom know "Who peed on the floor?", but it goes beyond this. The young roughnecks will constantly be watching or wrestling with one another; they won't have much attention left over to focus on what the human master of the house may wish. If dogs are a year or more apart in age, these problems can be avoided.

Teaching Your Dog to "Come" from a Distance

Teaching the dog recall, that is to "come", in the confines of a large room is simple and certainly useful. The problem is that your instructor, accustomed to tamed-down dogs, may leave you believing that this is all that is necessary to have your tracking dog handle in the woods and fields. Nothing could be farther from the truth. In typical obedience classes, reinforced by homework, a dog learns to respond to commands when his handler is close and has eye contact. In the hunting dog's mind this lesson has nothing to do with recalling from 200 yards away when his nose has alerted him to something interesting. The best solution is the remote or electric collar, gently and judiciously used. To the dog the "Big Magic" of the remote collar stimulation informs him that the master's influence extends far beyond the sphere of eye contact. Once this is realized, all of the prior recall training at close quarters begins to operate at long distances. The dog does not realize the exact limits of the magic, so he does not challenge the call to come in. To discuss remote collars here would get us off the main theme of the chapter. You will find information about remote collars and their use in Appendix E.

Exercise

At this point something needs to be said about why long distance recall is important. I have spoken with many people who assume that a dog, who tracks on lead, never has to be off lead anyway. They assume that walks around the block, and a few training blood lines are enough to keep the dog exercised and in shape. Until they are two years old, some dogs build up so much excess energy that it is difficult to make them focus on any specific task. On a challenging training line, they are jumping all over the place. With some of my own young dogs I find that I get much better tracking work out of them if they have a good run off lead before we begin.

The point is that you can't let them burn off that excess energy by running if they are going to disappear over the horizon, bump a healthy deer....or a fast moving vehicle. If you have to get out your ATV and road the dog on a long leash, that is a lot of extra work. I know one dedicated handler who would take his Dachshund out in the field behind his house on a very long leash, which was not the one he used for tracking. To be sure, the dog was safe from the numerous coyotes that haunted the area, but it definitely affected her working style when blood tracking. On the exercise lead she would swing back and forth in her enthusiasm to run. This bitch had a lot of talent, but even on a blood line she would continue to swing back and forth rather than work the line smoothly in the right direction. She knew where the line was, and she would return to it regularly, despite the windshield wiper style to which she had been conditioned. She would have been easier to handle and better at showing her handler blood sign if she had overcome this bad habit. Controlling her exercise session with a remote, electric collar would have worked better than keeping her on a long rope. In later life, after many natural tracks, this bitch did settle down and worked a line smoothly.

As was discussed in earlier training chapters, experience with other forms of hunting will usually enhance tracking performance while keeping the dog exercised. Intelligent dogs can make distinctions. When the tracking collar and leash go on, they will think "wounded deer", and not try to range out for pheasants. The free running possibilities with the various tracking breeds differ, but all of them require field obedience. A dog cannot live well by blood tracking alone. Middle aged dogs and older dogs will track better, and work longer, if they get exercise and mental stimulation year round.

Livestock

It is very desirable to expose your dog to the livestock that he may encounter around the house or on his trips. I can remember a time when a former neighbor acquired a flock of bantam chickens, which he allowed to forage in back of his house. I did not know about this, but my dogs discovered them on one of our walks through my nearby woods. These young dogs had never seen a chicken, but their instincts flashed the "GAME" message. The rest was feathers and dead meat. This cost me $50.

I went to a nearby poultry farm and purchased some worn-out layers, which were ready to become chicken soup. With these birds it was possible to set up a controlled training exercise and make the dogs aware that chickens were off limits. It worked.

I like to expose young dogs to sheep, cattle and horses in the field or the barn. Letting them sniff these animals, as cautions and reassurances are given, is very effective. You want a dog that will track through a pasture of grazing livestock if necessary.

Avoid Spaying and Neutering

The biggest problems with other domestic animals are likely to arise right in the household. Two dogs of the same sex are very likely to quarrel, and this can escalate into deadly combat. Most people who contemplate developing a tracking dog already have a dog of some sort in the house, or around the place. If you really like dogs, you already have one. There have been only a few painful years in my own life when I did not have a dog myself.

The best way to avoid problems is to buy a tracking prospect of the gender opposite that of the dog you already have. It is rare that a dog and a bitch don't get along reasonably well. In the real world, as distinguished from fantasy

Sheep and goats are not wounded big game. Joeri understands this.

lands of Disney dogs, males will often develop a rivalry. They should not be left together without supervision.

Bitches are, as a rule, more tolerant of one another, but deep-seated conflicts can become established in female cases as well. Veterinarians are very quick to recommend routine neutering and spaying of all dogs as a solution to everything. Eliminating the main source of testosterone in males does reduce aggressiveness between dogs in most cases. However, vets are more concerned about the nearly 5 million unwanted dogs put down each year in animal shelters.

Many vets, especially those who practice in the suburbs, fail to make a distinction between unwanted pets and working dogs that have been bred for a specific purpose. In some cases they use their professional positions to apply great pressure on new owners to castrate and spay young dogs that might become irreplaceable producers of desirable tracking traits. There may be too many mutts in the dog pounds, but for many years to come there will be a shortage of dogs that have the genetic qualities to become top tracking dogs. A dog neutered or spayed before his or her qualities are known will never reproduce. If a puppy is spayed before its male or female character develops, it will never acquire it. Personally I like my males to be masculine and my bitches feminine. I find that I can relate to the two positive gender types better than something bland and in between.

Neutered males usually have weight problems that require constant vigilance and diet restrictions. Health-wise there are real disadvantages, as well as advantages, in neutering males. Look into the matter thoroughly. Especially if a male is castrated while still a puppy, he is more likely to have uneven skeletal growth and joint problems later on. There is also a greater risk of several types of cancer.

The problems of weight gain and health complications are less severe with females, but various types of cancer occur more frequently in spayed bitches. We do spay our bitches once their reproductive careers are over and the health risks are reduced.

With good household management, the need to spay and neuter young dogs can usually be avoided.

Dog Fights

Fighting of any sort can generally be prevented if the owners make it clear to the canine family that fighting in any form will not be tolerated.

If dogs are made aware through early obedience training that there is a structure of desirable and forbidden behaviors, they will more readily accept the prohibition of fighting as part of the natural order. However, if you have more than two dogs together, the potential for serious fights increases, and a sound basis of obedience training may not be enough to ensure the peace.

If two dogs in your household pack begin to show serious aggressive behavior toward one another, graduated steps should be taken to nip this in the bud. First try using metal prong collars and check cords at least ten feet long. With two people present, one on each leash, set up a situation which is likely to provoke mutually aggressive behavior, and then, when the dogs begin growling with their tails up, jerk them hard and shout "No". This may sound like harsh treatment, but remember that dogs are capable of inflicting very serious damage upon one another if a fight develops. It is a kindness to prevent this behavior, and the injuries that can result, by imposing your authority by voice and by inflicting pain through the prong collars. Of course if one dog is being aggressive and the other is on the defensive, then punishment should be focused on the aggressor.

Remote collars (e-collars), set at a rather high intensity, are the next step, if the prong collars do not halt the aggression. The remote collars can be very effective both as a fight deterrent and for actually breaking up a fight that has begun in earnest. The remote collar has the advantage of being anonymous; neither fighter knows just what caused the painful shock. But you have to be prepared for a conflict that you know is brewing. You can't put the collars on after the fight starts, and you can't keep them on dogs all the time.

When an unexpected and all-out fight begins, the best break-up tool is a CO_2 fire extinguisher. Scott Leindecker, an Ontario Provincial Police Officer and a tracker writes:

"One of my duties, probably the most dangerous job a police officer does, was to enter people's homes with a search warrant. My specific task was to

be the first one through the door with a CO_2 fire extinguisher to take care of any dogs that might be in our way. I always volunteered for this job as my other team members would simply have shot any dog that gave us a problem.

The CO_2 extinguisher does three things to the dogs. The noise and burst of white gas scares the hell out of them and gets their attention right away. The gas, as it is being discharged, is freezing cold (a white cloud of snow) and cold on their faces. The gas, being CO_2, takes their breath away; that really gets their attention when they can't breath. The best thing about it is it does not hurt the dog at all."

Obviously it requires advanced planning to have this emergency equipment readily accessible. I have used a battery powered cattle prod successfully to break up a fight, but I think that Scott's solution is a better one.

Your own behavior toward each dog should reflect and enforce what appears to be the natural hierarchy of authority among them. You make things worse if you try to equalize relationships by favoring weaker dogs over stronger ones. Dogs do not appreciate equality as humans do, and stable inequality does not disturb them a bit.

Sometimes a stable relationship between two dogs, especially males, is unachievable. In this case the best and kindest thing to do is to find another home for one of them. Dogs are more loyal and devoted to us than are most other humans; but unlike humans they can shift their allegiance to a new master and family with surprising ease.

Humans usually suffer more and longer from such separations than do dogs.

Possessiveness

As discussed in Chapter 9 on training, your dog's possessiveness can be a problem when animals are found in the real world of tracking. You do not want your hunter to lose an ear as he rushes forth to kiss his trophy. Early training will greatly diminish the risks of a law suit.

When your puppy plays in the house he must learn that all his toys are to be shared with other members of the household. As he chews on a rawhide roll or a rubber bone, speak to him affectionately, put one restraining hand on his collar, and pick up the toy briefly. Give him a treat and then return his chewy to him with praise.

This exercise can be continued on the skin at the end of the training line and finally on the real dear that he finds.

Excessive possessiveness most commonly develops in males. The best way to deal with this is to head it off before it becomes an established behavior pattern.

Yards and Fences

People who have not had hunting dogs before sometimes assume that their new tracking prospect will be content to sniff around and do his business in his own back yard. If a young dog has "hunt", it is not possible to open the back door and let the dog out on his own. A fenced back yard, a fenced exercise pen or at least a secure kennel are essential. Otherwise, a bored dog will be off, looking for a rabbit or some other critter to chase. Even if you live out in the country on a hundred acres or more, there are plenty of ways that an unsupervised, young dog can get into trouble.

The electrified, "invisible fence", laid underground around your dwelling area may be a solution. If a bitch is not in season, she is pretty safe. Males, however, are always at risk. The invisible fence may keep your male in, but it will not keep other wandering males out, and they may kill your tracking dog. For example, a male Dachshund will usually defend his turf, even though the intruder is four times his size. The kind of dog that will track a bear would rather die than roll over and submit.

Summary

- Tracking dogs are strong-willed and frequently competitive.

- Dogs will try to establish themselves as high as possible on the family social ladder.

- Dogs are most at ease when they know that they live in a world of clear rules and boundaries.

- Avoid getting two puppies at the same time.

- Teaching a hunting dog to be obedient, when in eye contact with his handler, seldom extends naturally to obedience in the woods and fields.

- The remote collar, properly used, is usually the best way to enforce obedience commands at a distance.

- Expose your dog to livestock in a secure situation, so he will neither be frightened nor later assume that livestock is game to be pursued.

- Avoid buying a second dog of the same sex, particularly if you already have a male.

- Do not let yourself be coerced by veterinarians into spaying and neutering. There are often good reasons for not spaying and neutering.

- A CO_2 fire extinguisher is the quickest and safest way to stop a dog fight that has already started.

- Training your puppy to share his toys will help prevent possessiveness on game later on.

- A secure enclosure should be available to contain your young tracking dog when he is outside and unsupervised.

Chapter 24

The Tracking Dog for Guides and Outfitters

Tracking Dogs Are Good Business

An outfitting or guiding business depends upon satisfied hunters. By helping to maximize this satisfaction, a good tracking dog should prove to be a very worthwhile investment.

Not finding a dead deer is a bad experience for the hunter, and in many cases it also means that the hunter will go on to kill another deer, thereby reducing the number of quality trophies for future hunting clients. This is not good business.

Justin Richins of The Hunting Company in Utah calculates that his tracking dog Remi found just under $200,000 worth of wounded animals in his first three years.

An outfitter employs guides to work with his clients, but many guides work independently. In either of these situations, maximizing the quality of the hunting experience is the most important consideration. Of course it helps to be able to find any game the hunter shoots. Short of finding the animal, the hunter feels much better about his hunt if the tracking dog's work convinces him that he did not make a lethal hit and that the animal will survive for the future.

In Texas, and in "big buck" states of the Midwest like Illinois, outfitters leasing hunting rights on farmlands were quick to realize the advantages of a good tracking dog to help serve their clients. As of 2016 the use of tracking dogs by outfitters continues to expand. They are being used by outfitters in Quebec for moose and bear, and in the Rocky Mountain States for elk and mule deer.

Select a Dog Suitable for Your Hunting Situation

The first thing that an outfitter or guide thinks about when selecting a tracking dog is nose. He is running a professional operation, and the dog will be, among other things, a symbol of his professionalism. Often a guide, or a professional tracker who works for outfitters, will select a Bloodhound because of the breed's appearance and deserved reputation as the ultimate cold trailer.

The American Bloodhound, or one of the German "Schweiss" hounds may well be the best choice, but there are many factors, in addition to nose, that should be considered. Every breed has its advantages and disadvantages and these have been reviewed in Chapters 4 through 7. A Bloodhound class nose is not normally needed when a guide will be tracking for his client within

12 hours of when the animal has been shot. The risks of spoilage or coyote damage often preclude waiting longer.

There are disadvantages of tracking with "big nosed" dogs like Bloodhounds, who do not need to be right on the line to follow it. The Bloodhound can detect and follow the scent from 20 feet away. This makes it more difficult for the guide/handler to see and evaluate what little visible "blood sign" the wounded animal did leave behind.

On the other hand cases do arise in which animals must be tracked two or three days after they have been shot. A distant outfitter may call and ask him to find a bowel-shot that no one wanted to push out of the hunting lease to a competing outfitter. Often the hunter's main concern is the trophy antlers and he cares little about the condition of the venison. In cases like this the "biggest" nose is best.

The appropriate size of the guide's tracking dog has to be carefully considered. If tracking will be done in a state where it is mandatory to keep the dog on a tracking leash at all times, then there is no special advantage in having a large, strong dog. However, if the dog can be worked off leash or released when a wounded deer is jumped from the wound bed, then larger size is an advantage. A big dog can catch up to the deer and either pull it down, or what is more likely, bay it. This will dramatically reduce the time and distance required to approach the wounded deer.

Decisions about whether or not to release a dog go beyond the question of what is legal. Today, in parts of the South, a dog running loose after a wounded deer is likely to be shot by another hunter, who believes that his own hunting, or his property rights, are being threatened. Shooting a loose tracking dog may not be legal, but it happens just as it does in the North.

When it comes to water work, the nod must go to the larger bodied, longer legged dogs like Labs. In coastal marshes and in big swamps these retrievers will be able to work longer and farther than a Dachshund for example. This does not mean that small dogs will not rise to the occasion when an occasional swamp is encountered, but they are not designed for this sort of work on a daily basis.

Transportation factors must also be considered when decisions are made about the appropriate size of dog for a given situation. If some sort of modified pick-up truck is used to drive hunters out to their stands, then the same type of vehicle will serve very well to bring in the tracking dog later if he is needed. Size makes no difference in such situations.

However, if access to the hunting sites is restricted to ATVs, which can negotiate rough, narrow trails, then the smaller tracking dogs have their special merits.

I have found that our Dachshunds love to travel for miles perched ahead of me over the gas tank of an ATV. No matter how rough the ride, they seem totally at ease and are ready to start tracking once at their destination. Most of the time I keep one hand on the dog's collar. It's a good idea to have a small, rough-textured mat beneath the dog to assure a good surface for his nails to hang on to.

I know from my own experiments that a small, self-assured tracking dog will ride a horse, sitting on the front of the saddle ahead of the human rider without fuss. I would put a harness on the dog and provide rings on the sides of this harness to attach the dog securely to a pack saddle.

Getting a large dog to trot along with a pack train headed into elk country would require the right temperament and quite a bit of training as well. Probably a Lab would be better suited than a hound. Labs would better resist the temptation to take off after game on the ride into the hunting area than would the typical hound.

In Canada and Alaska guides and hunters are often flown by bush plane into their hunting area. Since weight is usually a consideration, the smaller tracking dog has its merits here.

Appropriate Breeds for Different Game Species

As has been discussed in previous chapters, bear, moose and elk all leave more scent to trail than whitetail deer. The guide selecting a tracking dog breed may not require a Bloodhound class nose, but he must consider the climate terrain and cover in which the dog will be worked.

Tracking dogs, mainly Wirehaired Dachshunds are being extensively used on wounded moose and bear in the dense, black spruce cover of Quebec. What is needed is a small, handy dog that can ride with the guide everywhere he goes as he picks up hunters.

Most bear hunted over bait are shot in the evening; this presents a choice for the outfitter. Tracking a wounded bear after dark can be hazardous, but the alternative of tracking the next day also presents problems. He may have to drive a long way back to where the bear was shot. There will still be plenty of scent the next morning, but other bears are likely to have visited the bait so the dog may be confused by many scent lines in the same immediate area. Often there is little or no bear blood on the ground because it has been absorbed by the dense, heavy coat. I know from personal experience that it is easy to get started on the wrong bear trail.

An Alaskan guide, Alisha Rosenbruch-Decker, said that she preferred to track wounded grizzly bears in the dark, almost right away after the shot. Her tracking dog, a Jack Russell Terrier called Braveheart, is well named; Alisha finds it more practical to find her client's bear with Braveheart before the track is overlain by the scent lines of other healthy bears.

My own preference would be to track even the less aggressive black bears the next morning. This requires an intelligent dog with good powers of scent discrimination.

In general the selection of a breed of tracking dog suitable for guides is based on the same considerations discussed in Chapters 4-7 that deal with tracking dog breeds. The dog has to be adapted to the climate and the terrain in which he will work. Poisonous snakes and alligators must be considered. Ordinarily a guide working with a hunter will be able to track a wounded deer within a few hours, so it may not be necessary to have a very cold-nosed dog capable of working 48 hour scent lines under poor conditions.

No matter what the circumstances, outfitters and guides are going to need a tracking dog that tolerates the hunter/clients around game that has been found. No outfitter needs a lawsuit from a mangled hunter, who did not realize that a tracking dog can be very possessive about "his" deer.

Bavarian Mountain Hound "Bear" recovered these bow-shot black bears in Quebec on the same morning in the span of less than two hours. Pictured are Jerry Russell and his son Luke Russell of Russell Outdoor Guides.

Care and Management of the Dog

The physical requirements for a guide's tracking dog are important, but the psychological environment in which the dog will live and work is even more fundamental.

Outfitters frequently call us to inquire about the availability of a "trained" tracking dog. As our conversation develops it becomes clear that they are thinking of a dog as another type of tool useful in their operation. They believe that a "trained" dog can be stored in a kennel out by the equipment shed. They realize that the dog must be fed, watered and cleaned up after regularly, but beyond that they assume he just stays and waits until the need arises for his services.

This scenario of a dog kept as a piece of equipment might be an extreme case, but in some quail or duck hunting operations this is often the reality.

Tracking dogs are different. They work best when they are closely in tune with their handler. They need to spend a lot of time with him. As explained earlier, tracking wounded deer is definitely not a command/obey activity like most duck retrieving.

Tara Plantation, near Vicksburg on the Mississippi is a fine example of how tracking dogs can be used effectively in a big deer hunting operation. Tara Wildlife maintains 27,000 acres of prime wildlife habitat along the "River". The deer herd is carefully managed to produce mature bucks and to keep the deer population in balance with the habitat. Elegant accommodations are provided for the hunters who come in for three day hunts. There is some firearm hunting limited to one part of the Tara acreage, but the great majority of the deer are taken by bowhunters. Statistics cannot capture all of the elements of quality deer hunting, but it is revealing to learn that in 2003 83% of the bucks taken were 3½ years old or older, and 41% of the bucks taken met the minimum standards of the Pope and Young record book. Deer hunting is taken very seriously by the Tara management and by the dedicated bowhunters who come there.

One of the explanations for the renown of Tara is the team of gifted and dedicated guides that have been recruited. They know the deer and the terrain of the 27,000 acres intimately. They maintain the food plots and internal road network; they hang the tree stands and cut the shooting lanes. And they handle the tracking dogs.

Significantly, the tracking Labs of Tara are not the property of Tara Wildlife Inc. They belong to the guides, and they live at home with the guides as part of their families. They are not restricted to a kennel. They ride around in the cabs of their owners' pick-ups when off duty. They are with their handlers when it is time for tasks like hanging tree stands and cutting shooting lanes. On hunting days the tracking dogs come in with the guides at 4 AM and then hang around outside the lodge until their services are needed. With the hunters they are polite, but somewhat aloof. They live for working with their owner and handler at the job they do so well together.

The way the dogs are trained and handled at Tara works in this special situation, but these methods would not be applicable everywhere. The Labs are worked off lead, with a bell or a GPS, which permits the guide to stay within a hundred yards of the dog until the deer is found dead or is bayed. At Tara we are dealing with many 1000s of contiguous acres of wooded land, largely isolated from other hunting properties by the broad Mississippi and by wide stretches of agricultural land beyond the Tara limits. It is highly unlikely that deer and dogs would run beyond the Tara boundaries. Outfitters who lease smaller blocks of land do not have this advantage.

Keep in mind that the Tara guides use Labs, a highly intelligent breed. These dogs are well aware that they work with their owner/handler as a team. The same system would not necessarily work with many hounds, which have a strong, innate prey drive, but generally do not handle as well off lead.

The system also works because young dogs work with the older ones, and many of the wounded deer that they track do not go far and are relatively easy to find. This is an ideal training situation. They learn by doing the real thing rather than by starting out on artificially placed blood lines.

Care and Management of the Hunter

Hunters at Tara are discouraged from trying to track their own deer if they run out of sight after they have been shot. The explanation for this, as stated in the 2003-4 Annual Report, is as follows. "Our guides realize that most of our clientele are proficient woodsmen, perfectly adept at recovering a mortally wounded animal. Nevertheless, most of our hunters are not totally familiar with property orientation, property boundaries, hunter placement and potentially hazardous features common to the batture (hunting area) habitat. Potential problems include over-exertion by the hunter, contamination of the blood trail, pushing the animal too fast to allow successful recovery, ruining someone else's hunt by stumbling on another hunter, getting lost, falling in a stump hole... At times it is warm enough for alligators to be active and since wounded deer often head for water, an encounter between a gator and an unsuspecting hunter would be interesting. We also have three species of poisonous snakes... Since any of the possibilities listed may take the hunter away from his/her specific location, timely recovery may not be possible. We can always find you where we leave you."

Not all of the considerations mentioned in the Tara report could be applied to a hunting area leased by an outfitter in the North. The outfitter's plan of operations might have to take into consideration the fact that he did not control all of the hunting rights in the immediate area. Property lines would present a greater problem than at Tara. And of course in most Northern States where tracking is allowed, it is done with the proviso that the dog must stay on the long leash at all times.

Outfitters and guides have to think about efficiency and cost effectiveness much more than hunters and trackers, who are working independently of a commercial organization. During normal hunting hours the guides must be concerned with placing their hunters on stand and picking them up at the end of the hunting period. Usually this involves a morning hunt, starting before daylight, and an afternoon hunt from mid-afternoon to the pickup at dark. Tracking must take place when the hunters are out of the woods and the guides are free. After dark is the best time to track when it appears that the deer could go a long way. Scenting conditions are better, and there is more time if the tracking runs into complications.

It is customary for independent hunters in the North to make every effort to track their own wounded deer before they consider calling in a tracking dog. The Tara report explains some of the reasons why this may not be practical in a guided hunt operation. In addition, for reasons of efficiency the Tara Labs are taken out on every search, even if there is a good blood trail leading to the deer 100 yards from the hit site. It cannot always be determined in advance whether a strong blood trail will bring the guide and hunter quickly to the deer, or whether the external bleeding will slack off making eye-tracking farther difficult or impossible. If the dog is needed, time will be lost going back for him. It is more efficient to have the dog with you from the start of the search. The easy lines are also an ideal way to develop a young dog. In much of the country dogs are trained in this way.

As a tracker who has never worked for an outfitter, I personally feel a bit uncomfortable about the procedure of using a tracking dog before any attempt has been made to track by eye. Often I am called upon to drive long distances to find a deer. I would not want to drive 60 miles, one way, to find a deer that was lying just out of sight of the hunter's stand. I come from a part of the country where skilled eye-tracking is considered an integral part of hunting, especially bowhunting. The circumstances can be very different in a guided hunt. Personally, I have to remind myself that all hunting situations and hunting customs are not the same everywhere in our country. To understand the big picture some flexibility is required.

A guided hunt is first of all focused on hunter satisfaction. And this means that the hunter should be involved in game recovery if he is physically capable. It is humiliating for a hunter to be told to stay in the truck or to stay in the lodge, treated as if he had "messed up", and must now let the pros clean up his mess. Everyone who has hunted seriously knows that occasionally even the experts do not kill cleanly. There are too many unpredictable factors involved such as game movement at the instant of the shot. Especially in bowhunting a vital artery can be missed by a quarter of an inch, and this will change the whole situation.

When the tracking dog is being worked at a moderate pace on a cold line, I think that it is useful for a number of reasons to give the hunter a roll of biodegradable tape so that he can mark any blood that he sees as he follows behind the dog and handler. This may be useful if the dog gets off the line, and psychologically it makes the client hunter feel that he is doing his part in the search operation. Even if the hunter misses a lot of sign, it is worth the trouble to do this.

If the tracking is done at night the hunter should be provided with a good, rechargeable light so that he can see well and also be seen at a distance if he gets separated from the rest of the tracking party. If there is any shooting to be done, the precise location of every person in the tracking party must be known.

When the dog is having a hard time working out a check, it should be explained to the hunter that he should stand in one spot and not contaminate the area as the dog searches. Some hunters don't like to be told not to smoke, but if they are told that they should smoke only downwind of the dog, they soon realize that smoking at all is more trouble than it's worth, even in this stressful situation.

Most hunters, who are not dog men, have no idea of what a good dog can do on a scent line that has little or no blood. They should be made to realize that it is their great good fortune to have the tracking assistance of an intelligent, trained dog with a remarkable nose. What could have been a very negative hunting experience can be transformed into an adventure that enriches hunting stories for many years to come, even if the deer is not recovered. Laid to rest are the nagging doubts that a beautiful buck was lost to die and be wasted.

When a hunter wounds a deer, he feels badly enough. There is no point in giving him a lecture. If he is shown the evidence of what and why things went wrong on his shot, he can put the correction together for himself; this will be much more effective than a sermon.

Putting down a mortally wounded deer is a delicate subject that has already been discussed. On guided hunts, clients are usually hunting for trophy deer. It should be kept in mind that bow-shot bucks, otherwise eligible for the Pope and Young Record Book, become unacceptable if finished off with a firearm. This is the case even if use of a firearm by the handler is legally permitted in that state. New York is a case in point. At Tara guides use a short spear to finish off wounded deer that are still alive.

It is also the guide's responsibility to keep his client out of a situation in which he might be hurt. Dogs are not the only ones to be charged and hooked by an angry buck. The third deer I ever tracked charged my dog, and then things went peacefully for more than 200 finds. In 2004, a buck, which was no trophy in the conventional sense, made very convincing contact with both Sabina and the author. A guide must not let this happen to his client!

The use of tracking dogs by outfitters and guides involves a special set of operating procedures and a special need to protect and satisfy the client. Ethical sensitivity is essential for a quality hunting experience, but the factors of financial profit and efficiency cannot be disregarded. Fortunately all of these concerns are compatible when the use of tracking dogs is considered.

Summary

- The practicality of a tracking dog to find deer, bear, moose and elk has been established.

- Selection of the appropriate type of dog depends on the game, climate, terrain and legal restrictions.

- Effective tracking dogs are best owned and cared for by the guide/handler who will use them.

- Small dogs are more transportable than large ones.

- Hunters should accompany the guide and tracking dog, but they must be provided with a good light and advice on how to participate in the tracking process.

- Tracking dogs can contribute significantly to client satisfaction.

- Tracking dogs can avoid wasteful depletion of the game animals that clients expect to hunt.

Chapter 25

Tracking Tests

Reasons for Testing

Finding real wounded deer should be the first priority of the tracking dog and handler, but taking tracking tests can be an absorbing substitute in the off-season. Preparation for the tests is excellent training for both dog and handler, and the tests themselves are certainly a useful tool for evaluating a dog. Tracking tests are more objective and useful than tall tales and bragging about the number of deer found. Almost any dog can compile quite a record if he tracks easy deer that the hunter could have found for himself. And it is easy to drop any mention of unproductive searches "since the deer couldn't have been hit very hard."

The natural test on actual wounded game is one alternative to the artificial one. This test is described at the end of the chapter, and it can be a very useful means of demonstrating a dog's competence when properly evaluated by experienced judges or witnesses. However, it is not a simple matter to bring together, on the spur of the moment, all necessary judges or witnesses. Artificial tests are certainly easier to organize than these natural tests.

A high score in an artificial blood tracking test will validate a record of many natural finds. It will strongly suggest that most of the natural successes were genuine and were achieved on difficult cases in which a dog was actually needed. It will also demonstrate how the work of one dog compares with that of another on a given day on similar blood lines.

It is best to gather all evidence available before purchasing a dog, evaluating the parents of your puppy or selecting a stud dog. Ask to see any test results that are available, but be aware that a blood tracking test does not tell the whole story. Blood tracking tests, like everything else, have their limitations. What a test can do is tell experienced buyers something about the working style of the dog, and a great deal about the skill of the handler.

Field Tests Versus Field Trials

Field tests, including blood tracking tests, are not something that is familiar to most Americans. These tests are set up quite differently from the competitive field trials that Americans have used as a way to maintain and improve the working qualities of their breeds. Americans are probably the most competitive people in the world, and they are enthusiastic about the idea of judging one dog against another. In the hunting breeds it has been the trial winners and the Field Champions who have been most used for breeding. This competitive approach to breed improvement does not always work well. It depends upon the breed, the type of event and the system of judging. In competitive events extreme and spectacular work is favored, and steady, reliable performance receives less recognition.

The alternative, European system, which has been adopted by the FCI (Fédération Cynologique Internationale, International Cynological Federation), judges dog performance against an objective standard instead of judging each dog's performance against that of the other competitors. Thus, in European tests, there can be two or more dogs awarded a Prize I. European tests are judged in the format of reaching a maximum number of points for each component in an event. This European system of testing has been spreading to North America in recent years. The development of these tests has been encouraged by what some bird dog people believe is a tendency of competitive trials to encourage stylish extremes of performance. When a judge has to select the very best from a number of excellent dogs, he may find himself basing his decision upon some fine point, or some stylistic quality, which has little practical application in hunting.

Whatever the original intent of the blood tracking test, the element of competition is still present. The handler strives to get the highest score of the day for his own dog. But he is not too disappointed if he shares the Prize I honors with others.

Blood Tracking Tests in America

Most of the blood tracking tests offered in the United States as of 2016 have clearly came out of the European, FCI tradition. The first blood tracking test given in America was the Deer Search Inc. certification test (1981). The rules for this Deer Search blood tracking certification test were translated and adapted from the tests of two German organizations: DTK, Deutscher Teckelklub (German Dachshund Club) and the JGV Jagdgebrauchshundverein (Useful Hunting Dog Union).

In 1998, the first JGV test was offered in New York State with two JGV judges imported from Germany. The third judge, who also organized the test, was Hans Klein, an American who had done a full judge's apprenticeship in Germany. The JGV testing system is used by the Verein Deutsch Drahthaar, Verein Deutsch Kurzhaar and other FCI clubs.

In 2001, the first North American Teckel Club blood tracking test was held, and a DTK/NATC blood tracking title was awarded.

The United Blood Trackers was founded in 2005, and they have subsequently developed a series of blood tracking "evaluations" and tests ranging from elementary evaluations for beginning handlers and puppies (UBT I and II) to the 20-hour UBT Test (UBT 20), which closely resembles the NATC 20-hour Test.

In the UBT Evaluations, which are Pass/Fail, the judge can intervene and instruct the handler as the dog progresses. In the UBT-20 Test, the handler is on his own, and the tracking dog is given a score for "Steadiness and Concentration, Tracking Accuracy and Williness to Track".

Currently, four different organizations offer 20-hour blood tracking tests in the United States: Deer Search Inc., JGV, DTK/NATC and UBT. Some of the European-based Versatile Hunting Dog Associations, such as the Verein Deutsch Drahthaar, also offer simpler tests with shorter, fresher lines. Useful generalizations can be made about all four of the major, 20-hour tests, which all have the same general format. For details and a representative test, the UBT-20 test, see the rules in Appendix B. The rules for UBT III Evaluation are given in Appendix C.

General Description

In all four tests, blood is dripped from a squeeze bottle or dabbed with a sponge on a stick over a distance of 1000 meters, or 800 to 1000 yards in the case of the DSI test. One fourth of a liter of blood, about half a pint, is applied over this distance. Deer blood has always been used in the United States, but the rules of the German tests allow for alternative types of blood if this is specified in the announcements of the tests. The blood trail incorporates three 90-degree turns within the distance, and three "wound beds" of about one meter in diameter, scraped out of the ground cover. At the end of the line, a carcass of a small deer or a frozen deer skin is placed to represent the "find." The line is aged for 20 hours, or for 40 hours in the more advanced JGV, DTK and UBT tests. Doubling the age of the blood line from 20 to 40 hours increases the difficulty to some degree, but it certainly does not make it twice as difficult. The test line is not like a normal human or animal scent line that consists of mobile scent particles. In contrast, the artificial blood line consists of small spots of blood that remain in place and continue to give off scent for several days.

In the DTK/NATC, Deer Search and standard UBT tests the trail is indicated with markers on the backs of trees. In this system markers cannot be seen by the handler upon his approach, yet the three judges know where the actual line runs. The handler is not allowed to look over his shoulder for the markers that would confirm that he is on the line. The JGV test substitutes detailed written notes for the marker system.

Challenges

From the scenting standpoint, the blood tracking tests are really not very difficult unless the scenting conditions are extremely poor. Unless there has been very heavy rain, there are physical traces of blood on the line that continue to give off scent, even if they have been diluted by rain and are invisible to the eye. Under most circumstances it is easier to track a 20-hour blood line than the 20-hour-old natural track of a human or a healthy deer. The scent particles from humans and animals volatilize or blow away in the breeze; in contrast, blood droplets stay put.

Most dogs fail tests, just as they fail to find wounded deer, because they are distracted by the fresher scent of healthy game. To an inexperienced dog, an aged blood line is about as exciting as a mathematics text book is to a teenager. The invisible, feather-scented cloud left by a flock of wild turkeys, or the tarsal gland reek of a passing buck wrench that young canine's attention away from the old, cold blood line.

Even mature dogs with excellent abilities and serious training can have serious problems if they have never been asked to work in an area that is saturated with fresh deer scent. The dog must either have extensive natural tracking experience or have had repeated tracking drills in deer bedding and feeding areas.

This point was impressed upon me as I handled my experienced Dachshund in a JGV test. As a challenge, I found this particular test as exciting as finding a difficult wounded deer.

An Experience With the JGV Blood Tracking Test

My first JGV Test, back in 1998, made me realize the importance of experience and maturity when it comes to dealing with the distractions of hot lines. This story also gives a sense of what a multi-breed test is like from a Dachshund owner's point of view.

I was working with a ten-year-old Wirehaired Dachshund named Gerte vom Dornenfeld, who had been born in Germany and had a DTK (Deutscher Teckelklub) registration number as well as one from the AKC. The DTK/FCI registration made her eligible for the test. Gerte weighed eighteen pounds, but in contrast to the rest of the dogs present, towering Drahthaar and Kurzhaar Pointers, she seemed like a mini. Certainly, in this company we looked a bit ridiculous, but only one of the big dog handlers ventured to point this out to me. Everyone else was extremely friendly.

There was no reason for me to be nervous as dogs and handlers assembled for the first day of the test. Gerte and I had considerable practical experience, and we were ready to do the best we could, even though those big-nosed, hard-eyed dogs seemed likely to do better. Calm as I was, it was strange that the doughnut I munched just would not go down. I finally had to spit it out behind a bush. At the drawing, Gerte and I drew the last line for the first day of the two-day test. This meant that we would probably run in the afternoon under hot, dry scenting conditions. This would be a challenge, but the biggest problem in such tests is to keep the dogs focused on the faint blood scent when their natural instinct is to follow the much fresher scent of healthy deer that have just passed. And the grounds where the test took place were alive with deer.

The undoing of many dogs in the test was this distraction of fresh deer scent. On the test grounds there were deer everywhere. It was late June and does seemed to be parading their fawns back and forth for the enjoyment of spectators and the frustration of the dogs. Tendrils of deer scent wafted in the light breeze; in the thickets it hung musky and enticing. Before Gerte's turn came, two big dogs had already failed, and one had registered a good score; all had been affected by the billowing abundance of deer scent.

Perhaps it was Gerte's small size that had helped her learn early in her tracking career that she would be overwhelmed in strength and speed by any deer that was normal and unhurt. Even when tracking a wounded deer, Gerte knew that she would need me close behind at the end of the 30 foot leash to dispatch the live wounded deer when the confrontation came. Gerte sensed, as I knew, that only through our cooperation could we accomplish our objective. In the test that was coming up, our practical experience together would greatly reduce the distraction problem of healthy deer moving through the tracking area.

But the line itself was not easy. A mini-shower the day before, shortly after the blood was placed, had diluted it to the point that all visible trace was gone. The scent remained, but there were no occasional telltale droplets to reassure me that we were on track.

Gerte seemed a little absent-minded and unfocused as we started down hill across a field. She did not look sharp; perhaps my efforts to keep her calm had actually put her to sleep. Bent blades of grass reflected light to show where the tracklayer had probably walked the day before; Gerte ambled down along this line angling into a graveled, interior road. She drew herself together as she slowly worked the scent along the road; the problem seemed to be that trucks, passing along the road, had smeared the scent out in their direction of travel and had blurred the point where the invisible line must have broken off the road and down into a ravine. As Gerte continued I could read declining confidence in her body language; there was something there but not enough. She cut to her right down into the ravine...nothing. As when tracking a deer, I looked for foot scrapes of the blood tracklayer on the steep bank... nothing. Gerte was searching, not working the line; we were in trouble.

I requested permission from the judges to pick Gerte up and reposition her. This is in conformity with the rules, and it is just the sort of thing that a cautious handler does when working a difficult live track of a wounded deer. We returned to the road and went back more than 50 yards to the point where we had first come out on the road from the field. This time we hugged the right side of the graveled road with Gerte pouring over the grass blades along the edge that might better hold the scent at the point where the line turned. Decisively she veered right down into the ravine. It looked good this time, but where were the tracks of the tracklayer that should have been there in the soft, steep bank? Across a muddy brook with a few big stones. Still no tracks. (Later it came to me that a seasoned German judge is much more clever than a deer!) I could do nothing but trust my dog... and she was right! There, right under Gerte's nose was the first, stylized "wound bed", one of the three round, scuffed areas that the track layer scrapes out along the line to simulate where a wounded deer has bedded temporarily.

Gerte was definitely on; the scent line had been at first an obscure, interrupted thread, barely distinguishable to her. As she gained concentration and focus, the scent line grew into a cord, a rope, a hawser, which guided her along with ease and certainty. The scent, which objectively could have been no stronger than before, became now the most obvious thing in Gerte's world. Once locked into this particular scent, nothing seemed difficult to her.

Gerte after her Prize I performance in a JGV blood tracking test (1998)

One of the three obligatory right angle turns required a few deft circles of reconnoiter, but we had no doubts. I knew that we were close to the 1000-meter end point when Gerte raised her head to test a slightest hint of breeze. Air scenting the goal, the road killed deer hidden out ahead, she coasted in to hugs, congratulations and the branch of oak leaves in her collar. Praise for small dogs!

In the European spirit, the tracking event was a test, and not a competition. I thought that her shaky start would detract more from her score, but the judges saw differently, gave her a Prize I rating, and found her to be the best blood tracker in the two days of the test. Gerte also seemed to be aware of what she had done and she shared my pleasure. One of the best aspects of this sport of tracking is that the dog knows that he has succeeded and soon realizes that this is the best means to become the center of attention.

In retrospect, the experience does not seem as amazing as it did at the time. Gerte was the oldest and the most experienced dog in the test. She had been specifically bred for this task, and using her nose to track game was her most fundamental hunting instinct. Like many other Dachshunds that I know, she was fully capable of holding her own when compared to the continental pointing breeds whose first instinct is to quarter back and forth, and to work air scent.

A hound, such as a Dachshund, will usually work more closely to the line than a pointing dog, and this can be an advantage in a test. However, the most important point is that the Drahthaars and Kurzhaars, who had failed in 1998, learned to do much better. In the JGV test of the following year, most of these dogs came back and passed with high scores because their trainers had worked with them in conditions similar to what they would encounter in the test.

Judges

The objective of this chapter is to make a case for the value of blood tracking tests. It is also designed to prepare the inexperienced handler and dog to take and pass such a test successfully. The handler will be more effective if he has a clear idea of the rules and knows what the judges will be looking for. The text of a representative set of rules, the UBT-20, can be found in the Appendix B. This general discussion of rules and judging is written to help the handlers, not to educate judges.

The judge of blood tracking tests should be experienced in natural blood tracking work so that he has a good understanding of the problems of scenting conditions and distractions. In addition, this judge should have handled a dog and passed blood tracking tests.

It is required of judges of all three testing systems to train and then pass a dog in the blood tracking test of that system. Training, and then handling a dog in the presence of three judges, gives a whole new perspective on the test! For one thing, a judge cannot understand the pressures upon the handler unless he has been there himself. A judge, who has had his own dog fail in a test, will be a better judge because he will be a more compassionate judge. An occasional failure is a good vaccination against arrogance. The standards cannot be weakened, but the judge who has gone through it will be better able to tactfully explain to the candidate what went wrong, and what mistakes were made.

The various organizations which offer blood tracking tests have qualification procedures for judges, which are too extensive to detail here. One component of all of these qualification procedures is an apprenticeship. The apprentice judge accompanies the three official judges and observes what they do. He usually reports his findings and scores to the senior judge, who points out where he is in error. In this way, the apprentice learns how the rules are interpreted and how rigorously they are applied.

The official judging is performed by three judges; the uneven number makes it unlikely that there will be deadlocks in scoring matters. The judges each maintain a score sheet with a place for notes and comments on what is observed.

Tracking Accuracy

In practical terms, the factor that plays the greatest single influence in determining scores is the dog's performance in staying close to or right on the blood line. This is described as "tracking accuracy", but it is, to a large degree, a manifestation of the dog's "steadiness and concentration". The dog should not be out of scenting contact with the line for more than an estimated 75 meters. If the dog happens to be paralleling the line, the direction of the wind must be considered. Downwind of the blood line, a dog tracking parallel to it at a distance of 10 yards, may be following scent that has blown with the wind. If he parallels upwind, he is just being lucky.

A dog that goes out farther than 75 meters from the blood line in a straight line is called back by the judges. But the handler should understand that his dog may also be called back by the judges for traveling 75 meters out of scent contact with the blood line even if he happens to stay within the 75 meter, straight-line, limit. Certain call-backs require judges' discretion. The judges have to decide whether the dog is actively searching for the line within the 75-meter limit and not just gambling or following a hot line that has nothing to do with the blood line. If the situation is not clear, the dog should be given the benefit of the doubt.

The rule of all the tests is "three call-backs and you're out." For the highest rating, a Prize I, no call-backs are normally allowed. For a Prize II, the maximum number of call-backs allowable is one; for a Prize III two call-backs are permitted. However, scoring a dog is based on much more than counting the call-backs.

Since a skilled handler can read his dog and probably has some general idea of where the line should be, he can pick up the dog and return to a point where he was confident that the dog was working the line. A skilled handler will do this when he senses that he is getting into trouble and wants to avoid a call-back. The handler must request permission from the judges to reestablish his dog on the line, and he should give a reason for doing so. It is perfectly correct to reestablish your dog on a sure point if you have doubts. A good handler, working a difficult natural line, sometimes does the same thing. Also, an inexperienced handler may make the mistake of taking his dog off the line when the dog is correct. Obviously, pick-ups with permission are to be desired over call-backs, but to many novices it is not so obvious that the pick-ups with permission have a price too.

A dog that gets through the test line only because of repeated pick-ups and corrections by a skilled handler is probably going to lose points on "steadiness and concentration" and "tracking accuracy" despite the lack of call-backs.

I had an opportunity to experience an extreme example of "Tracking without Accuracy" when I was handling a dog in a Deer Search Certification Test. My dog, Stone Apple Cleo, was a Southern Black Mouth Cur, extremely intelligent and an excellent wind scenter. However, she had an indifferent nose for ground scent, and to make things worse the scenting conditions were poor just before a thunderstorm. Somehow, thanks to good luck, Cleo's intelligence, and my experience, we managed to follow the line, in a rather loose way, for the thousand yards to the deer skin at the end, and we did it without a single call-back. The three judges were all experienced in both judging and in tracking. Two of the three wanted to give a Prize III with 50 points, the lowest possible passing score. The third, judge, who was, in my opinion, the best judge of all, wanted to fail the dog outright. After some discussion, the judges agreed to compromise on the Prize III with 50 points. These judges were perceptive and correct in their analysis. Cleo, the wind scenter, was a good natural deer finder, but her modest ground tracking abilities were not quite up to the challenging scenting conditions of that particular afternoon. Conditions have an impact upon performance, but they cannot be an excuse for non-performance. Cleo barely scraped by with a Prize III.

When the best dogs and performances are involved, call-backs seldom occur. In these cases the threat of damning call-backs plays little role in the thinking of either judges or handlers. When the dogs being tested are inexperienced, or of marginal ability, the call-back question can be quite important in the interplay between the handler and the judges. Judges must follow the handler and dog wherever the team goes. If they save steps and stay back around the blood line, it is a sure tip-off to the handler that his dog is off, and that corrections must be made. Instead of reading his dog, the handler reads the judges.

Once there has been a call-back, it is up to the judges to bring the handler back to his point of loss and show him where he should recommence working his dog. This opportunity for a fresh start on the line is the only good thing about a call-back.

Beyond Call-Backs

Good judges are most interested in the positive accomplishments and working style of the dog on the blood line. The tracking tests that we are discussing have three 90-degree turns, and the dog's work at these corners gives the judges a good opportunity to evaluate tracking accuracy. Usually the dog will overshoot the turn to some extent. Judges can evaluate the promptness with which the dog recognizes that he has gone too far, checks back and reestablishes the line. The dog will generally swing a circle to the left or to the right of his point of loss until he cuts the line going off at right angles. A fast moving Drahthaar will usually check in a bigger circle than a slower Dachshund, and all dogs cannot be judged in terms of the same, exact model. Different breeds of dogs, and even different dogs within the same breed, will perform differently. What the judge looks for is an efficient style with a minimum of wasted motion for both dog and handler.

Judges give some importance to the finding of wound beds along the blood trial. The handler is supposed to report to the judges these scraped circles in the ground litter. To do so is to demonstrate that the dog is staying close to the line and allowing the handler to evaluate evidence left by the "animal" he is tracking. Many good handlers are so intent on reading their dog that they miss the wound beds. To report the wound beds is positive evidence of accurate trailing for both handler and judges. The evidence is useful for the judges, and it can give emotional support to the handler! The wound bed is sure proof that he is on the line even though no blood can be seen.

In addition to the three wound beds, the JGV adds *Verweisepunkte*, or guide points. These *Verweisepunkte* consist of bits of deer lung placed on the track. If the dog finds all or most of these, it is an indication to the judges that he is doing close, careful work. In a natural tracking situation, a dog like this will show the handler blood, or other sign, which is useful in evaluating the status of the deer.

How fast should the dog work the line? I have seen an "American" German Wirehaired Pointer, working under ideal conditions, complete a test line in ten minutes. The handler was running to keep up with the dog. Under similar conditions good Dachshunds would take twice as long. The more difficult the conditions, the longer the tracking test will take, and a good dog should be able to adjust his speed to the circumstances. At least one and a half hours per dog should be allowed. In the German tests two hours are actually permitted, if circumstances warrant this. However, there is no reason to allow more than a half hour if the dog is not making substantial progress.

From what I have seen of European judging, rather rapid progress is expected at the higher levels of performance. In the emerging American tradition, judges are conditioned to deal with the very difficult lines produced in bowhunting. It is especially important to read the blood sign of bowshot deer in order to evaluate the nature of the wound. Speed on the line of a bowshot deer can be more a handicap than an advantage. As a result American judges have more appreciation for a slow, deliberate style.

In multi-breed blood tracking tests like those of Deer Search, the JGV and UBT, judges have to keep in mind that different breeds have strikingly different working styles. This involves more than simple speed. Any judge is going to have personal preferences, but he must not be influenced by them while judging. The Dachshund, which is a scent hound and a low stationed one, will usually stay closer to the blood line than the versatile hunting dogs. These pointing dogs have a tendency to quarter back and forth on the line, and they usually cover more ground to get from point "A" to point "B". Retrievers have a style somewhere between the Dachshund and versatile breed poles; they generally show less intensity on the track, but they still get the job done in their own way.

A good blood tracking judge has to be flexible. Breed templates cannot be crudely applied because there is considerable variation and individuality within breeds. The judge in a multi-breed test must ask the question, "Is this dog demonstrating that he is able to find a wounded deer effectively and efficiently?" Judging a multi-breed test fairly is a lot harder than writing about it!

Experienced judges realize that a tracking dog should use his intelligence and not be a tracking robot. For example, if the dog raises his head and goes 100 yards upwind to investigate the carcass of a dead deer, the dog should not be faulted with a call-back. By the same token, if a dog windscents the designated deer skin or carcass at the end of the line and leaves the blood line to go to it, the dog should not be faulted. Blood lines should be laid out with attention to the prevailing winds, but sometimes over a period of 20 or 40 hours, the wind will shift in unforeseen ways. The handler should recognize the head-up, windscenting attitude of his dog and inform the judges about what he believes is happening.

The behavior of the dog when the "game" is found should not be used as a basis for judging a dog's desire to do his job. Enthusiasm varies greatly between breeds and between individual dogs. Generally, Dachshunds are as aggressive as terriers and want to jump on the deer skin and shake it. They may be very possessive, growling at any strangers who approach their find. Labs and curs are more likely to sniff at a deer skin or deer carcass with mild curiosity. Some dogs track for the love of tracking and to please their handler. For others the motivation to conclude the search with a find is very important. In training it can be useful to let an enthusiastic dog worry the skin or carcass. European judges do not like to see a dog chew on the dead deer in a test because they believe it shows a willingness to damage and eat the game that has been found. They may be right, but when you have your dog on a tracking leash you are not going to let this happen. When training a dog, giving him a good "chew" on the deer skin can be a good motivator for the next session.

After the test for each dog has been concluded, the judges retire and decide upon an appropriate scoring for each category of the performance. At first, they may not always come up with identical scores, but they debate the numbers until they are in agreement on all points. The final scores are the same for each judge; these represent a reasoned consensus rather than an arithmetical average. After the judges are in agreement the handler is called over, and the results are stated and explained to him by the head judge.

Judges must know the rules of the test that they are judging very well, but they also must have extensive experience observing and handling a number of different dogs in natural searches as well as in tests. The capability to interpret the dog and to understand the problems that the dog is encountering comes only with experience.

To deal with the distractions of fresh wild game, training and a solid attention span are needed. Some dogs just never learn about hot lines, and these dogs will not be very useful in serious natural blood tracking either. The hyperactive, flighty tracking dog with an attention deficit disorder is going to reveal himself to the judges quickly. He will be given a low score for "steadiness and concentration".

To be truly useful and revealing, a good tracking test must be conducted in an area where there will be natural game trails fresher than the blood line. The purpose of the test is not to make the dogs look good. The test is supposed to indicate whether the dog has sufficient focus and concentration to stay on the line despite distractions of other wildlife.

Steadiness and intelligence are even more important than nose for a tracking dog. In the blood tracking tests, the dog's work is evaluated on a 0 to 4 basis in each of three performance categories. The score in each category is multiplied by a number so that the total perfect score adds up to a hundred. For example, the first category is "steadiness and concentration" (sometimes phrased as "working method on the blood line"). The multiplier is "10". A score of "4", multiplied by the "10", comes out as 40 points, which is the maximum for that category.

The multiplier for the second category, "tracking accuracy" is only "8". This lower multiplier indicates that "tracking accuracy" is not considered quite as important as "steadiness and concentration". Willingness to track, the third category, has a multiplier of 7.

On the next page we have included a representative copy of the Judge's Score Sheet used in the various 20 hour tests of different organizations. This will clarify the explanation of judging procedures.

The Handling Factor in Tests

The handler, who takes his dog into a blood tracking test, should have sufficient confidence in the dog's capabilities so that he interferes with the dog as little as possible. Novice handlers frequently pull the dog off the line when the dog is doing the right thing. As in natural tracking, it is difficult for a human to accept the fact that the dog knows more than he does. Preparing for and taking a blood tracking test develops the handler as much as it develops the dog. It provides training against over-handling a dog and interfering with correct tracking work.

Location	Notes
Date of Test	
Name of Dog	
Age of Dog	
Breed	
Sex	
Sire	
Dam	
Owner	
Handler	
Weather Conditions	

	MULTIPLIER	SCORE	POINTS	Comments
Time of Test:				
Finish				
Start				
Total Time				
Steadiness and Concentration	10			
Tracking Accuracy	8			
Willingness to Track	7			
Total Points				

Dog is qualified to track wounded deer   Yes ___   No ___

Scoring Key:

0 Unsatisfactory

1 Needs Improvement

2 Satisfactory   Signature of Judge

3 Good

4 Outstanding

Judge's Score Sheet used in the various 20-hour tests of different organizations

In tracking tests, as in natural tracking, it is very important to be able to "read" the body language of your tracking dog. You cannot learn your dogs "language" from a book because there is such a great difference in how individual dogs communicate what they are up to. The rhythm of tail wagging, the carriage of the head, and the curve of the back are all potential indicators. You must learn the individual body language of your dog by working him on well-marked artificial training lines, laid out where there are plenty of distractions of healthy deer, turkeys, rabbits or whatever. When your dog leaves the marked training line out of distraction, boredom or because he has lost the scent, you will learn to recognize how his body movements change. You will have a sense of when to correct him or ask, "Is that right?".

There is a fine balance between letting the dog do his own work and at the same time staying alert to the real risks of having the dog take off on a hot, or worse, a slightly warm line. Knowing when to intervene is the most difficult part of handling. It requires a close and intuitive reading of the dog. This is unlikely to happen if the handler has most of his own attention focused on a search for blood traces on the ground. Old, once-frozen blood is difficult to see when laid according to specifications. When it dries, it is brown, not red, and it blends with dead leaves and pine needles. In a test the handler will do better if he focuses on reading the dog instead of spending his time peering at the ground.

Blood tracking tests evaluate certain aspects of a dog's work, but the skill of the handler also plays a role, and the best dog can be neutralized by an unskilled handler. A test score that tells the most about a dog is one in which the dog is well handled but not guided.

By general acclaim one of the very best tracking dogs of the pioneering years of Deer Search was Adelheide von Spurlaut. Don Hickman co-owned her with his wife Penny, but it was Don who handled her almost always in the woods, at blood tracking tests and in competitions. Addie had earned a number of perfect 100, Prize Is and some of these in very tough conditions.

At one of the annual test/competitions of Deer Search everyone expected that Addie would earn another 100 point score; another dog might equal this score and also earn a Prize I, but it seemed unthinkable that Addie would be beaten. On this particular Saturday, Don had to work so his wife handled the dog. Addie was misread; Addie played games with hot lines and Addie was dropped from the competition for departing three times from the line in excess of 75 yards. There is a European saying that an excellent handler can do more with an average dog than a poor handler can do with an excellent dog. This saying has some limits in practical applications, but there is a lot to it.

Prize IIIs, the minimum passing scores, do not reveal much about a dog to those who were not present. An experienced test handler can pick up his dog repeatedly, take no chances and squeak through with a barely passing score if the judges feel charitable. Such a dog would have little chance if handled by a novice. When interpreting a test, give some thought to the handler. This will help you decide whether it was a ho-hum dog or a good dog having a bad day. Evaluate a dog by his best adult work, not by his lowest scores.

Preparing a Dog for the Blood Tracking Test

The methods of preparing a dog to take a blood tracking test are essentially the same as those used to prepare a dog to find wounded deer during hunting season. A mature dog, experienced in natural blood tracking, will likely do well in a test situation without any special preparations. However, for some younger dogs without much experience in natural tracking, there are nuances of difference in the specialized preparation for a test.

In Germany, a frequently prescribed preparation procedure is to mark the blood trail with great precision, and to correct the dog if he wanders off the track by even a meter or two. This is one way of producing a dog that stays precisely on the test line and gets the highest score for accuracy (*Spursicherheit*). It can be particularly useful for a dog that starts out being a bit wild and tends to move too fast. The problem is that this kind of training is not as likely to develop initiative as well as the alternative method of letting a dog make mistakes and correct them on his own.

On a test line, there will be a drop or dab of dried blood every meter or so. The dog will learn that the blood should be there, and that the task is to go from one drop or dab to the next. In a natural tracking situation, the blood is seldom laid out in a regular, linear pattern. There may be no blood, or scent of any kind, for 50 yards or more. A practical natural tracking dog must be able to "reach" intelligently for at least this distance to find wounded game, but if he does this in a test situation his scores will be lower. The handler must define his priorities as he trains his dog.

The Swedes recognize the special challenges created by gaps in a natural line. In their blood tracking test for Dachshunds, no blood is laid over a ten meter stretch of the test line. To continue, the Dachshund must reach across the gap and regain the blood scent on the other side.

As discussed in the chapter on Basic Training, the distractions of fresh, healthy game scent create more problems for a blood tracking dog than any other factor. Most rules for blood tracking tests require that the site be a game rich area; this requires that the later stages of training take place when and where there are plenty of deer on the move. Preparing your dog to withstand the temptation of following hot deer lines can be, quite literally, the difference between dazzling success and total failure. You cannot do all your training for a blood tracking test in a suburban park or on a golf course.

Tests are seldom given at a time of year when they would compete with or actually interfere with hunting. It is risky to schedule a test when snow is a possibility. The best times are undoubtedly in April, before the spring turkey seasons, but all too often tests are scheduled for months when the weather can be very warm. Your dog must be prepared for the all too frequent "unusually" hot weather.

Tracking for 1000 meters takes much more out of a dog than going for a stroll of the same distance. The dog has to concentrate, and he expands considerable nervous energy on his work. This can produce symptoms of overheating, which you would not expect. Water should be carried by the handler, but this is not enough; the dog should be prepared for hot weather. Exercise runs on a daily basis when the temperature is in the eighties will protect your dog against breakdowns during the test. It is not a good idea to work the dog on many blood lines during the heat of the day; this could quench enthusiasm.

Some dogs tend to be "hyper" and do not focus well, particularly in the first few hundred meters of the test. Exercising them hard, "to take the edge off", the day before or a few hours before the test, can be beneficial. You must know your dog and not overdo the exercise to the point of fatigue.

The dog should come into the test hungry. If he has been fed at the end of the training lines as part of the reward, then hunger will motivate him on the test line. After your test is over and congratulations have been expressed, you and your dog can have your own party with restoratives.

The Day of the Test

Artificial tracking tests can be nerve-wracking because the judges know where the line goes, while the handler does not have the same advantage. The judges see the handler's mistakes before he is aware of them. Try to keep in mind that the judges once went through the same experience themselves.

Psychologically, the best means of facing a test is to become so totally immersed in what you are doing that you are oblivious to everything but your dog and the terrain. This is easier to accomplish if the test goes well than if the dog is floundering.

The handler should realize that the first few hundred meters are usually the hardest. When the dog warms up mentally and locks in on the scent of the blood line, performance often improves dramatically.

Most of the techniques for finding real wounded deer apply in test situations. At the start, go through the ceremony of putting on the tracking leash and collar exactly as you would for a real search. In the German tests it is customary to first put the dog on sit/stay a few yards from the starting point. The handler is supposed to inspect the hit site, then return to his dog, buckle on the collar and urge him to begin tracking.

The judges will give you the direction of the line, and in some cases, the first 50 meters are marked. This simulates the live situation, in which the hunter gives you the direction from the point where the deer was shot, and frequently a blood line is visible. It is important to steady the dog and insist that he gets started on the right line. Talk to your dog and establish rapport.

In a test, the rules require the dog to work at, or nearly at, the full length of the tracking leash so that it is clear that the handler is not leading the dog. Normally you will not see very much blood, and your time is better spent observing your dog.

When you do see blood, or when your dog shows you blood, it is good strategy to mark this point so that you can return to it later if trouble develops.

Often you can be confident that you are on the line simply by watching the dog's body language. In these cases mark the "sure points" if there is any possibility that you will need to come back to them later.

These same precautions should be taken in natural searches unless you are very confident. If the handler can place the markers at eye level, he will see them much farther than if he places them on the ground. The best technique is to staple bright lengths of surveyors' tape to spring-loaded wooden clothespins. The clothespins can then be quickly attached to branches and twigs at eye level. These should be taken down after the test is over.

One handler arrived for a blood tracking test wearing a roll of toilet paper on a cord around her waist. A toilet paper roll is not the most elegant fashion accessory, but she did not lack for marking material. The problem with toilet paper is that these markers on the ground are more difficult to see than a marker at eye level. Especially if there is a time limit on your test, you do not want to waste time searching around for a sure spot to restart your dog.

As mentioned above, it is highly advisable to carry water for the dog if the weather is at all warm. A tracking dog burns a great deal of nervous energy on the line and heats up in the process, even if the purely physical exertion is not great. A refreshing drink also freshens the nasal membranes, and the pause can be an opportunity to settle down a dog agitated by distractions.

In handling a dog in a test, we cannot always do the same things that we do when trailing a real wounded deer. Sometimes on a difficult natural track the handler will get to a point where he has to allow his dog to search or reach 200 meters without any recognition of scent. If he gets the line going again, he is justified in what he does. But if he allows his tracking dog to reach more than 75 meters in an artificial blood tracking test, he is courting disaster. Callbacks will result, and the dog will do poorly or fail the test.

The handler must be able to read his dog, just as in natural searches. The difference between work on the old blood line of the test and smoking hot, very recent scent lines of healthy deer is easy to interpret in most cases. What gives experienced handlers more trouble are the lukewarm lines of healthy deer that passed several hours earlier. Here the interest of the dog is moderate and easier to confuse with proper work on the blood line. An experienced dog is not going to mislead his handler in situations like this. Younger dogs, just beginning their career, may go with a lukewarm line when they run out of the blood line and want to look as if they are doing something useful. Another JGV test taught me more about the pitfalls of warm lines.

Two years after the author's Gerte had the highest score in the JGV/USA test of 1998, the winds of fortune shifted. Branie, a distant Dachshund relative of Gerte, presented me with a very different lesson as she failed her test by getting three call-backs. Branie's turn also came shortly after midday. The weather was hot and there was a dry wind blowing. It was not likely that deer would be moving in such conditions. The first part of the line was in the sparse grass of worn-out fields. Branie began slowly, doing difficult work perfectly. But she was a young dog and psychologically too immature to maintain her concentration. Without showing the excitement that comes on a hot line, she turned 90 degrees where the correct turn might well have been. I noticed bent blades of grass where the tracklayer might well have walked. Not absolutely certain, I picked her up, went back to what had to be the line, and tried again. Branie repeated her moves slowly and deliberately. "All right then" I thought, "go ahead"; then came the judge's call-back. Instead of the blood scent line, it was a lukewarm deer line, probably several hours old. The grasses had been bent over reflecting light differently to the eye because a deer had passed, not a tracklayer. The handler in a blood tracking test should use his hunter's skills, just as he would on a real deer search, but nothing is foolproof.

Branie was in good physical condition to take the heat and well trained to work ordinary lines. This line was not beyond her abilities to follow, but the heat and confusion drained her will to concentrate. Water and a short rest did not help. Branie fumbled again, and then a third time. She was out. Branie knew that she was failing but she could not help herself. Psychological toughness and the ability to concentrate are the most important attributes of the tracking dog; they are more important than an exceptional nose. It is best if these characteristics are shown early. Sometimes they develop later. Sometimes they never develop at all. In training, the handler should try to develop psychological toughness so his dog does not wilt and go with the flow of what is easy. He does not always succeed.

The Dog and Handler as a Team

The handler should go into the test with a goal and strategy appropriate for the dog and circumstances. For a Prize I, the handler must take some risks and just trust his dog to stay out of trouble. The better the dog, the easier it is to move forward boldly and without questioning. If the handler second-guesses his dog and repeatedly picks him up and takes him back to a sure point, he will probably forfeit his chances for a Prize I score of 100 or 92. For a perfect score you have to let your dog do all of the work without interference.

If things do not go well, and the dog gets far enough off the line for a first call-back, then the handler may decide that discretion is the better part of valor. He may take a more cautious approach. When he has doubts about whether the dog is staying within the 75 meter limit, he will take the dog back to a sure point. This has its costs in the "accuracy" and "steadiness and concentration" categories, but at this point, a second call-back is even worse.

With two call-backs, a handler determined to survive becomes very conservative indeed. A third call-back will be fatal to hopes of passing the dog. No risks are taken and trust in the dog is minimal. On a simple course of straight lines and right angles, an excellent handler can get a marginal dog through the test with a just passing score of 50. When interpreting test results always consider the factor of handler influence.

Blood tracking is always a team performance. In a Prize I performance the dog is in control of the situation, and the handler's role is to focus the dog psychologically as needed. He should keep the tracking leash free of obstructions and otherwise not interfere with the dog. With weaker or less experienced dogs, the handler's role must be more assertive. Judges score the dog, but they cannot help but take into consideration the finesse of the handling as well. With the best dogs and the best handlers, the judges can recognize the intuitive bond of understanding within the working partnership. For the handler under pressure, it is a rare satisfaction to move into this mode where man and dog are in harmony and totally focused on the task of finding wounded game.

Tracking Tests for Young Dogs

In blood tracking there seems to be an exception to every generalization. Puppies of six or seven months often go through a period when their focus and attention span is much better than it will be when they reach adolescence at around a year old. Puppies, with little exposure to live game, will sometimes do exceedingly well in ignoring fresh game scent during a test. Sometimes young puppies are so naive that they have no awareness of live deer and how much fun it is to follow a steaming hot line. These puppies methodically follow the old bloodline and ignore everything else. Such puppies are capable of doing better on a test at six months than when they are a year old and primed with broader experiences. For this reason the DTK passed a rule that candidates for their blood tracking test must be at least a year old. The JGV requires that a dog be two years old or more.

I once owned a brilliant Dachshund puppy that would work any line, sober as a judge, when she was six months old. She was not turned on by hot lines because she didn't know what a hot line meant. When she became ten months old, she began to discover the world and kick up her heels. She blew sky high emotionally and did not settle back to earth in her tracking until she was three years old. Be thankful and proud if your puppy performs well on a blood line laid to official specifications. Your puppy undoubtedly has innate talent; it is a puppy to nurture and to cherish. But remember that your puppy has not arrived yet. The real tests for steadiness and intelligence are still to come. Any serious dog breeder has seen flashes in the pan, brilliant young dogs, who never realized their early promise. Usually, however, the talent shown by a young dog will return with maturity.

Some potentially excellent dogs seem to fall apart as they pass through those "early teenager years", which the psychologists call adolescence. This has been discussed in Chapter 10. Like many young humans, they have a temporary phase of "attention deficit disorder". Wait until this passes before you take your dog's tests too seriously.

When a dog begins finding wounded deer, he may pass through a phase in which he shows a low level of interest in an artificial blood line and does poorly on blood tracking tests. Confronted with an artificial blood line, this intelligent dog quickly recognizes it as a fake. "The blood scent is there, but where are all the other scents of the deer that should be there too?" On a test line his attitude is "Don't expect me to be interested in this phony nonsense."

Usually training with tracking shoes will prepare a dog to do well on tracking shoe tests and even on blood line tests. On the other hand there are a few dogs that excel in natural tracking, but never do very well when tested on artificially laid lines. Tests are useful, but they do not tell us everything.

Tracking Tests With Fährtenschuh

A scent shoe variant of blood tracking tests laid with deer blood has become increasingly popular in Europe and in 2005 an official DTK/NATC test was held for the first time in the United States. Training tracks laid with tracking shoes (*Fährtenschuhe*) were described earlier in Chapter 12; this means of laying a track was easily adapted to the test.

The format of the official DTK Fährtenschuh Test is similar, in many ways, to standard blood tracking tests. The 1000 meter distances and the aging time of 20 hours are familiar. However, this test is designed to be more natural; changes in direction are rounded, 90 degree curves rather than sharp corners. The amount of blood used may not exceed 1/10 of a liter, whereas the standard blood tracking test uses ¼ of a liter. Some blood is squirted from a squeeze bottle at the beginning to simulate where the animal was shot, but afterward the small blood "spritzes" have to be 7 to 10 meters apart.

Considering the reduced amount of blood used, one would expect tracking shoe tests to be much more difficult for the dog. When I observed this test, however, it did not seem to present greater scenting problems for the dogs. The interdigital scent from the deer feet, the "toe jam", seems to be very potent stuff. Hot, dry conditions did not diminish it as much as I had expected.

Heavy rainfall on a tracking shoe line does create problems. The interdigital scent washes out more rapidly than blood scent. To succeed after a cloud burst the dog must reach and search for the scent of the widely spaced blood drops that were placed up to 10 meters apart.

This tracking shoe test does not exactly replicate the scent line put down by a real wounded deer, but the dogs' enthusiasm and body language are comparable to what a handler sees when tracking a bow-shot deer with no visible blood.

Test Without Judges

A blood tracking test "without judges" has become popular in Europe as an entertaining and competitive alternative to the standard blood tracking tests. It certainly conserves the time of judges. A blood line is laid out in the traditional way (¼ liter of deer blood, 1000 meters), but five small markers (*Verweisepuncte*) are laid along the track. These markers can be 5 cm slices cut from a branch or a deer bone. They are numbered and must have deer blood on them.

No judge follows the dog/handler team on the track. Scoring is based first on the number of markers found and turned in by the handler at the end of the track. To pass this test the tracking team must find at least two markers. If two or more tracking teams find the same number of marking points, then the team with the shortest working time is placed higher. There is a maximum time limit of 1 ½ hours.

Obviously, the closer working dog has an advantage. In actual tests the majority of the teams do not find all five markers.

Natural Tests

Natural tests cannot be planned. They are organized on the spot under actual hunting conditions when a deer has been wounded. Certain minimum standards and controls are established. For example, in the German DTK natural test for Dachshunds the blood scent line must be at least 400 meters (437 yards) long, be in difficult terrain and must be at least four hours old. If there is snow, or patches of snow, the test is not allowed.

There are two ways that the natural blood tracking test can be officially approved and the title awarded.

1. Two qualified judges can approve the dog's work.
2. A signed application by the handler, complete with a thorough report of the dog's work, must be submitted to the Commission for the Recognition of Natural Work. Two witnesses, experienced in hunting matters, must confirm the report.

Blood Tracking Titles on European Pedigrees

If you are thinking about buying a dog that comes out of a European blood tracking background, it is useful to interpret pedigrees and determine what blood tracking titles were earned by the ancestors of your dog. Dachshunds, Jagdterriers, and all of the versatile hunting dog breeds such as Deutscher Drahthaars and Kurzhaars are likely to have blood tracking titles in their pedigrees.

After each dog's name on the pedigree, there will be list of the titles (*Leistungszeichen*) this ancestor has earned. Many of these titles refer to tests that have no direct connection to blood tracking, but you should keep your eyes open for titles that contain the letters Schwh for (Schweiss for blood and hund for dog in German). In some countries, France for an example, the "Schwh." notation is still used because the original test system did come from Germany. Here is a partial list of European blood tracking titles and a very short description of each:

SchwhK: 20-Hour Artificial Blood Tracking Test
             Schweißprüfung auf künstlicher Wundfährte
SchwhK/40:   40-Hour Artificial Blood Tracking Test

SchwhN:	Natural Blood Tracking Test
SchwhKF:	Tracking Test with the "Fährtenschuh"
SchwPoR:	Tracking Test without Judge
Sw:	JGV 20 Hour Artificial Blood Tracking Test
Vp:	Versatility Test which includes a 600 meter blood track

The shortcoming of these titles under the dog's name on the pedigree is that they do not tell us how well the dog performed. All you know is that the dog passed. If you have the opportunity to see the individual dog's pedigree, this document can tell you much more. On the back of a dog's official pedigree, the DTK pedigree of Max Wunderbar for example, the chief judge places a stamp for that particular test and writes in the number of points that Max earned. Therefore, you can determine whether Max did brilliantly with a Prize I, 100 points or just scraped by with a Prize III, 50 points. The total sum for certain tests can be more than 100 points.

The same information is available in annual European stud books or breed books. Even before the computer age, the Europeans, and especially the Germans, compiled seemingly endless annual statistics for the tests, shows and offspring of each dog.

Summary

- In most cases the handler should spend much more time "reading" his dog than searching for blood himself.

- Inform the judges when you pick up your dog and return him to a known point on the line.

- Carry disposable markers that will allow you to return to where you know you were on the line.

- You will be called back by the judges if your dog is out of scent contact with the line for more than 75 meters. Try not to let this happen. Three call-backs and you're out!

- By their animation dogs reveal that they have been distracted by a "hot line." Calm your dog down before you continue.

- Talk to your dog! Keep him focused and praise him for correct work.

- With each call-back the handler should become more conservative in his handling. Don't take risks when you have two call-backs.

- Carry water for your dog in hot weather.

Chapter 26

Questions and Answers

Ever since we began shipping the first edition of this book our days have been enlivened by phone calls and e-mails from all over North America. People have problems, or think that they might have problems, which were not dealt with specifically in the book. This chapter contains some of the most frequently asked questions that should be of general interest.

1. What is the best breed of tracking dog?

There is no "best" breed for everyone! The breed you choose for yourself should reflect your personal lifestyle and hunting interests, where you live in North America, and the circumstances in which you will be tracking.

If you and your spouse desire a small family dog, there is much to be said for a European type Dachshund out of tracking breeding. They are convenient for travel by land or air, and they are a good choice if most of your natural tracks will be 24 hours or less. If size of the dog is not important, a Lab or one of the German specialized tracking breeds should suit you. Understandably there are some trackers who feel ridiculous with a small dog, and they should choose a breed with which they feel comfortable.

If you will be using your dog primarily for bird hunting, one of the versatile pointing breeds (Drahthaar, etc.) is what you need. But pay attention to the working style of the parents. Many "versatile" pointing dogs are so high headed and birdy that they refuse to get their heads down to work old, cold tracks.

If you hunt squirrels or coons, a Catahoula or Black Mouth Cur should meet your needs. If you select one of the coonhound breeds, be sure that it comes from calm, "pleasure" hound, not "competition" hound breeding. Likewise, if you want a Beagle make sure that it comes from steady, responsive parents; avoid the high strung, hare hound types.

In the snake-ridden terrain of the Deep South and Texas a larger, longer legged dog makes sense. In these areas it is usually legal to track off lead. A large dog will usually make a better bay dog than a small one. In the off lead states coyotes are usually abundant, and a small dog is at greater risk than a large one.

If you are a professional tracker, working for outfitters who specialize in trophy deer, then one of the cold-nosed breeds such as Bavarian Mountain Hound, Hanover Hound or Bloodhound is a good choice. For tracking very old scent lines in "All I want is the rack!" situations, the extra nose power is important. And the Bloodhound appearance impresses clients.

If "hawgs" will be the main animal tracked, then consider the Jagdterrier. This breed combines aggressiveness with the agility necessary to stay alive.

2. Question: When I'm training my pup on a blood line that I have laid out for him, he tends to work too fast. And he doesn't work very close to where I put the blood line. How do you deal with this?

Most young dogs with strong tracking desire tend to track too fast. They are over-eager, and they get sloppy. This may not show up immediately, but it comes as the pup discovers what he loves to do.

Various steps can be taken to help slow the puppy down so that he will be ready to dig old, cold scent out of the grass roots when the time comes for this. Even if you plan to track with your dog off lead, it is very helpful to start with some work on a tracking leash. For this purpose I like to use 20 feet of plastic clothesline, which is light and almost friction free. The pup will not be distracted by it, but the trainer will have some control when he needs it. When the pup starts to race or jump around, the leash can be flipped down between his legs so that his head is pulled down into the track. You can also use the tone of your voice to reinforce the message of the leash restraint. Drawl "easy, easy" or "slowly, slowly". The tone of your voice is important.

Another way of slowing down a young dog is to loop a half hitch over his loins just ahead of the hind quarters. When the pup pulls in his enthusiasm, the tracking leash will pinch him.

A more basic reason for work that is too fast and sloppy is the freshness of the line. We don't have enough respect for a young dog's nose. A four-month-old pup may lack the mental maturity to process and interpret what he smells, but his ability to recognize the scent is already operational. He can smell a drop of blood that is many hours old.

Many trainers reason, "He's just a pup. I'll give him a training line a half hour old, or perhaps even an hour." When the pup is brought in to track a fresh line of blood and the air is still, he actually encounters a big "tunnel" of scent rather than a scent line on the ground. Because there is scent everywhere in this tunnel he doesn't pay any special attention to the blood line, even if it is clearly visible to his handler.

If there is a breeze, scent particles from the blood will have drifted downwind for 25 yards or more. There will be a wide swath of blood scent, and the puppy will run in "S" curves downwind of the actual blood drops.

The best way to get a pup to work slowly, and close to the line, is to give him one that is considerably older and colder. Your four-month-old pup should be able to work a line that is six, twelve or even twenty-four hours old. Remember that a line ages faster in the daytime than at night. The more challenging, older trail will hold the pup's attention better and force him to stay on the line and "dig for it" a little.

A blood trail laid out for training is very different from a game animal's track. Each blood drop stays in place and continues to give off scent particles for days. A day-old trail of blood drops, a yard apart, is a whole lot easier than a day old coon track. Unless the conditions are very good, the scent particles left by the coon will have largely blown away or burned off after half a day.

The whole process of slowing down a young dog will be easier if you do some obedience training while walking him on a short leash when tracking is not involved. Reverse your line of travel every time the dog lunges ahead. Use the verbal command "slowly" or "easy" so that he learns what the word means. In some cases you may have to use a prong collar with the short leash. but never use the prong collar when actually tracking on a training line.

Note the half hitch on the dog's loins.

3. Why is it so difficult to buy a fully trained tracking dog?

This would be a reasonable request for dogs asked to do certain kinds of work, but it doesn't apply very well to blood trackers. It's almost impossible to buy a tracking dog all set and ready for any tracking challenge that comes along. There are a number of reasons for this.

First of all, you can't train a dog up to the point where he is capable of handling old, cold lines with no visible blood unless he has acquired considerable live experience on real wounded deer. My own estimate is that a dog only develops to about 25% of his full potential by training on practice lines laid out with deer blood or with the European scent shoes, which have deer feet clamped to the soles. To go much beyond this level on artificial lines requires an enormous amount of time, which most trainers do not have.

Of course progress to that same primary, 25% level of performance can be reached by working the dog to find easy deer that could have been tracked by eye. It can also help considerably if the beginner dog is worked on live lines with an old veteran tracking dog; the young dog should be allowed to take the lead and work the line when he can.

There are many different ways to train a tracking dog, but none of them can completely replace the experience a young dog gains when he works to find a difficult deer on his own. This is what develops the confidence and initiative that we should expect in a completely trained dog. And it is difficult to give enough solo, live-tracking experiences to even one young dog. It becomes impossible to give this sort of experience to several dogs being trained for sale by a professional. There is a reason for this.

When I have a call from a hunter to find his wounded deer, the first priority is to find that deer, not to conduct a training session. That's why I go out with the "Varsity", an experienced dog that maximizes the chances of success. Sometimes we can work a "Junior Varsity" dog into the search if we have another handler, or if the tracking takes place fairly close to where we left the truck. Then I can go back and get the more experienced dog if needed. My point is that it's not so easy to give a young tracking dog the natural experience that would normally be provided for a duck retriever or a pointing dog.

Personally, I believe that I can honestly sell "started dogs" for sale, but I have never felt that I could offer a "fully trained dog". Started puppies or dogs have desire and line sense; they are aware that the scent of a wounded deer track leads to something good. They also have a general awareness that they are supposed to ignore the fresh scent of a healthy deer. They know that they are supposed to ignore the scent of a flock of turkeys. But all this training does not mean that these started dogs are going to be steady and reliable under pressure in all distraction situations. These things become solidly imprinted only through natural experience and maturity.

This leads us to a second point. The new owner or handler of a young tracking dog should have a relationship with that dog. The handler has to read the dog; usually it helps a lot if the dog also knows and can read the handler. Every dog has his own body language; if the handler has done some training with that dog, he will be able to recognize when his young tracker gets excited over some hot scent of unwanted game.

Some dogs are very easy to read in this respect; the head will come up, tail rhythm will accelerate and they may even yip in excitement. Others are very difficult to read. Certainly it's not a matter of "If you know one dog, you know 'em all".

On another level, the pack/partnership relationship, which underlies all dog social behavior, has to be established before dog and handler are going to work well together. If the dog does not know and respect the handler as his pack partner, then the dog is not likely to work as hard when the going gets tough.

There are dog jockeys who will tell a prospective buyer anything to get a sale. They will take advantage of the man who wants "a fully trained dog", something that he can use right away like a brand new shotgun. But money alone will not suffice to acquire a "fully trained tracking dog" unless time and personal attention are also invested. Beware of the dealer, who produces a "fully trained dog" by having that dog track a dragged deer hide a few times.

There is at least one more reason why "fully trained dogs" are hard to come by. If a handler works closely with a good dog through many tracking adventures, he finds a bond developing, even though he did not intend to have this happen. On a dark cold night both handler and dog understand that they are a team working together. They both sense that in working together, they will accomplish something that neither would be able to achieve alone. This bonding sinks in gradually over time. Then too, the handler becomes aware that his own reputation is tied up with the good dog he works with.

There's a saying in Germany that the opportunity to buy a really good tracking dog comes only when the owner/handler dies or becomes too old and sick to continue in the woods. Right now this certainly applies in North America too.

4. Which is better for tracking, a male or a female?

Many trackers in the Northeast, who have tracked primarily with bitches, firmly maintain that bitches are better. This is a myth that has been passed around by those who have not had extensive experience with both genders. My own view is that dogs and bitches develop differently, but in the end there are outstanding dogs as well as bitches. I never met a European tracking expert who would argue with this.

This said, I think that it is likely that a young bitch will mature psychologically somewhat faster than a male. Her adolescence will be less disruptive. She is more likely to be concerned about pleasing her master and focusing well in her early years.

Males are more likely to have an adolescence in which their powers of concentration regress. You may have to wait a little longer to see the young male's talents stabilize, but then he will be a very tough and efficient dog that doesn't know the meaning of "quit".

There are some exceptions to these gender generalizations. Clary, my best tracking dog ever, was useless for anything during her adolescence from 12 to 18 months. Sabina, my top tracking dog for eight years was one of the two toughest dogs that I've owned.

If your tracking dog is going to be worked off lead, all or part of the time, then a male is definitely better. No handler is going to want to cast loose a bitch in heat. That is one reason why you see fewer tracking females in the South where the leash is not mandatory. Another solution in the South would be to spay the bitch, but this is done infrequently.

5. I have an eight-year-old Beagle. Is she too old to train to track wounded deer?

A dog can certainly learn to track at the age of eight unless it is one of the very large breeds that is already slipping down into senility at this age. The problem is that natural experience plays such a large role in the development of any dog as an accomplished tracker. If you begin the formal training of a dog at eight, he will not get many years of potential natural experience before his brains and body begin to fail. In dogs this decline comes more abruptly than in humans.

6. Can you track with a bitch in heat?

I know that in many cases you can successfully work a leashed tracking bitch in heat. One time I found a deer with my Clary, and bred her the same day for a fine litter of pups. Of course the stability of bitches in heat will vary. There is no hard and fast rule on this.

If a bitch is subject to false pregnancies, this seems to be a much more distracting factor for tracking. Generally, it takes a month or so for a bitch to regain her sharpness after she has weaned a litter of pups.

7. I have a Black Mouth Cur, and I want to use him for tracking wounded deer. Will it hurt him if I squirrel hunt with him?

The Black Mouth Curs are very versatile dogs with the intelligence to focus on the task that they are being asked to perform. They won't automatically tune out squirrels when they are tracking a blood line, but they will learn to discriminate much more quickly than most hounds for example.

If you view your Black Mouth as primarily a squirrel dog, then I would start on squirrels and introduce the wounded deer tracking later under very controlled circumstances with the dog working on a leash. If blood tracking is first priority, then teach blood tracking first.

If you track wounded deer at night, there won't be any squirrels to offer a distraction. Nighttime offers a good opportunity to teach the dog that several tasks are important, but that they have to be kept separate.

At night you do run into coons, but they are not as numerous as squirrels in the daytime. When I worked my black mouth Cur Cleo on a tracking leash at night, she never seemed to be distracted by coon scent. However, if I took her out without the tracking leash and collar, she seemed to realize that we were after coons, and she became a straight cooner.

8. Last night my Wirehaired Dachshund got sprayed by a skunk. She smells so bad that my wife won't let her in the house. Does this mean that she won't be able to track a wounded deer?

Amazing as it may seem, a drenching with skunk spray does not have much effect on a dog's tracking capability. Clary, my best tracking dog, had one weakness; she would leave a line to attack a wandering skunk. She would kill a skunk, on or off lead, any time the opportunity presented itself. Once the skunk was dead she would go back about her own business, tracking or hunting. It seemed that she could use her nose just as well as before the spraying.

By the way, I never had much luck with tomato juice to reduce the impact of skunk scent. However, there is a product called Skunk-Off that breaks down skunk scent on the molecular level. It will do a good job of appeasing your spouse, and your tracking dog won't mind if you use it. The most effective home-made deskunking recipe includes 1 quart of 3% hydrogen peroxide, 1/4 cup of baking soda and 1 teaspoon of mild liquid soap. Wet the dog, and work the formula through his coat. Leave the mixture on for five minutes, and then rinse thoroughly.

9. Question: During bow season it gets pretty hot down here in North Carolina, and sometimes my Lab doesn't want to track. He just lies down and pants.

Labs have many qualities, but they are not the best dogs for taking heat. Their coats were designed to keep them warm in cold water. It can help a good deal if you take the dog out for walks, or to do retrieves when the temperature is over 80 degrees. Through exposure you can build up his heat tolerance significantly. However, a Lab will never approach the heat resistance of southern breeds like the Black Mouth and Catahoula Curs.

10. When I can pick up a road-killed deer, I bring it home in my truck and drag it around in the woods with my four wheeler. I leave the deer and the four wheeler at the end of the track, and my dog has no problem following it even four hours later. Isn't this a good and easy way to train a dog?

One drawback of this method is that it makes it too easy for the dog. A whole deer dragged along the ground leaves so much scent that the dog doesn't have to work at all. He can just stroll along with his head up. This will not prepare him to track a real wounded deer that has left very little blood. A more challenging scent line, laid with deer blood or a deer liver drag, will teach him to get his head down and concentrate.

Another problem with the "drag a deer method" is that it will encourage your dog to go with the scent path where another hunter has pulled a harvested deer out of the woods. You can recognize such a case because the drag marks and deer hair on the ground are aligned with the direction of travel. Still you don't need this kind of distraction.

11. I own six acres of woods in back of my house, and this is where I lay out training lines for my dog. At first this worked real well, but now

he sometimes goes the wrong way although he knows better. What's wrong?

A tracking dog has a very good nose and a remarkable memory for where things are located in horizontal space. Under most conditions your dog will be able to scent the blood droplets that you set down for last week's training exercise. Also the dog is very likely to remember the spot where you placed the deer skin and treats last week, or the week before that. Once the puppy is four months old, it is better to go to an entirely new area for each new training line

I'm convinced that many dogs have better spatial memories than we do. I see this in their unerring return to a point of loss when tracking. They remember very well where bones and other good things were two weeks ago.

12. What do you do when your leashed tracking dog takes you out into a deep beaver swamp. Is there an alternative to getting wet?

Dogs have a very good memory for a specific scent. If you have worked enough line with your dog so that he is thoroughly familiar with the scent of that particular wounded deer, then you can pick him up or lead him around to the other side of the swamp and work along the edge. The dog should be able to pick up the line again, even if there is no blood that you can see. I have done this many times.

Of course you have to be sure that there are no small hummocks or islands out in the swamp where the deer could bed down. They find security in such spots. Generally a deer will not bed down in standing water unless it suddenly runs out of gas while being pursued.

13. Everyone says "trust you dog", but I find that this is not easy to do. Sometimes when I get to the hunter's point of loss my dog will go off in three different directions. I will go out on one line, and then if I see no blood, I will bring him back to the point of loss. The second time he may go off in a different direction. How do I know when he is on the right line?

"Trust your dog" is the most important maxim for new handlers. Usually the dog is right, and the handler is wrong. As the handler/tracking dog relationship deepens it becomes easier to give the dog the benefit of the doubt when he follows what seems to be the wrong line. Hunters are notorious for insisting at the hit site, "I know the deer went the other way, not the way the dog is going." Actually they saw another deer running, and that was why they could not find the deer they shot.

Start at the hit site, in any case, because at the start the area will not be as tracked by the hunter, and there is likely to be visible blood. More serious problems for the tracking team are likely to arise at the hunter's point of loss.

At the point of loss the searching hunter has generally walked around with blood and deer scent on his boots greatly confusing the situation.

Consider the possibility of a back track beginning at the point of loss. If you find the fingers of blood splatters pointing in opposite directions, this is the probable reason for the young dog's confusion. I have found that whitetails backtrack quite frequently.

Once you have eliminated the cases of hunter exit tracks and deer back tracks, the next step is to go out, following the dog for 100 yards or so. If you see no blood sign, hang up a streamer of surveyors' tape with a knot tied in it. In the event that the dog leads you to this spot again, the knot will tell you that you are on an unconfirmed line previously traveled. If the dog takes you twice over this same knot-identified line, then you should go with the dog much farther, searching for evidence that the dog is on the right line.

Often this technique works better if you avoid the immediate point of loss and instead lead the dog in a fifty yard circle around this point. Of course the handler has to be able to read his dog, to recognize whether he has taken a fresher, more obvious hot line, is searching for the right line, or has found the right line and is actually following it.

Problems don't end after you have overcome the point of loss complications, but errors are less frequent. I have had good dogs make honest mistakes, especially when tracking a buck in rut. The dog may correct himself after a hundred yards or so and return to the point where he knew that he was right. When I begin to have doubts myself, I tug on the leash and ask the dog, "Is that right?" If the dog insists that he is right, then I trust him.

There are very rare situations in which a dog will deliberately lie. The story of Eda, who would pretend to track a fake scent line, is discussed in Chapter 3.

14. When you are tracking a gut-shot deer and you can't catch up, what do you do?

A gut shot deer will almost always die, but there is no certain way of knowing when this is going to happen. To begin with, you delay tracking as long as the weather and the coyote threat permits. This should be at least four and as many as eight hours of delay.

In my part of the county you risk losing everything but the antlers if you follow Grandpa's advice and wait until the following morning. The big coyote invasion in the Northeast came in the 1980s, and it changed everything.

Generally the farther back a deer is hit, the longer it will take to die, but a damaged kidney can bring about death within a half hour. Deer hit in the stomach may succumb within an hour or last more than a day. So much depends on whether major blood vessels in the stomach were ruptured. There is no way of being sure of the true situation on the basis of what the hunter can tell you. After a maximum of eight hours the tracker's best choice is to put his dog down on the line and go. Hopefully, the deer will be dead within a quarter mile, but I have found stomach shot deer that went unpushed for over two miles before they died. Never stop on a gut shot deer as long as you are still working a cold line and have not jumped him. You may find him dead at any time. He may pass through ideal bedding cover until he finds his own special spot where he chooses to bed down.

On the other hand, if you jump the gut shot deer, you have to look over your evidence and make a decision. If he lets you get close, within 25 yards, more than once, he will almost always go down for keeps within a half mile. However if he seems too strong, you may have to back off and let more time pass. For example, you do not want to push the deer onto a property where you cannot follow.

If possible, "park" the deer in a big thicket or some other spot, such as an island in a swamp, where he is likely to stay until you come back. Sometimes you can hang a big circle around the parking place and let your dog make sure that the deer did not exit.

I must admit that I have had mixed success with this "leave him and come back" strategy. Often it is a long drive back to where you left the deer, and the deer is not always there. This is a last resort, but it may be the best you can do.

It is in these situations, when a mortally wounded deer goes on and on, that the northern tracker may feel envy for his southern counterpart. If the dog can legally and safely be released, he will catch up to the deer and bay him within a quarter of a mile.

15. What do you think of working two dogs together on two leashes with two handlers?

With the right pair of tracking dogs I think that it can be very useful, from a training standpoint, to work two dogs together. If you have two, very competitive dogs together, they will pay too much attention to one another, and the final result will be negative. But if you have a steady, older dog, who will work calmly behind a less experienced lead dog and the handler, it's a great way to develop the young lead dog through natural experience.

If the young lead dog gets stalled on a difficult check, then it is possible to bring up the old veteran to solve the problem so that the younger dog can take over again.

Working a veteran dog behind an apprentice dog is one way of solving the dilemma that many serious handlers face. When you go out on a deer call, which dog do you take? You know that you must give natural experience to your younger dog so that he can take over when the senior dog retires. On the other hand, you realize that your first objective is to find the deer; it is not fair to the deer, or to the hunter, to treat the call as a training exercise for a young dog. And most of the time it is very inefficient and time consuming to have to go back to the truck and get a more experienced dog if the beginner fails on a tough line. Backing up the apprentice dog with an experienced dog, handled by a second person, is an excellent solution.

In Mississippi and in Texas, where tracking dogs are worked off lead, I have seen the same method used. The guides at Tara Plantation, and Roy Hindes in South Texas, all use this as the primary method of training their dogs. And when it comes to baying a big, mean buck, two dogs are definitely better than one.

16. What is the effect of rain on a training line?

When you have laid your training line with blood, up to an inch of rain does not create a problem for your dog if the blood has dried before the rain came. The rain may wash away the visible blood, but the blood scent goes down into the grass or dead leaves, and the dog can readily pick it up and follow. The circumstances are different if the blood did not dry before the rain. In this case the blood line is more difficult to follow but not impossible for a dog with some experience.

The interdigital scent left by tracking shoes doesn't hold up in the rain as well as blood. The dog will probably have more difficulty. If it seems that rain is coming, it works well to combine the tracking shoe scent with several ounces of blood.

These generalizations about training lines should be kept in mind when you are tracking the real thing during, or after a rain. Glandular scent of a real wounded deer does not hold up of the dog's nose as well as blood. When tracking wounded bear the same principle applies. The foot print scent of bear can be tracked for at least 24 hours, but rain will change this.

17. How long should you keep tracking after you stop seeing some blood?

After the first 100 yards or so some mortally wounded deer are not going to leave any visible blood traces at all. Many deer die of internal bleeding, particularly if they have been wounded in the stomach or the intestines. If you can determine where the deer has been hit from evidence at the hit site or along the early parts of the line, you can figure out if you should be seeing blood with any frequency. If I know that I have a gut shot or liver hit, I really don't worry about whether I am seeing blood. I just read my dog because I know that there is a high likelihood that we are tracking a dead deer. The greatest value of an occasional drop of blood is that you can show it to the hunter, and reassure him that the dog is still on the line of his deer.

Of course, if you can determine that you are dealing with a superficial muscle wound, you can pick up the dog after he gets to the point where the blood clotted and stopped flowing. There is no internal bleeding with such a flesh wound, and the deer can continue indefinitely. This is also the case for neck hits. Almost always you either find these neck-hit deer in a very short distance or you don't get them at all. There is not much point in tracking neck hits a long way after the bleeding has stopped.

In broken shoulders and legs, the presence of visible blood is much more important. You have to push these deer, make them bleed in order to catch up to them. Otherwise they will become coyote feed days down the road.

A deer with his leg broken and swinging may go four or five miles with nickel-sized drops of blood every few yards. It is important to realize that such a deer may stop bleeding on the outside for about two hundred yards before he goes down for the last time. Blood pressure drops to a point where there is no further loss of blood on the outside, but adrenaline carries the deer a bit farther.

To sum up I find that it's a good rule to track for another quarter of a mile after the situation seems hopeless. I have found a lot of deer in that last quarter of a mile.

18. I hear that some medications/drugs can affect dog's sense of smell? Which are they?

Veterinarian Tina Wismer compiled the following list of agents that may alter taste and olfaction: Allopurinol, Ampicillin (Amoxicillin is in same class of drugs), Azathioprine, Carprofen (Rimadyl), Chlorpheniramine, Corticosteroids, Doxorubicin, Griseofulvin, Metronidazole, Morphine, Phenylbutazone, Sulfasalazine, Tetracycline, Vincristine and Radiation Therapy.

19. My dog seems to have a lot of trouble following the scent line trail when it passes under high voltage electric power lines. Why does this happen and what can I do about it?

The magnetic field generated by the high voltage line ionizes the scent particles left by the wounded deer when he passed under the wires. This seems to neutralize the odor for the dog unless it is very fresh.

You deal with this as you do when encountering a creek or a wide highway. First have your tracking dog "reach" across the power line zone to the uncontaminated ground on the other side. Since the deer may have walked down along the power line for a ways, you and your dog may have to check along the edges, up and down, on both sides of the power line, in order to pick up the scent line again.

Chapter 27

Regional Tracking Traditions

For a southern deer hunter, a good deal of this book may seem like Yankee nonsense. Southerners have their own traditions for finding wounded deer that go way back. If a Yankee digs a little bit, he discovers that some southern hunters have been using dogs to find wounded deer from the days of the Early Republic. This is a very old tradition, and if it came from the British Isles, it came a long, long time ago. You would have to be in a dark Mississippi swamp, watching a black Lab working off lead with a Garmin Astro and flashing strobe light on his collar, to realize how different the southern tradition was and is.

Texas, when it comes to deer hunting, is truly an independent republic. Needless to say, the Texans have developed their own methods for finding wounded deer. These grew out of their use of dogs to work cattle.

More recent developments with leashed tracking dogs came in the Northeast and Midwest. These methods, which draw from the European experience, have been the primary focus of this book. The purpose of this chapter is to explain that the United States has at least three major traditions of the art of finding wounded deer: 1) the southern, 2) the Texan and 3) the northern USA/European. Laws, methods and ethical assumptions within the three traditions are quite different.

We might add the Canadians in Quebec have also developed a tracking tradition that comes independently from Europe. The Canadian story is not simple, but all North American trackers should be aware of its existence.

The Southern Tradition

In much of the Deep South, the use of hounds to drive deer, and to follow up on the wounded ones, was routine. After World War II, it became regulated to some degree, but it was never completely outlawed. In many southern states, where the deer cover is almost impenetrable, the use of deer dogs on a county option basis seems perfectly logical. Some southern deer hunters were mildly curious about the anti-dog uproar in the North.

In the South, hunting deer with dogs is now on the decline, but this is not because deer populations are in any danger. The problem is that deer hounds have not learned to read "posted" signs once landowners started putting them up. Rifle and bowhunters don't want a pack of hounds disrupting their more deliberate style of hunting. Recently, where Quality Deer Management (QDM) has been established, the best bucks are not shot until they have matured and sired many fawns. Hunters know that they cannot manage a herd for quality when the deer are frequently shot on the run, and when hounds may chase deer out of the whole management area for several days. Hunting deer with dogs is being phased out in the South, but one legacy of hound hunting is that Game Officials accept the principle of using a dog, under control, to find wounded deer. This open attitude grows out of the southern deer hunting experience.

Various hound breeds, from Beagles to Walker Foxhounds, were used and are still being used today in the South for driving deer to hunters on stand, who often use buckshot. Many a hound, not wanted in the North because he would run deer, has ended up in a southern deer pack where his talents were appreciated.

One problem that arose with the hounds used for full cry pursuit of deer was that they often failed to follow up on a deer that had been wounded. A number of southern hunters have explained this to me as they searched for a specialist, "wounded deer dog". They reported that deer hounds often had difficulty making the transition from the abundant scent of a small herd of deer to the fainter, solitary trail of a deer that had been shot and wounded. Better results were to be had if a "specialist", who had not been running with the pack, was brought in to follow up on the wounded deer. This specialist might be a wise old veteran hound that no longer had the speed to stay up with the deer pack.

As deer hunting with hounds and buckshot has declined, giving way to rifle and later to bowhunting, the use of dogs as wounded deer specialists has spread into these new forms of deer hunting.

Through my talks with southern handlers, I have learned that many different breeds were and are used as wounded deer trackers. Since these dogs are generally worked off lead, it is essential that they be calm, intelligent individuals responsive to their handler. Certain Bluetick, Redbone, and Black and Tan Coonhounds, Beagles and southern cur breeds are all being used successfully. In Georgia there is an active tradition of using coonhound breeds, on and off lead, to find wounded deer.

Curs, such as the Black Mouths and Catahoulas were discussed in the chapter on these breeds. Many of these curs in Louisiana and Mississippi are primarily feral "hawg" dogs, but their qualities of intelligence and responsiveness make them very useful for finding wounded deer also. They are excellent windscenters, and their noses are more than adequate for ground scent in the sorts of tracking circumstances that generally arise in southern deer hunting. The use of Lacys from Texas is beginning to spread across the South.

For good reason, it is the Labrador Retriever that is becoming the most popular and widely used deer tracker in the Deep South. Labs are most prevalent along the Mississippi Flyway, the mid-continent migration route of waterfowl. Here their first role is to retrieve ducks, but it has been found that they can be trained to find, if not retrieve, whitetails as well. As in the case of the curs, the strong points in favor of the Lab are intelligence and responsiveness to the handler. Unlike the curs, they are usually more tolerant of strangers around "their" wounded deer.

The southern tradition is well established, and without any lessons from Europe or from the northern states, it has proved to be very successful. The success rates of the best southern dogs are much better than anything that can be achieved up north. Handlers report finding over "50%" of the deer that their dogs track off lead. Still comparisons of tracking, North and South, are very difficult. This is due in large part to the differences in the nature of deer habitat and the different traditions and ethics of deer hunting in these two regions.

When a deer is shot in the dense cover down south, the hunter does not have the "find it yourself" compulsions of his Yankee counterpart. If a downed deer is not in sight, or if it is not obvious where the deer went, he calls for the tracking dog. The southern hunter believes that if he pushes into a dense thicket himself and flushes the deer from its first bed, he may never recover it. He knows that a big, strong dog like a Lab will be able to overtake a wounded deer in a few 100 yards and bay it or pull it down. The deer's fear and suffering will be ended quickly.

In the genteel southern tradition there is absolutely nothing wrong with having a professional help you find your deer. A German hunter would understand this southern system more easily than an American hunter from the North.

These generalizations about southern methods of tracking deer apply best to the lowlands of the coastal plains and the Mississippi Delta. Snakes and alligators are a threat to dogs, and big dogs like Labs and coonhounds are less at risk than small ones like Beagles and Dachshunds. In the upland, drier regions, the contrast with northern conditions is not as sharp. Cover is less dense and snakes are less numerous. In these situations, the use of smaller leashed tracking dogs seems to work well for those who have tried it. Of course coyotes are always a risk to small dogs working off lead.

The Texas Cowdog Tradition

Texas, has an off lead tradition distinctly different from what has been developed in the Deep South, where hounds were used, from early settlement times, to drive deer to hunters. Dogs were also used for deer hunting in East Texas, but in most of this vast state, stretching to the west, it was the cowdogs, working off lead, that became the primary trackers of wounded deer.

The methods used by Roy Hindes III, as described in Chapter 6, illustrate this American cattle country style of finding wounded deer. Modern technology, especially the GPS collar, has made working cowdogs off lead in the Texas tradition, even more effective.

The southwestern experience with wounded deer varies in many ways from what is encountered in the opposite corner of the county. I was surprised to learn that when using cowdogs, the mature, tough old bucks are the ones that are the easiest to stop. In Texas, the big, heavy racked buck is quickest to halt, turn and have a stand-off with the dog. Big, dominant bucks in Texas are used to having their own way, and they will not tolerate being harassed from the rear. A younger deer will flee and go much farther.

In the Northeast, catching up to a deer certainly does not happen in the same way; there the tough old bucks, which have the most stamina, use it to keep on moving out ahead of the handler and his leashed dog. The Texas system usually brings a buck to bay a few hundred yards out of his wound bed. In the Northeast, a similar deer might go for several miles.

South Texas is dry country. Between patches of cactus and brush, there is considerable bare clay or sand. Hunter tactics for following up on a wounded deer are adapted to this situation. Even if there is an obvious blood trail, the hunter backs off. He does not want to risk pushing the deer off its first wound bed. He reasons that if the deer stops bleeding while in the bed, there will be no way to follow it when it leaves. Even if a tracking dog handler is called for, it may be hours before he arrives. In the meantime, the scent will probably burn away in the sun and dryness.

These tactics, so unlike those of the Eastern tradition of "tracking your own deer", have a certain logic in South Texas. Scenting conditions tend to be very difficult, but on the other hand the hunter does not confuse the blood trail, or walk around at the point of loss. The average distance that the deer travels, or is pushed after the shot, is much shorter. Many of the wounded deer found by a dog in Texas, would be tracked and found in the North by the hunter himself. Northern hunters attempt to find a deer by themselves, even if it takes many hours of tracking; they only think about a tracking dog when all of their own efforts have failed. In the moister climate of the North, a good tracking dog can still prevail despite earlier interference by the hunter. A good tracking dog taken to arid South Texas would find it much harder to do the same thing. Again, as in the southern case, the special circumstances and tracking ethics of Texas permit the tracking dogs there to achieve a ratio of finds to non-recoveries that never could be equaled in the North.

The technique of baying big wounded bucks makes it possible to stop and dispatch deer that would never be found or approached in the North. In the North, a weakened, but not mortally wounded deer has a good chance of eluding the tracker and surviving if its legs are still working.

Texas law, as it pertains to tracking dogs, is applied on a county-by-county basis. In East Texas, in 2016, there were still 5 counties that had no legal provision for the use of tracking dogs. In the rest of Texas, up to two dogs can be worked off lead to find wounded deer. This creates a good situation for young dogs to learn from the experienced ones. This is the way that Roy Hindes' dogs learn their trade. Roy often tracks easy deer with young dogs to familiarize them with the task. On a more difficult, natural line, an experienced dog working off lead, does the hard work, and the young dog, following behind, is kept on a leash. When the scent line of the wounded deer is crossed, and the young dog reacts, praise is given. If the deer is jumped from the wound bed, the young dog is turned loose with the veteran.

But Texas is a huge state with many different types of habitat and many different ways of managing and hunting deer. This state is simply too big to be summed up in a discussion of how the cowdogs do it. Not every blood tracking dog in Texas today is a big cowdog or curdog. The use of the somewhat smaller Lacy is growing rapidly as this third edition goes to press.

There are many deer hunters in Texas, who do not live on a ranch, and who are not in a position to keep an 80 pounds plus cowdog to find wounded deer. Hunters have found that with care and the proper methods a smaller dog can be used in Texas, despite the rattlesnakes and the prickly pear.

As described in the chapter on scent hounds, a few imported Bavarian Mountain Hounds, which weigh around 50 pounds, are being used as cold-nosed specialists. And it is the Lacy that is becoming the most widely used tracking dog in Texas.

One common denominator runs through the accounts of every tracking dog handler that we have met, and this includes those from Texas. All agree that you have to be close with your dog and spend time with him in all seasons. Blood tracking is not for the handler who simply wants his dog to be a tool, used to find a deer once in a while and then put away.

Roy Hindes with Gus, son of Jethro, with Dale Jenkins' huge buck.
Photo courtesy of Roy Hindes

Regions With a Low Acceptance of Blood Tracking

When it comes to deer hunting, few things are a simple as 1, 2, 3. This also applies to the various traditions of finding wounded deer. Before we get into the tradition of leashed tracking dogs in the North, we should detour briefly down a few side roads to look at some minor North American developments in which tracking with dogs has been slow to catch on.

A. In British Columbia, Canada, the existence of tracking dog legislation did not have much of an impact at first. In 1998 when I visited the Ministry of Environment, Lands and Parks in Victoria, Deputy Director Mark Hayden told me that his office had no information on how the existing legislation was actually being used. At that time calls to a number of Guide Outfitters on the official registry uncovered only one guide that was using a tracking dog. By 2006, however, a tracking movement was beginning to take off. A Hanover Hound, several Bavarians and a Slovensky Kopov were being used (color Fig. 10). Michael Schneider, a guide/outfitter who came to British Columbia from Germany, made a strong effort to promote tracking dogs in the province but their use has been slow to expand, particularly among guides and outfitters. The difficult mountain terrain in the interior and poor communications have been negative factors.

B. There are currently some other scattered examples of enabling laws and regulations that never generated a great deal of blood tracking activity. The deer hunting laws and regulations in the United States are made by individual states; these laws are many and various.

In Nebraska the use of tracking dogs was never considered illegal and no law or written regulation was considered. According to Murray Johnson, a veteran Nebraska Conservation Officer, dogs were seldom being used in 2003. He speculated that there was a general assumption that dogs and deer hunting do not mix.

Nebraska is bird dog country, and apparently Nebraskans were thinking about other things that could be done with dogs. Not surprisingly the pioneer tracking dogs in this bird hunter's heaven have been the Drahthaars owned by Marty and Mikki Vlach.

For a time tracking dogs were legal or tolerated in certain hunting "zones" of California. They were being used by a few outfitters. As of 2016 an web search and calls to a legal authority in the central office of the California Fish and Game Department produced no record that tracking dogs were legal anywhere in California.

All legal provisions concerning tracking are subject to change, and the reader should consult his state game department for current information. The information above about tracking legalities in Nebraska and California does suggest something worth thinking about. Laws and regulations favorable to blood tracking with dogs don't guarantee, in themselves that tracking dogs will actually be used. Conservative hunting customs may limit the use of tracking dogs, and in some cases, hunters may simply be unaware of how successfully trained tracking dogs have been used to find wounded deer in other states and countries. If tracking with dogs works in South Texas (and it does), then tracking dogs will save game in any state of the Union.

Scattered through both the United States and Canada there have been instances in which dogs were used to find wounded deer. I have heard of Beagles, Labs and farm collies being used illegally by men not considered to be outlaws. As they explained it, leaving a wounded or dead deer in the woods seems a greater evil than breaking a "no dogs" law. Using the family dog to track a wounded deer seems like a fundamental and natural right to some people, but these isolated and unspoken cases cannot be considered a "tradition", widespread and recognized by law. The occasional use of tracking dogs around North America does not amount to a "tradition", known and accepted by many hunters and passed from one generation to the next.

The Tracking Tradition of the Northeast and the Upper Midwest

The legal use of leashed tracking dogs in the Northeast and Upper Midwest (the third tradition) is so recent that some might say it is pushing the definition of tradition to apply the term at all in this case. The term *tradition* is used in this chapter only because tracking in these regions is clearly an outgrowth of the much older tradition in Europe. Basic methods, and even the first breeds of dogs used (Wirehaired Dachshunds and Drahthaars), came from Europe. There has been no long-standing American tradition of using tracking dogs to find wounded deer that could be legally regulated and adapted to the Northeast. The idea of using dogs, in any way related to deer hunting, became an alien concept during the first three quarters of the 20th century. Of course, what seemed to Northeasterners to be a radical and untested innovation in deer hunting was the norm in most European countries. In many parts of the German speaking and the Scandinavian countries, the law mandates that all big game hunters must have access to a tracking dog.

The official status of tracking dogs in New York State was typical of the Northeast. Using a dog in any way to find a wounded deer was illegal, pure and simple. The legal definition of hunting in the Northeastern states included searching for or tracking wounded game. When whitetail deer were almost eliminated in this region, deer hunting with dogs was banned. It was an appropriate step for the time. Deer hunting with dogs was too efficient, especially at that time when so much of the Northeast had been cleared for agriculture. In the same era, state legislatures passed "bucks only" hunting laws as another means of restoring deer populations. Unlike many other laws, "bucks only" and "no dogs" both became sacred principles for concerned deer hunters. In the Northeast, and in some other parts of the country, shooting a dog running loose in the woods during deer season became a moral act. In the eyes of many hunters, shooting deer chasers, or probable deer chasers, was totally justifiable even though it might be technically illegal to take the law into your own hands.

In the Northeast, the strong opposition to the use of dogs, in any way associated with deer hunting, has moderated to the extent that the use of leashed tracking dogs is accepted in most states. However, there would be very strong opposition to any proposal to use tracking dogs off lead as is done in the South and in Texas. And it is still a fundamental belief that the use of tracking dogs is ethically correct only when all other methods of finding a wounded deer have failed. The use of leashed tracking dogs is a last resort, especially for bow hunters.

"Blood tracking" with leashed dogs was first introduced into New York State in 1976 on a research permit basis. The purpose of the research was to see if the leashed tracking dog method would work in New York, to see if the public would accept it, and to devise ways to prevent this from becoming a cover for jack lighters and other poachers. I was the first person to be granted a research permit, and at the time I had little awareness of what was going on in the rest of the United States. Later, it came as a surprise to me to learn that there were older and quite different American traditions of finding wounded deer with dogs. We have already discussed these southern and Texan traditions, but those off leash methods would never have been accepted in the North. It took considerable persuasion and politics to launch the idea of leashed tracking dogs in New York.

A slightly earlier attempt by Tom Scott to introduce the use of tracking dogs in Indiana during the 1970s failed for a number of reasons. Tom advocated releasing the big Drahthaars, which he favored, when a deer was jumped from the wound bed. This was acceptable to the Navy on the Crane Naval Ammunition Depot, where Tom launched his experiment. But Indiana sportsmen and Indiana authorities in the DNR did not buy it outside the vast 64,000 acre domain of the Navy. About 20 years later the Indiana DNR did come back to the concept, but tracking dogs, under the new law, were to be kept on a leash at all times.

The New York organization, Deer Search Inc., was responsible for the acceptance of tracking dogs in New York, and the word "leashed" was stressed from the beginning. The New York Legislature's provision for the leashed tracking dog license would never have happened without the fieldwork of this organization. The drive for a leashed tracking dog law was led by Deer Search President, Don Hickman, who spent hundreds of hours politicking when he was not out tracking or training dogs and handlers.

In the North, the idea of tracking dogs spread gradually. Wisconsin was the next state to introduce it in a somewhat different form. Larry Gohlke, a member of Deer Search, served as the first authorized handler in his home state. The Wisconsin Department of Natural Resources decided that their legal structure did not require new legislation; Larry's authorization was at first printed in a provisional form in a special DNR information book for Conservation Officers; the official regulation was not printed and generally distributed until 1999.

Next came Vermont with legislation and regulations closely patterned upon those of New York. In most states it required the determined efforts of a "point man" to win support from organized hunters and from the legislature. In Vermont, that person was Tim Nichols, a Deer Search member, who had moved across the Vermont border into New York in order to participate in the New York State tracking research. Then, using his Vermont roots for leverage, Tim won legal support for a leashed tracking dog law in his native state.

In the Northeast, Maine followed Vermont with another New York style program. In 2007 leashed tracking dogs were legalized in New Hampshire.

In the meantime, officials in the DNRs of Indiana and Michigan took the initiative to have leashed tracking dog laws passed in their respective states. These legal arrangements, as was discussed in Chapter 13, were significantly different from the New York model in that they specifically prohibited carrying a weapon. Maryland passed a leashed tracking dog law in 2000.

As this updated version of *Tracking Dogs for Finding Wounded Deer* goes to press, the number of "legal states" continues to grow. Since 2016 there have been major breakthroughs in the legalization of leashed tracking dogs for finding wounded big game. Six new states: New Jersey, Pennsylvania, Wyoming, North Dakota, Oklahoma and Minnesota have joined the tracking dog movement. In Pennsylvania, a major deer hunting state, this required 20 years of promotional effort.

The total number of "legal" states, North and South, on and off leash, has expanded to 40 as of December 2019. As shown by the map on the next page, we have included Texas as a "legal" state although there are still five counties along the Louisiana border that do not allow tracking in any form.

Five of the holdouts are extreme western states: Washington, Oregon, California, Nevada and Arizona. Here, there has been little expressed interest, and individuals have not emerged in these states to lead promotional efforts. State DNR officials are preoccupied with immediate crises, and they are concerned about adding new administrative costs. The experience in the USA as a whole has been that tracking programs are not expensive to administer.

The final holdouts are in a 'bundle" of three Southern New England states: Rhode Island, Connecticut and Massachusetts. In all three states some promotional leadership is present, but is encountering s wall of indifference from the DNR. Time will tell.

It has become almost impossible to present an accurate and up-to-date list of all the regulations involved. Details about the carrying and use of firearms to put down wounded deer vary, and these regulations are frequently being changed. Rather than presenting a complicated list of state regulations which would soon be out of date, we refer you to the DNR website of your own state.

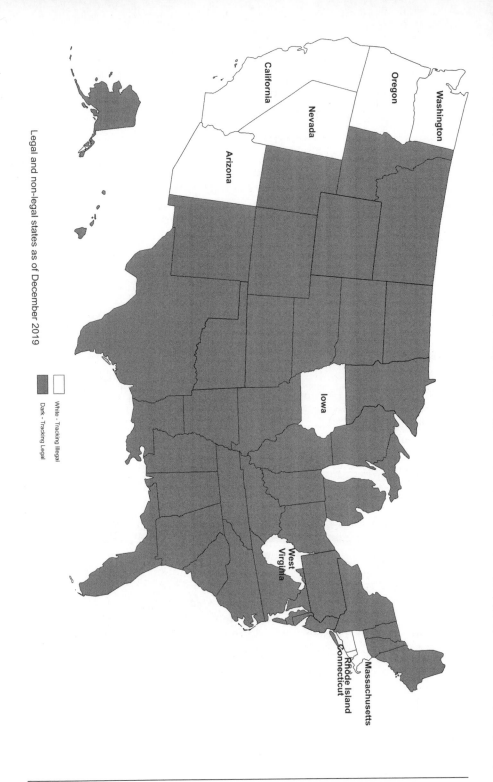

Legal and non-legal states as of December 2019

White - Tracking Illegal

Dark - Tracking Legal

Uniqueness of the Northern Tradition

The emerging of a northern tradition of tracking has more to it than sets of laws and regulations. In most cases, these rules reflect underlying regional and strongly held beliefs about what is ethical and appropriate. The legal tracking practices that have developed recently in the North stand out as distinctly different from the way things are done in the South and in Texas. When we compare these northern practices to what is done in Europe, we find, once again, that there are differences. Northern tracking does have its roots in Europe, but the new sprout growing up from these old roots, is developing a distinct form of its own.

For example, most American trackers emphasize night tracking more than the Europeans do. This is due, in good part, to the influence of American raccoon hunting. Like so many other handlers, I grew up spending long nights in the woods coon hunting. A coon hunter becomes comfortable and efficient in the dark. He also has access to specialized lights and other coon hunter's equipment that are not readily available to Europeans. Since coon hunting is an established and legal custom in the United States, it has been possible to convince American law enforcement agencies that a man in the woods at night with a gun and a light is not necessarily an outlaw. In Europe tracking is generally done in the daytime.

Bowhunting is another American custom that gives tracking here its unique character. As discussed in previous chapters, tracking bowshot deer is more difficult than tracking deer shot with firearms. During the long archery seasons, American tracking dogs routinely face difficult tracking challenges, which are less frequently encountered in Europe where bowhunting is not widespread. American dogs find many dead deer or deer doomed to die, but often they are called upon to track bow-shot deer that are superficially wounded and likely to recover. Evaluating the condition of such deer often involves a difficult tracking job.

There is an important link between blood tracking and bowhunting; some bowhunters were originally afraid of the public relations consequences of this. In fact, the use of tracking dogs is an honest improvement, which helps *all* types of deer hunters; it has not inspired criticism from the anti-hunters either. No one has tried to argue that the use of tracking dogs in bowhunting is evidence that bowhunting should be outlawed.

The most distinctive feature of the northern tradition is the "do-it-yourself" ethic. In the North, a hunter is expected to find his own deer using his best skills as a woodsman to track the wounded deer down, even if there is no blood to be seen. This ethic is especially emphasized in northern bowhunting. It is a matter of pride to find your own deer alone or with the help of a hunting buddy. If you are at one with the northern tradition, you will spend many hours on your hands and knees following pin prick drops of blood, a scuffed leaf here, a partial deer track there, before you concede that it will take another man and a dog to find your deer. The roots of this ethic come out of our frontier tradition in which a real hunter was one who could do everything for himself.

The South had its own frontier tradition, but, in contrast to the North, deer hunting evolved in a different way. It became much more a social and cooperative sport in which hunters, dogs and dog handlers were involved together. Hunting with dogs in the early days helped to establish a group hunting tradition. The solitary hunter could only be in one place at a time, and would not kill much game when deer were driven by hounds. Deer hunting leases, in which a number of partners participate, are much more widespread in the South than in the North, and this too enhances camaraderie and joint effort. Northern deer camps create a somewhat similar atmosphere, but they involve a much smaller percentage of the deer hunting population.

To conclude, the northern tracking tradition, with its recent European origins, has already begun to develop its own, distinctive character. Ties with Europe should be maintained and strengthened in the future, but we will be adapting European dogs and expertise to our American hunting customs, legislation and wild game.

Canada

As was mentioned earlier, British Columbia was the first Canadian Province to formally legalize tracking dogs to find wounded big game. This did not lead to extensive use of tracking dogs.

The Quebec Ministry of Natural Resources officially allowed the use of leashed tracking dogs in the Province in 2009. Actually there was some use of tracking dogs even earlier. The foundation brood stock of Wirehaired Dachshunds for tracking was imported from Belgium, and early in the 21st century certain aspiring handlers went to France for training seminars.

ACCSQ (Quebec Association of Tracking Dog Handlers) was founded in 2008, and it had much to do with the Ministry's acceptance of the leashed tracking dog idea. As an American I was invited to lead one tracking seminar in Quebec, but this was after the French influence was clearly established.

In 2004 new regulations in Nova Scotia formalized what had been a long standing tradition of using tracking dogs, usually bird dogs, to find wounded deer and bear.

As of 2013 the Ontario Ministry of Natural Resources has put in place the first regulations to authorize the use of tracking dogs for deer and moose. Bear were not mentioned. In contrast to the existing regulations in neighboring Quebec, tracking wounded game with a leashed dog in Ontario was defined by the MNR as a hunting activity subject to hunting regulations. This interpretation creates many complications, and the final outcome is not yet clear. At present it is illegal to track after dark because tracking is defined as a big game hunting activity. The present arrangement pleases the coyotes and grey wolves.

A small group of dog owners who hope for a workable system of regulations have organized themselves as Big Game Blood Trackers of Ontario (BGBTO). They seek to work with the MNR and with the hunting public to

---

expand a legalized tracking program as has been done in Quebec and Nova Scotia to the east. The number of trackers for the vast Province of Ontario was still very small in 2016. Contacts with trackers can be found at www.biggamesearchon.com.

The Canadian provinces will each develop their own tracking dog tradition or traditions because there is such a variation in terrain and wildlife.

As in the United States, the starting point in Canada has been European dogs and methods, but each province has tended to go its own way, both with respect to the rest of Canada and with the United States. Between British Columbia on the Pacific and Ontario far to the east there have been no new legalizations since 2013. The future will be interesting but it is unpredictable.

Evolving Traditions; What Does the Future Hold?

The current methods of screening calls are likely to change but there will never be a way to screen calls with total effectiveness. A broadbased study conducted in Quebec indicated that hunters were wrong in reporting where they had wounded animals 48% of the time. What hunters honestly perceive and report to trackers is not always reliable. And some wounded deer that seem likely to recover are actually more seriously wounded and could be found dead or in serious and deteriorating condition.

At present, with an inadequate number of handlers in most parts of this country, a handler has no choice. He must take the calls which are most likely to be productive. He is seldom in a position to take every call that **might** find the deer. We are still a long way from the European situation where there is a greater density of handlers.

In North America it is primarily the professional guides and outfitters who are in a position to take almost every possible call as a means of serving and pleasing their paying clients. But in most of North America we are still a very long way from the regulations established in many European states that make "control searches" mandatory.

A control search is a check on site, by an experienced tracking dog and handler to determine if a big game animal shot at was actually wounded seriously. An experienced handler can readily interpret his scenting dog's reactions around the hit site and determine whether it is worthwhile to follow the scent trail farther and gain further evidence to continue.

My own experience with Sabina, described in Chapter 18, where we had no sign for a half mile but ultimately caught up to the deer that charged us, convinced me that control searches can be valuable. In this case I was dealing with my own deer, but had a hunter told me the hit site details on the phone, I would have turned him down because of insufficient evidence.

A Danish study cited by Niels Sondergaard found that 25% of the control searches on roe deer led to the recovery of the animal. We are a long, long way from mandating control searches in North America. Such regulations would be very difficult to enforce in practice. Also, since hunting is associated here with an escape to freedom, much more than in Europe, mandated control searches would be opposed.

What we are likely to see, as the number of handlers increases, is a greater readiness to take somewhat dubious calls. Ethical considerations will be a factor, and the adventure of tracking will draw many impassioned handlers out into the brush and brambles.

Cash is likely to become the most important reason for a handler to take a call that does not seem very promising. If the hunter is so convinced that the deer can be recovered, the handler may reason, "What have I got to lose? The hunter has promised to pay me for my time and expenses."

Tracking On Lead and Off Lead

As we have discussed, the idea of working dogs off lead was never strongly opposed in the Deep South and in Texas. On the other hand it became an absolute taboo in most of the rest of the country. If the proponents of tracking dogs for finding wounded game in most of the rest of the country had insisted on releasing dogs on the track, it is doubtful that there would have been any legalizations at all. Those of us who participated in the legalization campaigns in more than 20 states were always careful to refer to **leashed** tracking dogs. This made all the difference.

Personally I cannot see far enough into the future to envision any political possibility of introducing the European methods of working the old, cold track on lead, but releasing the dog if the wounded game is jumped from its bed and takes off. This would transform many a long and sometimes fruitless pursuit on lead into a short run of a few hundred yards before the animal was stopped and "bayed" by the dog. As discussed in Chapter 13, releasing the dog, or working an experienced dog entirely off lead significantly raises the recovery rate.

Releasing tracking dogs would probably be more disruptive to hunting activity in much of the United States than has been the case in Europe. American hunting tends to be more individualistic and less regimented. If dogs were released in daylight hunting hours, the activities of hunters, especially bowhunters, would be disrupted. This would not be as great a problem if dogs were to be released only after hunting hours, but even this would be strongly opposed as a disturbance of normal deer movements and bedding sanctuaries. Coon hunting is legal during deer seasons, but landowners and lease holders, seriously interested in deer hunting, seldom allow coon dogs to range through their properties.

In the Northeast of the 1980s there was an invasion of coyotes with a strong infusion of grey wolf genes acquired during their migrations. This has made the nighttime woods unsafe for dogs off lead, particularly if they are Dachshunds. If the off lead use of tracking dogs is ever legalized in the North, one result will certainly be a shift to larger tracking dogs with more bay power and more resistance to the ever present coyote.

Wild Boars

The expansion of wild boars from South to North is another factor that will have an impact on the tracking of wounded big game in the United States. Wildlife biologists now refer to these animals as "Eurasian wild boars" while southern hunters continue to call their own, somewhat more domesticated strains as "wild hawgs". The toughest of these hybrid pigs survive snow and cold well; they are extending their range in the North as the climate warms.

Breeding populations are now established in Pennsylvania, New York, Michigan and probably in other northern states. Many of these "hog hotspots" originated with escapees from game farms, but the boars have shown that they can survive and reproduce on their own. Because of their early maturity and large litters, wild boars are likely to become a major big game species in the North. Boars are very destructive to agriculture, and few wildlife experts believe that they will be a desirable addition to the northern habitat. The fact remains that they are almost impossible to eliminate once they are established. Wild boars are here to stay.

If we look at Northern Europe, which has also experienced global warming, we have a preview of what may be coming here. Corn fields have to be fenced to keep the boars out. Pastures and hay fields are "rototilled" by the boars as they feed on grubs and roots. Boars come into towns and suburbs to feed on the contents of garbage cans. They are difficult to hunt, because they are nocturnal and move from one area to another. Today the great majority of all big game animals found in Europe by tracking dogs are wild boars.

In America the question will come up, "Will a dog trained to track wounded deer be willing and capable of tracking a wild boar?" Yes, there is no doubt that our American tracking dogs will do the job. When I was with forester/trackers in France and Germany, their dogs tracked wounded deer and boars interchangeably. The boars have a great deal of stamina and when wounded in a similar way, they seemed to bleed less than a deer. The boars left plenty of scent.

In the North it is unlikely that the Eurasian boars will be hunted with small packs of dogs as is the case with the feral "hawgs" down south. This would go against too many entrenched northern ideas about dogs running loose in the deer woods. As the Eurasian boars expand, aided by global warming, most of them are likely to be hunted by the same methods used for deer and black bear. Tracking dogs will have more work to do!

Summary

- Three distinctly different traditions and methods of finding deer with dogs exist in the United States.

- These traditions can be associated with the South, with Texas and with the Northeast/ Midwest areas. The Rocky Mountain elk hunting states are following in the leashed tracking dog tradition of the Northeast/ Midwest.

- Canada is developing its own methods and traditions.

- Quebec has rapidly become an important tracking region.

- Legalization of tracking dogs for finding wounded deer is not sufficient to encourage their use. A tracking tradition must be established. Education is required.

- American tracking traditions are likely to remain different from those in Europe for considerable time to come.

- The wild boar is likely to become an animal frequently tracked in the United States.

Recommendations to Deer Managers and Legislators

1. The tracking of wounded deer should be allowed day and night. This is the most direct and humane way to deal with a dying animal. The best and most avid trackers are likely to be hunters. Because of their job and family commitments, and because of their own desire to hunt during legal hours, they will be much more effective if they are allowed to track at night.

2. The tracker must be given some legal means of putting down live, but mortally wounded deer, when he finds them, day or night. There is no reliable way to determine in advance whether a wounded deer will be alive or dead when found. Wounded deer can be dangerous to tracking dogs and even to their handlers.

3. Handlers with tracking dogs should be required to notify a Conservation Officer before they assist a hunter in finding deer. The Northeastern experiment with this notification procedure has shown that game law violators find it unappealing. They are not tempted to exploit a tracking dog service for illegal purposes if they know that their names and their location are being reported to Law Enforcement.

Chapter 28

Conclusion

This book raises a fundamental question: How "effective" are leashed tracking dogs for finding wounded deer? I wish this simple question had a simple answer.

In the previous chapter, we discussed how different traditions and tracking methods have produced quite different "recovery rates". Valid comparisons or "averaged" results are impossible.

In addition to these regional factors, the individual handler's policy of selecting wounded deer calls has an enormous influence on the percentage of wounded deer found. If the handler only takes tracks that arise from wounds in the stomach and small intestines, he will have a high recovery rate of 70% or better. If he accepts every invitation to track a deer that comes in, he will have a recovery rate less than half as good. But the handler who takes every call will find *more* deer. Handlers can manipulate statistics about their tracking effectiveness, as they make decisions about what calls they will take. In a larger sense the handler, who has the highest percentage of recovered deer, may not be the handler who is most effective in reducing the number of mortally wounded deer that are never found.

To have a real understanding of what tracking dogs can do to reduce the loss of wounded deer, it is necessary to know what actually happens to all the deer that are wounded in a representative hunt. This requires thorough ground searches of the whole hunting area. Radio collars on the hunted deer and infrared searches by air can also be used in conjunction with ground searches. All of these evaluation methods are very costly, and none of these have yet been used to evaluate the effectiveness of tracking dogs.

In the 80s and 90s exaggerated criticisms were being made of bowhunting. In response to this, detailed and very expensive studies were conducted to determine how many deer are wounded by bowhunters, and what happens to these wounded deer. The best-known study is Wendy Krueger's *Aspects of Wounding White-tailed Deer by Bowhunters,* which was researched on a U.S. Army installation, Camp Ripley in Minnesota, during 1992 and 1993. Several leading deer biologists were involved in this study, which was supported by $250,000 in grant money from interested corporations and other organizations. Some other organizations, highly critical of hunting in general and bowhunting in particular, were invited to participate but chose not to do so. The Camp Ripley study used a helicopter equipped with infra-red video to establish the location of probable wounded or dead deer not found by bowhunters. Ground crews were then sent out to investigate these sites. It was a complex study that provided data on many different aspects of bowhunting, but the key piece of information, for our purposes here, was the percentage of deer mortally wounded and not recovered by the hunter. The Camp Ripley study concluded that 13% of the deer, which were killed in the hunts, were not recovered by the hunter who made the killing shot. Other hunters found more of these wounded deer since the concentration of hunters was high.

More data about the effectiveness of bowhunting was compiled in a smaller research project in McAlester, Oklahoma, conducted by Stephen S. Ditchkoff and five associates. Their study, *Wounding Rates of Whitetailed Deer with Traditional Archery Equipment*, was published in 1996, and found that 3 of the 11 deer, shot by traditional bowhunters and not found, actually died of their wounds. In other words, the mortality rate of wounded deer not found was 27%.

In this study, 80 male deer on the McAlester Army Ammunition Plant Reservation were trapped and fitted with radio collars that included a four-hour mortality sensor. When deer were hit and not found by the hunter, their location and condition were monitored every four to eight hours for about five days. When a deer died, researchers went in to determine the nature of the wound that caused death.

Neither the Camp Ripley, nor the McAlester study, used or considered the use of tracking dogs in any way. However, the structure of the McAlester study does provide a framework for better understanding the effectiveness of tracking dog work.

In the McAlester study, 22 radio-collared deer were shot and 11 of these were recovered by hunters. Of the 11 deer not recovered, eight deer survived non-mortal wounds, and three (about one in four) died but were never found by the hunters. Looking at this data in another way, half of the deer hit were not found by the hunter and would have been potential candidates for a tracking dog to follow.

These 11 wounded deer are representative of a pool of deer calls with which a tracking dog and handler has to deal. Of course, more accurate information was gathered on wounded deer at the McAlester Study than would have been available to a tracking dog handler, who has to depend upon the hopeful estimates of the hunters telephoning him. In the McAlester survey of the wounded deer not found by hunters, all three of the deer that died had damage to their stomach or gut. Two of the dead deer died within 24 hours, and the third lived for five to seven days.

Here is an estimate, based upon experience, of what would have happened if a good handler and dog had been used on the unretrieved wounded deer at McAlester. This is only an estimate, and it is not intended to prove anything. Some of the deer reported to the handler would probably have been rejected as "ungettable". For example, leg muscle wounds, or high back muscle wounds that stop bleeding are extremely unlikely to kill the deer. On all of the eight wounded deer that were survivors in the McAlester Study, the use or non-use of a leashed tracking dog would not have had any influence on final results. Possibly, a dog worked off leash, Southern or Texan style, would have caught up with some of these "survivor" deer.

Of the three "gut-shot" deer, any good dog, leashed or unleashed, would have been able to find the two that died within 24 hours. In the case of the deer that lived five to seven days, the results are more difficult to predict. If a handler and leashed dog had sufficient time to keep pressure on the deer and exhaust it, he could recover that deer. In the real world, this kind of time, one or two days, is seldom available. The Southerner or the Texan, with his dog off lead, would have had a better chance to catch up to this deer, but even here, the results are anything but certain. A deer wounded in the large bowel stays strong for a long time.

Wrapping up our discussion of this McAlester-based model, we could say that if the handler took all 11 deer calls and found only the two deer that died within 24 hours, then his recovery rate would be only 18%. If he rejected 1/3 of the least promising bow season calls, as most of us do, then his recovery rate would come up to 27%. Most of us who track with leashed tracking dogs during bow season come up with percentages close to this figure.

My own bow-shot recovery rates fluctuates quite a bit from one year to another. My "worst" year was in 1997 when my recovery rate was 11%, while in 2000 I recovered 41% of game tracked. It's useful to remember that in the great majority of cases where my dog did not find the deer, we were able to produce convincing evidence to the hunter that his deer would survive.

The most complete, detailed and reliable body of tracking statistics in North America has been compiled by Alain Ridel of the Quebec Association of Tracking Dog Handlers (ACCSQ). This provides a summary of 1359 tracking dog searches for whitetail deer, moose and bear in Quebec for the years 2009, 2010, 2011. This comprised searches for 685 deer, 631 moose and 43 bears. The total recovery rate was 41%, or 557 animals. The crossbow predominates in Quebec. Fifty-four percent of the animals tracked had been shot with a crossbow, as opposed to 27% by rifle and shotgun and 18% by bow.

In another survey conducted by ACCSQ on a smaller area (4 game management zones) over longer, and varied periods of time, 160 (6%) of a total 2676 animals harvested, were found with the aid of a tracking dog. These numbers strongly suggest that tracking dogs can have a significant impact from a game management standpoint!

For reasons that are not completely clear, recovery statistics in Quebec, where dogs must be kept on a leash, came in higher than in the "tracking leash required" states south of the border. The prevalence of crossbows and the heavily forested terrain may be part of the explanation.

Much of ACCSQ's statistical compilations had not yet been published as this revised 2nd edition went to press. I was given access to them thanks to Alain Ridel and to ACCSQ, which some years ago accepted me as a member.

No one really knows what the wounding and loss rates are in firearms hunting for deer. Estimates range from 10% to 30%. Although the great majority of deer are shot with firearms, the studies made on this aspect of deer hunting have been much less thorough. The researchers have relied primarily upon hunter reports with little or no follow-up field checking. A majority of hunters, who admit to wounding a deer, tend to exaggerate the possibility that they have killed it; the wounding loss is not likely to be as high as what they have reported. I speak to each hunter prior to taking a deer call. Most of them are convinced that the deer is down and dead or dying. Most of the time my dog proves otherwise.

Many special factors come into play during the firearms season. For example, snow makes it easier for hunters to track wounded deer. On the other hand, some mortally wounded deer give no visible sign of being hit, and the hunter never realizes or reports that he has wounded a deer. More research incorporating area searches is needed.

Why are we concerned about the loss of deer through wounding when the percentage is already low? Jay McAninch, one of the major deer biologists involved in the Camp Ripley study, said, "This study reinforced that the number of deer lost to bowhunting is not biologically significant". Of course, he is right. A tough winter can have much bigger impact than bowhunting losses upon the size and health of a deer herd.

But in the larger world of human emotions, human ethics and politics, the wounding of deer has an importance that goes beyond its purely biological significance.

Human factors can never be excluded from the deer management equation. On one level, we must maintain the acceptance of deer hunting in the political majority that does not hunt. Otherwise, we can lose the right to hunt, and wildlife biologists can lose their most important management tool.

Thirty years ago the National Shooting Sports Foundation polled non-hunters on the aspects of hunting that they did not like. At that time, five out of the top seven objections involved the wounding of game. In 2016, worries about the "gun culture" are more widespread, but the concerns of the public about wounded deer are certainly still with us. When a handler and tracking dog find wounded deer and report on the healthy survival of most of the others they track, it is, among other things, very good public relations. I have spoken with many non-hunters who are amazed that trackers and organizations like Deer Search and United Blood Trackers exist. This does not fit in at all with their preconceived notion of hunters as uncaring and irresponsible.

A strong case can be made for the use of tracking dogs, both as a means of reducing animal suffering, and as a way of avoiding the waste of a valuable natural resource. There are political and social implications involved that cannot be disregarded. Even if the wounding losses are much lower than the public has been misled to believe, there are very good reasons for reducing them still more. We should use statistical and rational arguments in explaining ourselves to the non-hunting public.

On a deeper level, we should be concerned about what we, as hunters, think and feel. Some of this goes beyond scientific studies and statistics and only has meaning to those who are hunters at heart. When a hunter wounds a deer and cannot find it, he does not think in terms of statistics or what is biologically significant. He has a personal, one-on-one relationship with that deer. He has a sense of responsibility that goes beyond a desire for venison and antlers.

Two tracking experiences in the fall of 2002 demonstrated to me the emotional and ethical factors that underlie our efforts to recover wounded deer. Both deer calls involved "bucks of a lifetime" and they ended very differently. Both were, in their own way, a success, although they were recorded statistically as a find and a deer not recovered.

It's easy to understand why Ryan Blothenburg's ten pointer, shown in the photo, was more than just a statistic to him. That's a fine deer anywhere, and it came out of a public hunting area on state land. Ryan grunted in the buck at the peak of the rut. His arrow took out the left lung, liver and stomach, but the buck ended up traveling four hundred yards in dense brush before it lay down. For a long way there was almost no blood. We were all worried about coyotes because the deer had been shot 17 hours earlier the previous day. When my Dachshund Elli came up on the dead buck, we saw the high, massive antlers before anything else. And the venison was untouched and still in fine shape. For the four men who participated in the find, there were whoops and back slaps. Elli was praised to the sky. Ryan Blothenburg's pure joy was something that went beyond numbers.

Later on in the season I tracked another big buck and the results were very different. Paul McCloskey described it as a "buck of a lifetime". The day before he had taken a long shot with his scoped and rifled shotgun. He held high to compensate for the distance. It seemed likely that he had shot too high because the buck had gone down instantly, and then had quickly risen to run across a field and disappear. It sounded like a high back shot to me. These hits above the spine, which deliver a shock to the spinal cord but do no permanent neurological damage, very seldom yield a deer that can ever be recovered. I said as much to Paul, but he begged me to come and check it out. He would not be able to sleep until he knew for sure what had happened. The site was

Elli with Ryan Blothenburg's 10 point buck. Author at left, Ryan at right.

only 15 miles away, so I met Paul there with Sabina, my most experienced tracking Dachshund.

It was tough to track past Paul's point of loss because the buck had abruptly changed direction. We "picked" the line across windswept open fields, finding occasional drops of blood to show that we were on the right track. The buck went across a major highway onto another property; with permission of the landowner, we tracked through thick cover, across a stream to a small, wooded plateau. There Sabina barked as the buck left his bed and we found that it contained only a small amount of blood. Eighteen hours had now passed since the shot, and from his actions the buck showed that he was strong and very likely to survive.

Paul had expected as much, and he seemed more relieved than disappointed. As he put it, he had closure, at least. There would be no nagging worries that his deer was dead or dying in a thicket, where only the coyotes would find and appreciate it.

Wildlife managers on deer leases, ranches and landowner associations are also concerned about the status of individual deer, although they can't afford to be as emotional about it as Ryan and Paul. When there is an intensive quality deer management in a localized area, it is important to know the status of each deer and especially the trophy deer. Is "Old Stickers" growing even bigger for next year or is he dead, wasted and out of the breeding herd? For the wildlife manager, the information provided by the tracking team, dog and observant handler, is valuable, even if there is no find and the deer does not end up on the meat pole. Trail cameras are important, but the tracking dog also plays a role.

There is more than one motivation for making every effort to find, or to account for every wounded deer. The reasons are almost as complex as the reasons why we hunt in the first place. Why do some hunters direct their passion into tracking those deer that are wounded? We can give clear and logical explanations, but some of the deep, driving forces motivating hunters and trackers are difficult to express. We have mixed feelings. When we are following a wounded deer, we become two different creatures at once. When we track, there is something of the predator in our feelings. The tracker is a hunter too, and we are a part of the natural world, "wild" humans seeking to track down our game before some wilder coyote finds it and devours it.

At the same time, we have another desire to do what is "right", although we know that this ethical sense comes from our civilized background and not from the natural world. We are aware that the natural world is cruel, that the lives of wild animals are destined to end through violence, disease or starvation. However, this does not change our conviction that we should intervene with a tracking dog, when this will reduce suffering, and when this will prevent waste. As hunters, and as trackers, we are predators, but we can be more humane predators than wolves and coyotes. We are predators ethically responsible for how we treat our prey. We are on the edge between the natural and the civilized worlds.

Appendix A

List of Equipment Suppliers

These suppliers and manufacturers are mentioned in the text, and they were offering the products that were referred to as of June 2015. In many cases, there are other manufacturers and suppliers of equal merit. This list is not intended to cover all the possible sources for the equipment that you may need.

In this age of the Internet, the reader is not limited to the suppliers listed below. A Google search will often turn up a supplier for the item you need. If you seek German equipment and find it unavailable in North America, it is always possible to purchase it online directly from Germany. To do this you must type in the appropriate German names as Google search words. For example, you would enter *Schweissriemen* or *Schweißriemen* if you were searching for a tracking leash. Tracking collar translates as *Schweisshalsung, Schweißhalsung* or *Schweißhundehalsung,* and *Fährtenschuh* is the German word for scent shoe.

Backcountry www.backcountry.com
2607 South 3200 West Suite A, West Valley, UT 84119; 1-800-409-4502;
The online retailer offers a broad selection of "recreational" ropes; some of them are suitable for tracking leash material.

Back Country Gear www.backcountrygear.com
1855 West 2nd Ave., Eugene, OR 97402, 1-800-953-5499
A good souce of mountain climbing ropes for tracking leashes.

Battery Junction.com www.batteryjunction.com
52 Donnelly Rd., Old Saybrook, CT 06475; 860-767-8888;
Wide selection of batteries and LED lights to be ordered online.

Bright Eyes Lights www.brighteyeslights.com
5061 Williamson Road, Rock Hill, SC 29730; 1-888-225-747;
Company makes and sells powerful lights suitable for tracking work.

Bushnell Performance Optics www.bushnell.com
9200 Cody, Overland Park, KS 66214; 1-800-423-3537;
Manufactures scopes, holographic sights.

Cabela's www.cabelas.com
400 E. Avenue A, Oshkosh, NE 69190; 1-800-237-4444;
Company sells hunting clothing, footwear, shooting accessories.

CSP Forestry www.cspforestry.com
(800) 592-6940;
Company sells forestry and engineering supplies including biogradable flagging tape.

E. Arthur Brown Company www.eabco.com
4088 County Road NW, Garfield, MN 56332, 320-950-9088;
Successor to Thompson Center Arms, barrels and some other accessories.

Eastern Mountain Sports www.ems.com
One Vose Farm Rd., Peterborough, NH 03458; 1-888-463-6367;
Source for mountain climbing rope, 80 retail stores around USA.

Filson www.filson.com
P.O. Box 34020, Seattle WA 98124; 1-800-624-0201;
Company manufactures and sells tough vests and other clothes for tough country. Products also sold by firms like Cabela's.

Foster & Smith www.drsfostersmith.com
2253 Air Park Road, P.O. Box 100, Rhinelander, WI 54501-0100; 1-800-381-7179;
Company sells many dog products.

Garmin International www.garmin.com
1200 E. 151st Street, Olathe KS 66062; (800) 800-1020
Company manufactures handhelds, collars for dog tracking and training, wearable devices etc.

GoPro www.gopro.com
1-888-600-4659
Manufacturer and distributer of GoPro action video cameras.

Gun Dog Supply www.gundogsupply.com
P.O. Box 80133, Starkville, MS 39759; 1-800-624-6378
Online vendor sells dog training supplies, including dog chest protectors.

James E. Mills mills_james@hotmail.com
606-305-4780
Custom made European style leashes, integral collar quick release leashes, various kinds of leather and synthetic tracking leashes.

Leerburg www.leerburg.com
PO Box 218, Menomonie, WI 54751; 715-235-6502
DVDs, videos on demand and online courses about dog training (for example the use of e-collars), also dog equipment and books.

L. L. Bean; www.llbean.com
1-800-441-5713;
Company sells hunting clothing and footwear, hunting dog supplies.

Master's Voice www.mastersvoice-dog.com
#17 Eagles Way Lane; Lake St. Louis, MO 63367; 1-800-520-8463;
Company produces and sells audio-tapes and CDs for conditioning dogs to prevent gunshyness.

New England Ropes www.neropes.com
848 Airport Road, Fall River, MA 02720; 508-678-8200; neropes@neropes.com
Company manufactures and sells rope suitable for tracking leashes.

Nite Lite www.huntsmart.com
Massengale Rd., Clarksville, AR 72830; (479) 754-5540; 1-800-332-6968;
Company sells variety of lights and hunting dog equipment.

Pistol Packaging Inc. www.pistolpackaging.com
5020 Highway 12, Maple Plain, MN 55359; 1-800-545-8016;
Company manufactures leather shoulder holsters for handguns.

Pivothead Wearable Imaging www.pivothead.com
Recording eyeware that captures hands-free first-person video.

Raymond Holohan rantler@ameritech.net
815-694-3767
Buck Shock Tracking Shoes avaialble in two sizes.

Ruffwear www.ruffwear.com
2843 NW Lolo Drive, Bend, OR 97701, 888-783-3932.
Manufacturer and distributor of popular dog harnesses.

Sicherheit für Alle GMBH www.sfa-bodoband.de
Vor dem Borstel 20 - 29646 Bispingen-Hützel, Germany; 49 5194 1484
Company sells a broad range of blood tracking equipment.

Stone Creek Hounds Hunting Supplies www.stonecreekhounds.com
R.D. #1, Box 29C, Hesston, PA 16647, 814-627-2316
Heavy Cordura nylon clothing for briar busting, hunting dog supplies.

The Sportsman's Guide www.sportsmansguide.com
411 Farwell Ave., So. St Paul, MN 55075;1-800-888-3006;
A good source for cheap but good LED hunter's lights.

Truglo, Inc.   www.truglo.com
Company manufactures sights for low-light conditions.

United Blood Trackers (UBT)   www.unitedbloodtrackers.org
Online store sells tracking dog supplies.

United States Plastic Corp.   www.usplastic.com
390 Neubrecht Road, Lima. Ohio 45801; 800-537-9724;
Plastic squeeze bottles for laying training blood line.

Waidewerk   www.waidwerk.de
Telefon (0 79 45) 94 10 100, Fax (0 79 45) 94 10 200 sells a wide range of German tracking equipment, including tracking shoes, and they have English speaking staff members.

Wildlife Materials International, Inc.   www.wildlifematerials.com
1202 Walnut St., Murphysboro, IL 62966; 1-800-842-453
Company manufactures and sells radio tracking collars.

Williams Gun Sight Company   www.williamsgunsight.com
7389 Lapeer Road, P.O. Box 329, Davison, MI 48423 1-800-530-9028,
Company manufactures and sells very durable "Fire Sights" for low-light conditions.

Appendix B

United Blood Trackers Inc.
20-Hour Artificial Blood Tracking Test (UBT-20)

Section I.   *Admission*

1. Dogs of any breed or combination of breeds are eligible for the test.
2. All dogs must be at least one year old.
3. The entry fees shall be established and announced by UBT.
4. A dog is not eligible to be entered under any judge that has bred,owned, boarded, trained, or handled the dog within 12 months prior to the date of the test.
5. No more than six dogs may be judged in the Artificial Blood Tracking Test on any given day.

Section II.   *Requirements for Judges*

1. Three judges are required for this test.
2. Judges must be approved by the UBT Board of Directors.
3. The chief judge must be a UBT member.

Section III.   *Preparation of the Track*

1. The track will be at least 1000 yards in length and will incorporate three (3) 90-degree turns. The track will stand at least 20 hours and must be laid in game-rich areas. The track will start in an area as natural as possible, e.g. deer trails or near the edge of pastures or fields.
2. Two (2) wound beds shall be distinctly marked on the track. These wound beds will not be placed within 50 yards of the 90 degree turns. The preparation of the wound bed will be made by clearing away all leaves and sticks to form a circle of bare ground at least one yard in diameter. Deer hair will be placed in the wound bed.
3. One of the test judges must be present either when the trail is marked or when the blood is placed.
4. Blood will either be dripped from a squeeze bottle or dabbed with a small sponge on a stick, approximately every three feet. The same technique will be used for all lines at an event and will be described in the official announcement of the test.
5. The blood lines for the test may not be laid on snow-covered grounds. At the judges' discretion, the lines may be run if some snow covers blood lines laid previously on bare ground.

6. Persons knowing the course of the track are not permitted to handle a dog in that test. If blood tracking tests are held repeatedly in one area, the course of the track must be altered each time.

Section IV.   Blood

1. A maximum of 8 ounces of blood will be used.
2. If possible, deer blood should be used. Chemical additives are not permitted. Deer blood, which has been frozen after collection, may be used.

Section V.   Dead Game Placed at the End of the Track

Normally a deer hide (if previously frozen, the hide must be thawed) will be placed at the end of the track shortly before the dog begins to work. An entire deer or fawn carcass, may be used. Track layers should consider the wind, or likely wind direction, so that the dog does not air scent the "deer" until he approaches it; however, the dog will not be penalized if he leaves the blood line and follows air scent to the "deer".

Section VI.   Evaluation of Performance

1. During the test, the dog must wear a tracking collar or harness attached to a leash which will be at least 18 feet, but no more than 50 feet, in length. The handler must be at a sufficient distance behind the dog to allow the judges to determine that the handler is not guiding the dog. When evaluating the performance of the dog, the judges will observe the behavior at the beginning of the track and the working style during the track, including any corrective actions taken to regain the line.
2. The handler will be shown the start and direction of the track by the judge.
3. Two call backs by the judges are allowed. A third call back will cause the dog to fail the test. If a dog has lost the track, it will be given sufficient time to correct itself. For this reason, the judges will make a call back only if the dog has clearly been out of contact with the line for 75 yards. The judges' behavior must not give any indication that the dog has lost the track. Corrections can be made by the handler. The handler may pick up the dog or lead the dog to the area that the dog was on the line; however, the handler must first announce his intention to do this to the judges. Repeatedly picking up the dog without explanation will result in the deduction of points or failure of the test, even if the "deer" is found. If the dog is called back, the judges should announce to the handler that it is a call back, and indicate the point where the tracking team left the line.
4. The test may be terminated when the performance can no longer be considered successful.

Section VII. Prize Classifications

The following categories of performance are tested and evaluated:
- A) Steadiness and Concentration (Multiplier number: 10)
- B) Tracking Accuracy (Multiplier number: 8)
- C) Willingness to Track (Multiplier number: 7)

Awarded Score Numbers
0 Unsatisfactory
1 Needs Improvement
2 Satisfactory
3 Good
4 Outstanding

The table of prize requirements below is intended as a guideline rather than a rigid framework in which a dog's performance is to be judged. Extenuating circumstances may be taken into consideration. For example on a dry, windy day tracking accuracy cannot be expected to be as good as when scenting conditions are good.

Minimum Requirements for a First Prize

	Index	Score	Points
Steadiness and Concentration	10	4	40
Tracking Accuracy	8	3	24
Willingness to Track	7	3	21
Total Points			85

Minimum Requirements for a Second Prize

	Index	Score	Points
Steadiness and Concentration	10	3	30
Tracking Accuracy	8	3	24
Willingness to Track	7	2	14
Total Points			68

Minimum Requirements for a Third Prize

	Index	Score	Points
Steadiness and Concentration	10	2	20
Tracking Accuracy	8	2	16
Willingness to Track	7	2	14
Total Points			50

Section VIII. Guidelines for Judging the Artificial Blood Track Test

General Commentary:

The speed and the body language with which dogs track differs from breed to breed and between individuals within a breed. Judges must be aware of differences in canine character and make appropriate allowances. For example, a Dachshund will generally show much more interest in the "deer" than a Lab or a cur.

Some dogs, pointing dogs for example, will generally work a line faster and less closely than a Dachshund. Judges should evaluate dogs on the basis of their effectiveness in finding game, not in terms of their conformity to a single model of working style. Still, if a dog works at an extremely rapid pace, the handler will not be able to observe the blood sign. A dog should not work at such an extremely rapid pace that in steep and wet terrain the dog would put the handler at risk of a fall. The dog being tested should be responsive to the handler's desire to move at an appropriate pace.

The number of "call backs" that a dog receives is one of the criteria for scoring a dog, but it is not the only one. For example, it is not required that a dog having 0 or 1 call-backs be given a "4" or a "3". A dog is also judged for its ability to stay in close contact with the blood line, to quickly recognize that it is off the line, and to efficiently return to the point of loss. A dog that parallels the line in a way that cannot be explained by wind drift, or a dog that overshoots turns by 50 yards, does not deserve the highest score for tracking accuracy even though the dog stays within the 75 yard limit at all times.

These guidelines are not applicable in all cases. For example, a dog may have no "call-backs" for clearly being out of contact with the line for over 75 yards, and yet may exhibit a lack of accuracy. Different varieties of dogs will show different working speeds, which should be taken into consideration.

Steadiness and Concentration

Score	
0	Dog does not attempt to track blood trail.
1	Dog attempts to track the blood line. Dog does not find the "deer" without numerous corrections from the handler and/or judges. Dog does not concentrate on the blood line.
2	Dog tracks the blood line too fast for accuracy and observation of sign by the handler. At the other extreme, the dog wastes time with needless pottering or periodically stops working. The dog concentrates on the blood line most of the time. Dog finds the "deer" with some corrections from the handler.
3	Dog tracks the blood line at a pace that would be appropriate for tracking a wounded deer. Dog is able to find the "deer" with little aid of the handler. Dog concentrates on the blood line very well with minor distractions and needs very little encouragement from the handler.
4	Dog tracks the blood line at a pace that would be appropriate for tracking a wounded deer. Dog is focused on the line at all times. Dog finds the "deer" without the aid of the handler. Dog needs no encouragement from the handler. Dog pays no attention to distractions and responds very little to hot deer tracks.
Note: If a dog does not work at a moderate pace, the handler will not be able to observe the blood sign.	

Tracking Accuracy

Score	
0	Dog acts as though it does not know what is expected of it.
1	Dog and is out of contact with the blood line in excess of 75 yards up to three times. Dog does not indicate the presence of the blood line.
2	Dog leaves the blood line in excess of 75 yards up to two times. Dog indicates the presence of the blood line.
3	Dog leaves the blood line in excess of 75 yards not more than once. Dog indicates blood sign on the line.
4	Dog works very close to the blood line at all times and the judges never have to call him back to the line. Dog finds and indicates blood sign and wound beds.

Willingness to Track

Score	
0	Dog is not willing to track the blood trail.
1	Dog is at first eager to track the blood line, but loses interest after a short while.
2	Dog is eager to track the blood line, but loses interest when other game tracks cross the line. The dog shows no interest when the "deer" is found.
3	Dog is eager to track the blood line. Dog shows that it likes to work the trail. Dog shows some interest when the "deer" is found.
4	Dog is eager to track the blood line. Dog does not lose interest in the track in hot or cold weather. Dog shows a great deal of interest when the "deer" is found.

Appendix C

United Blood Trackers Inc.
UBT III Evaluation

This is a pass/fail evaluation designed to demonstrate an experienced tracking dog and his handler's ability to solve together the problems that come up in natural tracking. Distractions are consciously introduced to judge the steadiness of the dog. UBT III is a one judge evaluation that does not require laying the scent line a long time in advance.

Purpose
The UBT-III demonstrates the ability to resolve situations often encountered on natural tracks. The test is designed to be both challenging and fun. Each test is likely to be unique, and handling teams may wish to take the test on multiple occasions.

Length
About ½ mile (800-1000 yards). The team's solution to the Directional Challenge may have an impact on the distance traveled.

Age
At least 4 hours. The emphasis of this test is the team's ability to resolve challenging situations, not on tracking cold trails.

Obstacles
Tracks may have 3-5 turns or arcs of any degree in addition to three of the challenges listed below. In addition, there will be 5 sign articles on the track. Examples of sign include bone fragments, hide, hair, blood on a broken branch, wound bed, etc. and will be indicated with a recoverable marker. The handler will pick up and return with any markers they encounter. A designation will be made on certificates issued to handling teams returning 3 or more articles. Judges will select one obstacle from each of the following categories (total of three), based on test site accommodations:

Directional Challenges (select one): star, circle or spiral configuration with random exit, loop with continuation, weaving up and down three or more standing corn or pine rows, back track or hairpin turn of 20 yards or more. Other challenging and realistic configurations may be used at the judge's discretion.

Surface Challenges (select one): track will cross or follow - water (less than knee deep for handler), very rocky terrain, paved or gravel road, paved driveway or parking area, or at least 10 yards on - bare or plowed ground, marsh/wetland or mud. Other challenging and realistic surfaces may be used at the judge's discretion.

Distracting Challenges (select one):
1. A dead animal (deer part or road kill) or a live animal (horse, goat, etc.) may be dragged or walked across the track after it has been laid.
2. Another dog may be walked 25 yards out and back from the start of the track, simulating another dog that was with the hunter.
3. The tracking dog may be stopped and kept waiting for five minutes at any point on the track, at the judge's command, simulating a wait for permission to cross property lines before resuming the track.
4. A car horn can be honked nearby periodically for at least three minutes.
5. The handler may be asked to leave the track by ten yards and to wait for two minutes, at the judge's command, before resuming tracking. This simulates injury or a need to adjust equipment.
6. A dead animal or gut pile may be placed within a yard of the track.
7. Other realistic distractions that a tracking team might find in the area of the test may be used. These must be legal and not dangerous.

Prerequisite
Successful completion of the UBT-II may be required, at the judge's discretion.

Preparation and Execution
Approximately 8 ounces of blood without the use of tracking shoes, or 3 ounces of blood with the use of tracking shoes, will be used over the course of the track. The handler will be shown the start, and given the general direction of the track.

Appendix D

The Schutzhund Approach to Training for Tracking

In this book it has been pointed out that some dogs do not learn well under training methods that assume that they have a natural, genetically based desire to track. This has been a problem with some of the versatile hunting dogs that are expected to range out well and wind scent birds, and then in another mode get their head down and slowly work out an old, cold blood line. Sometimes their "birdiness" is much stronger than their desire to track. There is some doubt in my own mind as to whether these high-headed super-birdy pointing dogs can ever be trained to be first class natural deer finders. But there is no doubt that they can be trained to excel in formal blood tracking tests and to be useful, if not outstanding, natural trackers.

Marty Ryan, a leading trainer and workshop leader in the Verein Deutsch Drahthaar, investigated the German method for teaching German Shepherds to man track; he adapted this "Schutzhund" method to the training of those Drahthaars that did not show natural aptitude and desire to work with a "deep nose" and to track an old line slowly and precisely. Marty acknowledges that much of the inspiration for his own method came from William Koehler and from Ed Frawley, whose Leerburg training videos helped to present the German Schutzhund approach to Americans.

In The Koehler *Method of Training Tracking Dogs* (1984), which deals with man tracking, not blood tracking, the author wrote, "If you have believed that training your dog was limited to only awakening and encouraging your dogs natural abilities, and you watched him bomb in a half dozen trials because he needed something more than 'natural desires,' this book can show you a realistic approach to the problem."

Ed Frawley's Leerburg Video 203 is entitled *Training a Competition Tracking Dog*. It focuses on man tracking with German Shepherds, and I think that is excellent for its intended purpose. Like William Koehler, Frawley does not rely on natural desire as a motivation. He states right at the beginning of Video 203 that "Tracking is an obedience exercise."

Frawley's training method is highly structured. The dog being trained is first commanded to track a short, fresh "scuffed in" track laid by his handler. Pieces of hot dog to reward the dog, are laid at close intervals along the line; the command emphasis, enforced with a short leash, is on working every inch of the line with precision and a deep nose. If the dog sniffs off the line, he is corrected. It is an obedience exercise. The length and age of the track is increased by small increments, but the slow, precise working style is always maintained with the same balance of discipline and reward. The exercises are short but repeated several times a day. Whether the dog becomes bored in the process is irrelevant.

Marty Ryan's adaptation of the Frawley/Schutzhund tracking approach begins with the same scuffed-in handler's track, which must be followed exactly. Marty uses the Leerburg training video in his own training workshops, but later moves beyond that format when he begins to dab deer blood along the footsteps of the training line. It would be a logical extension of this training approach to introduce the Fährtenschu, described in Chapter 12, at some advanced point in this training.

This Schutzhund-derived training approach is almost diametrically opposed to the methods that I advocate in my training chapters. It's important to realize that the two training systems have very different purposes and goals.

First, Marty Ryan's approach is designed for those versatile pointing dogs that excel in bird work, but may not have much natural inclination to track.

Another important difference is that the more traditional training method, advocated in my book has the goal of developing a dog with the initiative to solve difficult natural tracking problems in which the handler has no idea where the wounded deer actually went. He does not want a dog, who expects to be guided and corrected on a difficult check. He wants a dog that will "reach" intelligently to find the line again through water or on an actively used ATV trail.

Winning tracking competitions and finding difficult wounded deer are two very different things. There are dogs, who can do one much better than the other. Frequently an experienced veteran tracking dog begins to decline as a competition dog even as he improves in his natural work. He does not work as smoothly on a competition line; he is constantly checking for potential backtracks and other problems. He does not expect anything as straightforward and uncomplicated as a competition line because he has not been encountering this in his real world.

The owner of a dog lacking natural motivation to track has two choices. He can drop the idea of using him as a tracking dog, or he can train him by the structured obedience method.

The handler who puts wounded game tracking at the top of his list of priorities, will probably never be satisfied with a dog who lacks motivation and responds only to discipline. Such a dog is unlikely to show the initiative and die-hard persistence that is required in the most challenging tracking cases.

Other dog handlers emphasize versatility over specialized excellence in natural tracking. If they are primarily bird hunters, they may be satisfied with less than a top tracking dog. They are looking for a dog, who has a basic competence in natural tracking, if it is needed, and who can also do well on artificial blood tracking tests. This is a defensible position.

We should never forget that a dog that has to be commanded to track, is going to improve his natural skills through experience if he gets enough of it. His initiative and drive are likely to improve even though this was not encouraged in his early training.

Appendix E

Training with an Electronic Collar

In Chapter 23, "The Tracking Dog in the Family", we introduced the problems of exercising a tracking dog off lead. A dog with a strong desire to hunt will usually take off for the horizon, hunting on his own. Customary obedience training or "yard training", in itself, will not be enough to prevent this. The electronic collar, generally referred to as the e-collar, is the most effective way of making the dog realize that he still has to obey, even if eye contact has been broken. Dogs do not understand the "Big Magic" of the e-collar, which can reach out for 100s of yards to reinforce verbal commands or whistle beeps, but they quickly associate the sharp tingling sensation with ignoring the commands that come from the boss. They come to understand that they are hunting partners with the handler, only when they stay within the basic structure of his discipline.

The e-collar is not a substitute for obedience training. For example the dog should never be reprimanded with an unpleasant shock until he understands very clearly what "come" means. The standard approach is to train the dog to "come" by putting him on a sit-stay and then calling him a few feet to return to the handler. Sometimes this is referred to as training to "recall". First this is done on an ordinary walking leash. The next step is to go over the same lesson at a greater distance using a check cord of 20 to 40 feet. If you have a good relationship with the dog, there should be no need for a choke collar or prong collar. If you have eye contact with the dog, a tug on the cord, as the command is given, should suffice. Enthusiastic praise can serve as a reward, or you can supplement this with a small treat. I find that the treat is usually not necessary, but everything depends upon your relationship with your dog. If you use the check cord (not your tracking leash) while you have eye contact at forty feet, there is seldom a problem unless you try to rush things. It is normal for a dog to take 30 repetitions to get a command/response exercise though his head. Of course you should not attempt to cram all this into one lesson. The repetitions should be extended over several days of short sessions, which hold the dog's interest.

When it is crystal clear to the dog that he is supposed to come when called, you then can begin to use the e-collar with great care. It is a good idea to familiarize the dog with the weight and smell of the collar around his neck a week or so before the "e-day", but by no means give the dog any exposure to the electrical stimulation.

This brief appendix section is not the place to present complete instructions on how an e-collar should be used. Manufacturers of e-collars send their products to buyers with detailed recommendations set forth in a training booklet and also in a training video. These details for training are very important, but they are too lengthy for this appendix, which is intended only to give the reader an overview of recall training with an e-collar.

Before I use the e-collar on the dog, I like to try it on myself. I begin at the lowest setting and then work up one or two levels until the stimulation is mildly annoying to me. (I do not want to subject the dog to a violent, painful shock.) The individual dog's neck may be more or less sensitive than my own fingers, but this experiment will give me some sense of how the sensation increases as you move from one setting to another. When the e-collar is placed on the dog, it should be adjusted so that the two electrodes are in direct contact with the skin of his neck. This means that the e-collar has to be tighter than what would be appropriate for the dog's everyday collar.

As you make the transition from check cord to e-collar recall training, you should keep both items on the dog at the same time for several sessions. Then you can call, tug and give a mild electrical stimulation, all at the same time. Quickly the dog associates the mild stimulation with the tug on the check cord. They both mean the same thing to him because they occur simultaneously with the spoken command. Now you are ready to set aside the check cord and go to the open field.

For the details of e-training in the field you should consult the manufacturer's manual and video. The better e-collars have both a momentary and a continuous stimulation mode and in addition a vibration mode. Details of training techniques depend on the technical features of the collar you acquire. Avoid cheap, pet store products that do not include detailed instructions, and which do not state all of the necessary precautions to be taken.

All collar manufacturers seem to agree that the e-collar should be kept on the dog in training for a considerable time after it seems no longer necessary. Dogs have a way of relapsing or forgetting, especially when they are exposed to a powerful distraction. They can be reminded of their training by a vibration signal, followed by the electric shock if needed.

E-collars have many uses, both as a means of teaching a dog to perform, to come or to sit, and in teaching a dog not to do certain things. The manuals I have read do a good job of explaining how a dog is taught to do, or not to do, certain things.

However, the trainer of a tracking dog may face a situation that is not treated by the e-collar training manuals. How do you make your dog realize that it is "good" to track a wounded deer, but "bad" to chase a healthy deer? You don't want to come down with a hard electronic reprimand when he takes off on a healthy deer. This could end up turning him off tracking wounded deer as well.

The best approach is to avoid the whole problem before it develops to a point where the e-collar is necessary at all. Most of the time positive reinforcement for staying on the right line is enough to make the dog realize that his partnership with his handler only works if focus is maintained on the object of the search.

I have had only one experience with a dog that needed more than the positive reinforcement approach. Oslo was a Wirehaired Dachshund from eastern France, who had tremendous hunting desire. Oslo was firmly convinced that all wild game existed only for him to chase.

The first step was to teach Oslo basic recall in the field, as explained in the first part of this appendix. With Oslo this was not easy. Once Oslo was reliable on recall at a distance, I drove around until I spotted deer in a field. Then I would park the truck, and walk with Oslo off lead to the area where the deer had been feeding. When he reacted to the hot deer scent and began to follow a hot line, I would call him. When Oslo ignored my "Oslo come!", I "nicked" him with the e-collar set on a rather stiff level. I assume that Oslo associated the electrical jolt with his conscious act of ignoring his handler's command to come, even when he wanted to chase those deer so much.

I can only speculate about what actually went on in Oslo's head, but after three field sessions he began to turn back from a hot deer line at my call even when no electronic reminder was used. Oslo did go on to successfully track and find wounded deer, but he never became a top tracking dog. He lacked the calm focus and patience to work an old, cold line.

My experience with Oslo, many years ago, probably taught me more than it taught him. The e-collar is not the easy solution to all problems. It can only be useful if it is preceded by basic obedience training so that the dog understands clearly what he is supposed to do.

One other important point about the e-collar: used in ignorance or in anger, it can do serious psychological damage. Badly used it can permanently destroy the essential trust and affection that underlies the handler/tracking dog relationship. A tracking dog cannot be an electronically controlled robot, as some field trial retrievers appear to be. He must be ready to take the initiative, with no fear that the electronic wrath of God is about to strike him. In my own opinion the e-collar has no place whatever on a dog that is actually working a training line or the track of a real wounded deer.

There are numerous makes of e-collars; most, but not all of these are reliable. I would recommend an American-made collar from a manufacturer who maintains good support and repair services. The Tri-Tronics and Dogtra e-collars are well-respected by serious dog trainers, and they are sold through most mail order hunting catalogs. The Garmin Alpha collar combines a GPS system with the e-colllar. This is very useful for those who track off lead. With the Garmin Alpha the handler knows where his dog is located, and he can turn him away from danger.

Your choice of weight and model depend upon the size of your dog and the various ways in which you wish to use it as a training device. For example a big, heavy collar, designed for use at very long range to break coonhounds from running deer, is not what you should buy for use on a Beagle or Dachshund.

Appendix F

Blood Tracking Organizations in North America

United Blood Trackers
www.unitedbloodtrackers.org

This is a national, multi-breed blood tracking organization founded in 2005. UBT offers annual seminars (Trackfests) around the United States and gives advice on tracking and training through its website: www.unitedbloodtrackers.org and Facebook page www.facebook.com/unitedbloodtrackers and group www.facebook.com/groups/unitedbloodtrackers/.

One of the most useful features of the UBT website is the "Find a Tracker" page. A hunter in need of tracking services can go to the map of the United States, click on the state he is hunting in and find a list of the trackers and their contact info in that state.

UBT offers a series of blood tracking tests for dogs, and one of these, UBT-I, is a requirement for Michigan handlers who will track with an armed hunter. UBT offers simple, very elementary tracking tests like UBT-I and more advanced tests like UBT-20 that are comparable to tracking tests that have international recognition.

UBT is active in promoting blood tracking on a nationwide basis. Those who are campaigning for legalization in "new" states need information to help DNR officials and lawmakers understand how blood tracking has worked elsewhere. UBT provides that information.

Deer Search Inc.
www.deersearch.org

Deer Search was founded in 1978 as an organization of tracking dog handlers who were participating in a research project on the use of tracking dogs. This was authorized by a research permit issued by the New York State Department of Environmental Conservation (NYSDEC) to John Jeanneney. The research led to legalization of tracking dogs to find deer and bear. New York State was the first state in the North to legalize, and this example led to many other state legalizations.

Deer Search has remained a New York based organization, but it welcomes out of state members.

The organization acts as a dispatching agent bringing trackers and hunters together. It trains new handlers and tests tracking dogs. Deer Search hosts an annual blood tracking competition and serves as a liaison for communications with NYSDEC.

Deer Search began as a non-profit corporation that was later divided into chapters. The Western New York Chapter was created as an expansion of the original Founding Chapter in eastern New York. Then a Finger Lakes Chapter was organized for central New York.

Currently (2016) the chapters are separate, non-profit corporations that must be contacted individually through their websites. For eastern New York go to www.deersearch.org. For central New York, go to www.deersearchflc.com, and for western New York go to: www.deersearchwny.com/.

Texas Blood Trackers
www.texasbloodtrackers.com

Texas Blood Trackers is a Texas-based, multi-breed organization that also has members in the southern states to the east of Texas. It conducts training workshops, and three tracking tests of increasing difficulty that can be taken on or off lead.

The TBT website lists trackers and their locations. It is an important means of bringing hunters and trackers together.

Association des Conducteurs de Chiens de Sang du Québec
www.ACCSQ.com

This multi-breed tracking association operates in French, and its title can be translated as the Quebec Association of Tracking Dog Handlers, (ACCSQ). This is an organization with strong leadership that has a very productive relationship with the Quebec ministry governing wildlife affairs. Its educational and promotional formations (tracking workshops) are the best that I have observed in North America. The ACCSQ tracking statistics for the years 2009-2012 are detailed and very informative.

The web site includes a map showing the locations of tracking dog teams. A hunter can click on the nearest tracker icon and find the contact information needed. Most of the ACCSQ trackers are located in the broad St Lawrence River Valley of southern Quebec.

Big Game Blood Trackers of Ontario
www.biggamesearchon.com

Big Game Blood Trackers of Ontario (BGBTO) is a small organization formed in 2012 to promote blood tracking in a province where this was legalized only recently. Modifications of the Ontario tracking regulations are needed if they are to function efficiently, and BGBTO is working to enlighten the Ministry on this matter.

As of 2016 BGBTO is still at a stage where their primary objective is to attract and train new members so that there will be enough handlers and tracking dogs to serve the vast expanse of the province.

Organizations Offering Blood Tracking Tests

Check to make sure that your dog is of the correct breed and registration. In alphabethical order:

Club des Amateurs du Teckel de Canada, CATC

The Club des Amateurs de Teckel du Canada was founded by Patrick Mestadier, a certified judge of tracking tests in France. The CATC follows closely the testing procedures of the Federation Cynologique Internationale, FCI but the CATC organization and its test results are not officially recognized by the FCI. CATC is not directly affiliated with the French FCI teckel club. This complicated situation is the consequence of international agreements including those between the FCI and the Canadian Kennel Club.

With regard to testing, the CATC serves as a multi-breed organization. Dogs of FCI recognized breeds, such as Drahthaars and Bavarian Mountain Hounds are welcome in the CATC tests, but of course the results are not recognized by the FCI.

Jagdgebrauchshund-verein/USA
www.jgv-usa.org

The Jagdgebrauchshundverein-USA (JGV-USA) offers tracking tests for hunting dogs registered with the International Cynological Federation (FCI). Dachshunds with FCI registration are eligible for the Verband Schweiss Test (VSwP).

Klub für Bayerische Gebirgsschweißhunde
Arbeitsgruppe Nord Amerika
www.hillockkennels.com/breeding_and_importing.html

The KBGS-GNA in North America offers advanced blood tracking test for the BGS following the rules and regulations set forth by the the parent club in Germany (KBGS) and the JGHV. The dogs must be registered with the parent club in Germany. Numerous BMH dogs in the USA do not have the KBGS registration, and these dogs are not eligible for the tests.

North American Teckel Club
www.teckelclub.org

The North American Teckel Club is a "Group" within the Deutscher Teckelklub based in Germany. "Teckel" is one of the words the Germans use for their Dachshund. Once a year NATC offers blood tracking tests, and AKC registered Dachshunds are eligible to participate. The NATC tests and the Zuchtschau (breed show) are good occasions to learn about the European conception of the Dachshund.

Texas Trackers
www.texastrackers.com

Texas Blood Trackers has three tests of increasing difficulty that are especially designed for dogs working off lead. Handlers can work their dogs on lead, if they choose.

United Blood Trackers
www.unitedbloodtrackers.org

United Blood Trackers offers a series of blood tracking tests which are open to all breeds and mixed breeds. UBT I and UBT II are tests for beginner dogs and handlers. UBT- 20 is similar to other 20 hour tests of European origin. UBT III is a unique test designed to evaluate the stability and initiative of the mature, experienced tracking dog.

Verein Deutsch-Drahthaar
www. vdd-gna.org
Verein Deutsch-Kurzhaar
www.nadkc.org

The Verein Deutsch Drahthaar, Group North America, VDD-GNA, and the Verein Deutsch Kurzhaar, Group North America, VDK-GNA, are extensions of the German FCI breed clubs for German Wirehaired Pointers and German Shorthaired Pointers. These organizations offer advanced blood tracking tests following the rules of the parent testing organization, JGHV.

Appendix G

New York State Department of Environmental Conservation Division of Fish, Wildlife & Marine Resources Special Licenses, 5th Floor, 625 Broadway, Albany, New York 12233-4752 Phone: (518) 402-8985 • FAX: (518) 402-8925
Website: www.dec.state.ny.us

NYS Department of Environmental Conservation
Part 176: Leashed Tracking Dogs

(Statutory authority: Environmental Conservation Law, § 11-0928)
[Effective date: Sept 6, 1989]
[Last Amended: Sept 16, 2002]

§176.1 Definitions

For the purposes of this Part, the following terms have the indicated meanings:

(a) Department means the Department of Environmental Conservation.

(b) Certified leashed tracking dog means a dog which is used to track and find dead, injured, or wounded big game pursuant to a license issued as provided by this Part and which is licensed and identified as required by Article 7 of the Agriculture and Markets Law.

(c) License means a leashed tracking dog license issued pursuant to this Part, authorizing use of certified leashed tracking dogs as specified in this Part.

(d) Licensee means a person who is the holder of a leashed tracking dog license.

(e) Physically incapacitated means incapable of participating in the hunt due to physical injury.

(f) Dispatch means to humanely kill.

(g) Where notification of the department is required, such notification shall be directed to the Division of Fish, Wildlife and Marine Resources, New York State Department of Environmental Conservation, 625 Broadway, Albany, NY 12233.

§176.2 Prohibition

Except as permitted by section 176.4 of this Part, no person may use a dog to track dead, wounded or injured big game.
§176.3 Leashed tracking dog license

A leashed tracking dog license issued by the department entitles the licensee:

(a) use certified leashed tracking dogs at any time, with or without the aid of an artificial light, to track and recover dead, wounded or injured big game during all big game seasons, including Saturdays and Sundays, and the 24-hour period immediately following the last day of a big game season;

(b) dispatch wounded or injured big game animals which have been tracked and found in accordance with and pursuant to the conditions of such license;

(c) temporarily possess a big game animal which has been dispatched by the licensee, or reduced to possession by the licensee, until lawfully tagged or until delivered to an Environmental Conservation Officer pursuant to the conditions of such license;

(d) use certified leashed tracking dogs at any time, with or without an artificial light, to track and recover big game which are:

(1) dead, wounded or injured as the result of activities authorized by permit issued under the authority of Environmental Conservation Law §11-0521 or under the authority of Environmental Conservation Law §11-0523; or

(2) dead, wounded or injured as the result of an accident.

§176.4 Leashed tracking dog license; conditions

(a) A big game hunter who has killed, wounded or injured, or reasonably believes he or she has killed, wounded or injured, a big game animal during a big game season may engage a licensee to track and recover the animal. The hunter must, unless physically incapacitated, accompany the licensee when tracking the dead, wounded or injured animal. If the hunter is physically incapacitated, the licensee may track and dispatch the animal if the licensee is personally carrying a written signed instrument from the hunter listing

(1) the date,

(2) the hunter's name, address, telephone number and big game license number, and

(3) a certification that the hunter has engaged the licensee to track the animal, that the hunter has killed, wounded or injured such animal, and that the hunter is unable to accompany the licensee because of physical incapacitation.

(b) No person other than the licensee or, during legal hunting periods, the big game hunter who has engaged the licensee when specifically so authorized by the licensee, may carry a firearm or long bow of any description while tracking dead, wounded or injured big game pursuant to this Part.

(c) During legal hunting periods, the hunter who has engaged the licensee must dispatch the wounded or injured big game animal when found by the licensee by means which are lawful during the season in which it was wounded or injured and in a lawful manner reduce the animal to legal possession. However, the licensee must dispatch the wounded or injured animal if the legal hunting period has ended, when the hunter is not present, or, when in the judgement of the licensee it is unsafe or otherwise inappropriate for the hunter to do so.

(d)The licensee may dispatch a wounded or injured big game animal, during day or night, using any firearm provided that the licensee complies with the provisions of applicable Federal, State, or local laws or regulations concerning the possession and use of firearms.

(e) Before tracking a dead, wounded or injured animal, the licensee must notify, by telephone or in person, the Environmental Conservation Officer assigned to the area, or if unavailable the nearest available Environmental Conservation Officer, where the big game animal was killed, wounded or injured. Notification must include the

1) name of the licensee,

2) name, address, telephone number, and big game license number of the big game hunter engaging the licensee,

3) general location of the wounded or injured animal, and

4) the name of the landowner(s) where the search will be conducted.

(f) The licensee must use only certified leashed tracking dogs when conducting activities pursuant to such license.

(g) The licensee must maintain physical control of the certified leashed tracking dog(s) at all times while conducting activities pursuant to such license by means of a lead attached to the dog's collar or harness. This lead must be at least twelve (12) feet in length.

(h) The licensee may not provide services for hire unless the licensee possesses a valid guide's license issued pursuant to 6 NYCRR Part 197.

(i) After a big game animal has been dispatched, the licensed hunter must immediately fill out the carcass tag as required by section 11-0911 of the Environmental Conservation Law. If the hunter has not accompanied the licensee because of physical incapacitation, the hunter must immediately fill out the carcass tag upon delivery of the animal by the licensee. If the hunter is unavailable the licensee must report the incident to an Environmental Conservation Officer and deliver the animal to the officer.

(j) The licensee must personally carry a current big game license and a valid leashed tracking dog license when conducting activities pursuant to this Part.

(k) The licensee must notify the department in writing, of any change of address within 30 days of that change of address.

(l) The licensee must submit to the department a written request for license renewal within the 30 days prior to the expiration of such license.

§176.5 Leashed tracking dog license; qualifications

The applicant for a license must:

(a) Provide proof of possession of a current New York big game hunting license;

(b) Not have been convicted of, or pled guilty to, an offense under the Fish and Wildlife Law, or settled by civil settlement or otherwise therefore, within the previous five years which resulted in a revocation of the person's big game, hunting, or archery license;

(c) Submit a non-refundable application fee of $25.00 and a completed application to the department to be eligible to take the written examination;

(d) Receive a grade of 80 percent or higher on a written examination administered by the department. The examination will be offered at least once a year and will test the applicant's knowledge of the Environmental Conservation Law and appropriate regulations, dog training and handling methods and other areas of knowledge as deemed appropriate or relevant by the department.

§176.6 Leashed tracking dog license; issuance

(a) Effective January 1, 2003, applicants who meet the qualifications for a license must submit a $50 license fee to the department.

(b) A license is valid for five years from the date of issuance.

(c) A license is valid only for the individual identified on the license and is not transferable.

(d) Licensees who fail to renew their license within one year of the date of expiration must reapply and meet all the qualifications set forth in section 176.5 of this Part.

(e) The department may, in its discretion, include special conditions in the license which it deems appropriate or necessary. It may also waive or dispense with any requirement of this Part when it deems it to be in the public interest to do so.

(f) The renewal fee for this license is $50.

Appendix H

Tracking Training Report

Dog's Name	Age of Dog
Tracking Experience	
Date & Time of Exercise	Location
Atmospheric Conditions	
Method of Laying the Track	
Age of Line	Length
Description of Line	
Amount of Blood	Marked/Blind?
Training Objective	
Dog's Performance	
Behavior at Skin	

Recommended Reading

• Brown, Tom Jr., *The Science and Art of Tracking*, New York: Berkley, 1999. Eyetracking on the highest level.

• Bulanda, Susan, *Scenting on the Wind. Scentwork for Hunting Dogs*, Sun City, AZ: Doral 2002.
Excellent on flow of game scent in varying atmospheric conditions.

• *Deer and Deer Hunting, Advanced Whitetail Details*, Iola, WI: Krause Publ., 1991. Slender book has color overlays of whitetail anatomy and valuable text on deer physiology.

• Duffey, David Michael, *Hunting Hounds, the History, Training and Selection of America's Trail, Tree and Sight Hounds*, New York: Winchester Press, 1972. Best overview of American hunting hounds.

• Fält, Lars, Gustavsson, Tobias et al., *Tracking Dogs, Scents and Skills*, SWDI Publishing, Lindesberg (Lithuania), 2015. This book does not deal specifically with wounded big game tracking, but there are some useful tidbits about the nature of scent. Most of it deals with highly structured man tracking dog training. There is little attention paid to a dog's natural motivation or initiative. This a a good read after you have been deer tracking for ten years.

• Pearsall, Milo D., Verbruggen, Hugo, M.D., *Scent, Training to Track, Search, and Rescue*, Loveland, CO: Alpine Publications, 1982.
About man tracking, but offers good analysis of scent and how dogs respond to it.

• Scott, John Paul, Fuller John L., *Genetics and the Social Behavior of the Dog*, Chicago: University of Chicago Press, 1965.
A complex treasury of background material about canine psychological development.

• Schettler, Jeff, *Red Dog Rising*, Alpine Publishing, 2009.

• Schettler, Jeff, K-9 Tracking, *The Straightest Path,* Alpine Publishing, 2011.
The two books by Jeff Schettler describe training and techniques for human tracking, but there is much information that a wounded big game tracker can use.

• Smith, Richard P. *Tracking Wounded Deer, How to Find and Tag Deer Shot with Bow and Gun*, Harrisburg, PA: Stackpole Books, 1988.
Basic and indispensable book for identifying different types of wounds in the field. Suggests productive strategies for finding wounded deer by eyetracking.

• Sondergaard, Niels, *Working with Dogs for Deer*, Hornslet Bogtrykkeri (Denmark), 2006. This is an excellent book on tracking wounded big game in Europe.

• Syrotuck, William, *Scent and the Scenting Dog*, New York: Arner Publications, 1972. Valuable book for explaining dog's perception of ground scent.

• Trout, John Jr., *Finding Wounded Deer*, Bellvale, KY: Woods N Waters Inc., 2001. Practical guide covers same material as Richard P. Smith.

Recommended Video

Minns, A.J., Shacklett, Al, *Tracking 101, Train to Track*, 2013. The tracking training procedures that the video presents in this excellent DVD are very compatible with the methods presented in *Tracking Dogs for Finding Wounded Deer*. This is a very instructive video, and although it was filmed in Texas, it gives good attention to the techniques for working a young dog on a tracking leash. Available at www.texastrackingdogs.com.

Foreign Language Bibliography

There is a rich literature on deer tracking in European languages. The following books in German and French were useful to me, and there are many others. None of these books treat such North American subjects as tracking bow-shot deer. In general, European hunting customs are very different and their tracking dog methods, developed over many centuries, must be adapted to North American circumstances.

• Borngräber, Hans-Joachim, *Die Schweissarbeit, Lehrbuch für alle Gebrauchshundrassen,* Braunschweig: Venatus 1998.

• Engelmann, Fritz Bandel, Robert, *Der Dachshund, Geschichte, Kennzeichen, Zucht und Verwendung zur Jagd*, Melsungen: Neumann-Neudamm, 1981.

• Gruget, Robert, Ley, Ernest, Stoquert, Hubert, Titeux, Gilbert, Urban, Jean Georges. *La recherche du grand gibier blessé,* Sarreguemines, France: Marc Titeux, 1986.

• Lux, Hans, Von Hunden, *Schweiss und roten Hirschen*, Hamburg: Paul Parey, 1977.

• Numssen, Julia, Blake, Chris, *La Recherche du grand gibier blessé: Entrainement pratique du conducteur et du chien*, Gilbert Titeux, 2013.

• Richter, Klaus, *Schweissarbeit, Die Ausbildung von Jagdhunden Methoden und Voraussetzungen, Deutscher Landwurtschaftverlag*, Berlin, 1988.

• Union Nationale pour l'Utilization de Chiens de Rouge, (UNUCR) , *Traité de la recherche du grand gibier blessé,* Paris: Gerfaut, 1998.

Glossary

ATV: motorized all terrain vehicle, a "four-wheeler", designed for one rider in rough country

air scenter: a dog that uses his nose to detect body scent in the air

angulation: applied especially to "ideal" 90-degree angles formed by dog's rear leg bones

artificial line: a scent line of real blood applied by a human tracklayer

backtrack: (verb) to track back over a line just traversed; (noun) a track made when a game animal comes back over its own trail

bolt snap: simple metal snap opened by sliding back a spring-loaded bolt

Bringsel: a wide strap that hangs down from dog's collar

broadhead: the conventional steel arrowhead with fixed blades

button buck: young male deer that has "buttons" on his head where antlers will develop

canid: wolves, coyotes, dogs, foxes etc. of the zoological family Canidae

centerfire: pertaining to cartridges having the primer in center of base or to rifles firing such cartridges

check: point on scent line where dog loses scent and slows down to work out problem

cottontails: another term for the species of wild rabbit most common in the northeastern United States

cynological: pertaining to the study of dogs

dysplasia: a physical abnormality; hip dysplasia involves a shallow hip socket.

eye-tracking: tracking by visual signs only

Fährtenschuh: clog or sandal with clamps for a deer hoof to simulate a natural track

force train: gently but firmly compelling a dog to learn a given task

4 X 4: a pickup truck with four speed stick-shift and four wheel drive

gun-shyness: fearfulness at the sound of a firearm

heritability: the degree to which physical and mental traits are inherited

hot line: a fresh track with lots of scent

houndy: descriptive term applied to a dog showing drooping ears, muzzle and expression of a scenthound

interdigital glands: scent glands between the hoofs of a deer

jip, also **gyp**: southwestern or southern colloquial word for a female dog

lose: southern or southwestern colloquial for a check

mechanical head: a type of arrowhead with fold-out blades that expand on impact

olfactory: pertaining to scent and scenting

peritonitis: an infection of the abdomen cause by leakage of intestinal contents into body cavity

pulmonary: pertaining to the lungs

rumen: the large first stomach of deer, cows, etc. where first stage of digestion takes place

Schutzhund: guard or attack dog

slug: a single, solid projectile designed to be fired from a shotgun

spookiness: colloquial for shy

tarsal glands: scent glands on deer inside hocks on rear legs

Totverbellen: barking at dead big game

Totverweisen: dog returns to handler, indicates that dead game has been found and leads the handler to it.

tracking: closely following the scent of blood or footprints

trailing: following body scent particles that may have drifted over a broader area where the animal has passed

windscenting: using the wind to detect air-borne body scent

Index